LETTERS ON YOGA

Volume II

Sri Aurobindo

Letters on Yoga

Volume II

Sri Aurobindo Ashram
Pondicherry

First edition 1958
Fourth edition (revised and enlarged) 2013
Third impression 2020

Rs 290
ISBN 978-93-5210-060-6

© Sri Aurobindo Ashram Trust 1958, 2013
Published by Sri Aurobindo Ashram Publication Department
Pondicherry 605 002
Web http://www.sabda.in

Printed at Sri Aurobindo Ashram Press, Pondicherry
PRINTED IN INDIA

Publisher's Note

Letters on Yoga — II comprises letters written by Sri Aurobindo on the practice of the Integral Yoga. It is the second of four volumes of *Letters on Yoga*, arranged by the editors as follows:

I. Foundations of the Integral Yoga
II. Practice of the Integral Yoga
III. Experiences and Realisations in the Integral Yoga
IV. Transformation of Human Nature in the Integral Yoga

The letters in these volumes have been selected from the large body of letters that Sri Aurobindo wrote to disciples and others between 1927 and 1950. Other letters from this period are published in *Letters on Poetry and Art* and *Letters on Himself and the Ashram*, volumes 27 and 35 of THE COMPLETE WORKS OF SRI AUROBINDO. Letters written before 1927 are reproduced in *Autobiographical Notes and Other Writings of Historical Interest*, volume 36 of THE COMPLETE WORKS.

During Sri Aurobindo's lifetime, relatively few of his letters were published. Three small books of letters on Yoga were brought out in the 1930s. A more substantial collection came out between 1947 and 1951 in a four-volume series entitled *Letters of Sri Aurobindo* (including one volume of letters on poetry and literature). In 1958, many more letters were included in the two large tomes of *On Yoga — II*. A further expanded collection in three volumes entitled *Letters on Yoga* was published in 1970 as part of the Sri Aurobindo Birth Centenary Library. The present collection, also entitled *Letters on Yoga*, constitutes volumes 28 – 31 of THE COMPLETE WORKS. These volumes incorporate previously published letters and contain many new ones as well. About one-third of the letters in the present volume were not published in the Centenary Library.

The present volume is arranged by subject in three parts:

1. The Path of the Integral Yoga
2. The Synthetic Method of the Integral Yoga
3. The Integral Yoga and Other Spiritual Paths

The texts of all the letters have been checked against the available manuscripts, typescripts and printed versions.

CONTENTS

PART ONE
THE PATH OF THE INTEGRAL YOGA

Section One
The Path and the Goal

Seeking the Divine
The True Object of Spiritual Seeking	5
Motives for Seeking the Divine	8
Dedication to the Spiritual Life	15

The Aim of the Integral Yoga
A Yoga of Divine Life	19
A Yoga Not for Ourselves	20
Not Liberation But Transformation	22
Divinisation and Transformation	23

Section Two
Basic Requisites of the Path

The Call and the Capacity
The Call	27
Turning towards the Divine	29
Spiritual Destiny	30
Capacity for Yoga	31
Fitness for Yoga	32
Capacity of Westerners for Yoga	36

Qualities Needed for Sadhana
Indispensable Qualities	42
Conditions of the Yoga	43

Purity
Purification of the Nature	46
The Meaning of Purity	48

CONTENTS

Sincerity
- The Meaning of Sincerity — 50
- Sincerity in Sadhana — 51
- Earnestness and Straightforwardness — 54

Aspiration
- The Value of Aspiration — 55
- The Meaning of Aspiration — 56
- The Object of Aspiration — 57
- No Need of Words in Aspiration — 58
- The Necessity of Aspiration — 58
- Intensity of Aspiration and Vital Impatience — 59
- Aspiration and Desire — 60
- Aspiration and Pulling — 61
- Lack of Aspiration — 61
- Aspiration and Conversion — 63

Rejection
- Rejection of the Lower Impulses — 64

Surrender
- The Meaning of Surrender — 67
- A Free Surrender — 68
- The Will to Surrender — 69
- The Inner Surrender — 69
- The Central Surrender — 72
- Complete or Absolute Surrender — 72
- The Surrender of the Vital — 74
- Surrender and the Psychic — 76
- Surrender and Bhakti — 78
- Surrender and the Brahmic Condition — 78
- Surrender and Transformation — 79
- Passive or Tamasic Surrender — 79
- Surrender and Tapasya — 81
- Surrender and Personal Effort — 82

Faith
- Faith, Belief, Confidence, Trust — 88

CONTENTS

A Problem of Faith	90
Faith and Knowledge	91
Faith and Experience	92
The Gospel of Faith	95
Faith and Doubt	97
Types of Faith	99
Faithfulness	99
Keep Firm Faith	101

Consecration and Offering

Consecration	103
Offering	104

Opening

The Meaning of Opening	105
Opening to the Divine	106

Patience and Perseverance

Patience	110
Persistence	114
Perseverance	116
Endurance	117
Resolution	118
Firmness	118

Vigilance

Vigilance, Discrimination, Control	119

Section Three
The Foundation of the Sadhana

Peace — The Basis of the Sadhana

Peace Is the First Condition	123
Peace, Calm, Wideness	124
Difficulties, Disturbances and Peace	125

Equality — The Chief Support

Equality or Samata	129
Samata and Loyalty to Truth	131

CONTENTS

    Samata and Ego   133
    Equality and Detachment   133
    Equality in Times of Trouble and Difficulty   134

Quiet and Calm
    Quiet, Calm, Peace, Silence   137
    Quietude   138
    Quiet Mind   141
    Vacant Mind   145
    Calm   145

Peace
    Peace Is Something Positive   148
    Peace Comes Little by Little   149
    A Settled or Established Peace   149
    Peace in the Mind, Vital and Physical   151
    Peace in the Inner Being   153
    Passive Peace   154
    Peace and Inertia   154
    Peace and Force   155
    Peace, Love and Joy   155
    Peace, Happiness, Joy, Delight, Ananda   156

Silence
    Freedom from Thoughts   158
    Silence and True Knowledge   159
    Silence and Quietness of Mind   159
    Silence, Peace and Calm   162
    Silence and True Activity   162

Section Four
The Divine Response

The Divine Grace and Guidance
    The Divine Grace   167
    The Grace and Personal Effort   171
    Strength and Grace   172
    Grace and Tapasya   172

CONTENTS

No Insistence on the Grace	173
Trust in the Divine Grace	174
Withdrawal of Grace	174
The First Responses of the Divine	175
The Divine Guidance	175

The Divine Force
The Nature of Spiritual Force	179
The Divine Force Works under Conditions	185
Writing about Spiritual Force	186
Use and Misuse of the Divine Force	187
The Action of the Divine Force	187
Allow the Divine Force to Act	188

The Guru
Acceptance of the Guru	190
The Guru in the Supramental Yoga	192
Surrender to the Guru	193
Other Gurus	194
The Guru's Help in Difficulty	195
The Knowledge Given by the Guru	197
The Capacity of the Guru	199
The Bhakta and the Disciple	200

PART TWO
THE SYNTHETIC METHOD OF THE INTEGRAL YOGA

Section One
A Yoga of Knowledge, Works, Bhakti and Self-Perfection

The Central Processes of the Sadhana
Four Necessary Processes	207
The Need for Plasticity	208
Work, Meditation and Bhakti	209
Surrender and Self-Giving	212
Aspiration and Will of Consecration	214
Sadhana, Tapasya, Aradhana, Dhyana	215

CONTENTS

Combining Work, Meditation and Bhakti
    The Place of Work in Sadhana   216
    A Defence of Works   218
    Work and Meditation   221
    No Competition between Work and Meditation   222
    The Time Given to Work and Meditation   224
    Concentration, Meditation and Prayer   225
    Bhakti and Knowledge   227

Section Two
Sadhana through Work

Work and Yoga
    Work as Part of Sadhana   231
    Work without Personal Motives   232
    The Karmayoga of the Gita   234
    No Vital Demand in Work   238
    The Utility of Work   240
    Right Attitude in Work   242
    Equanimity in Work   243
    The Impersonal Worker   244
    Service of the Divine   245
    All Work Equal in the Eyes of the Spirit   246
    Interest in Work   250
    Joy in Work   251
    Loss of Inspiration in Work   252
    Thoughts of Sadhana during Work   253

Becoming Conscious in Work
    Working from Within   254
    Working with a Double Consciousness   256
    Absorption in Work   257
    Remembering the Presence in Work   258
    Inner Guidance about Work   260
    Knowing the Divine Will   263
    Freedom in Work   264

CONTENTS

The Divine Force in Work
Receiving the Divine Power or Force   266
The Working of the Force   268
The Force and the Peace in Action   271
Drawing upon the Force for Energy   272
Avoiding Overstrain   274

Practical Concerns in Work
Order and Rhythm   276
Rules, Discipline, Regularity, Thoroughness   277
Harmony   278
Avoiding Harshness, Severity, Anger   279
Working with Subordinates and Superiors   281
Overcoming the Instinct of Domination   282
Avoiding Disturbance   283
Avoiding Restlessness, Worry and Anxiety   284
Compliments and Criticism   286
Thinking about Work   287
Dealing with Physical Things   287

Creative Activity
The Arts and the Spiritual Life   290
Literature   291
Painting   292
Singing   294

Section Three
Sadhana through Concentration, Meditation and Japa

Concentration and Meditation
The Meaning of Concentration and Meditation   297
The Role of Concentration and Meditation
   (Dhyana) in Sadhana   298
The Object of Meditation   300
Meditation Not Necessary for All   300
Methods of Meditation and Concentration   301
Concentration on the Idea   305
Centres for Concentration   306

CONTENTS

Postures for Concentration or Meditation	311
Regularity, Length and Other Conditions	312
Coming out of Concentration or Meditation	313
The Difficulty of the Mechanical Mind	314
Surface Thoughts and Imaginations	315
Straining and Concentration	315
Relaxation and Concentration	316
Passive Meditation and Concentration	317
Inertia, Laziness, Tiredness in Meditation	317
Meditation, Sleep and Samadhi	319

Mantra and Japa

The Word	322
Mantras	323
The Mantra OM	323
The Mantra *So'ham*	324
The Gayatri Mantra	325
Mantras in the Integral Yoga	326
Namajapa or Repetition of the Name	327
Verses of the Gita Used as Japa	328
Success in Japa	328

Section Four
Sadhana through Love and Devotion

Divine Love, Psychic Love and Human Love

Divine Love and Its Manifestation	333
Divine Love and Psychic Love	336
Psychic Love	336
Universal Love and Psychic Love	337
Love for the Divine	338
Human Love in the Sadhana	341
Human Love and Divine Love	344
The Vital and Love for the Divine	347

Bhakti, Devotion, Worship

Turning the Emotions towards the Divine	350
Bhakti or Devotion	352

CONTENTS

Bhakti and Love	356
Emotional Bhakti	357
Vital Bhakti	358
Viraha or Pangs of Separation	359
Enmity to the Divine	360
Contact with the Divine	361
Contact and Union with the Divine	363
Outer Worship	364
Prayer	365

PART THREE
THE INTEGRAL YOGA AND OTHER SPIRITUAL PATHS

Section One
A Yoga of Transformation

Distinctive Features of the Integral Yoga

The Meaning of Purna Yoga	373
This-Worldliness and Other-Worldliness	374
The Importance of Descent in the Yoga	376
The Inclusiveness of the Yoga	379

Asceticism and the Integral Yoga

Not an Ascetic Path	380
Asceticism and Detachment	383
Two Methods of Living in the Supreme	384
The Human Approach to the Divine	385
Vairagya	387

A Realistic Adwaita

The World Not an Illusion	391
Shankara, Buddhism, Evolution	391

Transformation in the Integral Yoga

The Meaning of Transformation	398
Towards a Transformation of Earth Life	401
Spiritualisation and Transformation	404
The Attempt at Physical Transformation	407

CONTENTS

Section Two
Other Spiritual Paths and the Integral Yoga

The Newness of the Integral Yoga
Old and New Truth — 411
Spiritual Realisation and the Supramental
  Transformation — 412
Depreciation of the Old Yogas — 415
The Old Lines and This Line — 416

The Veda and the Upanishads
The Vedic Rishis — 417
The Veda and the Greeks — 420
No Incarnation of the Vedic Gods — 420
Terms and Verses of the Upanishads — 423
The Vedantin — 425

Jainism and Buddhism
Jainism — 428
Buddhism — 428
Buddhist Nirvana — 431
Different Kinds of Buddhism — 433
Buddhism and Vedanta — 434

Sankhya and Yoga
Sankhya — 437
Patanjali's Yoga — 437
The Yoga-Vasishtha — 439
Asanas and Pranayama — 439

The Yoga of the Bhagavad Gita
The Teaching of the Gita — 441
Apparent Contradictions in the Gita — 441
The Gita, the Divine Mother and the Purushottama — 443
The Gita and the Integral Yoga — 444

The Adwaita of Shankaracharya
Shankara's Mayavada — 447
Mayavada and Nirvana — 451

CONTENTS

The Illusionist Metaphors	457
Laya	457

Tantra
Tantra and the Integral Yoga	459
Kundalini, the Chakras and the Integral Yoga	460
Levels of Speech (Vak)	464

Bhakti Yoga and Vaishnavism
The Vaishnava Theory and Sadhana	465
Vaishnava Bhakti and the Integral Yoga	466
The True Vaishnava Attitude	467
The Sunlit Way of Yoga	469
Ordinary Life, Vaishnava Traditions and the Supramental Yoga	475
Different Approaches through Love and Bhakti	483
Love and Bhakti for Krishna	487
Love of Krishna and This Yoga	494

The Teachings of Some Modern Indian Yogis
Ramana Maharshi	496
Swami Ramatirtha	500
Swami Ramdas	500

Christianity and Theosophy
Christianity	504
Theosophy	511

NOTE ON THE TEXTS   515

Part One

The Path of the Integral Yoga

Section One

The Path and the Goal

Chapter One
Seeking the Divine

The True Object of Spiritual Seeking

To find the Divine is indeed the first reason for seeking the spiritual Truth and the spiritual life; it is the one thing indispensable and all the rest is nothing without it. The Divine once found, to manifest Him, — that is, first of all to transform one's own limited consciousness into the Divine Consciousness, to live in the infinite Peace, Light, Love, Strength, Bliss, to become that in one's essential nature and, as a consequence, to be its vessel, channel, instrument in one's active nature. To bring into activity the principle of oneness on the material plane or to work for humanity is a mental mistranslation of the Truth — these things cannot be the first or true object of spiritual seeking. We must find the Self, the Divine, then only can we know what is the work the Self or the Divine demands from us. Until then our life and action can only be a help or means towards finding the Divine and it ought not to have any other purpose. As we grow in the inner consciousness, or as the spiritual Truth of the Divine grows in us, our life and action must indeed more and more flow from that, be one with that. But to decide beforehand by our limited mental conceptions what they must be is to hamper the growth of the spiritual Truth within. As that grows we shall feel the Divine Light and Truth, the Divine Power and Force, the Divine Purity and Peace working within us, dealing with our actions as well as our consciousness, making use of them to reshape us into the Divine Image, removing the dross, substituting the pure gold of the Spirit. Only when the Divine Presence is there in us always and the consciousness transformed, can we have the right to say that we are ready to manifest the Divine on the material plane. To hold up a mental ideal or principle and impose that on the inner working brings the danger of limiting ourselves to a mental realisation or of impeding or even falsifying by a half-way formation the true growth into the full communion and union with the Divine and the free and intimate outflowing of His will in our life. This is a mistake of orientation to which the mind of today is especially prone. It is far better to approach the Divine for the Peace or Light or Bliss that the realisation of Him gives than to bring in these minor things which can divert us from the one thing needful. The divinisation of the material life also as well as the inner life is part of what we see as the Divine Plan, but it can only be fulfilled by an outflowing of the inner realisation, something that grows from within outward, not by the working out of a mental principle.

You have asked what is the discipline to be followed in order to convert the mental seeking into a living spiritual experience. The first necessity is the practice of concentration of your consciousness within yourself. The ordinary human mind has an activity on the surface which veils the real self. But there is another, a hidden consciousness within behind the surface one in which we can become aware of the real self and of a larger, deeper truth of nature, can realise the self and liberate and transform the nature. To quiet the surface mind and begin to live within is the object of this concentration. Of this true consciousness other than the superficial there are two main centres, one in the heart (not the physical heart, but the cardiac centre in the middle of the chest), one in the head. The concentration in the heart opens within and by following this inward opening and going deep one becomes aware of the soul or psychic being, the divine element in the individual. This being unveiled begins to come forward, to govern the nature, to turn it and all its movements towards the Truth, towards the Divine, and to call down into it all that is above. It brings the consciousness of the Presence, the dedication of the being to the Highest and invites the descent into our nature of a greater Force and Consciousness which is waiting above us. To concentrate in the heart centre with the offering of oneself to the Divine and the aspiration for this inward opening and for the Presence in the heart is the first way and, if it can be done, the natural beginning; for its result once obtained makes the spiritual path far more easy and safe than if one begins the other way.

That other way is the concentration in the head, in the mental centre. This, if it brings about the silence of the surface mind, opens up an inner, larger, deeper mind within which is more capable of receiving spiritual experience and spiritual knowledge. But once concentrated here one must open the silent mental consciousness upward to all that is above mind. After a time one feels the consciousness rising upward and in the end it rises beyond the lid which has so long kept it tied in the body and finds a centre above the head where it is liberated into the Infinite. There it begins to come into contact with the universal Self, the Divine Peace, Light, Power, Knowledge, Bliss, to enter into that and become that, to feel the descent of these things into the nature. To concentrate in the head with the aspiration for quietude in the mind and the realisation of the Self and Divine above is the second way of concentration. It is important, however, to remember that the concentration of the consciousness in the head is only a preparation for its rising to the centre above; otherwise one may get shut up in one's own mind and its experiences or at best attain only to a reflection of the Truth above instead of rising into the spiritual transcendence to live there. For some the mental concentration is easier, for some the concentration in the heart centre; some are capable of doing both alternately — but to begin with the heart centre, if one can do it, is the more desirable.

The other side of discipline is with regard to the activities of the nature, of the mind, of the life-self or vital, of the physical being. Here the principle is to accord the nature with the inner realisation so that one may not be divided into two discordant parts. There are here several disciplines or processes possible. One is to offer all the activities to the Divine and call for the inner guidance and the taking up of one's nature by a Higher Power. If there is the inward soul-opening, if the psychic being comes forward, then there is no great difficulty — there comes with it a psychic discrimination, a constant intimation, finally a governance which discloses and quietly and patiently removes all imperfections, brings the right mental and vital movements and reshapes the physical consciousness also. Another method is to stand back detached from the movements of the mind, life, physical being, to regard their activities as only a habitual formation of general Nature in the individual imposed on us by past workings, not as any part of our real being; in proportion as one succeeds in this, becomes detached, sees mind and its activities as not oneself, life and its activities as not oneself, the body and its activities as not oneself, one becomes aware of an inner Being within us — inner mental, inner vital, inner physical — silent, calm, unbound, unattached which reflects the true Self above and can be its direct representative; from this inner silent Being proceeds a rejection of all that is to be rejected, an acceptance only of what can be kept and transformed, an inmost Will to perfection or a call to the Divine Power to do at each step what is necessary for the change of the Nature. It can also open mind, life and body to the inmost psychic entity and its guiding influence or its direct guidance. In most cases these two methods emerge and work together and finally fuse into one. But one can begin with either, the one that one feels most natural and easy to follow.

Finally, in all difficulties where personal effort is hampered, the help of the Teacher can intervene and bring about what is needed for the realisation or for the immediate step that is necessary.

Motives for Seeking the Divine

Obviously to seek the Divine *only* for what one can get out of Him is not the proper attitude; but if it were absolutely forbidden to seek Him for these things, most people in the world would not turn towards Him at all. I suppose therefore it is allowed so that they may make a beginning — if they have faith, they may get what they ask for and think it a good thing to go on and then one day they may suddenly stumble upon the idea that this is after all not quite the one thing to do and that there are better ways and a better spirit in which one can approach the Divine. If they do not get what they want and still come to the Divine and trust in Him, well, that shows they are getting ready.

Let us look on it as a sort of infants' school for the unready. But of course that is not the spiritual life, it is only a sort of elementary religious approach. For the spiritual life to give and not to demand is the rule. The sadhak however can ask for the Divine Force to aid him in keeping his health or recovering it if he does that as part of his sadhana so that his body may be able and fit for the spiritual life and a capable instrument for the Divine Work.

*

First, it is a great exaggeration to deduce from your difficulties any idea of unfitness or of going away or being sent away or giving up the Yoga. I am certainly not going to pronounce you unfit because you want the Ananda; on such grounds I would have to pronounce myself unfit, because I have myself wanted it and many other things besides. And if I were to send you away because you are not entirely disinterested in the approach to the Divine, I should have, to be consistent, to send practically the whole Asram packing. I do not know why you are allowing yourself to indulge in such black and despondent thoughts — there is no ground for them at all, and I do not think I gave any grounds for them in my letter. Whatever your difficulties, the Mother and I have every intention of seeing you through them, and I think that you too, whatever suggestions your vital depression may make to you at the moment, have every intention of going through to the end of the Path. I imagine you have gone too far on it to go back and, if you wanted to, your psychic being which has persistently pushed you towards it, would not allow such a retreat.

Next, it was not my intention to say that it was wrong to aspire for the Ananda. What I wanted to point out was the condition for the permanent possession of the Ananda (intimations, visits, downrushes of it one can have before); the essential condition for it is a change of consciousness, the coming of peace, light, etc., all that brings about the transition from the normal to the spiritualised nature. And that being so, it is better to make this change of consciousness the first object of the sadhana. On the other hand, to press for the constant Ananda immediately in a consciousness which is not yet able to retain it, still more to substitute for it lesser (vital) joys and pleasures may very well stop the flow of these spiritual experiences which make the continuous ecstasy eventually possible. But I certainly never intended to say that the Ananda was not to be attained or to insist on your moving towards a *nirānanda* (joyless) Brahman. On the contrary, I said that Ananda was the crown of the Yoga, which surely means that it was part of the highest final *siddhi*.

Whatever one wants sincerely and persistently from the Divine, the Divine is sure to give. If then you want Ananda and go on wanting, you will surely have it in the end. The only question is what is to be the chief power in your seeking, a vital demand or a psychic aspiration manifesting through the heart and communicating itself to the mental and vital and physical consciousness. The latter is the greatest power and makes the shortest way — and besides one has to come to that way sooner or later.

*

Let us first put aside the quite foreign consideration of what we would do if the union with the Divine brought eternal joylessness, Nirananda or torture. Such a thing does not exist and to drag it in only clouds the issue. The Divine is Anandamaya and one can seek him for the Ananda he gives; but he has also in him many other things and one may seek him for any of them, for peace, for liberation, for knowledge, for power, for anything else of which one may feel the pull or the impulse. It is quite possible for someone to say: "Let me have Power from the Divine and do His work or His will and I am satisfied, even if the use of Power entails suffering also." It is possible to shun bliss as a thing too tremendous or ecstatic and ask only or rather for peace, for liberation, for Nirvana. You speak of self-fulfilment, — one may regard the Supreme not as the Divine but as one's highest Self and seek fulfilment of one's being in that highest Self; but one need not envisage it as a self of bliss, ecstasy, Ananda — one may envisage it as a self of freedom, vastness, knowledge, tranquillity, strength, calm, perfection — perhaps too calm for a ripple of anything so disturbing as joy to enter. So even if it is for something to be gained that one approaches the Divine, it is not a fact that one can approach Him or seek union only for the sake of Ananda and nothing else.

That involves something which throws all your reasoning out of gear. For these are aspects of the Divine Nature, powers of it, states of his being, — but the Divine Himself is something absolute, someone self-existent, not limited by his aspects, — wonderful and ineffable, not existing by them, but they existing because of him. It follows that if he attracts by his aspects, all the more he can attract by his very absolute selfness which is sweeter, mightier, profounder than any aspect. His peace, rapture, light, freedom, beauty are marvellous and ineffable, because he is himself magically, mysteriously, transcendently marvellous and ineffable. He can then be sought after for his wonderful and ineffable self and not only for the sake of one aspect or another of him. The only thing needed for that is, first, to arrive at a point when the psychic being feels this pull of the Divine in himself and, secondly, to arrive at the point when the mind, vital and each thing else begins to feel too that that was what it was wanting and the surface hunt after Ananda or what else was only an excuse for drawing the nature towards that supreme magnet.

Your argument that because we know the union with the Divine will bring Ananda, therefore it must be for the Ananda that we seek the union, is not true and has no force. One who loves a queen may know that if she returns his love it will bring him power, position, riches and yet it need not be for the power, position, riches that he seeks her love. He may love her for herself and could love her equally if she were not a queen; he might have no hope of any return whatever and yet love her, adore her, live for her, die for her simply because she is she. That has happened and men have loved women without any hope of enjoyment or result, loved steadily, passionately after age has come and beauty has gone. Patriots do not love their country only when she is rich, powerful, great and has much to give them; their love for country has been most ardent, passionate, absolute when the country was poor, degraded, miserable, having nothing to give but loss, wounds, torture, imprisonment, death as the wages of her service; yet even knowing that they would never see her free, men have lived, served and died for her — for her own sake, not for what she could give. Men have loved Truth for her own sake and for what they could seek or find of her, accepted poverty, persecution, death itself; they have been content even to seek for her always, not finding, and yet never given up the search. That means what? That men, country, Truth and other things besides can be loved for their own sake and not for anything else, not for any circumstance or attendant quality or resulting enjoyment, but for something absolute that is either in them or behind their appearance and circumstance. The Divine is more than a man or woman, a stretch of land or a creed, opinion, discovery or principle. He is the Person beyond all persons, the Home and Country of all souls, the Truth of which truths are only imperfect figures. And can He then not be loved and sought for his own sake, as and more than these have been by men even in their lesser selves and nature?

What your reasoning ignores is that which is absolute or tends towards the absolute in man and his seeking as well as in the Divine — something not to be explained by mental reasoning or vital motive. A motive, but a motive of the soul, not of vital desire; a reason not of the mind, but of the self and spirit. An asking too, but the asking that is the soul's inherent aspiration, not a vital longing. That is what comes up when there is the sheer self-giving, when "I seek you for this, I seek you for that" changes to a sheer "I seek you for you." It is that marvellous and ineffable absolute in the Divine that Krishnaprem means when he says, "Not knowledge nor this nor that, but Krishna." The pull of that is indeed a categorical imperative, the self in us drawn to the Divine because of the imperative call of its greater Self, the soul ineffably drawn towards the object of its adoration, because it cannot be otherwise, because it is it and He is He. That is all about it.

I have written all that only to explain what we mean when we speak of seeking the Divine for himself and not for anything else — so far as it is explicable. Explicable or not, it is one of the most dominant facts of spiritual experience. The call to self-giving is only an expression of this fact. But this does not mean that I object to your asking for Ananda. Ask for that by all means, so long as to ask for it is a need of any part of your being — for these are the things that lead on towards the Divine so long as the absolute inner call that is there all the time does not push itself to the surface. But it is really that that has drawn from the beginning and is there behind — it is the categorical spiritual imperative, the absolute need of the soul for the Divine.

I am not saying that there is to be no Ananda. The self-giving itself is a profound Ananda and what it brings, carries in its wake an inexpressible Ananda — and it is brought by this method sooner than by any other, so that one can say almost, "A self-less self-giving is the best policy." Only one does not do it out of policy. Ananda is the result, but it is done not for the result, but for the self-giving itself and for the Divine himself — a subtle distinction, it may seem to the mind, but very real.

*

No, what you write in your letter was not at all what the Mother was trying to tell you. The question of *ahaitukī bhakti* and its opposite was settled long ago and the Mother did not intend to return upon it; it is understood that whatever the motive immediately pushing the mind or the vital, an asking for Ananda or knowledge or power, yet if there is a true seeking for the Divine in the being, it must lead eventually to the realisation of the Divine. The soul within has always the inherent (*ahaitukī*) yearning for the Divine; the *hetu* or special motive is simply an impulsion used by it to get the mind and the vital to follow the inner urge. If the mind and the vital can feel and accept the soul's sheer love for the Divine for his own sake, then the sadhana gets its full power and many difficulties disappear; but even if they do not, they will get what they seek after in the Divine and through it they will come to realise something, even perhaps to pass beyond the limit of their original desire. I may say that the idea of a joyless God is an absurdity which only the ignorance of the mind could engender; the Radha love is not based upon any such thing, but means simply that whatever comes on the way to the Divine, pain or joy, *milana* or *viraha*, and however long the sufferings may last, the Radha love is unshaken and keeps its faith and certitude pointing fixedly like a star to the supreme object of Love.

All this, however, has nothing to do with what the Mother wished to say in the morning. What she told you was that you seemed to have a fixed notion about the Divine, as of a rather distant Being somewhere whom you expect to give you an article called Ananda, and, when there is some prospect of his giving it to you, you are on good terms with him, but when he doesn't, you quarrel and revolt and call him names! And she said a notion of the kind was in itself an obstacle, — because it is rather far from the Truth, — in the way of realising the Divine. What is this Ananda that you seek, after all? The mind can see in it nothing but a pleasant psychological condition, — but if it were only that, it would not be the rapture which the bhaktas and the mystics find in it. When the Ananda comes into you, it is the Divine who comes into you; just as when the Peace flows into you, it is the Divine who is invading you, or when you are flooded with Light, it is the flood of the Divine Himself that is around you. Of course, the Divine is something much more; many other things besides and in them all a Presence, a Being, a Divine Person; for the Divine is Krishna, is Shiva, is the Supreme Mother. But through the Ananda you can perceive the Anandamaya Krishna; for the Ananda is the subtle body and being of Krishna; through the Peace you can perceive the Shantimaya Shiva; in the Light, in the delivering Knowledge, the Love, the fulfilling and uplifting Power you can meet the presence of the Divine Mother. It is this perception that makes the experiences of the bhaktas and mystics so rapturous and enables them to pass more easily through the nights of anguish and separation — when there is this soul-perception, it gives to even a little or brief Ananda a force or value it would not otherwise have and the Ananda itself gathers by it a growing power to stay, to return, to increase. This was what the Mother meant when she said, "Don't ask the Divine to give you Ananda, ask Him to give you Himself" — signifying that in the Ananda and through the Ananda it would be Himself that He would give you. There would then be no cause to say, "I do not know the Divine. I have never felt or met Him"; it would be a gate too for other experiences and make it easier to see the Divine in the material object, in the human form, in the body.

It was not a condition that the Mother was laying down when she said this; it was simply a suggestion which, if something in you could seize and profit by it, would make things less slow and difficult than they actually are.

Dedication to the Spiritual Life

This Yoga demands a total dedication of the life to the aspiration for the discovery and embodiment of the Divine Truth and to nothing else whatever. To divide your life between the Divine and some outward aim and activity that has nothing to do with the search for the Truth is inadmissible. The least thing of that kind would make success in the Yoga impossible.

You must go inside yourself and enter into a complete dedication to the spiritual life. All clinging to mental preferences must fall away from you, all insistence on vital aims and interests and attachments must be put away, all egoistic clinging to family, friends, country must disappear if you want to succeed in Yoga. Whatever has to come as outgoing energy or action, must proceed from the Truth once discovered and not from the lower mental or vital motives, from the Divine Will and not from personal choice or the preferences of the ego.

*

It is a universally accepted principle of the spiritual endeavour that one must be prepared to sacrifice everything without reserve in order to reach the Divine through a spiritualised consciousness. If self-development on the mental, vital and physical plane is his aim that is another matter — that life is the life of the ego with the soul kept behind undeveloped or half developed.

But for the spiritual seeker the only development he seeks is the development of the psychic and spiritual consciousness and that too, only because it is necessary to reach and to serve the Divine, not for its own sake. Whatever mental, vital, physical development or use of faculties can be made part of the spiritual life and an instrumentation for the Divine can be kept on condition of surrender of them for transformation and restatement on the spiritual basis. But they must not be kept for their own sake or for the sake of the ego or considered as one's own possession or used for one's own purpose but only for the sake of the Divine.

As for James' statement[1] it is of course true except in so far as the politician can indulge in other things as hobbies for his leisure hours, but if he wants to succeed as a politician he must give his best energies to politics. Conversely if Shakespeare or Newton had spent part of their energies in politics they would not have been able to reach such heights in poetry and in science or even if they had they would have done much less. The main energies have to be concentrated on one thing; the others can only be minor pursuits at leisure or for distraction or interests rather than pursuits useful for keeping up a general culture.

*

All depends on the aim of the life. To one whose aim is to discover and possess the highest spiritual truth and the divine life, I do not think a University post can count for much, nor do I see that there can be any practical connection between them. It might be different if the aim were the life of a writer and thinker on the intellectual level only without any higher flight or deeper seeking. I do not see that your unwillingness to commit yourself to this kind of work is due to any weakness. It is rather that only a small part of your nature, and that not the deepest or strongest part, would be satisfied with it or with the atmosphere in which it would have to be done.

---

[1] *The correspondent wrote:* "*Prof. James even says* [in *Principles of Psychology*] *about the 'social me' and other 'me's, that one has to suppress several of them in order to achieve one or two main aims in life. A politician, in order to concentrate on politics alone, has to let go his tendency for music or painting or social fame or family affections.*" — *Ed.*

In these matters it is not the thinking mind but the vital being — the life-force and the desire nature — or some part of it at least, that usually determines men's action and their choice — when it is not some outward necessity or pressure that compels or mainly influences the decision. The mind is only an interpreting, justifying and devising agent. By your taking up the sadhana this part of your vital being has had a pressure put upon it from above and within which has discouraged its old turn of desires and tendencies, its past grooves, those which would have decided its direction before; this vital has, as is often one first result, fallen silent and neutral. It is no longer strongly moved towards the ordinary life; it has not yet received from or through the psychic centre and the higher mental will a sufficient illumination and impulse to take up a new vital movement and run vigorously on the road to a new life. That is the reason for the listlessness of which you speak and the mistiness of the future. Men do not know themselves and have not learned to distinguish these different parts of the being which are usually lumped together as mind; they do not understand their own states and actions, or, if at all, then only on the surface. It is part of the foundation of Yoga to become conscious of the complexity of the nature, see the different forces that move it and get over it a control of directing knowledge.

The remedy can only come from the parts of the being that are already turned towards the Light. To call in the light of the divine consciousness, bring the psychic being to the front and kindle a flame of aspiration which will awaken spiritually the outer mind and set on fire the vital being, is the way out. It is usually a psychic awakening or a series of strong experiences by which the sadhak comes out of this intermediary no man's land of the quiescent vital (few can avoid altogether this passage through a neutral vital indifference) into the full dynamic course of the spiritual movement.

*

It is not absolutely necessary to abandon the ordinary life in order to seek after the Light or to practise Yoga. This is usually done by those who want to make a clean cut, to live a purely religious or exclusively inner and spiritual life, to renounce the world entirely and to depart from the cosmic existence by cessation of the human birth and a passing away into some higher state or into the transcendental Reality. Otherwise it is only necessary when the pressure of the inner urge becomes so great that the pursuit of the ordinary life is no longer compatible with the pursuit of the dominant spiritual objective. Till then what is necessary is a power to practise an inner isolation, to be able to retire within oneself and concentrate at any time on the necessary spiritual purpose. There must also be a power to deal with the ordinary outer life from a new inner attitude and one can then make the happenings of that life itself a means for the inner change of nature and the growth in spiritual experience.

Chapter Two

The Aim of the Integral Yoga

A Yoga of Divine Life

You have apparently a call and may be fit for Yoga; but there are different paths and each has a different aim and end before it. It is common to all the paths to conquer the desires, to put aside the ordinary relations of life, and to try to pass from uncertainty to everlasting certitude. One may also try to conquer dream and sleep, thirst and hunger etc. But it is no part of my Yoga to have nothing to do with the world or with life or to kill the senses or entirely inhibit their action. It is the object of this Yoga to transform life by bringing down into it the Light, Power and Bliss of the divine Truth and its dynamic certitudes. This Yoga is not a Yoga of world-shunning asceticism, but of divine Life. Your object, on the other hand, can only be gained by entering into Samadhi and ceasing in it from all connection with world-existence.

*

The way of Yoga followed here has a different purpose from others, — for its aim is not only to rise out of the ordinary ignorant world-consciousness into the divine consciousness, but to bring the supramental power of that divine consciousness down into the ignorance of mind, life and body, to transform them, to manifest the Divine here and create a divine life in Matter. This is an exceedingly difficult aim and difficult Yoga; to many or most it will seem impossible. All the established forces of the ordinary ignorant world-consciousness are opposed to it and deny it and try to prevent it, and the sadhak will find his own mind, life and body full of the most obstinate impediments to its realisation. If you can accept the ideal whole-heartedly, face all the difficulties, leave the past and its ties behind you and are ready to give up everything and risk everything for this divine possibility, then only can you hope to discover by experience the Truth behind it.

The sadhana of this Yoga does not proceed through any set mental teaching or prescribed forms of meditation, mantras or others, but by aspiration, by a self-concentration inwards or upwards, by self-opening to an Influence, to the Divine Power above us and its workings, to the Divine Presence in the heart, and by the rejection of all that is foreign to these things. It is only by faith, aspiration and surrender that this self-opening can come.

*

The aim of the Yoga is to open the consciousness to the Divine, to live in the inner consciousness more and more while acting from it on the external life, to bring the inmost psychic into the front and by the power of the psychic to purify and change the being so that it may become ready for transformation and in union with the Divine Knowledge, Will and Love. Secondly, to develop the Yogic consciousness — i.e. to universalise the being on all the planes, become aware of the cosmic being and cosmic forces and be in union with the Divine on all the planes up to the Overmind. Thirdly, to come into contact with the transcendent Divine, beyond the Overmind, through the supramental consciousness, supramentalise the consciousness and the nature and make oneself an instrument for the realisation of the dynamic Divine Truth and its transforming descent into the earth-nature.

A Yoga Not for Ourselves

Well, I once wrote in my callow days, "Our Yoga is not for ourselves but humanity" — that was in the *Bande Mataram* times. To get out of the hole self-created I had to explain that it was no longer for humanity, but for the Divine. The "not for ourselves" remained intact.

*

Quite possible and practical and a very rapturous thing [*is absolute surrender to the Divine*] as anyone who has done it can tell you. It is also the easiest and most powerful way of "getting the Divine". So it is the best policy also. The phrase ["*for the Divine*"], however, means that the object of the Yoga is to enter into and be possessed by the Divine Presence and Consciousness, to love the Divine for the Divine's sake alone, to be turned in our nature into nature of the Divine and in our will and works and life to be the instrument of the Divine. Its object is not to be a great Yogi or a superman (although that may come) or to grab at the Divine for the sake of the ego's power, pride or pleasure. It is not for salvation though liberation comes by it and all else may come; but these must not be our objects. The Divine alone is our object.

*

To come to this Yoga merely with the idea of being a superman would be an act of vital egoism which would defeat its own object. Those who put this object in the front of their preoccupations invariably come to grief, spiritually and otherwise. The aim of this Yoga is, first, to enter into the divine consciousness by merging into it the separative ego (incidentally, in doing so one finds one's true individual self which is not the limited, vain and selfish human ego but a portion of the Divine) and, secondly, to bring down the supramental consciousness on earth to transform mind, life and body. All else can be only a result of these two aims, not the primary object of the Yoga.

The extreme difficulty of these two aims has never been concealed from the sadhakas; on the contrary, difficulties and dangers have been overemphasised, rather than minimised. If still they choose and persist in this path, it is supposed that they are ready to risk everything, sacrifice everything, surrender everything in order to achieve this end or help towards its achievement.

*

You must get out of certain wrong ideas that you seem to have about Yoga, for these are dangerous and ought to be thrown away by every sadhak:

(1) The object of Yoga is not to become "like" Sri Aurobindo or the Mother. Those who cherish this idea easily come to the further idea that they can become their equals and even greater. This is only to feed the ego.

(2) The object of Yoga is not to get power or to be more powerful than others or to have great siddhis or to do great or wonderful or miraculous things.

(3) The object of Yoga is not to be a great Yogi or a superman. This is an egoistic way of taking the Yoga and can lead to no good; avoid it altogether.

(4) To talk about the supramental and think of bringing it down in yourself is the most dangerous of all. It may bring an entire megalomania and loss of balance. What the sadhak has to seek is the full opening to the Divine, the psychic change of his consciousness, the spiritual change. Of that change of consciousness, selflessness, desirelessness, humility, bhakti, surrender, calm, equality, peace, quiet, sincerity are necessary constituents. Until he has the psychic and spiritual change, to think of being supramental is an absurdity and an arrogant absurdity.

All these egoistic ideas, if indulged, can only aggrandise the ego, spoil the sadhana and lead to serious spiritual dangers. They should be rejected altogether.

*

Making fulfilment etc. the aim encourages an ego-centric attitude. Fulfilment, liberation, bliss etc. will come, but as a result of union with the Divine, not as a personal object of the sadhana.

Not Liberation But Transformation

Peace is a necessary basis, but peace is not sufficient. Peace if it is strong and permanent can liberate the inner being which can become a calm and unmoved witness of the external movements. That is the liberation of the Sannyasin. In some cases it can liberate the external also, throwing the old nature out into the environmental consciousness, but even this is liberation, not transformation.

*

Spiritual liberation means to be free from ego and from the imprisonment in the mind and vital and physical nature and to be conscious of the spiritual Self and live in that consciousness.

Spiritual perfection and fulfilment means that the nature should be spiritualised, new-formed in the consciousness of the free Self and the divine consciousness of infinity, purity, light, power, bliss and knowledge.

*

In the Brahmanic condition one feels the self to be untouched and pure — but the nature remains imperfect. The ordinary Sannyasin does not care about that, because it is not his object to perfect the nature, but to separate himself from it.

*

The negative means [*of sadhana*] are not evil — they are useful for their object which is to get away from life. But from the positive point of view, they are disadvantageous because they get rid of the powers of the being instead of divinising them for the transformation of life.

Divinisation and Transformation

The fundamental difference is in the teaching that there is a dynamic divine Truth (the Supermind) and that into the present world of Ignorance that Truth can descend, create a new Truth-consciousness and divinise Life. The old Yogas go straight from mind to the absolute Divine, regard all dynamic existence as Ignorance, Illusion or Lila: when you enter the static and immutable Divine Truth, they say, you pass out of cosmic existence.

*

They [*the ancient Yogas*] aimed at realisation and did not care about divinisation, except the Tantric and some others. The aim however even in these was rather to become saints and siddhas than anything else.

*

If your soul always aspires for the transformation, then that is what you have to follow after. To seek the Divine or rather some aspect of the Divine — for one cannot entirely realise the Divine if there is no transformation — may be enough for some, but not for those whose soul's aspiration is for the entire divine change.

*

Unless the external nature is transformed, one may go as high as possible and have the largest experiences — but the external mind remains an instrument of the Ignorance.

*

If the presence of the Divine is established, it means that the being is ready for the transformation which proceeds naturally.

*

The full transformation is the result of union with the divine consciousness.

*

To be in full union with the Divine is the final aim. When one has some kind of constant union, one can be called a Yogi, but the union has to be made complete. There are Yogis who have only the union on the spiritual plane, others who are united in mind and heart, others in the vital also. In our Yoga our aim is to be united too in the physical consciousness and on the supramental plane.

Section Two

Basic Requisites of the Path

Chapter One

The Call and the Capacity

The Call

This Yoga is a special way to a high and difficult spiritual achievement. It is given only when there is sufficient evidence of capacity or an irresistible call. Inner peace is not its object; that is only one of the elementary conditions for it.

*

The goal of Yoga is always hard to reach, but this one is more difficult than any other, and it is only for those who have the call, the capacity, the willingness to face everything and every risk, even the risk of failure, and the will to progress towards an entire selflessness, desirelessness and surrender.

*

This Yoga implies not only the realisation of God, but an entire consecration and change of the inner and outer life till it is fit to manifest a divine consciousness and become part of a divine work. This means an inner discipline far more exacting and difficult than mere ethical and physical austerities. One must not enter on this path, far vaster and more arduous than most ways of Yoga, unless one is sure of the psychic call and of one's readiness to go through to the end.

*

By readiness I did not mean capacity but willingness. If there is the will within to face all difficulties and go through, no matter how long it takes, then the path can be taken.

*

A mere restless dissatisfaction with the ordinary life is not a sufficient preparation for this Yoga. A positive inner call, a strong will and a great steadiness are necessary for success in the spiritual life.

*

Knowledge of the way is not enough — one must tread it, or if one cannot do that, allow oneself to be carried along it. The human vital and physical external nature resist to the very end, but if the soul has once heard the call, it arrives, sooner or later.

*

What you write [*about the urge of the soul*] is quite accurate about the true soul, the psychic being. But people mean different things when they speak of the soul. Sometimes it is what I have called in the *Arya* the desire soul, — that is the vital with its mixed aspirations, desires, hungers of all kinds good and bad, its emotions, finer and grosser, or sensational urges crossed by the mind's idealisings and psychic stresses. But sometimes it is also the mind and vital under the stress of a psychic urge. The psychic so long as it is veiled must express itself through the mind and vital and its aspirations are mixed and coloured there by the vital and mental stuff. Thus the veiled psychic urge may express itself in the mind by a hunger in the thought for the knowledge of the Divine, what the Europeans call the intellectual love of God. In the vital it may express itself as a hunger or hankering after the Divine. This can bring much suffering because of the nature of the vital, its unquiet passions, desires, ardours, troubled emotions, cloudings, depressions, despairs. The psychic can have a psychic sorrow when things go against its diviner yearnings, but this sorrow has in it no touch of torment, depression or despair. Nevertheless all cannot approach, at least cannot at once approach the Divine in the pure psychic way — the mental and vital approaches are often necessary beginnings and better from the spiritual point of view than an insensitiveness to the Divine. It is in both cases a call of the soul, the soul's urge — it only takes a form or colour due to the stress of the mind or vital nature.

*

For those who have within them a sincere call for the Divine, however the mind or vital may present difficulties or attacks come or the progress be slow and painful, — even if they fall back or fall away from the path for a time, the psychic always prevails in the end and the Divine Help proves effective. Trust in that and persevere — then the goal is sure.

*

There is only one logic in spiritual things: when a demand is there for the Divine, a sincere call, it is bound one day to have its fulfilment. It is only if there is a strong insincerity somewhere, a hankering after something else — power, ambition, etc. — which counterbalances the inner call that the logic is no longer applicable. Supramental realisation is another matter: I am speaking now of the realisation of the Divine, of the contact with the Divine, through whatever lever, heart or mind, or both. In your case it is likely to come through the heart, through increase of bhakti or psychic purification of the heart: that is why I was pressing the psychic way upon you. I do not mean that nothing can come through meditation for you, but probably — barring the unexpected — only after the heart-experience.

Do not allow these wrong ideas and feelings to govern you or your state of depression to dictate your decisions: try to keep a firm central will for the realisation — you can do so if you make up your mind to it — these things are not impossible for you; they are within the scope of your nature which is strong. You will find that the obstinate spiritual difficulty disappears in the end like a mirage. It belongs to the maya and, where the inner call is sincere, cannot hold even the outer consciousness always: its apparent solidity will dissolve.

Turning towards the Divine

An idealistic notion or a religious belief or emotion is something quite different from getting spiritual light. An idealistic notion might turn you towards getting spiritual light, but it is not the light itself.

It is true however that "the spirit bloweth where it listeth", and that one can get some initial impulse or touch of mental realisation of spiritual things from almost any circumstance, as Bilwamangal got it from the words of his courtesan mistress. Obviously it happens because something is ready somewhere, — if you like, the psychic being waiting for its chance and taking some opportunity in mind, vital or heart to knock open a window somewhere.

*

Mental idealism can only have an effect if one has a strong will in the mind capable of forcing the vital to follow.

*

The push to drown oneself in the Divine is very rare. It is usually a mental idea, a vital fumbling or some quite inadequate reason that starts the thing — or else no reason at all. The only reality is the occult psychic push behind of which the surface consciousness is not aware or else hardly aware.

*

Your influence on him for turning towards the Yoga was good, but it was not able to change his vital nature. No human influence — which can only be mental and moral — can do that. You can see that he is just what he was before. It is only from the sadhak's own soul turning towards the Divine [*that the change can come*].

*

It is so with everybody. Part of the nature turns to the Divine, another part does not give its consent at all; it either revolts or remains dully discontented or only pretends to acquiesce. It is only by making the whole being turn whole-heartedly to the Divine that one can enter fully into the Yoga.

Spiritual Destiny

When someone is destined for the Path all circumstances,

through all the deviations of mind and life, help in one way or another to lead him to it. It is his own psychic being within him and the Divine Power above that use to that end the vicissitudes both of mind and outward circumstance.

*

A spiritual opportunity is not a thing that should be lightly thrown away with the idea that it will be all right some other time — one cannot be so sure of the other time. Besides, these things leave a mark and at the place of the mark there can be a recurrence.

*

The spiritual destiny always stands — it may be delayed or seem to be lost for a time, but it is never abolished.

Capacity for Yoga

All can do some kind of Yoga according to their nature, if they have the will to it. But there are few of whom it can be said that they have capacity for this Yoga. Only some can develop a capacity, others cannot. What X wants is peace and something to carry her through the trials of life — she is not ready for more.

*

In sadhana it is not by the personal capacity that things are done. It is the Divine Power that works and if one makes oneself its instrument, even what is impossible for the personal capacity can be done.

*

When one once enters into the true (Yogic) consciousness, then you see that everything can be done, even if at present only a slight beginning has been made; but a beginning is enough, once the Force, the Power are there. It is not really on the capacity of the outer nature that success depends, (for the outer nature all self-exceeding seems impossibly difficult), but on the inner being and to the inner being all is possible. One has only to get into contact with the inner being and change the outer view and consciousness from the inner — that is the work of the sadhana and it is sure to come with sincerity, aspiration and patience.

*

You must realise that these moods are attacks which should be rejected at once — for they repose on nothing but suggestions of self-distrust and incapacity which have no meaning, since it is by the Grace of the Divine and the aid of a Force greater than your own, not by personal capacity and worth that you can attain the goal of the sadhana. You have to remember that and dissociate yourself from these suggestions when they come, never accept or yield to them. No sadhak even if he had the capacity of the ancient Rishis and Tapaswis or the strength of a Vivekananda can hope to keep during the early years of his sadhana a continuous good condition or union with the Divine or an unbroken call or height of aspiration. It takes a long time to spiritualise the whole nature and until that is done, variations must come. A constant trust and patience must be cultivated — must be acquired — not least when things go against — for when they are favourable, trust and patience are easy.

*

Spiritual capacity means simply a natural capacity for true spiritual experience and development. It can be had on any plane, but the natural result is that one gets easily into touch with the Self and the higher planes.

Fitness for Yoga

Nobody is fit for the sadhana — i.e. nobody can do it by his sole capacity. It is a question of preparing oneself to bring in fully the Force not one's own that can do it with one's consent and aspiration.

*

It is useless to raise the question of fitness. No one is fit — for all human beings are full of faults and incapacities — even the greatest sadhaks are not free. It is a question only of aspiration, of believing in the divine Grace and letting the Divine work in you, not making a refusal.

*

It is difficult to say that any particular quality makes one fit or the lack of it unfit. One may have strong sex impulses, doubts, revolts and yet succeed in the end, while another may fail. If one has a fundamental sincerity, a will to go through in spite of all things and a readiness to be guided, that is the best security in the sadhana.

*

Fitness for Yoga is a very relative term — the real fitness comes by the soul's call and the power to open oneself to the Divine. If you have that, you have the fitness, and your past actions cannot stand in the way: the past cannot bind the future. Of course, you have to finish with it, reject it and turn into the new ways — otherwise the past remains the present. But that is the question of the will in you and the soul's call. If you are faithful to your soul's call there is no reason why you should not be able to do Yoga. All that you have to do is to keep your aspiration and not lose the inner connection that has been made — then the Mother's thought and the help will be with you and you will find your way.

*

You speak of your possible unfitness, but it is not a question of fitness or unfitness. There is nobody who can go on in his own strength or by right of his fitness to the goal of the sadhana. It is only by the Divine Grace and reliance on the Divine Grace that it can be done. It is in a strength greater than your own that you must put your first and last reliance. If your faith falters you have to call on that to sustain you; if your force is insufficient against the ill-will and opposition that surround you, open yourself to receive that force in its place.

*

The Mother's help and mine are always there for you. You have only to turn fully towards it and it will act on you. What has come across is these wrong ideas about your unfitness, about bad things in you that prevent you from receiving the Mother's grace, about the lack of aspiration which prevents you from having realisation and experience. These thoughts are quite wrong and untrue — they are not even your own thoughts, they are suggestions thrown on you just as they are thrown on the other sadhaks and intended to produce depression. There is no unfitness, no bad thing inside that comes across, no lack of aspiration causing the cessation of experience. It is the depression, the self-distrust, the readiness to despair which are the only cause; there is no other. To all sadhaks, as I wrote to you, even to the best and strongest there come interruptions in the flow of the sadhana; that is not a cause for thinking oneself unfit and wanting to go away with the idea that there is no hope. A little quietude would bring back the flow. You were having the necessary experiences, the necessary progress and it was only a coming forward of some difficulties of the physical consciousness that stopped them for a time. That happens to all and is not particular to you, as I explained to you. These difficulties always come and have to be overcome. Once overcome by the working of the Force, the sadhana goes on as before. But you began to entertain this wrong idea of unfitness and lack of aspiration as the cause and got entirely depressed. You must shake all that off and refuse to believe in the thought-suggestions that come to you. No sadhak ought ever to indulge thoughts of unfitness and hopelessness — they are quite irrelevant because it is not one's personal fitness and worthiness that makes one succeed, but the Mother's grace and power and the consent of the soul to her grace and the workings of her Force.

Turn from these dark thoughts and look to the Mother only, not with impatience for the result and desire, but with trust and confidence and let her workings bring you quietude

The Call and the Capacity 35

and the renewal of the progress towards the psychic opening and realisation. That will bring surely and without doubt the fuller faith and the love which you seek.

*

I repeat what I said before (though your physical mind does not yet believe) that these experiences show at once that your inner being is a Yogi capable of trance, ecstasy, intensest bhakti, fully aware of Yoga and Yoga consciousness, and showing himself the very moment you get inside yourself, even as the outer man is very much the other way round, modernised, externalised, vigorously outward-vital (for the Yogi is inward-vital and psychic) and knowing nothing of Yoga or the world of inner experience. I could see at once when I saw you that there was this inner Yogin and your former experiences here were quite convincing to anyone who knows anything at all about these things. When there is this inner Yogin inside, the coming to the way of Yoga is sure and not even the most externalised surface consciousness — not even a regular *homo Russelicus* outside and you are not that, only a little *Russelicatus* on the surface, — can prevent final success in the Yoga. But the tussle between the inward and the outward man can create a lot of trouble, because the inward man pushes towards the Divine and will not let go and the outward man regrets, repines, pulls back, asks what is this shadowy thing to which he is being brought, this Unknown, this (to him) far-off Ineffable. That, and not merely sex, food or society, is the genesis of the struggle and trouble in you. And yet it is all a misunderstanding — for if the outer gave way entirely to the inner Yogi, he would find that what he lost or thought he was losing would be repaid a hundredfold — though he would get it in another spirit and consciousness, not any longer the transient and deceptive delight of the world for its own sake, but the delight of the Divine in the world, a thousand times more intense, sweet and desirable.

*

The vision of the Light and the vision of the Lord in the form of

Jagannath are both of them indications that he has the capacity for Yoga experience and that there is a call of the Divine on his inner being. But capacity is not enough; there must be also the will to seek after the Divine and courage and persistence in following the path. Fear is the first thing that must be thrown away and, secondly, the inertia of the outer being which has prevented him from responding to the call.

The Light is the light of the Divine Consciousness. The aim of this Yoga is first to come into contact with this consciousness and then to live in its light and allow the light to transform the whole nature, so that the being may live in union with the Divine and the nature become a field for the action of the Divine Knowledge, the Divine Power and the Divine Ananda.

He can succeed in that only if he makes it the supreme object of his life and is prepared to subordinate everything else to this one aim. Otherwise all that can be done is only to make some preparation in this life — a first contact and some preliminary spiritual change in part of the nature.

Capacity of Westerners for Yoga

The best way to answer your letter will be, I think, to take separately the questions implied in it. I will begin with the conclusion you have drawn of the impossibility of the Yoga for a non-Oriental nature.

I cannot see any ground for such a conclusion; it is contrary to all experience. Europeans throughout the centuries have practised with success spiritual disciplines which were akin to Oriental Yogas and have followed too ways of the inner life which came to them from the East. Their non-Oriental nature did not stand in their way. The approach and experiences of Plotinus and the European mystics who derived from him were identical, as has been shown recently, with the approach and experiences of one type of Indian Yoga. Especially, since the introduction of Christianity Europeans have followed its mystic disciplines which were one in essence with those of Asia, however much they may have differed in forms, names and symbols.

If the question be of Indian Yoga itself in its own characteristic forms, here too the supposed inability is contradicted by experience. In early times Greeks and Scythians from the West as well as Chinese and Japanese and Cambodians from the East followed without difficulty Buddhist or Hindu disciplines; at the present day an increasing number of occidentals have taken to Vedantic or Vaishnava or other Indian spiritual practices and this objection of incapacity or unsuitableness has never been made either from the side of the disciples or from the side of the Masters. I do not see, either, *why* there should be any such unbridgeable gulf; for there is no essential difference between spiritual life in the East and spiritual life in the West, — what difference there is has always been of names, forms and symbols or else of the emphasis laid on one special aim or another or on one side or another of psychological experience. Even here differences are often alleged which do not exist or else are not so great as they appear. I have seen it alleged by a Christian writer (who does not seem to have shared your friend X's objection to these scholastic (?) distinctions) that Hindu spiritual thought and life acknowledged or followed after only the Transcendent and neglected the Immanent Divinity while Christianity gave due place to both Aspects; but, in matter of fact, Indian spirituality, even if it laid the final stress on the Highest beyond form and name, yet gave ample recognition and place to the Divine immanent in the world and the Divine immanent in the human being. Indian spirituality has, it is true, a wider and more minute knowledge behind it; it has followed hundreds of different paths, admitted every kind of approach to the Divine and has thus been able to enter into fields which are outside the less ample scope of occidental practice; but that makes no difference to the essentials, and it is the essentials alone that matter.

Your explanation of the ability of many Westerners to practise Indian Yoga seems to be that they have a Hindu temperament in a European or American body. As Gandhi is inwardly a moralistic Westerner and Christian, so, you say, the other non-Oriental members of the Asram are essentially Hindus in outlook. But what exactly is this Hindu outlook? I have not myself seen anything in them that can be so described nor has the Mother. My own experience contradicts entirely your explanation. I knew very well Sister Nivedita (she was for many years a friend and a comrade in the political field) and met Sister Christine, — the two closest European disciples of Vivekananda. Both were Westerners to the core and had nothing at all of the Hindu outlook; although Sister Nivedita, an Irishwoman, had the power of penetrating by an intense sympathy into the ways of life of the people around her, her own nature remained non-Oriental to the end. Yet she found no difficulty in arriving at realisation on the lines of Vedanta. Here in this Asram I have found the members of it who came from the West (I include especially those who have been here longest) typically occidental with all the quality and also all the difficulties of the Western mind and temperament and they have had to cope with their difficulties, just as the Indian members have been obliged to struggle with the limitations and obstacles created by *their* temperament and training. No doubt, they have accepted in principle the conditions of the Yoga; but they had no Hindu outlook when they came and I do not think they have tried to acquire one. Why should they do so? It is not the Hindu outlook or the Western that fundamentally matters in Yoga, but the psychic turn and the spiritual urge, and these are the same everywhere.

What are the differences after all from the viewpoint of Yoga between the sadhak of Indian and the sadhak of occidental birth? You say the Indian has his Yoga half done for him, — first, because he has his psychic much more directly open to the Transcendent Divine. Leaving out the adjective, (for it is not many who are by nature drawn to the Transcendent, most seek more readily the Personal, the Divine immanent here, especially if they can find it in a human body), there is there no doubt an advantage. It arises simply from the strong survival in India of an atmosphere of spiritual seeking, and a long tradition of practice and experience, while in Europe the atmosphere has been lost, the tradition interrupted and both have to be rebuilt. There is an absence too of the *essential* doubt which so much afflicts the minds of Europeans or, it may be added, of Europeanised Indians, although that does not prevent a great activity of a practical and very operative kind of doubt in the Indian sadhak. But when you speak of indifference to fellow human beings in any deeper aspect, I am unable to follow your meaning. My own experience is that the attachment to persons — to mother, father, wife, children, friends — not out of sense of duty or social relationship, but through close heart-ties is quite as strong as in Europe and often more intense; it is one of the great stumbling blocks in the way, some succumbing to the pull and many even advanced sadhaks being still unable to get it out of their blood and their vital fibre. The impulse to set up a "spiritual" or a "psychic" relationship with others — very usually covering a vital mixture which distracts them from the one aim — is a persistently common feature. There is no difference here between Western and Eastern human nature. Only the teaching in India is of old standing that all must be turned towards the Divine and everything else either sacrificed or changed into a subordinate and ancillary movement or made by sublimation a first step only towards the seeking for the Divine. This no doubt helps the Indian sadhak if not to become single-hearted at once, yet to orientate himself more completely towards the goal. It is not always for him the Divine alone, though that is considered the highest state, but the Divine chief and first is easily grasped by him as the ideal.

The Indian sadhak has his own difficulties in his approach to the Yoga — at least to this Yoga — which a Westerner has in less measure. Those of the occidental nature are born of the dominant trend of the European mind in the immediate past. A greater readiness of essential doubt and sceptical reserve; a habit of mental activity as a necessity of the nature which makes it more difficult to achieve a complete mental silence; a stronger turn towards outside things born of the plenitude of active life (while the Indian commonly suffers from defects born rather of a depressed or suppressed vital force); a habit of mental and vital self-assertion and sometimes an aggressively vigilant independence which renders difficult any completeness of internal surrender even to a greater Light and Knowledge, even to the divine Influence — these are frequent obstacles. But these things are not universal in Westerners, and they are on the other hand present in many Indian sadhaks, and they are, like the difficulties of the typical Indian nature, superstructural formations, not the very grain of the being. They cannot permanently stand in the way of the soul, if the soul's aspiration is strong and firm, if the spiritual aim is the chief thing in the life. They are impediments which the fire within can easily burn away if the will to get rid of them is strong, and which it will surely burn away in the end, — though less easily — even if the outer nature clings long to them and justifies them — provided that central will, that deeper impulse is behind all, real and sincere.

This conclusion of yours about the incapacity of the non-Oriental for Indian Yoga is simply born of a too despondently acute sense of your own difficulties, — you have not seen those, equally great, that have long troubled or are still troubling others. Neither to Indian nor to European can the path of Yoga be smooth and easy; their common human nature is there to see to that. To each his own difficulties seem enormous and radical and even incurable by their continuity and persistence and induce long periods of despondency and crises of despair. To have faith enough or enough psychic sight to react at once or almost at once and prevent these attacks is given hardly to two or three in a hundred. But one ought not to settle down into a fixed idea of one's own incapacity or allow it to become an obsession; for such an attitude has no true justification and unnecessarily renders the way harder. Where there is a soul that has once become awake, there is surely a capacity within that can outweigh all surface defects and can in the end conquer.

If your conclusion were true, the whole aim of this Yoga would be a vain thing; for we are not working for a race or a people or a continent or for a realisation of which only Indians or only Orientals are capable. Our aim is not, either, to found a religion or a school of philosophy or a school of Yoga, but to create a ground and a way of spiritual growth and experience which will bring down a greater Truth beyond the mind but not inaccessible to the human soul and consciousness. All can pass who are drawn to that Truth, whether they are from India or elsewhere, from the East or from the West. All may find great difficulties in their personal or common human nature; but it is not their physical origin or their racial temperament that can be an insuperable obstacle to their deliverance.

*

I am not sure about the last matter.[1] After all India with her mentality and method has done a hundred times more in the spiritual field than Europe with her intellectual doubts and questionings. Even when a European overcomes the doubt and questioning, he does not find it as easy to go as fast and far as an Indian with the same force of personality because the stir of mind is still greater. It is only when he can get beyond that that he arrives, but for him it is not so easy.

On the other hand however your statement is correct. It [*the tendency to doubt and question*] is "natural considering the times" and the occidental mentality prevalent everywhere. It is also probably necessary that this should be faced and overcome before any supramental realisation is possible in the earth-consciousness — for it is the attitude of the physical mind to spiritual things and as it is in the physical that the resistance has to be overcome before the mind can be overpassed in the way required for this Yoga, the strongest possible representation of its difficulties was indispensable.

---

[1] *The correspondent suggested that in this Yoga a disciple with an occidental mentality might be "even better off" than a disciple with a traditional Indian mentality of humility and respect for the Guru. — Ed.*

Chapter Two
Qualities Needed for Sadhana

Indispensable Qualities

It goes without saying that the qualities you speak of are helpful in the approach to the spiritual path, while the defects you enumerate are each a serious stumbling-block in the way. Sincerity especially is indispensable to the spiritual endeavour, and crookedness a constant obstacle. The sattwic nature has always been held to be the most apt and ready for the spiritual life, while the rajasic nature is encumbered by its desires and passions. At the same time, spirituality is something above the dualities, and what is most needed for it is a true upward aspiration. This may come to the rajasic man as well as to the sattwic. If it does, he can rise by it above his failings and desires and passions, just as the other can rise beyond his virtues, to the Divine Purity and Light and Love. Necessarily this can only happen if he conquers his lower nature and throws it from him; for if he relapses into it, he is likely to fall from the path or at least to be, so long as the relapse lasts, held back by it from inner progress. But for all that the conversion of great sinners into great saints, of men of little or no virtue into spiritual seekers and God-lovers has frequently happened in religious and spiritual history — as in Europe St. Augustine, in India Chaitanya's Jagai and Madhai, Bilwamangal and many others. The house of the Divine is not closed to any who knock sincerely at its gates, whatever their past stumbles and errors. Human virtues and human errors are bright and dark wrappings of a divine element within which once it pierces the veil, can burn through both towards the heights of the Spirit.

Humility before the Divine is also a *sine qua non* of the spiritual life, and spiritual pride, arrogance, or vanity and self-assurance press always downward. But confidence in the Divine and a faith in one's spiritual destiny (i.e. since my heart and soul seek for the Divine, I cannot fail one day to reach Him) are much needed in view of the difficulties of the Path. A contempt for others is out of place, especially since the Divine is in all. Evidently, the activities and aspirations of men are not trivial and worthless, for all life is a growth of the soul out of the darkness towards the Light. But our attitude is that humanity cannot grow out of its limitations by the ordinary means adopted by the human mind, politics, social reform, philanthropy, etc., —these can only be temporary or local palliatives. The only true escape is a change of consciousness, a change into a greater, wider and purer way of being, and a life and action based upon that change. It is therefore to that that the energies must be turned, once the spiritual orientation is complete. This implies no contempt, but the preference of the only effective means over those which have been found ineffective.

*

Such qualities as faith, sincerity, aspiration, devotion etc. make up the perfection indicated in our language of the flowers.[1] In ordinary language it would mean something else such as purity, love, benevolence, fidelity and a host of other virtues.

Conditions of the Yoga

I have never said that this Yoga was a safe one — no Yoga is. Each has its dangers as has every great attempt in human life. But it can be carried through if one has a central sincerity and a fidelity to the Divine. These are the two necessary conditions.

*

The first conditions of this Yoga are:
(1) A complete sincerity and surrender in the being. The divine life and the transformation of the lower human into the higher divine nature must be made the sole aim of all the life.

---

[1] *The Mother named the* Plumeria *flower "Psychological perfection" and said that its five elements were faith, sincerity, aspiration, devotion and surrender.* — Ed.

No attachments, desires or habits of the mind, heart, vital being or body should be clung to which come in the way of this one aspiration and one object of the life. One must be ready to renounce all these completely as soon as the demand comes from above and from the divine Shakti.

(2) A fundamental calm, peace and purity in the mind, vital being and all the nature.

The hours of meditation should be devoted to the formation of these two conditions in you, by aspiration and by self-observation and rejection of all that disturbs the nature or keeps it troubled, confused and impure. Aspiration if rightly done, quietly, earnestly and sincerely, brings the divine help from above to effect this object.

As to the hours devoted to work, needs, family, etc., hey can be made an aid only on the following conditions.

(1) To regard all these things as not belonging to yourself, your inner being, but as things external, work to be done so long as it remains on your shoulders to the best of your ability without desire or attachment of any kind.

(2) To do all work as a sacrifice without any egoistic motive.

(3) To establish and deepen the inner calm and quiet. If that is done, all these things will be felt more and more as external and the falling off of desire and attachment will become possible.

For getting rid of passion the same condition. If you separate yourself from these movements and establish calm and peace inside, the passions may still rise on the surface, but they will be felt to be external movements and you can deal with them or call down the divine aid to get rid of them. So long as the mind does not fall quiet, it is not possible to deal finally with the vital being from which these forces rise.

*

The way to realise is through a quiet mind and a vital free from desires. To reject the desires and demands of the vital and to quiet the excessive activity of the mind, so that a true consciousness and spiritual perception and knowledge may take the place of the mind's activity, are the requisite conditions of the Yoga.

The further method is, — (1) To concentrate in the heart and aspire and (2) to call to the divine Mother to enter there and purify the mind and vital and unveil the psychic being so that her constant guidance and presence in it may be felt always and (3) to concentrate in the quiet mind and (in the head) open oneself first to the divine force and light which is always above the mind and call to it to descend into the body and the whole being — either of these or both, according to the capacity of the sadhaka.

Yoga must be done not for oneself or what one can get but for the sake of the Divine and to be united with the Divine.

If he can do any of these things (not minding how long it takes) in this spirit, then let him do Yoga; if he cannot, then there is no use in doing it.

Chapter Three

Purity

Purification of the Nature

A certain amount of purification is necessary before there can be any realisation of the Divine and that is what has been going on in you. It is after all not a very long time since the real purification began and it is never an easy work. So the impatience may be natural, but it is not exactly reasonable.

*

Purification — rejecting from one's nature all that is egoistic or of the nature of rajasic desire.
 Aspiration for peace and calm and a perfect equality.
 Purification and a basis of calm are the first necessary steps in the spiritual life.

*

The aspiration must be for entire purification, especially (1) purification from sex, so that no sex imaginations may enter and the sex impulse may cease, (2) purification from desires and demands, (3) purification from depression which is the result of disappointed desires. It is the most important for you. Particularly what you must aspire for is peace in all the being, complete equanimity, samata. The feeling that peace is not enough must go. Peace and purity and equanimity once established, all the rest must be the Mother's free gift, not a result of the demand from the being.
 You can mix normally with people keeping as much as possible an inner quietude. In future when the purification is done and a continuous experience possible we can reconsider the matter.

*

Very often the earlier stage of the sadhana is successful, because there is an opening of the mind to first workings of the Force — afterwards the lower vital consciousness and the physical rise up and if these are not ready or inclined for the sadhana, it ceases. The sadhaka has first to purify and open them and call in the Force to work there and make all ready until he can bring the true consciousness and experience there. Yoga implies a long and difficult work and one must be ready to accept the necessity of years of preparation and purification and increasing consecration before the greater results can come.

*

By meditation alone and trying to concentrate you will never succeed. There must be an aspiration from the heart and a giving up of all yourself to Krishna.

In your nature there are many obstacles, chiefly a great activity of the outward-going mind and a thick crust of the impure lower Prakriti that covers the heart and the vital being. Quieting of the mind and purification of the nature are what you must have before you can fulfil your aim. Aspire for these two things first; ask for them constantly from above. You will not be able to achieve them by your own unaided effort.

*

As for the way out of the impasse, I know only of the quieting of the mind which makes meditation effective, purification of the heart which brings the divine touch and in time the divine presence, humility before the Divine which liberates from egoism and the pride of the mind and of the vital, the pride that imposes its own reasonings on the ways of the spirit and the pride that refuses or is unable to surrender, sustained persistence in the call within and reliance on the Grace above. Meditation, japa, prayer or aspiration from the heart can all succeed, if they are attended by these or even some of these things. But I do not know that you can be promised what you always make the condition of any inner endeavour, an immediate or almost immediate realisation or beginning of concrete realisation. I fully believe on the other hand that one who has the call in him cannot fail to arrive, if he follows patiently the way towards the Divine.

*

I can only hope that the depression and the suggestions it brings will pass away soon. You were making very good progress before it touched you. There is no impossibility in the purification of the heart which was the thing you were trying for and when the heart is purified, other things which seemed impossible before become easy — even the inner surrender which now seems to you impracticable. I at any rate will go on trusting in your spiritual destiny until the performance of the "miracle".

The Meaning of Purity

Purity is to accept no other influence but only the influence of the Divine.

*

It [*purity*] is more a condition than a substance. Peace helps to purity — since in peace disturbing influences cease and the essence of purity is to respond only to the Divine Influence and not to have an affinity with other movements.

*

Purity means freedom from soil or mixture. The divine Purity is that in which there is no mixture of the turbid ignorant movements of the lower nature. Ordinarily purity is used to mean (in the common language) freedom from vital passion and impulse.

*

The Divine Purity is a more wide and all-embracing experience than the psychic.

*

Purity or impurity depends upon the consciousness; in the divine consciousness everything is pure, in the ignorance everything is subject to impurity, not the body only or part of the body, but mind and vital and all. Only the self and the psychic being remain always pure.

*

A pure mind means a mind quiet and free from thoughts of a useless or disturbing character.

*

X pretends to be pure and surrendered to the will of God. How can he be pure when his whole trouble has come from the indulgence of impure desires? He pretends to act according to God's will, but his actions are moved by three things, desire, vanity and self-will. The devil makes suggestions supported by one or another of these three motives and persuades him that it is the will of God.

Ignorance is not a state of innocence or purity; that is an old blunder. Only a consciousness full of light can be pure. For instance, when you are conscious, your mind is clear and you have the right ideas about things and people; your mind is pure of ignorance. But when the mind is clouded by some impurity, — say, anger, jealousy or pride or some unreasonable desire, — you at once become ignorant and mistake and misunderstand everything.

Again, when your heart is turned to the Mother and satisfied with her love, when you are full of peace, contentment and happiness, then there is no room for wrong feelings and desires; your heart is pure.

This is what the Mother meant by purity; to be free from false ideas, wrong feelings, desires, demands etc. is to be pure.

*

Purity in the consciousness and purity in the conduct is what is usually meant by these terms [*inner and outer purity*].

Chapter Four

Sincerity

The Meaning of Sincerity

There is one indispensable condition, sincerity.

*

What is meant by "sincere"? Sincerity means to accept the Divine influence only and not that of lower forces.

*

Sincerity means to be turned wholly to the Divine and accept only the Divine impulses — it means also the true and constant will or effort to be like this.

*

Sincere is simply an adjective meaning that the will must be a true will. If you simply think "I aspire" and do things inconsistent with the aspiration, or follow your desires or open yourself to contrary influences, then it is not a sincere will.

*

Sincerity means more than mere honesty. It means that you mean what you say, feel what you profess, are earnest in your will. As the sadhak aspires to be an instrument of the Divine and one with the Divine, sincerity in him means that he is really in earnest in his aspiration and refuses all other will or impulse except the Divine's.

*

[*Sincerity*:] To allow no part of the being to contradict the highest aspiration towards the Divine.

*

All sincere aspiration has its effect; if you are sincere, you will grow into the divine life.

To be entirely sincere means to desire the divine Truth only, to surrender yourself more and more to the Divine Mother, to reject all personal demand and desire other than this one aspiration, to offer every action in life to the Divine and do it as the work given without bringing in the ego. This is the basis of the divine life.

One cannot become altogether this at once, but if one aspires at all times to it and calls in always the aid of the Divine Shakti with a true heart and straightforward will, one grows more and more into this consciousness.

Sincerity in Sadhana

Men are always mixed and there are qualities and defects mingled together almost inextricably in their nature. What a man wants to be or wants others to see in him or what he is sometimes on one side of his nature or in some relations can be very different from what he is in the actual fact or in other relations or on another side of his nature. To be absolutely sincere, straightforward, open, is not an easy achievement for human nature. It is only by spiritual endeavour that one can realise it — and to do it needs a severity of introspective self-vision, an unsparing scrutiny of self-observation of which many sadhaks or Yogins even are not capable and it is only by an illumining Grace that reveals the sadhak to himself and transforms what is deficient in him that it can be done. And even then only if he himself consents and lends himself wholly to the divine working.

*

It is quite natural that there should be much mixture in the attitude till all is clear — the ordinary nature clings to the action and the transformation in its completeness cannot be sudden. What is necessary is that the basic consciousness should become firmly established in the Divine, then the mixture in the rest can be seen and steadily weeded out. To have this outwardly as well as inwardly is a great progress.

*

It is true that a central sincerity is not enough except as a beginning and a base; the sincerity must spread as you describe through the whole nature. But still unless there is a double nature (without a central harmonising consciousness) the basis is usually sufficient for that to happen.

*

I do not think there is any reason for anxiety about your sadhana. We feel always a great depth and sincerity of aspiration in you which keeps you in constant and close relation with us, and where there is this depth and sincerity and this closeness the progressive opening of the being is assured; for the openness already exists.

*

You speak of insincerity in your nature. If insincerity means the unwillingness of some part of the being to live according to the highest light one has or to equate the outer with the inner man, then this part is always insincere in all. The only way is to lay stress on the inner being and develop in it the psychic and spiritual consciousness till that comes down in it which pushes out the darkness from the outer man also.

*

It is not sincerity to express only what the adverse forces suggest or what you feel when you are in a bad condition full of obscurity and a wrong outlook. When you are in the Truth, you feel quite the opposite and it is not insincerity to cling to that and recall it. It is only by bringing it back that the Truth can grow in you.

The trouble in your chest comes only from a vital resistance and it continues because you identify yourself with that resistance. It is only by quietude and opening to the Mother that these things can disappear. There is no other way to progress.

If you have not got quietude, you can always aspire first and a sincere aspiration will bring it back.

*

All need vital sincerity, it is the most difficult to have and the most needful.

*

To perceive one's own weaknesses is one result of sincerity.

*

One cannot be perfect in discrimination at once or in rejection either. The one indispensable thing is to go on trying sincerely till there comes the full success. So long as there is complete sincerity, the Divine Grace will be there and assist at every moment on the way.

*

If he [*the sadhak*] is sincere, there is bound to be devotion. Sincerity in Yoga means to respond to the Divine alone and if he has no devotion he cannot do it.

*

It is difficult for the ordinary Christian to be of a piece, because the teachings of Christ are on quite another plane from the consciousness of the intellectual and vital man trained by the education and society of Europe — the latter, even as a minister or priest, has never been called upon to practise what he preached in entire earnest. But it is difficult for the human nature anywhere to think, feel and act from one centre of true faith, belief or vision. The average Hindu considers the spiritual life the highest, reveres the Sannyasi, is moved by the Bhakta; but if one of the family circle leaves the world for spiritual life, what tears, arguments, remonstrances, lamentations! It is almost worse than if he had died a natural death. It is not conscious mental insincerity — they will argue like Pandits and go to Shastra to prove you in the wrong; it is unconsciousness, a vital insincerity which they are not aware of and which uses the reasoning mind as an accomplice.

That is why we insist so much on sincerity in the Yoga — and that means to have all the being consciously turned towards the one Truth, the one Divine. But that for human nature is one of the most difficult of tasks, much more difficult than a rigid asceticism or a fervent piety. Religion itself does not give this complete harmonised sincerity — it is only the psychic being and the one-souled spiritual aspiration that can give it.

Earnestness and Straightforwardness

In the major part of your being you are very much in earnest. But of course there are always parts or rather parts of parts that are not equally ready to change. But that is not hypocrisy. It is so with everybody, otherwise there would be no difficulty in the transformation.

*

Straightforwardness means simply to be honest with oneself and with the Divine and not to be crooked in one's ways.

Self-justification is unwillingness to recognise a mistake and an attempt to prove oneself right even against the censure of the Mother.

Chapter Five

Aspiration

The Value of Aspiration

What you say is quite true. A simple, straight and sincere call and aspiration from the heart is the one important thing and more essential and effective than capacities. Also to get the consciousness to turn inwards, not remain outward-going is of great importance — to arrive at the inner call, the inner experience, the inner Presence.

The help you ask will be with you. Let the aspiration grow and open the inner consciousness altogether.

*

One has only to aspire sincerely and keep oneself as open as possible to the Mother's Force. Then whatever difficulties come, they will be overcome — it may take some time, but the result is sure.

*

One has to suppose that [*the Mother's*] force everywhere around and call it in — if one feels it, so much the better, but even otherwise if there is faith and power in the call, it can flow in.

*

One must rely on the Divine and yet do some enabling sadhana — the Divine gives the fruits, not by the measure of the sadhana but by the measure of the soul and its aspiration. Also worrying does no good — "I shall be this, I shall be that, what shall I be?" Say "I am ready to be not what I want, but what the Divine wants me to be" — all the rest should go on that base.

*

I mean by the measure of the soul's sincerity a yearning after the

Divine and its aspiration towards the higher life.

*

But why allow *anything* to come in the way between you and the Divine, any idea, any incident; when you are in full aspiration and joy, let nothing count, nothing be of any importance except the Divine and your aspiration. If one wants the Divine quickly, absolutely, entirely, that must be the spirit of approach, absolute, all-engrossing, making that the one point with which nothing else must interfere.

What value have mental ideas about the Divine, ideas about what he should be, how he should act, how he should not act — they can only come in the way. Only the Divine Himself matters. When your consciousness embraces the Divine, then you can know what the Divine is, not before. Krishna is Krishna, one does not care what he did or did not do; only to see Him, meet Him, feel the Light, the Presence, the Love, the Ananda is what matters. So it is always for the spiritual aspiration — it is the law of the spiritual life.

Don't waste time any longer in these ideas of the mind or in any starts of the vital — blow these clouds away. Keep fixed on the one thing indispensable.

The Meaning of Aspiration

There is no deep meaning [*of aspiration*] — the meaning is plain. It is the call of the being for higher things — for the Divine, for all that belongs to the higher or Divine Consciousness.

*

It [*aspiration*] is the call in the being for the Divine or for the higher things that belong to the Divine Consciousness. (To "aspire" always means to call for higher things.)

*

Aspiration is a turning upward of the inner being with a call, yearning, prayer for the Divine, for the Truth, for the

Consciousness, Peace, Ananda, Knowledge, descent of Divine Force or whatever else is the aim of one's endeavour.

*

Aspiration is to call the forces. When the forces have answered, there is a natural state of quiet receptivity concentrated but spontaneous.

*

Aspiration is a call to the Divine, — will is the pressure of a conscious force on Nature.

*

Aspiration is a call in the being, it is not opening.

The Object of Aspiration

The aspiration should be for the full descent of the Truth and the victory over falsehood in the world.

*

Aspire for the constant contact and the light. It is in the Light that the being will get organised in the Truth.

*

Aspire for your will to be one with the Divine will, concentrate in the heart and be plastic to whatever experience comes, neither forcing nor resisting any spiritual experience.

*

The aspiration for the supramental would be premature. What you have to aspire for is for the psychic change and the spiritual change of the whole being — which is the necessary condition before one can even think of the supramental.

*

To want to be a superman is a mistake, it only swells the ego.

One can aspire for the Divine to bring about the supramental transformation, but that also should not be done till the being has become psychic and spiritualised by the descent of the Mother's peace, force, light and purity.

No Need of Words in Aspiration

There is no need of words in aspiration. It can be expressed or unexpressed in words.

*

The aspiration need not be in the form of thought — it can be a feeling within that remains even when the mind is attending to the work.

The Necessity of Aspiration

It depends on the stage which one has reached. Personal aspiration is necessary until there is the condition in which all comes automatically and only a certain knowledge and assent is necessary for the development.

*

Even if there is no rising up, the aspiration connects you with the higher consciousness and helps or prepares to bring down something from it.

*

It [*the higher consciousness*] may not come exactly according to the aspiration, but the aspiration is not ineffective. It keeps the consciousness open, prevents an inert state of acquiescence in all that comes and exercises a sort of pull on the sources of the higher consciousness.

*

Aspiration during the period of experience is not so necessary.

It is in the intervals that it should be there.

*

Why do you write "If I get" [*aspiration*] — one can always aspire. It is your mistake to think that everything must come of itself and nothing is within your own power to do. This kind of belief in the necessity of passivity to all movements should be thrown aside. Will, aspiration, surrender are things that you must do yourself — although even in doing them you must call in the Divine Power to help your will, aspiration and surrender and make them effective.

*

Why "getting" aspiration? Aspiration is an act of the will and one can always aspire.

*

Activity in aspiration, tapasya, rejection of the wrong forces, passivity to the true working, the working of the Mother's force are the right things in sadhana.

*

One has to aspire to the Divine and surrender and leave it to the Divine to do what is true and right with the Adhar once it is perfected.

Intensity of Aspiration and Vital Impatience

Intense aspiration is always good, but let there also be calm and peace and joy in the mind and heart, and a confidence that all will be done in its due time.

*

There can be an intense but quiet aspiration which does not disturb the harmony of the inner being.

*

Yes — that is the way. The intensity of the aspiration brings the intensity of the experience and by repeated intensity of the experience the change.

*

The impatience and restless disquietude come from the vital which brings that even into the aspiration. The aspiration must be intense, calm and strong (that is the nature of the true vital also) and not restless and impatient, — then alone it can be stable.

*

It is the psychic that gives the true aspiration — if the vital is purified and subjected to the psychic, then the vital gives intensity — but if it is unpurified it brings in a rajasic intensity with impatience and reactions of depression and disappointment. As for the calm and equality needed, it must come down from above through the mind.

*

That [*fiery aspiration*] is all right, that is the psychic aspiration, the psychic fire. Where the vital comes in is in the impatience for result and dissatisfaction if the result is not immediate. That must cease.

Aspiration and Desire

One should be satisfied with what one gets and still aspire quietly, without struggle, for more — till all has come. No desire, no struggle — aspiration, faith, openness — and the grace.

*

There is no doubt the mixture of desire in what you do, even in your endeavour of sadhana, that is the difficulty. The desire brings a movement of impatient effort and a reaction of disappointment and revolt when difficulty is felt and the immediate result is not there and other confusing and disturbing feelings. Aspiration should be not a form of desire, but the feeling of an inner soul's need, and a quiet settled will to turn towards the Divine and seek the Divine. It is certainly not easy to get rid of this mixture of desire entirely — not easy for anyone; but when one has the will to do it, this also can be effected by the help of the sustaining Force.

*

If there are good desires, bad desires will come also. There is a place for will and aspiration, not for desire.

If there is desire there will be attachment, demand, craving, loss of equanimity, sorrow at not getting, all that is unyogic.

Aspiration and Pulling

Pulling comes usually from a desire to get things for oneself — in aspiration there is a self-giving for the higher consciousness to descend and take possession — the more intense the call, the greater the self-giving.

*

It is certainly a mistake to bring down the light by force — to pull it down. The supramental cannot be taken by storm. When the time is ready it will open of itself — but first there is a great deal to be done and that must be done patiently and without haste.

Lack of Aspiration

Naturally the more one-pointed the aspiration the swifter the progress. The difficulty comes when either the vital with its desires or the physical with its past habitual movements comes in — as they do with almost everyone. It is then that the dryness and difficulty of spontaneous aspiration come. This dryness is a well-known obstacle in all sadhana. But one has to persist and not be discouraged. If one keeps the will fixed even in these barren periods, they pass and after their passage a greater force of aspiration and experience becomes possible.

*

You are finding it still difficult to bear the interval periods when all is quiet and nothing being done on the surface. But such interval periods come to all and cannot be avoided. You must not cherish the suggestion that it is because of your want of aspiration or any other unfitness that it is so and, if you had the constant ardent aspiration, then there would be no such periods and there would be an uninterrupted stream of experiences. It is not so. Even if the aspiration were there, the interval periods would come. If even in them one can aspire, so much the better — but the main thing is to meet them with quietude and not become restless, depressed or despondent. A constant fire can be there only when a certain stage has been reached, that is when one is always inside consciously living in the psychic being, but for that all this preparation of the mind, vital, physical is necessary. For this fire belongs to the psychic and one cannot command it always merely by the mind's effort. The psychic has to be fully liberated and that is what the Force is working to make fully possible.

*

No doubt the true and strong aspiration is needed, but it is not a fact that the true thing is not there in you. If it had not been, the Force could not have worked in you. But this true thing was seated in the psychic and in the heart and whenever these were active in the meditation it showed itself. But for the sake of completeness the working had to come down into the physical consciousness and establish the quietude and the openness there. The physical consciousness is always in everybody in its own nature a little inert and in it a constant strong aspiration is not natural, it has to be created. But first there must be the opening, a purification, a fixed quietude, otherwise the physical vital will turn the strong aspiration into over-eagerness and impatience or rather it will try to give it that turn. Do not therefore be troubled if the state of the nature seems to you to be too neutral and quiet, not enough aspiration and movement in it. This is a passage necessary for the progress and the rest will come.

Aspiration and Conversion

Those who come here have an aspiration and a possibility — something in their psychic being pushes and if they follow it, they will arrive; but that is not conversion. Conversion is a definite turning of the being away from lower things towards the Divine.

*

Aspiration can lead hereafter to conversion; but aspiration is not conversion.

*

Conversion is a spontaneous movement of the consciousness, a turning of it away from external things towards the Divine. It comes usually as the result of a touch from within and above. Self-consecration may help to open one to the touch or the touch may come of itself. But conversion may also come as the culmination of a long process of aspiration and tapasya. There is no fixed rule in these things.

If the psychic being comes to the front, then conversion becomes easy or may come instantaneously or the conversion may bring the psychic being to the front. Here again there is no rule.

Chapter Six

Rejection

Rejection of the Lower Impulses

It is no part of the sadhana to accept the uglinesses of the lower nature on the ground that they exist — if that is what is meant by realism. Our object is not to accept or enjoy these things but to get rid of them and create a life of spiritual beauty and perfection. So long as we accept these things, that cannot be done. To observe that these things are there and reject them, refusing to allow them to touch you, is one thing; to accept and acquiesce in them is quite another.

*

Who is able to reject the lower nature fully? All one can do is to aspire and reject the lower impulses and call in the Divine to do the rest.

*

There are no right positive vibrations of devious impulses — these are wrong vibrations of the mind or vital. The right vibrations I speak of are those that come from the psychic or from the spiritual above or take place in the mind or vital under the influence of the psychic or spiritual. If one aspires sincerely and rejects what has to be rejected, as far as one can, then the psychic and spiritual influences will more and more work, bring more and more true discrimination, support, stimulate and create the right vibrations, detect, discourage and eliminate the wrong ones. That is the method the Mother and I advise to all.

*

Rejection is a principle element in this sadhana. But what I say is that one can reject best by bringing in the positive psychic and spiritual forces through the pursuit of positive things like brahmacharya and the rest.

*

I do not know what you mean by dissolution [*of desires*]. The principle of the Yoga is rejection — throwing out of the being. It is true that rejected from the mind it often goes to the vital, rejected by the vital, to the physical, rejected by the physical to the subconscient. Rejected from the subconscient also, it can still linger in the environmental consciousness — but there it has no longer any possession of the being and can be thrown away altogether.

*

That is a known fact that everything comes from outside, from universal Nature. But the individual is not bound to accept everything that comes; he can accept and he can reject. The rejection may not succeed at once, if there is a strong habit of past acceptance; but if it is steadily persisted in, the rejection will succeed in the end.

What you should do, is always to reject the lower experiences and concentrate on a fixed and quiet aspiration towards the one thing needed, the Light, the Calm, the Peace, the Devotion that you felt for two or three days. It is because you get interested in the lower vital experiences and in observing and thinking about them that they take hold, and then comes the absence of the Contact and the confusion. You have surely had enough of this kind of experience already and should make up your mind to steadily reject it when it comes.

*

The effort should be to reject the restlessness and its suggestions altogether. These things come to everybody in the early stages of the sadhana and are sometimes very persistent, even later on they continue — but the sadhak rejects them and regards them as no part of his true consciousness or worthy to determine his action and life, but as untrue suggestions which he has to overcome. If that is always done, they begin after a time to lose their force of invasion and become superficial things; finally they disappear.

*

The peace and the equality are there above you, you have to call them down into the mind and the vital and the body. And whenever something disturbs you have to reject the thing that disturbs and the disturbance.

*

What do you mean by active means [*to overcome inertia*]? The power to refuse, to reject is always there in the being and to go on rejecting till the rejection is effective. Nothing can obstruct a quiet aspiration except one's own acquiescence in the inertia.

*

The practice of rejection prevails in the end; but with personal effort only, it may take a long time. If you can feel the Divine Power working in you, then it should become easier.

There should be nothing inert or tamasic in the self-giving to the guidance and it should not be made by any part of the vital into a plea for not rejecting the suggestions of lower impulse and desire.

Chapter Seven

Surrender

The Meaning of Surrender

The Divine gives itself to those who give themselves without reserve and in all their parts to the Divine. For them the calm, the light, the power, the bliss, the freedom, the wideness, the heights of knowledge, the seas of Ananda.

*

Surrender is giving oneself to the Divine — to give everything one is or has to the Divine and regard nothing as one's own, to obey only the Divine will and no other, to live for the Divine and not for the ego.

*

Self-surrender is to give up yourself and all that is yours, mind and everything else to the Divine, so that the Divine Force may take everything and change it.

*

Surrender means to consecrate everything in oneself to the Divine, to offer all one is and has, not to insist on one's ideas, desires, habits etc., but to allow the divine Truth to replace them by its knowledge, will and action everywhere.

*

Surrender means to be entirely in the Mother's hands and not to resist in any way by egoism or otherwise her Light, Knowledge, Will, the working of her Force etc.

*

The essence of surrender is not to ask the Mother before doing anything — but to accept whole-heartedly the influence and the guidance, when the joy and peace come down to accept them without question or cavil and let them grow, when the Force is felt at work to let it work without opposition, when the Knowledge is given to receive and follow it, when the Will is revealed to make oneself its instrument.

*

To believe that one is being constantly guided by the Divine in the heart is not necessarily surrender. It is necessary to be detached, to see what are the divine forces and undivine and to reject the undivine forces. It is only by this discrimination that one can make a true surrender to the Divine in the heart.

*

It [*true surrender*] begins when there is the true self-offering.

A Free Surrender

The Divine can lead, he does not drive. There is an internal freedom permitted to every mental being called man to assent or not to assent to the Divine leading — how else can any real spiritual evolution be done?

*

All the play in this world is based on a certain relative free will in the individual being. Even in the sadhana it remains and his consent is necessary at each step — even though it is by surrender to the Divine that he escapes from ignorance and separateness and ego, it must be at every step a free surrender.

*

Each person has his own freedom of choice up to a certain point — unless he makes the full surrender — and as he uses the freedom, has to take the spiritual or other consequences. The help can only be offered, not imposed. Silence, absence of frank confession, means a desire in the vital to go its own way. When there is no longer concealment, when there is the physical self-opening to the Divine, then the Divine can intervene.

The Will to Surrender

All can be done by the Divine, the heart and nature purified, the inner consciousness awakened, the veils removed, if one gives oneself to the Divine with trust and confidence — and even if one cannot do so fully at once, yet the more one does so, the more the inner help and guidance comes and the contact and the experience of the Divine grows within. If the questioning mind becomes less active and humility and the will to surrender grow in you, this ought to be perfectly possible. No other strength and tapasya are then needed, but this alone.

*

Surrender cannot be made at once — it is not so easy; for there is much in the being that resists. But one must have the will to surrender. It is the same with becoming an instrument. If one has the will and calls on the Mother and opens oneself as much as possible to her, then gradually these things develop in the nature.

*

If the difficulties that arise are in the nature itself, it is inevitable that they should rise and manifest themselves. Surrender is not easy, it is resisted by a large part of the nature. If the mind forms the will to surrender, all these inner obstacles are bound to show themselves; the sadhak has then to observe them and detach himself from them, reject them from his nature and overcome. This may take a very long time but it has to be done.

Outer obstacles cannot prevent the inner surrender unless they are supported by a resistance in the nature itself.

The Inner Surrender

It was never my intention to suggest that there was only a faint hope of your sadhana depending on the *if* of surrender. I have always said the contrary, that since your soul wants the Divine truly, you are sure to reach him; only if you give up — and that is why I strongly object to these despondencies apart from the suffering they inflict, because they try to drive you to that — can it be frustrated or rather postponed to a far future.

What I wrote was in answer to your statement about your former idea of the Yoga that if one wanted the Divine, the Divine himself would take up the purifying of the heart and develop the sadhana and give the necessary experiences. I meant to say that it can and does happen in that way if one has trust and confidence in the Divine and the will to surrender. For such a taking up involves one's putting oneself in the hands of the Divine rather than trusting to one's own efforts alone and it implies one's putting one's trust and confidence in the Divine and a progressive self-giving. It is in fact the principle of sadhana that I myself followed and it is the central part of the Yoga as I envisage it. It is, I suppose, what Ramakrishna meant by the method of the baby cat in his image. But all cannot follow that at once; it takes time for them to arrive at it — it grows most when the mind and vital fall quiet.

What I meant by surrender was this inner surrender of the mind and vital. There is of course the outer surrender also, the giving up of all that is found to conflict with the spirit or need of the sadhana, the offering, the obedience to the guidance of the Divine, whether directly, if one has reached that stage, or through the psychic or to the guidance of the Guru. I may say that *prāyopaveśana* does not seem to me to have anything to do with surrender; it is a form of tapasya of a very austere and in my opinion very excessive kind, often dangerous. But what I was speaking of in my letter was the inner surrender.

The core of this inner surrender is trust and confidence in the Divine. One takes the attitude, "I want the Divine and nothing else." I do not know why you should think that you can be asked to give up that — if there is not that, then the Yoga cannot be done. "I want to give myself entirely to him and since my soul wants that, it cannot be but that I shall meet him and realise him. I ask nothing but that and his action in me to bring me to him, his action secret or open, veiled or manifest. I do not insist on my own time and way; let him do all in his own time and way, I shall believe in him, accept his will, aspire steadily for his light and presence and joy, go through all difficulties and delays relying on him and never giving up. Let my mind be quiet and turn to him and let him open it to his light; let my vital be quiet and turn to him alone and let him open it to his calm and joy. All for him and myself for him. Whatever happens, I will keep to this aspiration and self-giving and go on in perfect reliance that it will be done." That is the attitude into which one must grow; for, certainly, it cannot be made perfect at once; mental and vital movements come across; but if one keeps the will to it, it will grow in the being. The rest is a matter of obedience to the guidance when it makes itself manifest — not allowing one's mental or vital movements to interfere.

It was not my intention to say that this way is the only way and sadhana cannot be done otherwise — there are so many others by which one can approach the Divine. But this is the only one I know by which the taking up of the sadhana by the Divine becomes a sensible fact before the preparation of the nature is done. In other methods the Divine action and help may be felt from time to time, but it remains mostly behind the veil till all is ready. In some sadhanas the Divine action is not recognised; all must be done by tapasya. In most there is a mixing of the two, the tapasya finally calling the direct help and intervention. The idea and experience of the Divine doing all belongs to the Yogas based on surrender.

But whatever way is followed, the one thing to be done is to be faithful and go to the end. You have so often taken that decision — stand by it, do not let the storms of the vital quench the aspiration of your soul.

*

It depends on the sadhak [*whether the surrender should begin from within*]. Some may find it necessary to surrender the external activities first so as to bring the inner surrender.

The Central Surrender

I have said that if one has the principle of surrender and union in the mind and heart there is no difficulty in extending it to the obscurer parts of the physical and the subconscient. As you have this central surrender and union, you can easily complete it everywhere. A quiet aspiration for complete consciousness is all that is needed. Then the material and subconscient will become penetrated by the light like the rest and there will come in a quietude, wideness, harmony free from all reactions that will be the basis of the final change.

*

When the psychic being and the heart and the thinking mind have surrendered, the rest is a matter of time and process — and there is no reason for disturbance. The central and effective surrender has been made.

Complete or Absolute Surrender

If you are surrendered only in the higher consciousness, with no peace or purity in the lower, certainly that is not enough and you have to aspire for the peace and purity everywhere.

*

It [*surrender*] cannot be absolutely complete in the beginning, but it can be true — if the central will is sincere and there is the faith and the Bhakti. There may be contrary movements, but these will be unable to stand for long and the imperfection of the surrender in the lower part will not seriously interfere with the power and pervasiveness of the inner attitude.

*

A complete surrender is not possible in so short a time, — for a complete surrender means to cut the knot of the ego in each part of the being and offer it, free and whole, to the Divine. The mind, the vital, the physical consciousness (and even each part of these in all its movements) have one after the other to surrender separately, to give up their own way and to accept the way of the Divine. But what one can do is to make from the beginning a central resolve and self-dedication and to implement it in whatever way one finds open, at each step, taking advantage of each occasion that offers itself to make the self-giving complete. A surrender in one direction makes others easier, more inevitable; but it does not of itself cut or loosen the other knots, and especially those which are very intimately bound up with the present personality and its most cherished formations may often present great difficulties, even after the central will has been fixed and the first seals put on its resolve in practice.

*

You can get the full surrender only by degrees. Meanwhile you have to go on the straight path not regarding the suggestions that are put into you through the vital or physical parts.

*

It is on that consciousness of complete surrender that the psychic foundation of sadhana can be made. If once it fixes itself, then, whatever difficulties remain to be overcome, the course of the sadhana becomes perfectly easy, sunlit, natural like the opening of a flower. The feeling you have is an indication of what can and must develop in you.

*

It depends on what is meant by absolute surrender — the experience of it in some part of the being or the fact of it in all parts of the being. The former may easily come at any time; it is the latter that takes time to complete.

*

The absolute surrender must be not only an experience in meditation, but a fact governing all the life, all the thoughts, feelings, actions. Till then the use of one's own will and effort is necessary, but an effort in which also there is the spirit of surrender, calling in the Force to support the will and effort and undisturbed by success or failure. When the Force takes up the sadhana, then indeed effort may cease, but still there will be the necessity of the constant assent of the being and a vigilance so that one may not admit a false Force at any point.

*

It is never too early to make the complete surrender. Some things may need to wait, but not that.

The Surrender of the Vital

The surrender of the vital is always difficult, because of the unwillingness of the forces of the universal vital Ignorance. But that does not mean a fundamental incapacity.

*

The ordinary vital is never willing to surrender. The true inmost vital is different — surrender to the Divine is as necessary to it as to the psychic.

*

If there is any identification with the vital demands or outcries, that necessarily diminishes the surrender for the time.

*

What is this surrender to which there is no response? Surrender and demands don't go together. Evidently the vital is not afraid of thinking illogical and self-contradictory nonsense. So long as the vital keeps up its demand, these things will come.

*

It was from your description of the reaction that I said there was a vital demand. In the pure psychic or spiritual self-giving there are no reactions of this kind, no despondency or despair, no saying, "What have I gained by seeking the Divine?", no anger, revolt, abhiman, wish to go away — such as you describe here — but an absolute confidence and a persistence in clinging to the Divine under all conditions. That is what I wanted you to have; it is the only basis in which one is free from troubles and reactions and goes steadily forward.

*

Not to impose one's mind and vital will on the Divine but to receive the Divine's will and follow it, is the true attitude of sadhana. Not to say, "This is my right, want, claim, need, requirement, why do I not get it?" but to give oneself, to surrender and to receive with joy whatever the Divine gives, not grieving or revolting, is the better way. Then what you receive will be the right thing for you.

*

The Divine is not bound to do that [*supply all one's real needs*], He can give or not give; whether He gives or does not give makes no difference to the one who is surrendered to Him. Otherwise, there is an arrière-pensée in the surrender which is not then complete.

*

Most of the sadhaks have similar thoughts [*of hostility and ingratitude*] — or had them at one time or another. They rise from the vital ego which either does not want the Divine or wants It for its own purpose and not for the Divine's purpose. It gets furious when it is pressed to change or when its desires are not satisfied — that is at the root of all these things. That is why we insist on surrender in this Yoga — because it is only by the surrender (especially of the vital ego) that these things can go — to accept the Divine for the Divine's sake and for no other motive and in the Divine's way and not in one's own way or on one's own conditions.

*

Difficult? It is the first principle of our sadhana that surrender is the means of fulfilment and so long as ego or vital demand

and desire are cherished, complete surrender is impossible — the self-giving is incomplete. We have never concealed that. It may be difficult and it is; but it is the very principle of the sadhana. Because it is difficult it has to be done steadily and patiently till the work is complete.

*

Your mind and psychic being are concentrated on the spiritual aim and open to the Divine — that is why the Influence comes down into the head and as far as the heart. But the vital being and nature and the physical consciousness are under the influence of the lower nature. As long as the vital and physical being are not surrendered or do not on their own account call for the higher life, this struggle is likely to continue.

Surrender everything, reject all other desires or interests, call on the divine Shakti to open the vital nature and bring down calm, peace, light, Ananda into all the centres. Aspire, await with faith and patience the result. All depends on a complete sincerity and an integral consecration and aspiration.

The world will trouble you so long as any part of you belongs to the world. It is only if you belong entirely to the Divine that you can become free.

Surrender and the Psychic

For surrender it is necessary not to insist on the mind's opinions, ideas and preferences, the vital's desires and impulses, the physical's habitual actions, the life of the ego — all such insistence is contrary to surrender. All egoism and self-will has to be abandoned and one must seek to be governed only by the Divine Shakti. No complete surrender is possible without the psychic opening.

*

It is impossible to become like a child giving oneself entirely until the psychic is in control and stronger than the vital.

*

Surrender

It is the psychic coming forward that brings the force of surrender.

*

The power of experience is not gone — but what is most important now is to develop the psychic condition of surrender, devotion, love and cheerful confidence in the Mother, an unshaken faith and a constant inner closeness, and also to bring down from above the peace, wideness, purity etc. of the higher Self which is that of the Mother's consciousness. It is these things that are the basis of the siddhi in this Yoga — other experiences are only a help, not the basis.

*

It is the psychic surrender in the physical that you have begun to experience.

All the parts are essentially offered, but the surrender has to be made complete by the growth of the psychic self-offering in all of them and in all their movements separately and together.

To be enjoyed by the Divine is to be entirely surrendered so that one feels the Divine Presence, Power, Light, Ananda possessing the whole being rather than oneself possessing these things for one's own satisfaction. It is a much greater ecstasy to be thus surrendered and possessed by the Divine than oneself to be the possessor. At the same time by this surrender there comes also a calm and happy mastery of self and nature.

*

No surrender to the psychic being is demanded, the surrender is to the Divine. One approaches the Divine through faith; concrete experience comes as a result of sadhana. One cannot demand a direct experience without doing anything to prepare the consciousness for it. If one feels the call, one follows it — if there is no call, then there is no need to seek the Divine. Faith is sufficient to start with — the idea that one must first understand and realise before one can seek is a mental error and if it were true would make all sadhana impossible — realisation can come only as a result of sadhana, not as its preliminary.

*

There is no need of all this complication. If the psychic manifests, it will not ask you to surrender to it, but to surrender to the Mother.

*

The surrender must be to the Mother — not even to the Force, but to the Mother herself.

Surrender and Bhakti

Surrender and love-bhakti are not contrary things — they go together. It is true that at first surrender can be made through knowledge by the mind, but it implies a mental bhakti and, as soon as the surrender reaches the heart, the bhakti manifests as a feeling and with the feeling of bhakti love comes.

*

Self-surrender at first comes through love and bhakti, more than through Atmajnana. But it is true that with Atmajnana the complete surrender becomes more possible.

Surrender and the Brahmic Condition

There can be [*devotion and surrender on the higher spiritual planes*], but it is not inevitable as in the psychic. In the higher mind one may be too conscious of identity with the "Brahman" to have devotion or surrender.

*

The Brahmic condition brings a negative peace of shanti and mukti in the soul. Self-giving brings a positive freedom which can become also a dynamic force of action in the nature.

*

One can have the Brahmic condition without self-giving, because it is the impersonal Brahman to which one turns. Renunciation of desires and of all identification with Nature is its condition. One can have self-giving of the nature to the Divine as well as of the soul and reach by it the Brahmic condition which is not only negative but positive, a release of the nature itself and not only a release from the nature.

Surrender and Transformation

If there is no surrender, there can be no transformation of the whole being.

*

A surrender by any means is good, but obviously the impersonal is not enough — for surrender to that may be limited in result to the inner experience without any transformation of the outer nature.

Passive or Tamasic Surrender

Active surrender is when you associate your will with the Divine Will, reject what is not the Divine, assent to what is the Divine. Passive surrender is when everything is left entirely to the Divine — that few can really do, because in practice it turns out that you surrender to the lower nature under pretext of surrendering to the Divine.

*

I wanted to stress two things, that is why I have written so much about them.

(1) There must be no tamasic (inert, passive) surrender to the Mother — for that will bring as its reaction a passive inert helplessness before the lower or hostile forces or suggestions, an unresisting or helplessly resisting acquiescence or sufferance of these inroads. A passive condition can bring much peace, quietude, joy even, but it disperses the being instead of concentrating it in wideness and the will becomes atrophied. Surrender

must be luminous, active, a willed offering to the Mother and reception of her Force and support to its workings, at the same time a strong vigilant will to reject all that is not hers. Too many sadhaks cry before the attacks of their lower nature, "I am helpless, I cannot react, it comes and makes me do what it wants." This is a wrong passivity.

(2) One must not get into the habit of a state in which one is always in a struggle with suggestions and forces. People very easily fall into this and make it a habit — the vital part takes a sort of glowing satisfaction in crying out, "I am attacked, overborne, suffering, miserable! How tragic is my fate! Why do you not help, O Divine? There is no help, nor divine Grace? I am left to my misery and downfall etc. etc. etc." I do not want one more sadhak to fall into this condition — that is why I am calling Halt! before you get entangled in this kind of habit of constant struggle. It is what these forces want — to make you feel helpless, defeated, overborne. You must not allow it.

*

You are always expecting the Mother to do it [*remove vital dissatisfaction and revolt*] — and here again the laziness and tamas come in — it is the spirit of tamasic surrender. If the Mother puts you back into a good condition, your vital pulls you down again. How is that to stop so long as you say Yes to the vital and accept its discouragement and restlessness and anguish and the rest of it as your own? Detachment is absolutely necessary.

*

Talk of surrender or a mere idea or tepid wish for integral consecration will not do; there must be the push for a radical and total change.

It is not by taking a mere mental attitude that this can be done or even by any number of inner experiences which leave the outer man as he was. It is this outer man who has to open, to surrender and to change. His every least movement, habit, action has to be surrendered, seen, held up and exposed to the divine Light, offered to the divine Force for its old forms and motives to be destroyed and the divine Truth and the action of the transforming consciousness of the Divine Mother to take their place.

*

It [*the idea that the sadhana is done by the Divine rather than by oneself*] is a truth but a truth that does not become effective for the consciousness until or in proportion as it is realised. The people who stagnate because of it are those who accept the idea but do not realise — so they have neither the force of tapasya nor that of the Divine Grace. On the other hand those who can realise it feel even behind their tapasya and in it the action of the Divine Force.

Surrender and Tapasya

Yoga is an endeavour, a tapasya — it can cease to be so only when one surrenders sincerely to a higher Action and keeps the surrender and makes it complete. It is not a fantasia, devoid of all reason and coherence or a mere miracle. It has its laws and conditions and I do not see how you can demand of the Divine to do everything by a violent miracle.

*

When the will and energy are concentrated and used to control the mind, vital and physical and change them or to bring down the higher consciousness or for any other Yogic purpose or high purpose, that is called Tapasya.

*

Tapasya has predominated in your sadhana, for you have a fervour and active energy which predisposes you to that. No way is entirely easy, and in that of surrender the difficulty is to make a true and complete surrender. Once it is made, it certainly makes things easier — not that things are all done in no time or that there are no difficulties, but there is an assurance, a support, an absence of tension which gives the consciousness rest as well as strength and freedom from the worst forms of resistance.

*

Yes, of course you are right. The process of surrender is itself a Tapasya. Not only so, but in fact a double process of Tapasya and increasing surrender persists for a long time even when the surrender has fairly well begun. But a time comes when one feels the Presence and the Force constantly and more and more feels that that is doing everything — so that the worst difficulties cannot disturb this sense and personal effort is no longer necessary, hardly even possible. That is the sign of the full surrender of the nature into the hands of the Divine. There are some who take this position in faith even before there is this experience and if the Bhakti and the faith are strong it carries them through till the experience is there. But all cannot take this position from the beginning — and for some it would be dangerous since they might put themselves into the hand of a wrong Force thinking it to be the Divine. For most it is necessary to grow through Tapasya into surrender.

*

Yes, if there is the sense of the Divine Will behind all the Tapasya and receiving it and bestowing the fruit — it is at least a first form of surrender.

Surrender and Personal Effort

There are always two ways of doing the Yoga — one by the action of a vigilant mind and vital seeing, observing, thinking and deciding what is or is not to be done. Of course it acts with the Divine Force behind it, drawing or calling in that Force — for otherwise nothing much can be done. But still it is the personal effort that is prominent and assumes most of the burden.

The other way is that of the psychic being, the consciousness opening to the Divine, not only opening the psychic and bringing it forward, but opening the mind, the vital and the physical, receiving the Light, perceiving what is to be done, feeling and seeing it done by the Divine Force itself and helping constantly by its own vigilant and conscious assent to and call for the Divine working.

Usually there cannot but be a mixture of these two ways until the consciousness is ready to be entirely open, entirely submitted to the Divine's origination of all its action. It is then that all responsibility disappears and there is no personal burden on the shoulders of the sadhak.

*

There are two possibilities, one of purification by personal effort, which takes a long time, another by a direct intervention of the Divine Grace which is usually rapid in its action. For the latter there must be a complete surrender and self-giving and for that again usually it is necessary to have a mind that can remain quite quiet and allow the Divine Force to act supporting it with its complete adhesion at every step, but otherwise remaining still and quiet. This last condition which resembles the baby cat attitude spoken of by Ramakrishna, is difficult to have. Those who are accustomed to a very active movement of their thought and will in all they do, find it difficult to still the activity and adopt the quietude of mental self-giving. This does not mean that they cannot do the Yoga or cannot arrive at self-giving — only the purification and the self-giving take a long time to accomplish and one must have the patience and steady perseverance and resolution to go through.

*

If there is not a complete surrender, then it is not possible to adopt the baby cat attitude, — it becomes mere tamasic passivity calling itself surrender. If a complete surrender is not possible in the beginning, it follows that personal effort is necessary.

*

In the early part of the sadhana — and by early I do not mean a short part — effort is indispensable. Surrender of course, but surrender is not a thing that is done in a day. The mind has its ideas and it clings to them; the human vital resists surrender, for what it calls surrender in the early stages is a doubtful kind of self-giving with a demand in it; the physical consciousness is like a stone and what it calls surrender is often no more than inertia. It is only the psychic that knows how to surrender and the psychic is usually very much veiled in the beginning. When the psychic awakes, it can bring a sudden and true surrender of the whole being, for the difficulty of the rest is rapidly dealt with and disappears. But till then effort is indispensable. Or else it is necessary till the Force comes flooding down into the being from above and takes up the sadhana, does it for one more and more and leaves less and less to individual effort — but even then, if not effort, at least aspiration and vigilance are needed till the possession of mind, will, life and body by the Divine Power is complete. I have dealt with this subject, I think, in one of the chapters of *The Mother*.

On the other hand, there are some people who start with a genuine and dynamic will for a total surrender. It is those who are governed by the psychic or are governed by a clear and enlightened mental will which having once accepted surrender as the law of the sadhana will stand no nonsense about it and insists on the other parts of the being following its direction. Here there is still effort, but it is so ready and spontaneous and has so much the sense of a greater Force behind it that the sadhak hardly feels that he is making an effort at all. In the contrary case of a will in mind or vital to retain self-will, a reluctance to give up your independent movement, there must be struggle and endeavour until the wall between the instrument in front and the Divinity behind or above is broken. No rule can be laid down which applies without distinction to everybody — the variations in human nature are too great to be covered by a single trenchant rule.

*

It is not possible to get rid of the stress on personal effort at once — and not always desirable; for personal effort is better than tamasic inertia.

The personal effort has to be transformed progressively into a movement of the Divine Force. If you feel conscious of the Divine Force, then call it in more and more to govern your effort, to take it up, to transform it into something not yours, but the Mother's. There will be a sort of transfer, a taking up of the forces at work in the personal adhar — a transfer not suddenly complete but progressive.

But the psychic poise is necessary: the discrimination must develop which sees accurately what is the Divine Force, what is the element of personal effort, and what is brought in as a mixture from the lower cosmic forces. And until the transfer is complete, which always takes time, there must always be as a personal contribution, a constant consent to the true Force, a constant rejection of any lower mixture — that is very important.

At present to give up personal effort is not what is wanted, but to call in more and more the Divine Power and govern and guide by it the personal endeavour.

*

It is not advisable in the early stages of the sadhana to leave everything to the Divine or expect everything from it without the need of one's own endeavour. That is only possible when the psychic being is in front and influencing the whole action (and even then vigilance and a constant assent are necessary) or else, later on in the ultimate stages of the Yoga when a direct or almost direct supramental force is taking up the consciousness; but this stage is very far away as yet. Under other conditions this attitude is likely to lead to stagnation and inertia. (See *The Mother*, Part I.)

It is only the more mechanical parts of the being that can truly say they are helpless: the physical (material) consciousness, especially, is inert in its nature and moved either by the mental and vital or by the higher forces. But one has always the power to put the mental will or vital push at the service of the Divine. One cannot be sure of the immediate result, for the obstruction of the lower Nature or the pressure of the adverse forces can often act successfully for a time, even for a long time, against the necessary change. One has then to persist, to put always the will on the side of the Divine, rejecting what has to be rejected, opening oneself to the true Light and the true Force, calling it down quietly, steadfastly, without tiring, without depression or impatience, until one feels the Divine Force at work and the obstacles beginning to give way.

You say you are conscious of your ignorance and obscurity. If it is only a general consciousness, that is not enough. But if you are conscious of it in the details, in its actual working, then that is sufficient to start with; you have to reject steadfastly the wrong workings of which you are conscious and make your mind and vital a quiet and clear field for the action of the Divine Force.

*

Certainly one ought not to fret [*about whether one will achieve one's end*] — and certainly one ought to dedicate [*one's desire to achieve it*] to the Divine. But our experience is that merely leaving the Divine to do everything (to fulfil) does not carry one very far. There must be a cooperation, a consent, an aspiration, a will to change.

*

If there were no conditions at all [*in Yoga*], then there would be no need of sadhana; all would be done automatically by the Force or help without any need of effort by the sadhak. The help is always there and it has pulled you out of many difficulties and attacks. It is, I suppose, because of the feeling "I do not want to do anything" that you have not been able to receive the help, but that is a temporary inertia of the physical mind and will. I do not see the use of your going back for a few months to a life which could not now satisfy you. The only course is to shake off the inertia of the will and persevere.

*

So long as there is not the full presence and conscious working of the higher Force, some amount of personal effort is indispensable. To do the sadhana for the sake of the Divine and not for one's own sake is of course the true attitude.

*

Faith, reliance upon God, surrender and self-giving to the Divine Power are necessary and indispensable. But reliance upon God must not be made an excuse for indolence, weakness and surrender to the impulses of the lower nature; it must go along with untiring aspiration and a persistent rejection of all that comes in the way of the Divine Truth. The surrender to the Divine must not be turned into an excuse, a cloak or an occasion for surrender to one's own desires and lower movements or to one's ego or to some Force of the ignorance and darkness that puts on a false appearance of the Divine.

*

It is always better to make an effort in the right direction; even if one fails the effort bears some result and is never lost.

*

For those who do not make any effort, — that absence of effort is itself a difficulty — they do not progress.

Chapter Eight
Faith

Faith, Belief, Confidence, Trust

Faith is a general word = *śraddhā* — the soul's belief in the Divine's existence, wisdom, power, love and grace — confidence and trust are aspects of faith and results of it.

Confidence is a feeling of sureness that the Divine will hear when sincerely called and help and that all the Divine does is for the best.

Trust is the mind's and heart's complete reliance on the Divine and its guidance and protection.

*

Faith — a dynamic entire belief and acceptance.
Belief — intellectual acceptance only.
Conviction — intellectual belief held on what seem to be good reasons.
Reliance — dependence on another for something, based on trust.
Trust — the feeling of sure expectation of another's help and reliance on his word, character etc.
Confidence — the sense of security that goes with trust.

*

Faith is a feeling in the whole being, belief is mental; confidence means trust in a person or in the Divine or a feeling of surety about the result of one's seeking or endeavour.

*

You have seized the right principle again, to be all for the Mother and to have full confidence that one has only to go on quietly in that confidence and all will come that needs to come and all be done that the Divine wills to be done. The workings of the world are too subtle and strange and complex for the human mind to understand it — it is only when the knowledge comes from above and one is taken into the higher consciousness that the understanding can come. Meanwhile what one has to follow is the dictates of the deeper psychic heart within based on that faith and love which is the only sure guiding star.

*

Faith in its essence is a light in the soul which turns towards the truth even when the mind doubts or the vital revolts or the physical consciousness denies it. When this extends itself to the instruments, it becomes a fixed belief in the mind, a sort of inner knowledge which resists all apparent denial by circumstances or appearances, a complete confidence, trust, adhesion in the vital and in the physical consciousness, an invariable clinging to the truth in which one has faith even when all is dark around and no cause of hope seems to be there.

*

Faith in the spiritual sense is not a mental belief which can waver and change. It can wear that form in the mind, but that belief is not the faith itself, it is only its external form. Just as the body, the external form, can change but the spirit remains the same, so it is here. Faith is a certitude in the soul which does not depend on reasoning, on this or that mental idea, on circumstances, on this or that passing condition of the mind or the vital or the body. It may be hidden, eclipsed, may even seem to be quenched, but it reappears again after the storm or the eclipse; it is seen burning still in the soul when one has thought that it was extinguished for ever. The mind may be a shifting sea of doubts and yet that faith may be there within and, if so, it will keep even the doubt-racked mind in the way so that it goes on in spite of itself towards its destined goal. Faith is a spiritual certitude of the spiritual, the divine, the soul's ideal, something that clings to that even when it is not fulfilled in life, even when the immediate facts or the persistent circumstances seem to deny it. This is a common experience in the life of the human being; if it were not so, man would be the plaything of a changing mind or a sport of circumstance.

A Problem of Faith

How to conciliate these two notions:
(1) that the Divine's Will is behind all movements and happenings,
(2) that the Divine Will is distorted in the manifestation.

There are two kinds of faith:
The faith that calls down the equanimity and the faith that calls down the realisation.

These two faiths correspond to two different aspects of the Divine.

There is the Transcendent Divine and there is the Cosmic Divine.

The Will of realisation is that of the Transcendent Divine.

The Cosmic Divine is what is concerned with the actual working out of things under the present circumstances. It is the Will of that Cosmic Divine which is manifested in each circumstance, each movement of this world.

The Cosmic Will is not, to our ordinary consciousness, something that acts as an independent power doing whatever it chooses; it works through all these beings, through the forces at play in the world and the law of these forces and their results. It is only when we open ourselves and get out of the ordinary consciousness that we can feel it intervening as an independent power and overriding the ordinary play of the forces.

Then too we can see that even in the play of the forces and in spite of their distortions the Cosmic Will is working towards the eventual realisation of the Will of the Transcendent Divine.

The supramental realisation is the Will of the Transcendent Divine which we have to work out. The circumstances under which we have to work it out are those of an inferior consciousness in which things can be distorted by our own ignorance, weaknesses and mistakes, and by the clash of conflicting forces. That is why faith and equanimity are indispensable.

We have to have the faith that in spite of our ignorance and errors and weaknesses and in spite of the attacks of hostile forces and in spite of any immediate appearance of failure the Divine Will is leading us, through every circumstance, towards the final realisation. This faith will give us equanimity; it is a faith that accepts what happens not definitively but as something that has to be gone through on the way. Once equanimity is established there can be established too another kind of faith, supported by it, which can be made dynamic with something from the supramental consciousness and can overcome the present circumstances and determine what will happen and help to bring down the realisation of the Will of the Transcendent Divine.

The faith that goes to the Cosmic Divine is limited in the power of its action by the necessities of the play.

To get entirely free from these limitations one must reach the Transcendent Divine.

Faith and Knowledge

Faith is a thing that precedes knowledge, not comes after knowledge. It is a glimpse of a truth which the mind has not yet seized as knowledge.

*

Until we know the Truth (not mentally but by experience, by change of consciousness) we need the soul's faith to sustain us and hold on to the Truth — but when we live in the knowledge, this faith is changed into knowledge.

Of course I am speaking of direct spiritual knowledge. Mental knowledge cannot replace faith; so long as there is only mental knowledge, faith is still needed.

*

The phrase ["*blind faith*"] has no real meaning. I suppose they mean they will not believe without proof — but the conclusion formed after proof is not faith, it is knowledge or it is a mental opinion. Faith is something which one has before proof or knowledge and it helps you to arrive at knowledge or experience. There is no proof that God exists, but if I have faith in God, then I can arrive at the experience of the Divine.

Faith and Experience

Mental theories are of no fundamental importance, for the mind forms or accepts the theories that support the turn of the being. What is important is that turn and the call within you.

The knowledge that there is a Supreme Existence, Consciousness and Bliss which is not merely a negative Nirvana or a static and featureless Absolute, but dynamic, the perception that this Divine Consciousness can be realised not only beyond but here, and the consequent acceptance of a divine life as the aim of Yoga, do not belong to the mind. It is not a question of mental theory — even though mentally this outlook can be as well supported as any other, if not better, — but of experience and, before the experience comes, of the soul's faith bringing with it the mind's and the life's adhesion. One who is in contact with the higher Light and has the experience can follow this way, however difficult it may be for the lower members to follow; one who is touched by it, without having the experience, but having the call, the conviction, the compulsion of the soul's adherence, can also follow it.

*

There is much in your letter that would need long explanation for an adequate reply — but I want to say something about the faith which you say you don't have and can't have in the absence of experience. First of all, faith does not depend upon experience; it is something that is there before experience. When one starts the Yoga, it is not usually on the strength of experience, but on the strength of faith. It is so not only in Yoga and the spiritual life, but in ordinary life also. All men of action, discoverers, inventors, creators of knowledge proceed by faith and, until the proof is made or the thing done, they go on in spite of disappointment, failure, disproof, denial, because of something in them that tells them that this *is* the truth, the thing that must be followed and done. Ramakrishna even went so far as to say, when asked whether blind faith was not wrong, that blind faith was the only kind to have, for faith is either blind or it is not faith but something else — reasoned inference, proved conviction or ascertained knowledge.

Faith is the soul's witness to something not yet manifested, achieved or realised, but which yet the Knower within us, even in the absence of all indications, feels to be true or supremely worth following or achieving. This thing within us can last even when there is no fixed belief in the mind, even when the vital struggles and revolts and refuses. Who is there that practises the Yoga and has not his periods, long periods of disappointment and failure and disbelief and darkness — but there is something that sustains him and even goes on in spite of himself, because it feels that what it followed after was yet true and it more than feels, it knows. The fundamental faith in Yoga is this, inherent in the soul, that the Divine exists and the Divine is the one thing to be followed after — nothing else in life is worth having in comparison with that. It was this faith growing in you that made you come for Yoga and this faith has not died or diminished — to judge from what you say in your letters, it has become more insistent and abiding. So long as a man has that, he is marked for the spiritual life and I will say that, even if his nature is full of obstacles and crammed with denials and difficulties, and even if he has many years of struggle, he is marked out for success in the spiritual life.

What you really have not yet a fixed faith in is the guidance of the Divine, his will to manifest to you or your capacity to receive him. It is this that the adverse attacks which began when you were on the threshold of the inner experience — as so often happens in the Yoga — try constantly to fix in your brain. They want to have a fixed mental formation there, so that whenever you make the attempt there will be in the physical mind an expectation of difficulty, a dwelling on the idea of difficulty and unsuccess and incapacity, if not always in the front of the mind, yet at the back and by that they hope to prevent the experience from coming. It is these mental formations that you must reject, for they are a much greater obstacle than the vital failings to which you give such an exaggerated importance. It is not a fact that you have not had experiences — you had them but you did not give them their full value, because you were expecting something else. Otherwise the sense of the Divine Guidance and the faith in attainment would have formed in spite of difficulties and relapses such as everyone has in the Yoga. It is this faith that you need to develop, — a faith which is in accordance with reason and common sense — that if the Divine exists and has called you to the Path, as is evident, then there must be a Divine Guidance behind and that through and in spite of all difficulties you will arrive. Not to listen to the hostile voices that suggest failure or to the voices of impatient vital haste that echo them, not to believe that because great difficulties are there, there can be no success or that because the Divine has not yet shown himself he will never show himself, but to take the position that everyone takes when he fixes his mind on a great and difficult goal, "I will go on till I succeed and I will succeed — all difficulties notwithstanding." To which the believer in the Divine adds, "The Divine exists, he is there, and since he exists, my following after the Divine cannot fail. I will go on through everything till I find him."

*

I am rather surprised at Krishnaprem's surprise about my statement of faith. I thought he had said once you should not hanker after experiences. As for experience being necessary for faith and no faith possible without it, that contradicts human psychology altogether. Thousands of people have faith before they have experience and it is the faith that helps them to the experience. The doctrine "No belief without proof" applies to physical science, it would be disastrous in the field of spirituality — or for that matter in the field of human action. The saints or bhaktas have the faith in God long before they get the experience of God — the man of action has the faith in his cause long before his cause is crowned with success — otherwise they would not have been able to struggle persistently towards their end in spite of defeat, failure and deadly peril. I don't know what Krishnaprem means by true faith. For me faith is not intellectual belief but a function of the soul; when my belief has faltered, failed, gone out the soul has remained steadfast, obstinately insisting, "This path and no other; the Truth I have felt is the Truth whatever the mind may believe or not believe." On the other hand experiences do not necessarily lead to faith. One sadhak writes to me, "I feel the grace of the Mother descending into me, but I cannot believe it because it may be a vital imagination." Another has experiences for years together, then falls down because he has, he says, "lost faith". All these things are not my imagination, they are facts and tell their own tale.

All that, however, is by the way. I have no objection to you or anybody having experiences. I am not a fool. Let everybody have as many experiences as possible. What I say is that the hankering for experiences should not be there in such a way as to replace the true attitude and bring disappointment and revolt. Bhakti is not an experience, it is a state of the heart and soul. It is a state which comes when the psychic being is awake and prominent. It is for that reason that I asked you to cleave to the psychic way and not go back to that of vital desire. I have not said that your psychic being was "in front" in such a way as to be proof against all attack. What I said was that it was becoming awake and active, giving you the right attitude and helping you towards the change of your nature. I certainly did not mean a moral but a spiritual change. Freedom from ego is not a moral but a spiritual change — a moral man may be chock full of ego, an ego increased by his sense of goodness and rectitude. Freedom from ego is spiritually valuable because then one can be centred, no longer in one's personal self, but in the Divine, and that too is the condition of bhakti.

The Gospel of Faith

I spoke of a strong central and if possible complete faith because your attitude seemed to be that you only cared for the full response — that is, realisation, the Presence, regarding all else as quite unsatisfactory, and your prayer was not bringing you that. But prayer by itself does not usually bring that at once — only if there is a burning faith at the centre or a complete faith in all the parts of the being. That does not mean that those whose faith is not so strong or surrender complete cannot arrive, but usually they have to go at first by small steps and to face the difficulties of their nature until by perseverance or tapasya they make a sufficient opening. Even a faltering faith and a slow and partial surrender have their force and their result, otherwise only the rare few could do sadhana at all. What I mean by the central faith is a faith in the soul or the central being behind, a faith which is there even when the mind doubts and the vital despairs and the physical wants to collapse, and after the attack is over, reappears and pushes on the path again. It may be strong and bright, it may be pale and in appearance weak, but if it persists each time in going on, it is the real thing. Fits of despair and darkness are a tradition in the path of sadhana — in all Yogas oriental and occidental they seem to have been the rule. I know all about them myself — but my experience has led me to the perception that they are an unnecessary tradition and could be dispensed with if one chose. That is why whenever they come in you or others I try to lift up before them the gospel of faith. If still they come, one has only to get through them as soon as possible and get back into the sun. Your dream of the sea was a perfectly true one — in the end the storm and swell do not prevent the arrival of the state of Grace in the sadhak and with it the arrival of the Grace itself. That I suppose is what something in you is always asking for — the suprarational miracle of Grace, something that is impatient of the demand for tapasya and self-perfection and long labour. Well, it can come, it has come to several here after years upon years of blank failure and difficulty or terrible internal struggles. But it comes usually in that way — as opposed to a slowly developing Grace — after much difficulty and not at once. If you go on asking for it in spite of the apparent failure of response, it is sure to come.

Faith and Doubt

I see you have let the demons of self-doubt and doubt in general and melancholy get inside again and sit down at your table. There is no other reason for your troubles than this readiness to listen to their knock and open the door. You speak of X, but that is why X gets on because when they knock, he turns them out at once. If you resolutely do that, you will arrive also at security and perfect ease — for there are only two things that create insecurity — doubt and desire. If you desire only the Divine, there is an absolute certitude that you will reach the Divine. But all these questionings and repinings at each moment because you have not yet reached, only delay and keep an impeding curtain before the heart and the eyes. For at every step when one makes an advance, the opposite forces will throw this doubt like a rope between the legs and stop one short with a stumble — it is their *métier* to do that. One must not give them that advantage. Instead of saying, "I want only the Divine, why is the Divine not already here?", one must say, "Since I want only the Divine, my success is sure, I have only to walk forward in all confidence and his own hand will be there secretly leading me to him by his own way and at his own time." That is what you must keep as your constant mantra and it is besides the only logical and reasonable thing to do — for anything else is an irrational self-contradiction of the most glaring kind. Anything else one may doubt — whether the supermind will come down, whether this world can ever be anything but a field of struggle for the mass of men, — these can be rational doubts — but that he who desires only the Divine shall reach the Divine is a certitude much more certain than that two and two make four. That is the faith every sadhak must have in the bottom of his heart, supporting him through every stumble and blow and ordeal. It is only false ideas still casting their shadow on your mind that prevent you from having it. Push them aside for good and see this simple inner truth in a simple and straightforward way — the back of the difficulty will be broken.

*

As for the doubts, such occurrences happen to almost all sadhaks from time to time so long as there is not such a fixity of continuous experience as makes any fundamental doubt impossible, although there may still be questionings about this or that until the knowledge and experience are made complete.

The nature of the doubts and misbeliefs were such as are always suggested to everybody when this kind of Influence envelops — the part of the mind which responds to them is the physical mind — for the other parts are covered over at such times and the physical mind left to itself naturally doubts everything supraphysical and believes only in its own domain.

Mental faith is very helpful, but it is a thing that can always be temporarily shaken or quite clouded — until the higher consciousness and experience get fixed for good. What endures even if concealed is the inner being's aspiration or need for something higher which is the soul's faith. That too may be concealed for a time but it reasserts itself — it undergoes eclipse but not extinction.

*

It is quite sufficient if there is the firm and constant will towards faith and self-offering. It is understood that it is not possible for the human nature to be always without movements of doubt, obscurity or things not yet offered until the inner consciousness has sufficiently grown to make these impossible. It is because it is so that the will is necessary so that the Force may work to remove these things with full consent and will of the mind and heart of the sadhak. To try to reject these things and make the will permanent is sufficient, — for it is this effort that brings eventually the permanence.

*

It is possible for anyone to attain to a complete and living faith in the Divine if he has the sincere will to do so, even though he may not be sattwic in his nature; but, if he is sattwic, it will be easier for him — he will not be hampered by doubts and revolts such as afflict the rajasic man on his way.

Types of Faith

Mental faith combats doubt and helps to open to the true knowledge; vital faith prevents the attacks of the hostile forces or defeats them and helps to open to the true spiritual will and action; physical faith keeps one firm through all physical obscurity, inertia or suffering and helps to open to the foundation of the true consciousness; psychic faith opens to the direct touch of the Divine and helps to bring union and surrender.

*

Faith can be tamasic and ineffective, e.g. "I believe the Mother will do everything, so I will do nothing. When she wants, she will transform me." That is not a dynamic but a static and inert faith.

Faithfulness

When I spoke of being faithful to the light of the soul and the divine Call, I was not referring to anything in the past or to any lapse on your part. I was simply affirming the great need in all crises and attacks, — to refuse to listen to any suggestions, impulses, lures and to oppose to them all the call of the Truth, the imperative beckoning of the Light. In all doubt and depression, to say "I belong to the Divine, I cannot fail"; to all suggestions of impurity and unfitness, to reply "I am a child of Immortality chosen by the Divine; I have but to be true to myself and to Him — the victory is sure; even if I fell, I would be sure to rise again"; to all impulses to depart and serve some smaller ideal, to reply "This is the greatest, this is the Truth that alone can satisfy the soul within me; I will endure through all tests and tribulations to the very end of the divine journey." This is what I mean by faithfulness to the Light and the Call.

*

I do not see how the method of faith in the cells can be likened to eating a slice of the moon. Nobody ever got a slice of the moon, but the healing by faith in the cells is an actual fact and a law of Nature and has been demonstrated often enough even apart from Yoga. The way to get faith and everything else is to insist on having them and refuse to flag or despair or give up until one has them — it is the way by which everything has been got since this difficult world began to have thinking and aspiring creatures upon it. It is to open always, always to the Light and turn one's back on the darkness. It is to refuse the voices that cry persistently, "You cannot, you shall not, you are incapable, you are the puppet of a dream" — for these are the enemy voices, they cut one off from the result that was coming by their strident clamour and then triumphantly point to the barrenness of result as a proof of their thesis. The difficulty of the endeavour is a known thing, but the difficult is not the impossible — it is the difficult that has always been accomplished and the conquest of difficulties makes up all that is valuable in the earth's history. In the spiritual endeavour also it shall be so.

*

For the sadhana, your strong distaste (to say the least) for the methods which we find most useful but you find grim and repellent, makes a great obstacle. But I maintain my idea that if you remain faithful to the seeking for the Divine, the day of grace and opening will come. Nobody will be more pleased than ourselves if it comes over there in the Himalayas, or for that matter anywhere. The place does not matter — the thing itself is all.

*

I ask you to have faith in the Divine, in the Divine Grace, in the truth of the sadhana, in the eventual triumph of the spirit over its mental and vital and physical difficulties, in the Path and the Guru, in the existence of things other than are written in the philosophy of Haeckel or Huxley or Bertrand Russell, because if these things are not true, there is no meaning in the Yoga.

*

If his faith depends on the perfection of the sadhaks, obviously it must be a rather shaky thing! Sadhaks and sadhikas are not supposed to be perfect. It is only siddhas for whom one can claim perfection and even then not according to a mental standard.

Keep Firm Faith

Do not allow any discouragement to come upon you and have no distrust of the Divine Grace. Whatever difficulties are outside you, whatever weaknesses are inside you, if you keep firm hold on your faith and your aspiration, the secret Power will carry you through and bring you back here. Even if you are oppressed with opposition and difficulties, even if you stumble, even if the way seems closed to you, keep hold on your aspiration; if faith is clouded for a time, turn always in mind and heart to us and it will be removed. As for outer help in the way of letters we are perfectly ready to give it to you. But keep firm on the way — then in the end things open out of themselves and circumstances yield to the inner spirit.

*

Whatever adverse things present themselves you must meet them with courage and they will disappear and the help come. Faith and courage are the true attitude to keep in life and work always and in the spiritual experience also.

*

In moments of trial faith in the Divine protection and the call for that protection; at all times the faith that what the Divine wills is the best.

It is what turns you towards the Divine that must be accepted as good for you — all is bad for you that turns you away from the Divine.

*

That is the true resolution. Keep it firm inside you even if waves of other consciousness cover on the surface. If one plants a faith or resolution like that firmly in oneself, then it remains and even if the mind for a time gets clouded or the resolution dimmed, yet one finds it reemerging automatically like a ship out of a covering wave, and goes invincibly on with the journey through all vicissitudes till it reaches the harbour.

*

They [*faith, surrender and samata*] have to be put into every part and atom of the being so that there may be no possibility of a contrary vibration anywhere.

*

You must keep the faith always that however the lower nature may rise or hostile forces attack, victory will be yours and the transformation is sure.

*

Keep firm faith in the victory of the Light and face with calm equanimity the resistances of Matter and human personality to their own transformation.

*

Even if there is much darkness — and this world is full of it and the physical nature of man also — yet a ray of the true Light can prevail eventually against a tenfold darkness. Believe that and cleave to it always.

Chapter Nine
Consecration and Offering

Consecration

Consecration is a process by which one trains the consciousness to give itself to the Divine.

*

The general principle of self-consecration and self-giving is the same for all in this Yoga, but each has his own way of consecration and self-giving. The way that X takes is good for X, just as the way that you take is the right one for you because it is in consonance with your nature. If there were not this plasticity and variety, if all had to be cut in the same pattern, Yoga would be a rigid mental machinery, not a living power.

When you can sing out of your inner consciousness in which you feel the Mother moving all your actions, there is no reason why you should not do it. The development of capacities is not only permissible but right, when it can be made part of the Yoga; one can give not only one's soul, but all one's powers to the Divine.

*

It is very evident that X has had a sudden opening to spiritual experience — a surprisingly sudden opening, one would think, but it happens often in that way, especially if there is a sceptical mind outside and a soul ready for experience within. In such cases also it comes often after a blow such as his brother's illness, but I think there was already a turning of the mind which prepared it. This sudden and persistent visualisation also shows that there is a faculty within that has broken the gates which shut it in — the faculty of supraphysical vision. The coming up of the word "consecration" is also a familiar phenomenon of these experiences — it is what I call the voice of the psychic, an intimation from his own soul to the mind as to what it wants him to do. Now he has to accept it, for the assent of the nature, of the outward man to the inner voice, is necessary so that it may be effective. He is standing at the turning point and has been given an indication of the new road his inner being, the Antaratman, wants him to follow — but, as I say, the assent of his mind and vital is necessary. If he can decide to consecrate, he must make the *saṅkalpa* of consecration, offer himself to the Divine and call for the help and the guidance. If he is not able to do that at once let him wait and see, but keeping himself open, as it were, to the continuation and development of the experience that has begun till it becomes definitely imperative to his own feeling. He will receive help and, if he becomes conscious of it, then there can be no further question — it will be easy for him to proceed on the way.

Offering

One offers to the Divine in order to get rid of the illusion of separation — the very act of offering implies that all belongs to the Divine.

*

Have attachment to nothing [*in order to offer all to the Divine*] — aspire until you get the consciousness of the Divine — call on the Divine to control and take up all you are and have.

*

(1) Offer yourself more and more — all the consciousness, all that happens in it, all your work and action.

(2) If you have faults and weaknesses, hold them up before the Divine to be changed or abolished.

(3) Try to do what I told you, concentrate in the heart till you constantly feel the Presence there.

*

Remain quiet, put your will always on the side of the Truth, offer yourself entirely to the Divine.

Chapter Ten

Opening

The Meaning of Opening

Opening is a change of the consciousness by which it becomes receptive to the Divine.

*

Opening means that the consciousness becomes opened to the Truth or the Divine to which it is now shut — it indicates a state of receptivity.

*

Opening is a thing that happens of itself by sincerity of will and aspiration. It means to be able to receive the higher forces that come from the Mother.

*

Opening means only to be able to receive the Mother's force. Whether one is open or not is shown by two things. If one is conscious of the force working in one, then one is open. But even if one is not conscious, yet if results of the working happen, then that also means that in the inner being some opening has been made. Aspiration, sincerity and the quietude of the mind are the three best conditions for opening.

*

These [*calling the Mother, praying to her*] are acts of the mind, openness is a *state* of consciousness which keeps it turned to the Mother, free from other movements, expecting and able to receive what may come from the Divine.

*

There is a state in which the sadhak is conscious of the Divine Force working in him or of its results at least and does not obstruct its descent or its action by his own mental activities, vital restlessness or physical obscurity and inertia. That is openness to the Divine. Surrender is the best way of opening; but aspiration and quietness can do it up to a certain point so long as there is not the surrender.

*

The object of the self-opening is to allow the force of the Divine to flow in bringing light, peace, Ananda etc. and to do the work of transformation. When the being so receives the Divine Shakti and it works in him, produces its results (whether he is entirely conscious of the process or not), then he is said to be open.

Opening to the Divine

In this Yoga the whole principle is to open oneself to the Divine Influence. It is there above you and, if you can once become conscious of it, you have then to call it down into you. It descends into the mind and into the body as Peace, as a Light, as a Force that works, as the Presence of the Divine with or without form, as Ananda. Before one has this consciousness, one has to have faith and aspire for the opening. Aspiration, call, prayer are forms of one and the same thing and are all effective; you can take the form that comes to you or is easiest to you. The other way is concentration; you concentrate your consciousness in the heart (some do it in the head or above the head) and meditate on the Mother in the heart and call her in there. One can do either and both at different times — whatever comes naturally to you or you are moved to do at the moment. Especially in the beginning the one great necessity is to get the mind quiet, reject at the time of meditation all thoughts and movements that are foreign to the sadhana. In the quiet mind there will be a progressive preparation for the experience. But you must not become impatient if all is not done at once; it takes time to bring entire quiet into the mind; you have to go on till the consciousness is ready.

*

In this Yoga all depends on whether one can open to the Influence or not. If there is a sincerity in the aspiration and a patient will to arrive at the higher consciousness in spite of all obstacles, then the opening in one form or another is sure to arrive. But it may take a long or a short time according to the prepared or unprepared condition of the mind, heart and body; so if one has not the necessary patience, the effort may be abandoned owing to the difficulty of the beginning. There is no method in this Yoga except to concentrate, preferably in the heart, and call the presence and power of the Mother to take up the being and by the workings of her force transform the consciousness; one can concentrate also in the head or between the eyebrows, but for many this is a too difficult opening. When the mind falls quiet and the concentration becomes strong and the aspiration intense, then there is a beginning of experience. The more the faith, the more rapid the result is likely to be. For the rest one must not depend on one's own efforts only, but succeed in establishing a contact with the Divine and a receptivity to the Mother's Power and Presence.

*

A Fire in the heart is usually the psychic fire and that should rather grow and be fed by the tendency or aspiration to the personal sadhana. The main principle of the personal sadhana is the surrender, the aspiration to the Divine touch, presence, control in the heart — the opening of the psychic being from within and its coming in front to govern and change mind, vital, physical consciousness. There are two openings that are necessary, one from above, the other from within. The one from above which can come by the impersonal Path or by the personal and impersonal together, seems to have come to you. Your feeling about the Personal probably comes from the push from within for the psychic to emerge fully. It is this aspiration therefore that should be the beginning of the personal path and a reliance on the Inner Power to guide and do what is needed.

*

Well, that is the idea in Yoga — that by a right passivity one opens oneself to something greater than one's limited self, and effort is only useful for getting that condition. There is also a notion that even in the ordinary life the individual is only an instrument in the hands of a Universal Energy though his ego takes the credit of all he does.

*

It is the law of the sadhana to open to the influences of the higher worlds.

*

It is true that through whatever is strongest in him a sadhak can most easily open to the Divine.

*

In the practice of Yoga, what you aim at can only come by the opening of the being to the Mother's force and the persistent rejection of all egoism and demand and desire, all motives except the aspiration for the Divine Truth. If this is rightly done, the Divine Power and Light will begin to work and bring in the peace and equanimity, the inner strength, the purified devotion and the increasing consciousness and self-knowledge which are the necessary foundation for the siddhi of the Yoga.

*

Open with sincerity. That means to open integrally and without reservation: not to give one part of you to the divine working and keep back the rest; not to make a partial offering and keep for yourself the other movements of your nature. All must be opened wide; it is insincerity to hold back any part of you or keep it shut to the Divine.

Open with faithfulness. That means to be open constantly and always; not to open one day and withdraw the next.

*

The opening is the same for all. It begins with an opening of the mind and heart, then of the vital proper — when it reaches the lower vital and physical the opening is complete. But with the opening there must be the full self-giving to what comes down, which is the condition of the complete change. It is this last stage that is the real difficulty and it is there that everyone stumbles about till it is overcome.

*

It takes time to open all the parts fully. Let the mind and heart remain open and the rest will follow. Clouds that pass and coverings that come cannot prevent it.

*

It is certainly not by merely repeating "to will" and "to open" (with the mental idea), that the will or the opening will come. It is by using the will that the will becomes effective, it is by using the aspiration and the will also that the opening comes. The first thing is to call down the calm into the mind and the vital; with the calm established or in course of preparation to invite more and more the Mother's workings and grow conscious of them within you and give your assent to them and refuse all else. All the rest then comes in its time and by the proper process.

*

It is by confidence in the Mother that the opening needed will come when your consciousness is ready. There is no harm in arranging your present work so that there will be time and energy for some meditation, but it is not by meditation alone that what is needed will come. It is by faith and openness to the Mother.

*

Keep yourself open to the Mother, remember her always and let her Force work in you, rejecting all other influences — that is the rule for Yoga.

Chapter Eleven
Patience and Perseverance

Patience

It is certain that an ardent aspiration for the Divine helps to progress, but patience is also needed. For it is a very big change that has to be made and, although there can be moments of great rapidity, it is never all the time like that. Old things try to stick as much as possible; the new that come have to develop and the consciousness takes time to assimilate them and make them normal to the nature.

Keep this firm faith in your mind that the thing needed is being done and will be done fully. There can be no doubt about that.

*

There are always difficulties and a hampered progress in the early stages and a delay in the opening of the inner doors until the being is ready. If you feel whenever you meditate the quiescence and the flashes of the inner Light and if the inward urge is growing so strong that the external hold is decreasing and the vital disturbances are losing their force, that is already a great progress. The road of Yoga is long, every inch of ground has to be won against much resistance and no quality is more needed by the sadhak than patience and single-minded perseverance with a faith that remains firm through all difficulties, delays and apparent failures.

*

Determination is needed and a firm patience, not to be discouraged by this or that failure. It is a change in the habit of the physical nature and that needs a long patient work of detail.

*

One who has not the courage to face patiently and firmly life and its difficulties will never be able to go through the still greater inner difficulties of the sadhana. The very first lesson in this Yoga is to face life and its trials with a quiet mind, a firm courage and an entire reliance on the Divine Shakti.

*

It is true that a great patience and steadfastness is needed. Be then firm and patient and fixed on the aims of the sadhana, but not over-eager to have them at once. A work has to be done in you and is being done; help it to be done by keeping an attitude of firm faith and confidence. Doubts rise in all, they are natural to the human physical mind — reject them. Impatience and over-eagerness for the result at once are natural to the human vital; it is by firm confidence in the Mother that they will disappear. The love, the belief in her as the Divine to whom your life is given, — oppose with that every contrary feeling and then those contrary feelings will after a time no longer be able to come to you.

*

It is an impatience and restlessness in the vital which makes it feel as if it were no use staying here because things are not moving forward. Sadhana is a thing which takes time and needs patience. There are often periods of quiescence in which a working is going on behind of which the mind is not aware — all seems then to be inert and dull; but if one has patience and confidence, the consciousness passes through these periods to new openings and things which seemed to be impossible to effect at that time, get done. The impulse to rush away is always a mistake — perseverance in the path is the one rule to cling to and with that finally all obstacles are overcome.

*

Impatience is always a mistake, it does not help but hinders. A quiet happy faith and confidence is the best foundation for sadhana; for the rest a constant opening wide of oneself to receive with an aspiration which may be intense, but must always be calm and steady. Full Yogic realisation does not come all at once, it comes after a long preparation of the Adhara which may take a long time.

*

In a more deep and spiritual sense a concrete realisation is that which makes the thing realised more real, dynamic, intimately present to the consciousness than any physical thing can be. Such a realisation of the personal Divine or of the impersonal Brahman or of the Self does not usually come at the beginning of a sadhana or in the first years or for many years. It comes so to a very few; mine came fifteen years after my first pre-Yogic experience in London and in the fifth year after I started Yoga. That I consider extraordinarily quick, an express train speed almost — though there may no doubt have been several quicker achievements. But to expect and demand it so soon and get fed up because it does not come and declare Yoga impossible except for two or three in the ages would betoken in the eyes of any experienced Yogi or sadhaka a rather rash and abnormal impatience. Most would say that a slow development is the best one can hope for in the first years and only when the nature is ready and fully concentrated towards the Divine can the definitive experience come. To some rapid preparatory experiences can come at a comparatively early stage, but even they cannot escape the labour of the consciousness which will make these experiences culminate in the realisation that is enduring and complete. It is not a question of my liking or disliking your demand or attitude. It is a matter of fact and truth and experience, not of liking or disliking, two things which do not usually sway me. It is the fact that people who are grateful and cheerful and ready to go step by step, even by slow steps, if need be, do actually march faster and more surely than those who are impatient and in haste and at each step despair or murmur. It is what I have always seen — there may be instances to the contrary and I have no objection to your being one, — none at all. I only say that if you could maintain "hope and fervour and faith", there would be a much bigger chance — that is all.

This is just a personal explanation — a long explanation but which seemed to be called for by your enhancement of my glory — and is dictated by a hope that after all in the long run an accumulation of explanations may persuade you to prefer the sunny path to the grey one. My faith again perhaps? But, sunny path or grey one, the one thing wanted is that you should push through and arrive.

*

You say after several years you have not changed your nature. I only wish the external nature were so easy to transform that it could be done in a few years. You forget also that the real problem — to get rid of the pervading ego in this nature — is a task you have seriously tackled only a short time ago. And it is not in a few months that that can be done. Even the best sadhaks find after many experiences and large changes on the higher planes that here much remains to be done. How do you expect to get rid of it at once unlike everybody else? A Yoga like this needs patience, because it means a change both of the radical motives and of each part and detail of the nature. It will not do to say — "Yesterday I determined this time to give myself entirely to the Mother, and look it is not done, on the contrary all the old opposite things turn up once more; so there is nothing to do but to proclaim myself unfit and give up the Yoga." Of course when you come to the point where you make a resolution of that kind, immediately all that stands in the way does rise up — it invariably happens. The thing to be done is to stand back, observe and reject, not to allow these things to get hold of you, to keep your central will separate from them and call in the Mother's Force to meet them. If one does get involved as often happens, then to get disinvolved as soon as possible and go forward again. That is what everybody, every Yogin does — to be depressed because one cannot do everything in a rush is quite contrary to the truth of the matter. A stumble does not mean that one is unfit, nor does prolonged difficulty mean that for oneself the thing is impossible.

The fact that you have to give up your ordinary work when

you get depressed does not mean that you have not gained in steadiness — it only means that the steadiness you have gained is not a personal virtue but depends on your keeping the contact with the Mother — for it is her Force that is behind it and behind all the progress you can make. Learn to rely on that Force more, to open to it more completely and to seek spiritual progress even not for your own sake but for the sake of the Divine — then you will go on more smoothly. Get the full psychic opening in the most external physical consciousness. That and not despondency is the lesson you ought to draw from your present adverse experience.

*

They [*patience and peace*] go together. By having patience under all kinds of pressure you lay the foundations of peace.

Persistence

Your attitude towards the change needed and new life is the right one. A quiet, vigilant but undistressed persistence is the best way to get it done.

For the intimacy within to be reestablished the quietude must deepen so that the psychic may come out in the physical as it had done in the higher parts.

*

Things that have long acted on the nature take some time to go altogether, but they are bound to go since you have the sincere desire and your psychic being is growing in your nature. Our help is there always with you. You have to persist in faith and quietude and let the psychic grow more and more, then all will come right and you will no longer have this trouble.

*

It is so with all things in the path of sadhana — one must persist however long it takes, so only one can achieve.

*

What I want of you besides aspiring for faith? Well, just a little thoroughness and persistence in the method! Don't aspire for two days and then sink into the dumps, evolving a gospel of earthquake and Schopenhauer plus the jackal and all the rest of it. Give the Divine a full sporting chance. When he lights something in you or is preparing a light, don't come in with a wet blanket of despondency and throw it on the poor flame. You will say it is a mere candle that is lit — nothing at all? But in these matters, when the darkness of human mind and life and body has to be dissipated, a candle is always a beginning — a lamp can follow and afterwards a sun — but the beginning must be allowed to have a sequel — not get cut off from its natural *sequelae* by chinks of sadness and doubt and despair. At the beginning and for a long time the experiences do usually come in little quanta with empty spaces between — but, if allowed their way, the spaces will diminish and the quantum theory give way to the Newtonian continuity of the spirit. But you have never yet given it a real chance. The empty spaces have become peopled with doubts and denials and so the quanta have become rare, the beginnings remain beginnings. Other difficulties you have faced and rejected, but this difficulty you dandled too much for a long time and it has become strong — it must be dealt with by a persevering effort. I do not say that all doubts must disappear before anything comes — that would be to make sadhana impossible, for doubt is the mind's persistent assailant. All I say is, don't allow the assailant to become a companion, don't give him the open door and the fireside seat. Above all don't drive away the incoming Divine with that dispiriting wet blanket of sadness and despair!

To put it more soberly, — accept once for all that this thing has to be done, that it is the only thing left for yourself or the earth. Outside are earthquakes and Hitlers and a collapsing civilisation and — generally speaking — the jackal in the flood? All the more reason to tend towards the one thing to be done, the thing you have been sent to aid in getting done. It is difficult and the way long and the encouragement given meagre? What then? Why should you expect so great a thing to be easy or that there must be either a swift success or none? The difficulties have to be faced and the more cheerfully they are faced, the sooner they will be overcome. The one thing to do is to keep the mantra of success, the determination of victory, the fixed resolve, "Have it I must and have it I will." Impossible? There is no such thing as an impossibility — there are difficulties and things of *longue haleine*, but no impossibles. What one is determined fixedly to do, will get done now or later — it becomes possible.

There — that is my counterblast to your variations on Schopenhauer. I conclude — drive out dark despair and go bravely on with your poetry, your novels — and your Yoga. As the darkness disappears, the inner doors too will open.

Perseverance

Whatever method is used, persistence and perseverance are essential. For whatever method is used, the complexity of the natural resistance will be there to combat it.

*

One who fears monotony and wants something new would not be able to do Yoga or at least this Yoga which needs an inexhaustible perseverance and patience. The fear of death shows a vital weakness which is also contrary to a capacity for Yoga. Equally, one who is under the domination of his passions, would find the Yoga difficult and, unless supported by a true inner call and a sincere and strong aspiration for the spiritual consciousness and union with the Divine, might very easily fall fatally and his effort come to nothing.

*

There can be no doubt about the Divine Grace. It is perfectly true also that if a man is sincere, he will reach the Divine. But it does not follow that he will reach immediately, easily and without delay. Your error is there, to fix for God a term, five years, six years, and doubt because the effect is not yet there. A man may be centrally sincere and yet there may be many things that have to be changed in him before realisation can begin. His sincerity must enable him to persevere always — for it is a longing for the Divine that nothing can quench, neither delay nor disappointment nor difficulty nor anything else.

You have got troubled again because you have allowed your mind to become active again in its ignorance, questioning, trying to refute the simplest and most established spiritual truths, trying to decide without waiting for the inner knowledge. Throw all that away and go on in quietude, not minding if it takes short or long for things to open up. That was what you had undertaken to do. Keep to it and, however slowly, the consciousness will open and light come.

*

Keep quietude, persevere. These are the clouds that cover the growing Light; but the true consciousness is there increasing behind the clouds.

*

There is no such impossibility of your victory over the harder parts of your nature as you imagine. There is only needed the perseverance to go on till this resistance breaks down and the psychic which is not absent nor unmanifest is able to dominate the others. That has to be done whether you stay here or not and to go is likely only to increase the difficulty and imperil the final result — it cannot help you. It is here that the struggle however acute has, because of the immediate presence of the Mother, the best chance and certitude of a solution and successful ending.

Endurance

[*Endurance:*] The power to go through effort, difficulty or trouble without getting fatigued, depressed, discouraged or impatient and without breaking off the effort or giving up one's aim or resolution.

Resolution

A resolution means the will to try to get a thing done by the given time. It is not a binding "promise" that the thing will be done by that time. Even if it is not, the endeavour will have to continue, just as if no date had been fixed.

Firmness

Whether by tapasya or surrender does not matter, the one thing is to be firm in setting one's face to the goal. Once one has set one's feet on the way, how can one draw back from it to something inferior? If one keeps firm, falls do not matter, one rises up again and goes forward. If one is firm towards the goal, there can be on the way to the Divine no eventual failure. And if there is something within you that drives, as surely there is, falterings or falls or failures of faith make no eventual difference. One has to go on till the struggle is over and there is the straight and open and thornless way before us.

*

One cannot say whether the conquest is near or not — one has to go on steadily with the process of the sadhana without thinking of near and far, fixed on the aim, not elated if it seems to come close, not depressed if it still seems to be far.

*

You have only to remain quiet and firm in your following of the path and your will to go to the end. If you do that, circumstances will in the end be obliged to shape themselves to your will, because it will be the Divine Will in you.

Chapter Twelve
Vigilance

Vigilance, Discrimination, Control

Yes, the vigilance is very necessary — to remain *jāgrat* and *apramatta* was always considered as a main requisite by the Yogins.

*

Openness and, whenever needed, passivity, but to the highest consciousness, not to anything that comes.
   Therefore, there must be a certain quiet vigilance even in the passivity. Otherwise there may be either wrong movements or inertia.

*

Yes; vigilance should not be relaxed. In fact, it is only as the automatic knowledge and action are established in the being that the constant vigilance ceases to be needed — even then it cannot be given up absolutely until there is the full Light.

*

To give up restraint would be to give free play to the vital and that would mean leave for all kinds of forces to enter in. So long as there is not the supramental consciousness controlling and penetrating everything, in all the being from the overmind downwards, there is an ambiguous play of forces, and each force, however divine in origin, may be used by the Powers of light or intercepted as it passes through the mind and the vital by the Powers of darkness. Vigilance, discrimination, control cannot be abandoned till the complete victory has been won and the consciousness transmuted.

*

Grace is all right, but there should also be care and vigilance.

In putting the cycle, you should first observe and be sure that it will stand steady before you withdraw your hand from it or loosen too much your hold.

*

If you want the divine life, you must remain absolutely *unexcited and quiet*. Not careless, but always on your guard, sober, vigilant. "Madcaps" cannot contain the Power of the Mother, only those who are calm, poised, balanced. So do not be "something of a madcap".

Section Three

The Foundation of the Sadhana

Chapter One

Peace — The Basis of the Sadhana

Peace Is the First Condition

Peace and purity of the consciousness are the very foundation of the necessary change in the nature.

*

Peace is necessary for all; without peace and an increasing purity, even if one opens, one cannot receive perfectly all that comes down through the opening. Light too is necessary for all — without light one cannot take full advantage of all that comes down.

*

Peace is necessary for the higher states to develop.

*

Equanimity and peace in all conditions in all parts of the being is the first foundation of the Yogic status. Either Light (bringing with it knowledge) or Force (bringing strength and dynamism of many kinds) or Ananda (bringing love and joy of existence) can come next according to the trend of the nature. But peace is the first condition without which nothing else can be stable.

*

The first thing that you have to bring down is a positive, complete and enduring peace from above — that is the only foundation on which the rest can be done, i.e. the development of the higher consciousness, force, knowledge, love, Ananda.

*

What you are doing is entirely the right thing and nothing more is needed. The peace you feel is the basis, the foundation for the transformation, all the rest will be built on it. To open to the Divine Forces with a quiet and strong aspiration, to become conscious of their working, to allow quietly that working and calmly to contain it, seconding it with one's aspiration, getting more and more knowledge and understanding of what is being done as one goes on — this is the sound and natural way of the Yoga.

*

A quiet aspiration can be as effective as an intense call. Peace is the basis of the sadhana.

*

The meditation experience seems to be developing in the right direction. Before it was only an opening; but to get something settled, there must be this assimilation and the growth in stability, in peace. Peace is the basis of the spiritual change — all the rest falls into the peace and is sustained on it as on a sure foundation.

*

Stability is indeed a great — the first necessity, like the foundations of a house. I am so glad to hear that you feel it growing in you.

Peace, Calm, Wideness

At last you have the true foundation of the sadhana. This calm, peace and surrender are the right atmosphere for all the rest to come, knowledge, strength, Ananda. Let it become complete.

It does not remain when engaged in work because it is still confined to the mind proper which has only just received the gift of silence. When the new consciousness is fully formed and has taken entire possession of the vital nature and the physical being (the vital as yet is only touched or dominated by the silence, not possessed by it), then this defect will disappear.

The quiet consciousness of peace you now have in the mind

must become not only calm but wide. You must feel it everywhere, yourself in it and all in it. This also will help to bring the calm as a basis into the action.

The wider your consciousness becomes, the more you will be able to receive from above. The Shakti will be able to descend and bring strength and light as well as peace into the system. What you feel as narrow and limited in you is the physical mind; it can only widen if this wider consciousness and the light come down and possess the nature.

The physical inertia from which you suffer is likely to lessen and disappear only when strength from above descends into the system.

Remain quiet, open yourself and call the divine Shakti to confirm the calm and peace, to widen the consciousness and to bring into it as much light and power as it can at present receive and assimilate.

Take care not to be over-eager, as this may disturb again such quiet and balance as has been already established in the vital nature.

Have confidence in the final result and give time for the Power to do its work.

*

Wideness and calmness are the foundation of the Yogic consciousness and the best condition for inner growth and experience. If a wide calm can be established in the physical consciousness, occupying and filling the very body and all its cells, that can become the basis for its transformation; in fact, without this wideness and calmness the transformation is hardly possible.

Difficulties, Disturbances and Peace

Aspire, concentrate in the right spirit and, whatever the difficulties, you are sure to attain the aim you have put before you.

It is in the peace behind and that "something truer" in you that you must learn to live and feel it to be yourself. You must regard the rest as not your real self, but only a flux of changing or recurring movements on the surface which are sure to go as the true self emerges.

Peace is the true remedy; distraction by hard work is only a temporary relief — although a certain amount of work is necessary for the proper balance of the different parts of the being. To feel the peace above or about your head is a first step; you have to get connected with it and it must descend into you and fill your mind and life and body and surround you so that you live in it — for this peace is one sign of the Divine's presence with you, and once you have it all the rest will begin to come.

Truth in speech and truth in thought are very important. The more you can feel falsehood as being not part of yourself, as coming on you from outside, the easier it will be to reject and refuse it.

Persevere and what is still crooked will be made straight and you will know and feel concretely the truth of the Divine's presence and your faith will be justified by direct experience.

*

So long as the mind is restless, it is not possible to get at the inner Truth. Calm, peace, quietude — that is the first necessary condition.

*

To be calm, undisturbed and quiet is not the first condition for sadhana but for siddhi. It is only a few people (very few, one, two, three, four in a hundred sadhaks) who can get it from the first. Most have to go through a long preparation before they can get anywhere near it. Even afterwards when they begin to feel the peace and calm, it takes time to establish it — they swing between peace and disturbance for a fairly long time until all parts of the nature have accepted the truth and the peace. So there is no reason for you to suppose you cannot progress or arrive. You are finding a great difficulty with one part of your nature which has been accustomed to open itself to these feelings, separation from the Mother and attachment to relatives, and is not willing to give them up — that is all. But everybody finds such obstinate difficulties in that part of the nature, even the most successful sadhaks here. One has to persevere until the light conquers there.

*

It is the quietness in which the Force can act and an entire reliance on that Force to do for you what is necessary — and for the rest a quiet vigilance not to consent to the confusion and restlessness — that you must achieve. It has been evident throughout since the working in you began that this is the only possible foundation for your sadhana.

*

That is the right way — to keep the peace of the higher consciousness, then even if there is vital disturbance, it will be only on the surface. The foundation will remain till the Force can release the true vital.

*

Detachment, silence, inner peace are certainly indispensable for the spiritual progress — a quiet peace-filled detachment. In that peace the Force must do its work. Attacks of confusion, pains etc. — the one thing to arrive at is to be able to stand back from them, to feel detachment from them, separate and call down the Force to act. Whenever one can do that, the attack, the difficulty after a time retires — or even if it lasts a little cannot disturb what has been gained.

*

The depression and vital struggle must have been due to some defect of over-eagerness and straining for a result in your former effort — so that when a fall in the consciousness came it was a depressed, disappointed and confused vital that came to the surface giving full entry to the suggestions of doubt, despair and inertia from the adverse side of Nature. You have to move towards a firm basis of calm and equality in the vital and physical no less than in the mental consciousness; let there be the full downflow of Power and Ananda, but into a firm adhara capable of containing it — it is a complete equality that gives that capacity and firmness.

*

When the peace of the higher consciousness descends, it brings always with it this tendency towards equality, samata, because without samata peace is always liable to be attacked by the waves of the lower nature.

Chapter Two
Equality — The Chief Support

Equality or Samata

There can be no firm foundation in sadhana without equality, *samatā*. Whatever the unpleasantness of circumstances, however disagreeable the conduct of others, you must learn to receive them with a perfect calm and without any disturbing reaction. These things are the test of equality. It is easy to be calm and equal when things go well and people and circumstances are pleasant; it is when they are the opposite that the completeness of the calm, peace, equality can be tested, reinforced, made perfect.

*

Yogic Samata is equality of soul, equanimity founded on the sense of the one Self, the one Divine everywhere — seeing the One in spite of all differences, degrees, disparities in the manifestation. The mental principle of equality tries to ignore or else to destroy the differences, degrees and disparities, to act as if all were equal there or to try and make all equal. It is like Hriday, the nephew of Ramakrishna, who when he got the touch from Ramakrishna began to shout, "Ramakrishna, you are the Brahman and I too am the Brahman; there is no difference between us", till Ramakrishna, as he refused to be quiet, had to withdraw the power. Or like the disciple who refused to listen to the Mahout and stood before the elephant, saying, "I am Brahman", until the elephant took him up in his trunk and put him aside. When he complained to his Guru, the Guru said, "Yes, but why didn't you listen to the Mahout Brahman? That was why the elephant Brahman had to lift you up and put you out of harm's way." In the manifestation there are two sides to the Truth and you cannot ignore either.

*

Samata means a wide universal peace, calm, equanimity, an equal feeling of all in the Divine.

*

Equality is to remain unmoved within in all conditions.

*

Equality is the chief support of the true spiritual consciousness and it is this from which the sadhak deviates when he allows a vital movement to carry him away in feeling or speech or action. Equality is not the same thing as forbearance, — though undoubtedly a settled equality immensely extends, even illimitably, a man's power of endurance and forbearance.

Equality means a quiet and unmoved mind and vital; it means not to be touched or disturbed by things that happen or things said or done to you but to look at them with a straight look, free from the distortions created by personal feeling, and to try to understand what is behind them, why they happen, what is to be learnt from them, what is it in oneself which they are cast against and what inner profit or progress one can make out of them; it means self-mastery over the vital movements, anger and sensitiveness and pride as well as desire and the rest, not to let them get hold of the emotional being and disturb the inner peace, not to speak and act in the rush and impulsion of these things, always to act and speak out of a calm inner poise of the spirit. It is not easy to have this equality in any full and perfect measure, but one should always try more and more to make it the basis of one's inner state and outer movements.

Equality means another thing — to have an equal view of men and their nature and acts and the forces that move them; it helps one to see the truth about them by pushing away from the mind all personal feeling in one's seeing and judgment and even all mental bias. Personal feeling always distorts and makes one see in men's actions, not only the actions themselves, but things behind them which, more often than not, are not there. Misunderstanding and misjudgment which could have been avoided are the result; things of small consequence assume

Equality — The Chief Support

large proportions. I have seen that more than half of the untoward happenings of this kind in life are due to this cause. But in ordinary life personal feeling and sensitiveness are a constant part of human nature and may be needed there for self-defence, although, I think, even there, a strong, large and equal attitude towards men and things would be a much better line of defence. But, for a sadhak, to surmount them and live rather in the calm strength of the spirit is an essential part of his progress.

The first condition of inner progress is to recognise whatever is or has been a wrong movement in any part of the nature, — wrong idea, wrong feeling, wrong speech, wrong action, — and by wrong is meant what departs from the Truth, from the higher consciousness and higher self, from the way of the Divine. Once recognised it is admitted, — not glossed over or defended, — and it is offered to the Divine for the Light and Grace to descend and substitute for it the right movement of the true consciousness.

*

Complete samata takes long to establish and it is dependent on three things — the soul's self-giving to the Divine by an inner surrender, the descent of the spiritual calm and peace from above and the steady, long and persistent rejection of all egoistic, rajasic and other feelings that contradict samata.

The first thing to do is to make the full consecration and offering in the heart — the increase of the spiritual calm and the surrender are the condition for making the rejection of ego, rajoguna etc. effective.

Samata and Loyalty to Truth

No doubt hatred and cursing are not the proper attitude. It is true also that to look upon all things and all people with a calm and clear vision, to be uninvolved and impartial in one's judgments is a quite proper Yogic attitude. A condition of perfect samata can be established in which one sees all as equal, friends and enemies included, and is not disturbed by what men do or by what happens. The question is whether this is all that is demanded from us. If so, then the general attitude will be one of a neutral indifference to everything. But the Gita, which strongly insists on a perfect and absolute samata, goes on to say, "Fight, destroy the adversary, conquer." If there is no kind of general action wanted, no loyalty to Truth as against Falsehood except for one's personal sadhana, no will for the Truth to conquer, then the samata of indifference will suffice. But here there is a work to be done, a Truth to be established against which immense forces are arranged, invisible forces which use visible things and persons and actions for their instruments. If one is among the disciples, the seekers of this Truth, one has to take sides for the Truth, to stand against the Forces that attack it and seek to stifle it. Arjuna wanted not to stand for either side, to refuse any action of hostility even against assailants; Sri Krishna, who insisted so much on samata, strongly rebuked his attitude and insisted equally on his fighting the adversary. "Have samata," he said, "and seeing clearly the Truth, fight." Therefore to take sides with the Truth and to refuse to concede anything to the Falsehood that attacks, to be unflinchingly loyal and against the hostiles and the attackers, is not inconsistent with equality. It is personal and egoistic feeling that has to be thrown away; hatred and vital ill-will have to be rejected. But loyalty and refusal to compromise with the assailants and the hostiles or to dally with their ideas and demands and say, "After all we can compromise with what they ask from us", or to accept them as companions and our own people — these things have a great importance. If the attack were a physical menace to the work and the leaders and doers of the work, one would see this at once. But because the attack is of a subtler kind, can a passive attitude be right? It is a spiritual battle inward and outward; by neutrality and compromise or even passivity one may allow the enemy Forces to pass and crush down the Truth and its children. If you look at it from this point you will see that if the inner spiritual equality is right, the active loyalty and firm taking of sides is as right, and the two cannot be incompatible.

    I have of course treated it as a general question apart from all particular cases or personal questions. It is a principle of action that has to be seen in its right light and proportions.

*

It [*samata*] is to face it [*an attack*] without being disturbed and to reject it calmly. Whether one tries to remedy or not remedy should make no difference. Only when one acts against it, one must do it calmly, without anger, excitement, grief or any other disturbing movement.

Samata and Ego

Samata does not mean the absence of ego, but the absence of desire and attachment.

*

I have said "samata" shows absence of desire and attachment — the ego-sense may disappear or it may remain in a subtilised and widened form — it depends on the person.

Equality and Detachment

As for the detachment of which you speak, it comes by attaining the poise of the Spirit, the equality of which the Gita speaks always, but also by sight, by knowledge. For instance, looking at what happened in 1914 — or for that matter at all that is and has been happening in human history — the eye of the Yogin sees not only outward events and persons and causes, but the enormous forces which precipitate them into action. If the men who fought were instruments in the hands of rulers and financiers etc., these in turn were mere puppets in the clutch of these forces. When one is habituated to see the things behind, one is no longer prone to be touched by the outward aspects — or to expect any remedy from political, institutional or social changes; the only way out is through the descent of a consciousness which is not the puppet of these forces but is greater than they are and can force them either to change or disappear.

*

The Yogic attitude consists in calm, detachment, equality, universality — added to this the psychic element, bhakti, love, devotion to the Divine.

Equality in Times of Trouble and Difficulty

Equality is a very important part of this Yoga; it is necessary to keep equality under pain and suffering — and that means to endure firmly and calmly, not to be restless or troubled or depressed or despondent, to go on in a steady faith in the Divine Will. But equality does not include inert acceptance. If, for instance, there is temporary failure of some endeavour in the sadhana, one has to keep equality, not to be troubled or despondent, but one has not to accept the failure as an indication of the Divine Will and give up the endeavour. You ought rather to find out the reason and meaning of the failure and go forward in faith towards victory. So with illness — you have not to be troubled, shaken or restless, but you have not to accept illness as the Divine Will, but rather look upon it as an imperfection of the body to be got rid of as you try to get rid of vital imperfections or mental errors.

*

To be free from all preference and receive joyfully whatever comes from the Divine Will is not possible at first for any human being. What one should have at first is the constant idea that what the Divine wills is always for the best even when the mind does not see how it is so, to accept with resignation what one cannot yet accept with gladness and so to arrive at a calm equality which is not shaken even when on the surface there may be passing movements of a momentary reaction to outward happenings. If that is once firmly founded, the rest can come.

*

It is very good that you have had this experience; for this kind of consciousness full of equality (samata) is just the thing that has to be acquired and the very basis on which a sound Yogic consciousness full of the Mother can be built up. If it can be fixed, then most of the trouble and difficulty of sadhana disappears — all necessary changes can proceed quietly without these disturbances and upsettings which break and hamper the progress. Also in it there can grow a right and clear understanding of people and things and how to deal with them without friction which can make work and action much more easy. Once this consciousness has come, it is bound to return and increase.

*

Through an equality gained by strong mental control [*the worldly man is able to bear all kinds of difficulty*] — but that is not *samatā*, it is *titikṣā*, the power to bear which is only a first step or a first element of *samatā*.

*

It is not enough to have that equality and silence and freedom only when you are in communion with the sky and sea. It is at all times that you must be able to receive it from above — then there will be a true foundation of the sadhana.

*

You must establish a basis of equanimity within — the peace of the inner being which these surface movements cannot touch, — then if they come on the surface, there will be no violent reaction and they can be rejected with more ease.

*

The sadhak has to keep his quietude and faith and equanimity in all conditions — even when the higher consciousness and experience are not there.

*

One has to proceed on a basis of firm quietude and equanimity with a steady aspiration. It is only if there is a vital excitement that progress becomes a strain and relaxation is needed; for this demand for relaxation is the vital's counterpart of excitement and its way of relief from it.

*

A perfect spiritual equanimity throughout the being is a sure defence against all the perturbations that might come through the environmental nature.

*

The difficulty of getting the perfect equanimity is a fact, but not for you alone — it has been so for all of us — it is too universal for you to make it a legitimate ground of discouragement. Nothing is more necessary, but nothing is more difficult. So there is no reason why you should discount my encouragement. My encouragement is given in spite of difficulties and not because I think there are none. Never mind these momentary mishaps — shake off the mood and once more *en avant*.

Chapter Three
Quiet and Calm

Quiet, Calm, Peace, Silence

The words "peace, calm, quiet, silence" have each their own shade of meaning, but it is not easy to define them.
Peace — *śānti*.
Calm — *sthiratā*.
Quiet — *acañcalatā*.
Silence — *niścala-nīravatā*.
Quiet is a condition in which there is no restlessness or disturbance.
Calm is a still, unmoved condition which no disturbance can affect — it is a less negative condition than quiet.
Peace is a still more positive condition; it carries with it a sense of settled and harmonious rest and deliverance.
Silence is a state in which either there is no movement of the mind or vital or else a great stillness which no surface movement can pierce or alter.

*

Quiet is rather negative — it is the absence of disturbance.
Calm is a positive tranquillity which can exist in spite of superficial disturbances.
Peace is a calm deepened into something that is very positive amounting almost to a tranquil waveless Ananda.
Silence is the absence of all motion of thought or other vibration of activity.

*

Quietness is when the mind or vital is not troubled, restless, drawn about by or crowded with thoughts and feelings. Especially when either is detached and looks at these as a surface movement, we say that the mind or vital is quiet.

Calmness is a more positive condition, not merely an absence of restlessness, over-activity or trouble. When there is a clear sense of great or strong tranquillity which nothing troubles or can trouble, then we say that calm is established.

*

Calm is a strong and positive quietude, firm and solid — ordinary quietude is mere negation, simply the absence of disturbance.

Peace is a deep quietude where no disturbance can come — a quietude with a sense of established security and release.

In complete silence there are either no thoughts or, if they come, they are felt as something coming from outside and not disturbing the silence.

Silence of the mind, peace or calm in the mind are three things that are very close together and bring each other.

*

These [*tranquillity and stillness*] are general words, of a general and not a special Yogic significance. Quiet, calm and peace can all be described as tranquillity, silence is akin to what is meant by stillness.

Quietude

Quiet means to keep the inner quietude and keep turned to the Mother with the aspiration towards or call for the return of the right condition.

*

Remember first that an inner quietude, caused by the purification of the restless mind and vital, is the first condition of a secure sadhana. Remember, next, that to feel the Mother's presence while in external action is already a great step and one that cannot be attained without a considerable inner progress. Probably, what you feel you need so much but cannot define is a constant and vivid sense of the Mother's force working in you, descending from above and taking possession of the different planes of your being. That is often a prior condition for the twofold movement of ascent and descent; it will surely come in time. These things can take a long time to begin visibly, especially when the mind is accustomed to be very active and has not the habit of mental silence. When that veiling activity is there, much work has to be carried on behind the mobile screen of the mind and the sadhak thinks nothing is happening when really much preparation is being done. If you want a more swift and visible progress, it can only be by bringing your psychic to the front through a constant self-offering. Aspire intensely, but without impatience.

*

Your mind is too full of demands and desires. If you want to be able to practise the Yoga here, you must throw them from you and learn quietude, desirelessness, simplicity and surrender. It is these you must get first; other things can come afterwards — for this is the only true foundation of the sadhana.

*

Always get back to quietude. It is through the quietude that the right attitude and understanding and movements come back. It is natural for the lower vital to be made up of feelings, impulses and desires and to be attached to outer things — but that is only a part of you. There is also the psychic and the higher mind and higher vital which only need quietude and the help of the Force and Peace behind them to come forward more strongly and dominate over the lower vital and help to change it.

*

You are too easily invaded by these things [*from outside*]. You must call for a calm quietness in the vital and physical and a Force in you and around you which will repel all foreign forces the moment they appear. If there is entire quietude and strength in the nerves, these outside forces will not easily be able to touch you.

*

You should realise that while quiet surroundings are desirable, the true quiet is within and no other will give you the condition you want.

*

The inner spiritual progress does not depend on outer conditions so much as on the way we react to them from within — that has always been the ultimate verdict of spiritual experience. It is why we insist on taking the right attitude and persisting in it, on an inner state not dependent on outer circumstances, a state of equality and calm, if it cannot be at once of inner happiness, on going more and more within and looking from within outwards instead of living in the surface mind which is always at the mercy of the shocks and blows of life. It is only from that inner state that one can be stronger than life and its disturbing forces and hope to conquer.

To remain quiet within, firm in the will to go through, refusing to be disturbed or discouraged by difficulties or fluctuations, that is one of the first things to be learned on the Path. To do otherwise is to encourage the instability of consciousness, the difficulty of keeping experience of which you complain. It is only if you keep quiet and steady within that the lines of experience can go on with some steadiness — though they are never without periods of interruption and fluctuation; but these, if properly treated, can then become periods of assimilation and exhaustion of difficulty rather than denials of sadhana.

A spiritual atmosphere is more important than outer conditions; if one can get that and also create one's own spiritual air to breathe in and live in it, that is the true condition of progress.

*

If you can achieve quietude followed by an upward openness, it is better than the effort which sways between strong experiences and strong adverse reactions.

*

Even to have the quietude and calm somewhere behind or in

a passive way is more important and helpful than it seems. It provides a sort of permanent ground on which ultimately a lasting peace, power and joy can be built. If one can feel one part of the being always quiet in spite of the disturbances in another part, then one has made the first firm step towards a permanent change.

*

This state of emptiness and quietude and absence of reactions is regarded by Yogins as a great step in advance, especially the equality and indifference to what is said or done. For the moment it is a neutral condition only, but that it is usually at first. Afterwards it changes into peace or even into an equal Ananda undisturbed by anything that can happen.

*

The quiet and calm have to be increased so as to be a firm basis for the love and Ananda.

Quiet Mind

A quiet mind is a mind that does not get disturbed, is not restless and always vibrating with the need of mental action.

*

It is not possible to make a foundation in Yoga if the mind is restless. The first thing needed is quiet in the mind. Also, to merge the personal consciousness is not the first aim of the Yoga; the first aim is to open it to a higher spiritual consciousness and for this also a quiet mind is the first need.

*

The first step is a quiet mind — silence is a farther step, but quietude must be there, and by a quiet mind I mean a mental consciousness within which sees thoughts arrive to it and move about, but does not itself feel that it is thinking or identify itself with the thoughts or call them its own. Thoughts, mental movements may pass through it as wayfarers appear and pass from elsewhere through a silent country — the quiet mind observes them or does not care to observe them but in either case does not become active or lose its quietude. Silence is more than quietude; it can be gained by banishing thought altogether from the inner mind keeping it voiceless or quite outside; but more easily it is established by a descent from above — one feels it coming down, entering and occupying, or surrounding the personal consciousness which then tends to merge itself in the vast impersonal silence.

*

To get rid of the random thoughts of the surface physical mind is not easy. It is sometimes done by a sudden miracle as in my own case, but that is rare. Some get it done by a slow process of concentration, but that may take a very long time. It is easier to have a quiet mind with things that come in passing on the surface, as people pass in the street, and one is free to attend to them or not — that is to say, there develops a sort of double mind, one inner silent and concentrated when it pleases to be so, a quiet witness when it chooses to see thoughts and things, — the other meant for surface dynamism. It is probable in your case that this will come as soon as these descents of peace, intensity or Ananda get strong enough to occupy the whole system.

*

How can you throw away the mind unless you want to disappear from manifested existence? It has first to be made quiet and open to the higher consciousness and transformed by the descent of the higher consciousness.

*

First aspire and pray to the Mother for quiet in the mind, purity, calm and peace, an awakened consciousness, intensity of devotion, strength and spiritual capacity to face all inner and outer difficulties and go through to the end of the Yoga. If the consciousness awakens and there is devotion and intensity of aspiration, it will be possible for the mind, provided it learns quietude and peace, to grow in knowledge.

*

It is in the quiet mind that the true observation and knowledge come.

*

You have to become conscious [*in writing poetry*] as in Yoga. The mind has to be silent and you have to become aware of the inspiration as it comes and its source and of the mixture that comes on the way. The more the mind becomes quiet, the more all this is possible.

*

All quietude of the mind makes good conditions for the receptivity to act.

*

As I have said already, in all matters, work and study as well as in the inner progress in the Yoga, the same thing is needed if you want perfection — quietude of mind, becoming aware of the Force, opening to it, allowing it to work in you. To aim at perfection is all right, but restlessness of mind is not the way towards it. To dwell upon your imperfections and be always thinking how to do and what to do, is not the way either. Remain quiet, open yourself, allow the consciousness to grow — call the Force to work. As it grows and as the Force works, you will become aware not only of what is imperfect, but of the movement which will take you (not at one step, but progressively) out of the imperfection and you will then only have to follow that movement.

If you overstrain yourself by too prolonged work or a restless working, that disturbs or weakens the nervous system, the vital-physical, and lays one open to the action of the wrong forces. To work but quietly so as to have a steady progress is the right way.

*

1. A quiet mind makes consciousness easier.

2. If you keep a quiet mind and a constant contact with myself and the Mother and the true Light and Force, then things will become easy and straight — it is the *only* way to get to the realisation.

3. It is a mistake to think that this method will not lead you to the supramental realisation. It is the only way to advance towards the supramental change.

4. It is because you become doubtful and begin to follow after other ways and other (lower) experiences that you get again confused and full of incertitudes.

5. Keep to *one* way, the way shown to you by me. It is by following this way that you can reach the wideness you want — if you run about on many ways, that will bring not wideness but confusion.

6. Here in the lower nature there are many things, but they are in a state of disharmony, so to follow them all together means disharmony, confusion, want of organisation, fight. In the higher (supramental) nature there is a greater wideness and much more is there than in the lower nature; but all is harmony, organisation, peace. Follow therefore the one way that leads to the higher supramental nature.

7. Do not be impatient, because full knowledge does not come to you at once. In quietude of mind keep the contact, let the true Light and Force work and with time all knowledge will come and the Truth will grow in you.

*

Do you imagine that a quiet mind cannot reject anything and it is only the unquiet mind that can do it? It is the quiet mind that can best do it. Quiet does not mean inert and tamasic.

*

That is absurd. Doing nothing with the mind is not quiet or silence. It is inactivity that keeps the mind thinking mechanically and discursively instead of concentrating on an object — that is all.

*

Keeping the mind without occupation is not the same thing as peace or silence.

Vacant Mind

Keep the quietude and do not mind if it is for a time an empty quietude; the consciousness is often like a vessel which has to be emptied of its mixed or undesirable contents; it has to be kept vacant for a while till it can be filled with things new and true, right and pure. The one thing to be avoided is the refilling of the cup with the old turbid contents. Meanwhile wait, open yourself upwards, call very quietly and steadily, not with a too restless eagerness, for the peace to come into the silence and, once the peace is there, for the joy and the presence.

*

The difference between a vacant mind and a calm mind is this, that when the mind is vacant, there is no thought, no conception, no mental action of any kind, except an essential perception of things without the formed idea; but in the calm mind, it is the substance of the mental being that is still, so still that nothing disturbs it. If thoughts or activities come, they do not rise at all out of the mind, but they come from outside and cross the mind as a flight of birds crosses the sky in a windless air. It passes, disturbs nothing, leaving no trace. Even if a thousand images or the most violent events pass across it, the calm stillness remains as if the very texture of the mind were a substance of eternal and indestructible peace. A mind that has achieved this calmness can begin to act, even incessantly and powerfully, but it will keep its fundamental stillness — originating nothing from itself but receiving from Above and giving it a mental form without adding anything of its own, calmly, dispassionately, though with the joy of the Truth and the happy power and light of its passage.

Calm

It is the first secret of Yoga, to maintain the inner calm always and from that calm to meet everything.

*

It is not necessary [*in a calm mind*] that there should be no thought. When there is no thought, it is silence. But the mind is said to be calm when thoughts, feelings, etc. may pass through it, but it is not disturbed. It feels that the thoughts are not its own; it observes them perhaps; but it is not perturbed by anything.

*

What you have written about your condition seems to be correct as a whole. There is certainly a greater calm within and a freedom of the inner being which was not there once. It is this which gives you the equality you feel there and the capacity to escape from the more serious disturbances. When one has this basis of inner calm, the difficulties and imperfections of the surface can be dealt with without upsets, depressions, etc. The power to go among others without any invasion is also due to the same cause.

*

Do not attach so much importance to mistakes or insist on your non-receptiveness and unconsciousness. You have only to turn always to the Force that gives you calmness and in the calmness you will become progressively more and more conscious and receptive.

*

Calm, even if it seems at first only a negative thing, is so difficult to attain that to have it at all must be regarded as a great step in advance.

In reality, calm is not a negative thing; it is the very nature of the Sat-Purusha and the positive foundation of the divine consciousness. Whatever else is aspired for and gained, this must be kept. Even Knowledge, Power, Ananda, if they come and do not find this foundation, are unable to remain and have to withdraw until the divine purity and peace of the Sat-Purusha are permanently there.

Aspire for the rest of the divine consciousness, but with a calm and deep aspiration. It can be ardent as well as calm, but not impatient, restless or full of rajasic eagerness.

Only in the quiet mind and being can the supramental Truth build its true creation.

*

The calm from above came to you and established your connection with the Above, — and if you hold firmly to it, you will be able to remain calm. But to be rid of these vital disturbances from outside, you have to get down the Power and Will that is also there above — or at least so to be connected with it that it will act whenever you call upon it against the forces of the Ignorance.

*

It is the calm that has come down from above, only you are feeling it from there (mind and heart) and not from above the mind. But you have to find it below the heart and not only from the heart above, — the calm has to spread lower down.

*

The first [*calmness with disturbances on the surface*] is the ordinary fundamental calm of the individual Adhar — the second [*perfect stillness in the body and in the surrounding atmosphere*] is the fundamental limitless calm of the cosmic consciousness, a calm which abides whether separated from all movements or supporting them.

This [*limitless stillness*] is the calm of the Atman, the Self above, silent, immutable and infinite.

Chapter Four

Peace

Peace Is Something Positive

Peace is more positive than calm — there can be a negative calm which is merely an absence of disturbance or trouble, but peace is always something positive bringing not merely a release as calm does but a certain happiness or Ananda of itself. There is also a positive calm, something that stands firm against all things that seek to trouble, not thin and neutral like the negative calm, but strong and massive. Very often the two words are used in the same sense, but one can distinguish them in their true sense as above.

*

In peace there is besides the sense of stillness a harmony that gives a feeling of liberation and full satisfaction.

*

It is very good news. The peace settling in the system and with it a happy activity — that is the basis for your Yoga which I always wanted you to have — a sunny condition in which what has to come in will come in and expand like a bud into flower and what has to fall off will fall off in its time like a slough discarded.

*

The quietude and silence which you feel and the sense of happiness in it are indeed the very basis of successful sadhana. When one has got that, then one may be sure that the sadhana is placing itself on a sound footing. You are also right in thinking that if this quietude is fully established all that is concealed within will come out. It is true also that the happiness of this peace is far greater than anything outer objects can bring — there can be no comparison. To become indifferent to the attraction of outer objects is one of the first rules of Yoga, for this non-attachment liberates the inner being into peace and the true consciousness. It is only when one sees the Divine in all things that objects get a value for the Yoga, but even then not for their own sake or as objects of desire, but for the sake of the Divine within and as a means of the divine work and manifestation.

Peace Comes Little by Little

To nobody does the divine calm and peace come uninterruptedly in the early stages of the Yoga — it comes little by little — it is sometimes absent for long periods together, or there are strong attacks which cloud it over. It is by long sadhana that one gets the permanent peace.

*

In the beginning the peace and calmness comes like that only for a short time. The Adhar cannot keep it, its own natural condition being different. But afterwards the power of holding increases until in some part of the being at least it is constant.

A Settled or Established Peace

It is very good indeed. The peace and silence must settle deep in, so deep that whatever comes from outside can only pass over the surface without troubling the settled calm within — it is good also that the meditation comes of itself. It means that the Yoga-Force is beginning to take up the sadhana.

*

Yes, a settled peace and strength supporting the intensity and from which everything foreign falls off, is the true basis.

*

The first thing to do in the sadhana is to get a settled peace and silence in the mind. Otherwise you may have experiences, but nothing will be permanent. It is in the silent mind that the true consciousness can be built.

A quiet mind does not mean that there will be no thoughts or mental movements at all, but that these will be on the surface and you will feel your true being within separate from them, observing but not carried away, able to watch and judge them and reject all that has to be rejected and to accept and keep to all that is true consciousness and true experience.

Passivity of the mind is good, but take care to be passive only to the Truth and to the touch of the Divine Shakti. If you are passive to the suggestions and influences of the lower nature, you will not be able to progress or else you will expose yourself to adverse forces which may take you far away from the true path of Yoga.

Aspire to the Mother for this settled quietness and calm of the mind and this constant sense of the inner being in you standing back from the external nature and turned to the Light and Truth.

The forces that stand in the way of sadhana are the forces of the lower mental, vital and physical nature. Behind them are adverse powers of the mental, vital and subtle physical worlds. These can be dealt with only after the mind and heart have become one-pointed and concentrated in the single aspiration to the Divine.

*

If the peace or silence is once absolutely established, no amount of movements on the surface can impair or abolish it. It can bear all the movements of the universe and yet be the same.

*

When the peace is fully established everywhere in the being, these things [*reactions in the lower vital*] will not be able to shake it. They may come first as ripples on the surface, then only as suggestions which one looks at or does not care to look at, but in either case they don't get inside, affect or disturb at all.

It is difficult to explain, but it is something like a mountain at which one throws stones — if conscious all through the mountain may feel the touch of the stones, but the thing would be so slight and superficial that it would not be in the least affected. In the end even that reaction disappears.

*

The peace liberates from all dependence on outer contacts — it brings what the Gita calls the *ātmarati*. But at first there is a difficulty in keeping it intact when there is the contact with others because the consciousness has the habit of running outwards in speech or external interchange or else of coming down to the normal level. One must therefore be very careful until it is fixed; once fixed it usually defends itself, for all outer contacts become surface things to a consciousness full of the higher peace.

*

Even when there is the peace and the wideness, these things [*imaginations about old enjoyments*] can float on the surface and try to come in — only then they do not occupy the consciousness but touch it merely. It is what was regarded by the old Yogis as a mechanical remnant of Prakriti, a continuation of its blind habit which remained after the essential liberation of the self. It was treated lightly as of no importance — but that view is not tenable in our sadhana which aims not only at a liberation of the Purusha but at a *complete* transformation of the Prakriti also.

*

That is of course how it should be. It should go so far indeed that you will feel this peace and vastness as your very self, the abiding stuff of your consciousness — unchangeably there.

Peace in the Mind, Vital and Physical

Yes, certainly, there is a mental peace, a vital peace, a peace of the physical Nature. It is the peace of a higher consciousness that descends from above.

*

The silence and peace are there waiting to manifest. Let the mind and vital give all themselves and they will pour in and reveal themselves.

*

There can be peace in the mind even when the vital is not quite at rest or peace in the inner being even if the surface is disturbed. Consciousness cannot feel at rest and free, if there is no peace.

*

If you get peace, then to clean the vital becomes easy. If you simply clean and clean and do nothing else, you go very slowly — for the vital gets dirty again and has to be cleaned a hundred times. The peace is something that is clean in itself — so to get it is a positive way of securing your object. To look for dirt only and clean is the negative way.

*

When the light and peace are full in the vital and physical consciousness, it is this that remains always as a basis for the right movement of the whole nature.

*

It is the same peace [*in the physical as in the vital*] — but is felt materially in the material substance, concretely in the physical mind and nervous being, as well as psychologically in the mind and vital or subtly in the subtle body.

*

I presume that [*feeling peace concretely between the lobes of the brain*] would mean that the peace had become or was becoming very material and solid and physically tangible — "peace in the cells". Everything is a "substance" — even peace, consciousness, ananda, — only there are different orders of substance.

*

Certainly, peace, purity and silence can be felt in all material things — for the Divine Self is there in all.

*

Nature by itself is always full of peace — a peace which is fundamental and even the perturbations of mind and life cannot break.

Peace in the Inner Being

It is quite usual to feel an established peace in the inner being even if there is disturbance on the surface. In fact that is the usual condition of the Yogi before he has attained the absolute samata in all the being.

*

When the peace is deep or wide, it is usually in the inner being. The outer parts do not ordinarily go beyond a certain measure of quietude — they get deep peace only when they are flooded with it from the inner being.

*

The peace starts in the inner being — it is spiritual and psychic but it overflows the outer being — when it is there in the activity, it means either that the ordinary restless mind, vital, physical has been submerged by the flood of the inner peace or, at a more advanced stage, that they have been partially or wholly changed into thoughts, forces, emotions, sensations which have in their very stuff an essence of inner silence and peace.

*

If peace becomes permanent in the inner being, then the subnature becomes an external and superficial thing — one part of the consciousness is then free; unmoved by anything that happens, it regards the surface turmoil as something not belonging to itself. If the peace extends in the same way into the external parts also, then the whole being becomes free and the inferior nature is felt only as something moving about in the atmosphere, trying to enter but unable to do so. But this of course happens only when the descents of Peace have turned into a massive stability of Peace.

*

Yes, the inward move is the right one. To live within in the peace and silence is the first necessity. I spoke of the wideness because in the wideness of silence and peace (which the Yogins recognise as the realisation of self at once individual and universal) is the basis for harmonising the inward and the outward. It will come.

*

Peace is never easy to get in the life of the world and never constant, unless one lives deep within and bears the external activities as only a surface front of our being.

Passive Peace

Passive peace is not supposed to do anything. It is by the complete solid presence of peace alone that all disturbance is pushed out to the surface or outside the consciousness.

*

It is not the innate character of passive peace that it can only concentrate in inaction. It can be there and concentrate in or behind action also.

Peace and Inertia

The Peace is not of the nature of inertia, but the inertia (tamas) is a degradation of peace or rest as rajas is a degradation of divine Force. So when the physical is invited to peace and cannot receive it, it brings up inertia instead.

*

Rest of the being from effort, disturbance etc.[1] The Spirit is

---

[1] *The correspondent wrote to Sri Aurobindo, "You have said, 'The inertia (tamas) is a degradation of peace or rest.' What sort of rest do you mean?"* — Ed.

eternally at rest even in the midst of action — peace gives this spiritual rest. Tamas is a degradation of it and leads to inaction.

Peace and Force

The peace is the condition of the right play of the Force. Force and Peace are two different powers of the Divine.

*

Peace is the first condition, but peace of itself does not bring Force — it is a receptacle of Force, not a bringer of Force.

*

A peaceful state is the basis of the Yogic consciousness. It is only when that is complete and fully established that the true intensity and energy can come.

*

The greater the quietude, the greater the energy that can be received.

Peace, Love and Joy

It is the Vaishnava feeling that the Vedantic peace is not enough, the love and joy of the Divine is more precious. But unless the two things go together, the love and joy felt is perhaps intense, but impermanent, and it is also true that it gets easily mixed, misdirected or turns to something that is not the true thing at all. Peace and purity must be got as the foundation of the consciousness, otherwise there is no firm standing ground for the divine play.

*

Active experience of the joy, peace, love, etc. when the direct contact is there; but even when it is not there, a quiet mind, heart and vital waiting and aspiring for the contact and the Presence — this should always be the condition.

No disturbance or confusion due to mere vital-physical impressions and experiences. To throw these away always, not to want them or get interested when they come — this is what is very much needed in you.

Always either the contact and the true experience *or* the quiet peace and aspiration.

Peace, Happiness, Joy, Delight, Ananda

To be full of peace, the heart quiet, not troubled by grief, not excited by joy is a very good condition. As for Ananda, it can come not only with its fullest intensity but with a more enduring persistence when the mind is at peace and the heart delivered from ordinary joy and sorrow. If the mind and heart are restless, changeful, unquiet, Ananda of a kind may come, but it is mixed with vital excitement and cannot abide. One must get peace and calm fixed in the consciousness first, then there is a solid basis on which the Ananda can spread itself and in its turn become an enduring part of the consciousness and the nature.

*

The peace need not be grave or joyless — there should be nothing grey in it — but the gladness or joy or sense of lightness that comes in the peace must be necessarily something internal, self-existent or due to a deepening of experience — it cannot, like the laughter of which you speak, be conveyed by an external cause or dependent upon it, e.g. something amusing, exhilarating etc.

*

It is when one is full of peace that one laughs most gladly. It is an inner condition, not something external like being silent or not laughing. It is a condition of serenity and stillness within in which there is no disturbance even if things go wrong or people are unpleasant or the body feels unwell — the state of serene inner gladness remains the same. It is self-existent.

*

Happiness is a condition of gladness, sense of inner ease and welfare, contentment, a sunlit life — it is more quiet in its nature than joy and delight.

Joy (*harṣa*) is more intense. It is a strong movement of great gladness with an exultation, a leaping up of the vital to take some happiness, good fortune or other thing pleasant to the being.

Delight is an intense joy or an intense pleasure in something or an intensely joyful condition. At its most intense it becomes what is called rapture or ecstasy when one is "carried away" or "lifted out of" oneself by the intensity of the delight.

*

Joy is a vital movement, exciting, restless and transient.

In Ananda there is no excitement, it is a calm and happy and intense spiritual state or spiritual movement.

*

The joy also should be deep within, then it will not conflict with the deeps of peace and inner consciousness.

*

Shanti is peace or calm — it is not Ananda. There can of course be a calm Ananda.

*

Peace is a sign of mukti — Ananda moves towards siddhi.

*

There are two conditions, one of Ananda, another of great calm and equality in which there is no joy or grief. If one attains the latter, afterwards a greater more permanent Ananda becomes possible.

*

The active Ananda can culminate in the shanta Ananda. Also when the shanta Ananda is established, it is the base from which active Ananda arises without disturbing its calmness.

Chapter Five

Silence

Freedom from Thoughts

Silence means freedom from thoughts and vital movements — when the whole consciousness is quite still.

*

It is the silence of the mind and vital — silence implying here not only cessation of thoughts but a stillness of the mental and vital substance. There are varying degrees of depth of this stillness.

*

It is not possible to establish a deep silence all at once unless you can separate yourself from the thoughts, feel them as coming from outside and reject them before they enter. But everybody cannot do that at once.

*

It is quite possible for thoughts to pass without disturbing the silence — but for that you must be perfectly detached from the thoughts and indifferent to them.

*

If there is absolute silence within it is quite natural that the thoughts on entering and touching it should fall off. It is the way in which silence of the outer mind usually comes.

*

In the entirely silent mind there is usually the static sense of the Divine without any active movement. But there can come into it all higher thought and aspiration and movements. There is then no absolute silence but one feels a fundamental silence behind which is not disturbed by any movement.

Silence and True Knowledge

A silent mind is the first step towards true knowledge and the experience of the Divine.

*

I have read again the message of the Yogi quoted in X's letter but apart from the context nothing much or very definite can be made out of it. There are two statements which are clear enough —

"In Silence is wisdom" — it is in the inner silence of the mind that true knowledge can come; for the ordinary activity of the mind only creates surface ideas and representations which are not true knowledge. Speech is usually only the expression of the superficial nature — therefore to throw oneself out too much in such speech wastes the energy and prevents the inward listening which brings the word of true knowledge.

"In listening you will win what you are thinking of" means probably that in the silence will come the true dynamic thought formations which can effectuate or realise themselves. Thought can be a force which realises itself, but the ordinary surface thinking is not of that kind, there is in it more waste of energy than anything else. It is in the thought that comes in a quiet or silent mind that there is power.

"Talk less and gain power" has essentially the same meaning. Not only a truer knowledge, but a greater power comes to one in the quietude and silence of a mind that instead of bubbling on the surface can go into its own depths and listen for what comes from a higher consciousness.

It is probably this that is meant — these are things known to all who have some experience of Yoga.

Silence and Quietness of Mind

Silence is a state of the consciousness which comes of itself from above when you open to the Divine Consciousness — you need not trouble about that now.

A quiet mind, receiving things and looking at them without effervescence or haste, not rushing about or throwing up random ideas, is what is necessary.

*

It is not an undesirable thing for the mind to fall silent, to be free from thoughts and still — for it is oftenest when the mind falls silent that there is the full descent of a wide peace from above and in that wide tranquillity the realisation of the silent Self above the mind spread out in its vastnesses everywhere. Only, when there is the peace and the mental silence, the vital mind tries to rush in and occupy the place or else the mechanical mind tries to raise up for the same purpose its round of trivial habitual thoughts. What the sadhaka has to do is to be careful to reject and hush these outsiders, so that during the meditation at least the peace and quietude of the mind and vital may be complete. This can be done best if you keep a strong and silent will. That will is the will of the Purusha behind the mind; when the mind is at peace, when it is silent one can become aware of the Purusha, silent also, separate from the action of the nature.

To be calm, steady, fixed in the spirit, *dhīra*, *sthira*, this quietude of the mind, this separation of the inner Purusha from the outer Prakriti is very helpful, almost indispensable. So long as the being is subject to the whirl of thoughts or the turmoil of the vital movements one cannot be thus calm and fixed in the spirit. To detach oneself, to stand back from them, to feel them separate from oneself is indispensable.

For the discovery of the true individuality and building up of it in the nature, two things are necessary, first, to be conscious of one's psychic being behind the heart and, next, this separation of the Purusha from the Prakriti. For the true individual is behind veiled by the activities of the outer nature.

*

Silence is always good; but I do not mean by quietness of mind entire silence. I mean a mind free from disturbance and trouble,

Silence

steady, light and glad so as to be open to the Force that will change the nature. The important thing is to get rid of the habit of the invasion of troubling thoughts, wrong feelings, confusion of ideas, unhappy movements. These disturb the nature and cloud it and make it more difficult for the Force to work; when the mind is quiet and at peace, the Force can work more easily. It should be possible to see things that have to be changed in you without being upset or depressed; the change is the more easily done.

*

Let us not exaggerate anything. It is not so much getting rid of mental activity as converting it into the right thing. Krishnaprem has mental activity, but it is a mind that has gone inside and sees things from there, an intuitive mind; I have mental activity (in the midst of silence) whenever necessary, but it is a mind that has gone up and sees things from above, an overmind action. What has to be surpassed and changed is the intellectual reason which sees things from outside only by analysis and inference — when it does not do it rather by taking a hasty look and saying "So it is" or "So it is not". But you can't get the inner or upper mind unless the old mental activity becomes a little quiet. A quiet mind does not involve itself in its thoughts or get run away with by them; it stands back, detaches itself, lets them pass, without identifying itself, without making them its own. It becomes the witness mind watching the thoughts when necessary, but able to turn away from them and receive from within and from above. Silence is good, but absolute silence is not indispensable, at least at this stage. I do not know that to wrestle with the mind to make it quiet is of much use; usually the mind gets the better of that game. It is this standing back, detaching oneself, getting the power to listen to something else other than the thoughts of the external mind that is the easier way. At the same time one can look up, as it were, imaging to oneself the Force as there just above and calling it down or quietly expecting its help. That is how most people do it till the mind falls gradually quiet or silent of itself or else silence begins to descend from above. But it is important not to allow the depression or despair to come in because there is no immediate success; that can only make things difficult and stop any progress that is preparing.

Silence, Peace and Calm

The silence and peace are themselves part of the higher consciousness — the rest comes in the silence and peace.

*

When the mind is silent, there is peace and in peace all things that are divine can come. When there is not the mind, there is the Self which is greater than the mind.

*

You have attained the silent inner consciousness, but that can be covered over by disturbance — the next step is for calm and silence to be established as the basis in the more and more outer consciousness — probably these [higher] forces are working for that. Then the play of the ordinary forces will be only on the surface and can be more easily dealt with.

Silence and True Activity

The silence is the silence of the inner consciousness and it is in that silence unmoved by outward things that the true activity of the consciousness can come without disturbing the silence — true perceptions, will, feelings, action. There also one can feel more easily the Mother's working. As for the heat, it must be the heat of Agni, the fire of purification and tapasya; it often feels like that when the inner work is going on.

*

It is not possible for the spontaneous silent condition to last always at once, but that is what must grow in one till there is a constant inner silence — a silence which cannot be disturbed by any outward activity or even by any attempt at attack or disturbance.

The condition you describe shows precisely the growth of this inner silence. It has to fix itself eventually as the basis of all spiritual experience and activity. It does not matter if one does not know what is going on within behind the silence. For there are two conditions in the Yoga, one in which all is silent and there is no thought, feeling or movement even though one is acting outwardly as others do — another in which a new consciousness becomes active bringing knowledge, joy, love and other spiritual feelings and inner activities, but yet at the same time there is a fundamental silence or quietude. Both are necessary in the development of the inner being. The absolutely silent state, which is one of lightness, voidness and release, prepares the other and supports it when it comes.

*

The passive silence is that in which the inner consciousness remains void and at rest, not making any reaction on outer things and forces.

The active silence is that in which there is a great force that goes out on things and forces without disturbing the silence.

*

It is on the Silence behind the cosmos that all the movement of the universe is supported.

It is from the Silence that the peace comes; when the peace deepens and deepens, it becomes more and more the Silence.

In a more outward sense the word silence is applied to the condition in which there is no movement of thought or feeling etc., only a great stillness of the mind.

But there can be an action in the Silence, undisturbed even as the universal action goes on in the cosmic Silence.

Section Four

The Divine Response

Chapter One

The Divine Grace and Guidance

The Divine Grace

The Divine Will works in all things — it may work out anything whatever. The Divine Grace comes in to help and save.

*

If you would know what is the Divine Grace, it is necessary first to realise that it is something which contradicts the law of the world, for it is outside its normal rule and not of its nature. There is here something which does not seem to govern at all the cosmic action, but only to intervene, and yet it is always there; an element without which this universe would be either a tremendous machine or a fortuitously and yet inexorably ordered chance. For to our observation all here is a process, a mechanism of Ignorance and Inconscience manifesting a precarious consciousness distressed by a nostalgia of Truth that exists somewhere and yet seems to be unseizable and unrealisable, — a mechanism of Law that controls a frightening whirl of Forces, a mechanism of implacable justice measuring things by a mysterious and to us unintelligible balance, a mechanism of evolution with matter and inconscience as its starting point, a precarious and groping life and consciousness as its highest realised term and as its final uncertain poise some possibility of the Divine. Our senses can discover no visible presence of the Divine, our intellect can do without any idea of its intervention — but it is another experience than that of the intellect and the senses which once it is there will no longer let us escape from the Presence or refuse to see the intervening Will or Grace.

This world is a world of Ignorance and by Ignorance a world of strife, seeking, error and suffering. We start by knowing nothing and have to learn everything; because our knowledge is a mixture of truth and falsehood and our will constantly mistaken when not perverted, we stumble at every step and pay the price of experience in pain and grief and sorrow. It would seem as if nothing could save us but thought and knowledge translated into right will and action and it is that for which man by his intellect is seeking and yet by his intellect he has never found it and it looks as if by his intellect he would never find it. Then there is probably something else beyond the intellect which alone can give him the Light — something beyond his mind and greater than himself — a Grace that intervenes, the law of a supernormal Light and Will, a help, an opening from above.

*

I should like to say something about the Divine Grace — for you seem to think it should be something like a Divine Reason acting upon lines not very different from those of human intelligence. But it is not that. Also it is not a universal Divine Compassion either, acting impartially on all who approach it and acceding to all prayers. It does not select the righteous and reject the sinner. The Divine Grace came to aid the persecutor (Saul of Tarsus), it came to St. Augustine the profligate, to Jagai and Madhai of infamous fame, to Bilwamangal and many others whose conversion might well scandalise the puritanism of the human moral intelligence; but it can come to the righteous also — curing them of their self-righteousness and leading to a purer consciousness beyond these things. It is a power that is superior to any rule, even to the Cosmic Law — for all spiritual seers have distinguished between the Law and Grace. Yet it is not indiscriminate — only it has a discrimination of its own which sees things and persons and the right times and seasons with another vision than that of the Mind or any other normal Power. A state of Grace is prepared in the individual often behind thick veils by means not calculable by the mind and when the state of Grace comes then the Grace itself acts. There are these three powers: (1) the Cosmic Law, of Karma or what else; (2) the Divine Compassion acting on as many as it can reach through the nets of the Law and giving them their chance; and (3) the Divine Grace which acts more incalculably but also more irresistibly than the others. The only question is whether there is something behind all the anomalies of life which can respond to the call and open itself with whatever difficulty till it is ready for the illumination of the Divine Grace — and that something must be not a mental and vital movement but an inner somewhat which can well be seen by the inner eye. If it is there and when it becomes active in front, then the Compassion can act, though the full action of the Grace may still wait attending the decisive decision or change; for this may be postponed to a future hour, because some portion or element of the being may still come between, something that is not yet ready to receive.

*

Each mind can have its own way of approaching the supreme Truth and there is an entrance for each as well as a thousand ways for the journey to it. It is not necessary to believe in the Grace or to recognise a Godhead different from one's highest Self — there are ways of Yoga that do not accept these things. Also for many no form of Yoga is necessary — they arrive at some realisation by a sort of pressure of the mind or the heart or the will breaking the screen between it and what is at once beyond it and its own source. What happens after the breaking of the screen depends on the play of the Truth on the consciousness and the turn of the nature. There is no reason therefore why X's realisation of his being should not come in its own way by growth from within, not by the Divine Grace if his mind objects to that description, but let us say by the spontaneous movement of the Self within him.

For, as to this "Grace", we describe it in that way because we feel in the infinite Spirit or Self of existence a Presence or a Being, a Consciousness that determines — that is what we speak of as the Divine, — not a separate Person, but the one Being of whom our individual self is a portion or a vessel. But it is not necessary for everybody to regard it in that way. Supposing it is the impersonal Self of all only, yet the Upanishad says of the Self and its realisation, "This understanding is not to be gained by reasoning nor by tapasya nor by much learning, but whom this Self chooses, to him it reveals its own body." Well, that is the same thing as what we call the Divine Grace, — it is an action from above or from within independent of mental causes which decides its own movement. We can call it the Divine Grace; we can call it the Self within choosing its own hour and way to manifest to the mental instrument on the surface; we can call it the flowering of the inner being or inner nature into self-realisation and self-knowledge. As something in us approaches it or as it presents itself to us, so the mind sees it. But in reality, it is the same thing and the same process of the being in Nature.

I could illustrate my meaning more concretely from my own first experience of the Self, long before I knew even what Yoga was or that there was such a thing, at a time when I had no religious feeling, no wish for spiritual knowledge, no aspiration beyond the mind, only a contented agnosticism and the impulse towards poetry and politics. But it would be too long a story, so I do not tell it here.

*

It is not indispensable that the Grace should work in a way that the human mind can understand, it generally doesn't: it works in its own "mysterious" way. At first usually it works behind the veil, preparing things, not manifesting. Afterwards it may manifest, but the sadhak does not understand very well what is happening. Finally, when he is capable of it, he both feels and understands or at least begins to do so. Some feel and understand from the first or very early; but that is not the ordinary case.

*

"The ordinary action of the Divine is a constant intervention within the actual law of things" — that may or may not be but is not usually called the Divine Grace. The Divine Grace is something not calculable, not bound by anything the intellect can fix as a condition — though ordinarily some call, aspiration, intensity of the psychic being can awaken it, yet it acts sometimes without any apparent cause even of that kind.

The Grace and Personal Effort

Without the Grace of the Divine nothing can be done, but for the full Grace to manifest the sadhak must make himself ready. If everything depends on the Divine intervention, then man is only a puppet and there is no use of sadhana, and there are no conditions, no law of things — therefore no universe, but only the Divine rolling things about at his pleasure. No doubt in the last resort all can be said to be the Divine cosmic working, but it is through persons, through forces that it works — under the conditions of Nature. Special intervention there can be and is, but all cannot be special intervention.

*

The Divine Grace and Power can do everything, but with the full assent of the sadhak. To learn to give that full assent is the whole meaning of the sadhana. It may take time either because of ideas in the mind, desires in the vital or inertia in the physical consciousness, but these things have to be and can be removed with the aid or by calling in the action of the Divine Force.

*

There are three main possibilities for the sadhak — (1) To wait on the Grace and rely on the Divine. (2) To do everything himself like the full Adwaitin and the Buddhist. (3) To take the middle path, go forward by aspiration and rejection etc. helped by the Force.

*

Everything should be for the sake of the Divine, this [*aspiration for the Divine's Presence*] also. As for leaving the result to the Divine, it depends on what you mean by the phrase. If it implies dependence on the Divine Grace and equanimity and patience in the persistent aspiration, then it is all right. But it must not be extended to cover slackness and indifference in the aspiration and endeavour.

Strength and Grace

There is nothing unintelligible in what I say about strength and Grace. Strength has a value for spiritual realisation, but to say that it can be done by strength only and by no other means is a violent exaggeration. Grace is not an invention, it is a fact of spiritual experience. Many who would be considered as mere nothings by the wise and strong have attained by Grace; illiterate, without mental power or training, without "strength" of character or will, they have yet aspired and suddenly or rapidly grown into spiritual realisation, because they had faith or because they were sincere. I do not see why these facts which are facts of spiritual history and of quite ordinary spiritual experience should be discussed and denied and argued as if they were mere matters of speculation. Strength, if it is spiritual, is a power for spiritual realisation; a greater power is sincerity; the greatest power of all is Grace. I have said times without number that if a man is sincere, he will go through in spite of long delay and overwhelming difficulties. I have repeatedly spoken of the Divine Grace. I have referred any number of times to the line of the Gita:

Ahaṁ tvā sarvapāpebhyo mokṣayiṣyāmi mā śucaḥ
"I will deliver thee from all sin and evil, do not grieve."

Grace and Tapasya

Your experience about the meditation is common enough — I used to have it or analogous things hundreds of times. I suppose it is to teach us first that grace is more effective than tapasya and, secondly, that either equanimity or a cheerful spontaneous happy self-opening is as effective, to say the least, as the grimmest wrestling for a result. But it would be dangerous to assume from that that no tapasya and no endeavour is needful — for that might very well mean inertia. I have seen too that very often a long tapasya with doubtful results prepares the moment of grace and the spontaneous downflow. All which seem to be contradictions, but are not in a whole view of things.

*

The Divine Grace and Guidance

What X says about tapasya is of course true. If one is not prepared for labour and tapasya, control of the mind and vital, one cannot demand big spiritual gains — for the mind and vital will always find tricks and excuses for prolonging their own reign, imposing their likes and dislikes and staving off the day when they will have to become obedient instruments and open channels of the soul and spirit. Grace may sometimes bring undeserved or apparently undeserved fruits, but one can't demand Grace as a right and privilege — for then it would not be Grace. As you have seen one can't claim that one has only to shout and the answer must come. Besides I have always seen that there has been really a long unobserved preparation before the Grace intervenes and, also, after it has intervened one has still to put in a good deal of work to keep and develop what one has got — as it is in all other things — until there is the complete siddhi. Then of course labour finishes and one is in assured possession. So tapasya of one kind or another is not avoidable.

You are right again about the imaginary obstacles. Good Lord! what mountains of them you have piled up on the way — a regular Abyssinia. It is why we always express depreciation of mental constructions and vital formations — because they are the defence works mind and vital throw up against their capture by the Divine. However the first thing is to become conscious of all that as you have now become, — the next thing is to be firm in knocking it all down and making a *tabula rasa*, a foundation of calm, peace, happy openness for the true building.

No Insistence on the Grace

I have surely never said that you should not want the Divine Response. One does Yoga for that. What I have said is that you should not expect or insist on it at once or within an early time. It can come early or it can come late, but come it will if one is faithful in one's call — for one has not only to be sincere but to be faithful through all. If I deprecate insistence, it is because I have always found it creates difficulties and delays — owing to a strain and restlessness which is created in the nature and despondencies and revolts of the vital when the insistence is not satisfied. The Divine knows best and one has to have trust in His wisdom and attune oneself with His will. Length of time is no proof of an ultimate incapacity to arrive — it is only a sign that there is something in oneself which has to be overcome and if there is the will to reach the Divine it can be overcome.

Suicide solves nothing — it only brings one back to life with the same difficulties to be faced in worse conditions. If one wishes to escape from life altogether, it can only be by the way of complete inner renunciation and merging oneself in the Silence of the Absolute or by a bhakti that becomes absolute or by a karmayoga that gives up one's own will and desires to the will of the Divine.

I have said also that the Grace *can* at any moment act suddenly, but over that one has no control, because it comes by an incalculable Will which sees things that the mind cannot see. It is precisely the reason why one should never despair, — that and also because no sincere aspiration to the Divine can fail in the end.

Trust in the Divine Grace

Face all these things [*inner disturbances*] quietly and firmly with perseverance in the endeavour of the sadhana. Trust firmly in the Divine Grace and the Divine Grace will not fail you.

*

The best possible way [*to "repay" the Divine Grace*] is to allow the Divine Grace to work in you, never to oppose it, never to be ungrateful and turn against it — but to follow it always to the goal of Light and Peace and unity and Ananda.

Withdrawal of Grace

As for withdrawal of Grace, it might be said that few are those from whom the Grace withdraws, but many are those who withdraw from the Grace.

*

If the will of the individual is towards perdition, if his ego becomes hostile to the Divine, then the Divine is not bound to show him a Grace he does not want at all and kicks at.

The First Responses of the Divine

What you describe in your letter as the response of the Divine would not be called that in the language of Yogic experience — this feeling of greater peace, light, ease, trust, difficulties lessening, certitude would rather be called a response of your own nature to the Divine. There is a Peace or a Light which is the response of the Divine, but that is a wide Peace, a great Light which is felt as a presence other than one's personal self, not part of one's personal nature, but something that comes from above, though in the end it possesses the nature — or there is the Presence itself which carries with it indeed the absolute liberation, happiness, certitude. But the first responses of the Divine are not often like that — they come rather as a touch, a pressure one must be in a condition to recognise and to accept, or it is a voice of assurance, sometimes a very "still small voice", a momentary Image or Presence; a whisper of Guidance sometimes, — there are many forms it may take. Then it withdraws and the preparation of the nature goes on till it is possible for the touch to come again and again, to last longer, to change into something more pressing and near and intimate. The Divine in the beginning does not impose himself — he asks for recognition, for acceptance. That is one reason why the mind must fall silent, not put tests, not make claims — there must be room for the true intuition which recognises at once the true touch and accepts it.

The Divine Guidance

The question you have put[1] raises one of the most difficult and complicated of all problems and to deal with it at all adequately

---

[1] *The correspondent said that this unhappy world seems doomed to falsehood and suffering, for it is filled with selfishness, pettiness and heartless greed. Why should one embrace such a world, he asked, "where the divine guidance seems so accidental, almost out of place"? — Ed.*

would need an answer as long as the longest chapter of *The Life Divine*. I can only state my own knowledge founded not on reasoning but on experience that there is such a guidance and that nothing is in vain in this universe.

If we look only at outward facts in their surface appearance or if we regard what we see happening around us as definitive, not as processes of a moment in a developing whole, the guidance is not apparent; at most we may see interventions occasional or sometimes frequent. The guidance can become evident only if we go behind appearances and begin to understand the forces at work and the way of their working and their secret significance. After all, real knowledge — even scientific knowledge — comes by going behind the surface phenomena to their hidden process and causes. It is quite obvious that this world is full of suffering and afflicted with transience to a degree that seems to justify the Gita's description of it as "this unhappy and transient world", *anityam asukham*. The question is whether it is a mere creation of Chance or governed by a mechanic inconscient Law or whether there is a meaning in it and something beyond its present appearance towards which we move. If there is a meaning and if there is something towards which things are evolving, then inevitably there must be a guidance — and that means that a supporting Consciousness and Will is there with which we can come into inner contact. If there is such a Consciousness and Will, it is not likely that it would stultify itself by annulling the world's meaning or turning it into a perpetual or eventual failure.

This world has a double aspect. It seems to be based on a material Inconscience and an ignorant mind and life full of that Inconscience; error and sorrow, death and suffering are the necessary consequence. But there is evidently too a partially successful endeavour and an imperfect growth towards Light, Knowledge, Truth, Good, Happiness, Harmony, Beauty, — at least a partial flowering of these things. The meaning of this world must evidently lie in this opposition; it must be an evolution which is leading or struggling towards higher things out of a first darker appearance. Whatever guidance there is must be given under these conditions of opposition and struggle and must be leading towards that higher state of things. It is leading the individual, certainly, and the world, presumably, towards the higher state, but through the double terms of knowledge and ignorance, light and darkness, death and life, pain and pleasure, happiness and suffering; none of the terms can be excluded until the higher status is reached and established. It is not and cannot be, ordinarily, a guidance which at once rejects the darker terms or still less a guidance which brings us solely and always nothing but happiness, success and good fortune. Its main concern is with the growth of our being and consciousness, the growth towards a higher self, towards the Divine, eventually towards a highest Light, Truth and Bliss; the rest is secondary, sometimes a means, sometimes a result, not a primary purpose.

The true sense of the guidance becomes clearer when we can go deep within and see from there more intimately the play of the forces and receive intimations of the Will behind them. The surface mind can get only an imperfect glimpse. When we are in contact with the Divine or in contact with an inner knowledge and vision, we begin to see all the circumstances of our life in a new light and can observe how they all tended without our knowing it towards the growth of our being and consciousness, towards the work we had to do, towards some development that had to be made, — not only what seemed good, fortunate or successful but the struggles, failures, difficulties, upheavals. But with each person the guidance works differently according to his nature, the conditions of his life, his cast of consciousness, his stage of development, his need of farther experience. We are not automata but conscious beings and our mentality, our will and its decisions, our attitude to life and demand on it, our motives and movements help to determine our course; they may lead to much suffering and evil, but through it all, the guidance makes use of them for our growth in experience and consequently the development of our being and consciousness. All advance by however devious ways, even in spite of what seems a going backwards or going astray, gathering whatever experience is necessary for the soul's destiny. When we are in close contact with the Divine, a protection can come in which helps or directly guides or moves us; it does not throw aside all difficulties, sufferings or dangers, but it carries us through them and out of them — except where for a special purpose there is need of the opposite.

It is the same thing though on a larger scale and in a more complex way with the guidance of the world-movement. That seems to move according to the conditions and laws or forces of the moment through constant vicissitudes, but still there is something in it that drives towards the evolutionary purpose, although it is more difficult to see, understand and follow than in the smaller and more intimate field of the individual consciousness and life. What happens in a particular juncture of the world-action or the life of humanity, however catastrophical, is not ultimately determinative. Here too one has to see not only the outward play of forces in a particular case or at a particular time but also the inner and secret play, the far-off outcome, the event that lies beyond and the Will at work behind it all. Falsehood and Darkness are strong everywhere on the earth and have always been so and at times they seem to dominate; but there have also been not only gleams but outbursts of the Light. In the mass of things and the long course of Time, whatever may be the appearances of this or that epoch or moment, the growth of Light is there and the struggle towards better things does not cease. At the present time Falsehood and Darkness have gathered their forces and are extremely powerful; but even if we reject the assertion of the mystics and prophets since early times that such a condition of things must precede the Manifestation and is even a sign of its approach, yet it does not necessarily indicate the victory — even temporary — of the Falsehood. It merely means that the struggle between the Forces is at its acme. The result may very well be the stronger emergence of the best that can be; for the world-movement often works in that way. I leave it at that and say nothing more.

Chapter Two

The Divine Force

The Nature of Spiritual Force

All the world, according to Science, is nothing but a play of Energy — a material Energy it used to be called, but it is now doubted whether Matter, scientifically speaking, exists except as a phenomenon of Energy. All the world, according to Vedanta, is a play of a power of a spiritual entity, the power of an original consciousness, whether it be Maya or Shakti, and the result an illusion or real. In the world so far as man is concerned we are aware only of mind energy, life energy, energy in matter; but it is supposed that there is a spiritual energy or force also behind them from which they originate. All things, in either case, are the results of a Shakti, energy or force. There is no action without a Force or Energy doing the action and bringing about its consequence. Farther, anything that has no Force in it is either something dead or something unreal or something inert and without consequence. If there is no such thing as spiritual consciousness, there can be no reality of Yoga, and if there is no Yoga force, spiritual force, Yoga Shakti, then also there can be no effectivity in Yoga. A Yoga consciousness or spiritual consciousness which has no power or force in it, may not be dead or unreal but it is evidently something inert and without effect or consequence. Equally a man who sets out to be a Yogi or Guru and has no spiritual consciousness or no power in his spiritual consciousness — a Yoga force or spiritual force — is making a false claim and is either a charlatan or a self-deluded imbecile; still more is he so if having no spiritual force he claims to have made a path others can follow. If Yoga is a reality, if spirituality is anything better than a delusion, there must be such a thing as Yoga force or spiritual force.

It is evident that if spiritual force exists, it must be able to produce spiritual results — therefore there is no irrationality in the claim of those sadhaks who say that they feel the force of the Guru or the force of the Divine working in them and leading towards spiritual fulfilment and experience. Whether it is so or not in a particular case is a personal question, but the statement cannot be denounced as *per se* incredible and manifestly false because such things cannot be. Farther, if it be true that spiritual force is the original one and the others are derivative from it, then there is no irrationality in supposing that spiritual force can produce mental results, vital results, physical results. It may act through mental, vital or physical energies and through the means which these energies use, or it may act directly on mind, life or matter as the field of its own special and immediate action. Either way is *prima facie* possible. In a case of cure of illness, someone is lying ill for two days, weak, suffering from pains and fever; he takes no medicine but finally asks for cure from his Guru; the next morning he rises well, strong and energetic. He has at least some justification for thinking that a force has been used on him and put into him and that it was a spiritual power that acted. But in another case medicines may be used, while at the same time the invisible force may be called for to aid the material means, for it is a known fact that medicines may or may not succeed — there is no certitude. Here for the reason of an outside observer (one who is neither the user of the force nor the doctor nor the patient) it remains uncertain whether the patient was cured by the medicines only or by the spiritual force with the medicines as an instrument. Either is possible, and it cannot be said that because medicines were used, therefore the working of a spiritual force is *per se* incredible and demonstrably false. On the other hand it is possible for the doctor to have felt a force working in him and guiding him or he may see the patient improving with a rapidity which, according to medical science, is incredible. The patient may feel the force working in himself bringing health, energy, rapid cure. The user of the force may watch the results, see the symptoms he works on diminishing, those he did not work upon increasing till he does work on them and then immediately diminishing, the doctor working according to his unspoken suggestions, etc. etc. until the cure is done. (On the other hand he may see forces working against the cure and conclude that the spiritual force has to be contented with a withdrawal or an imperfect success.) In all that the doctor, the patient or the user of force is justified in believing that the cure is at least partly or even fundamentally due to the spiritual force. Their experience is valid of course for themselves only, not for the outside rationalising observer. But the latter is not logically entitled to say that their experience is incredible and must be false.

Another point. It does not follow that a spiritual force must either succeed in all cases or, if it does not, that proves its non-existence. Of no force can that be said. The force of fire is to burn, but there are things it does not burn; under certain circumstances it does not burn even the feet of the man who walks barefoot on red-hot coals. That does not prove that fire cannot burn or that there is no such thing as force of fire, Agni-shakti.

I have no time to write more; it is not necessary either. My object was not to show that spiritual force must be believed in, but that the belief in it is not necessarily a delusion and that this belief can be rational as well as possible.

*

The invisible Force producing tangible results both inward and outward is the whole meaning of the Yogic consciousness. Your question about Yoga bringing merely a feeling of Power without any result was really very strange. Who would be satisfied with such a meaningless hallucination and call it Power? If we had not had thousands of experiences showing that the Power within could alter the mind, develop its powers, add new ones, bring in new ranges of knowledge, master the vital movements, change the character, influence men and things, control the conditions and functionings of the body, work as a concrete dynamic Force on other forces, modify events, etc. etc., we would not speak of it as we do. Moreover, it is not only in its results but in its movements that the Force is tangible and concrete. When I speak of feeling Force or Power, I do not mean simply having a vague sense of it, but feeling it concretely and consequently being able to direct it, manipulate it, watch its movement, be conscious of its mass and intensity and in the same way of that of other perhaps opposing forces; all these things are possible and usual by the development of Yoga.

It is not, unless it is supramental Force, a Power that acts without conditions and limits. The conditions and limits under which Yoga or sadhana has to be worked out are not arbitrary or capricious; they arise from the nature of things. These including the will, receptivity, assent, self-opening and surrender of the sadhak have to be respected by the Yoga-force — unless it receives a sanction from the Supreme to override everything and get something done — but that sanction is sparingly given. It is only if the supramental Power came fully down, not merely sent its influences through the Overmind, that things could be very radically altered in this respect — and that is why my main effort is directed towards that object — for then the sanction would not be rare! For the Law of the Truth would be at work not constantly balanced by the law of the Ignorance.

Still the Yoga-force is always tangible and concrete in the way I have described and has tangible results. But it is invisible — not like a blow given or the rush of a motor car knocking somebody down which the physical senses can at once perceive. How is the mere physical mind to know that it is there and working? By its results? but how can it know that the results were that of the Yoga-force and not of something else? One of two things it must do. Either it must allow the consciousness to go inside, to become aware of inner things, to believe in and experience the invisible and the supraphysical, and then by experience, by the opening of new capacities it becomes conscious of these forces and can see, follow and use their workings just as the scientist uses the unseen forces of Nature. Or one must have faith and watch and open oneself and then it will begin to see how things happen; it will notice that when the Force was called in, there began after a time to be a result, — then repetitions, more repetitions, more clear and tangible results, increasing frequency, increasing consistency of results, a feeling and awareness of the Force at work — until the experience becomes daily, regular, normal, complete. These are the two main methods, one internal, working from in outward, the other external, working from outside and calling the inner force out till it penetrates and is sensible in the exterior consciousness. But neither can be done if one insists always on the extrovert attitude, the external concrete only and refuses to join to it the internal concrete — or if the physical Mind at every step raises a dance of doubts which refuses to allow the nascent experience to develop. Even the scientist carrying out a new experiment would never succeed if he allowed his mind to behave in that way.

*

Concrete? what do you mean by "concrete"?[1] It [*spiritual force*] has its own concreteness; it can take a form (like a stream for instance) of which one is aware and can send it quite concretely in whatever "direction" or on whatever object one chooses.

This is a statement of fact about the power inherent in spiritual consciousness. What I was speaking of was a willed use of any subtle force (it may be spiritual or mental or vital) to secure a particular result at some point in the world. Just as there are waves of unseen physical forces (cosmic waves etc.) or currents of electricity, so there are mind waves, thought currents, waves of emotion, e.g. anger, sorrow, etc., which go out and affect others without their knowing whence they come or that they come at all — they only feel the result. One who has the occult or inner senses awake can feel them coming and invading him. Influences good or bad can propagate themselves in that way; that can happen without intention, automatically, but also a deliberate use can be made of them. There can also be a purposeful generation of force, spiritual or other. There can be too the use of the effective will or idea acting directly without the aid of any outward action, speech or other instrumentation which is not concrete in that sense, but is all the same effective.

*

---

[1] *The correspondent asked whether the spiritual force Sri Aurobindo put on him was "concrete". — Ed.*

Leave aside the question of Divine or undivine, no spiritual man who acts dynamically is limited to physical contact — the idea that physical contact through writing, speech, meeting is indispensable to the action of the spiritual force is self-contradictory, for then it would not be a spiritual force. The spirit is not limited by physical things or by the body. If you have the spiritual force, it can act on people thousands of miles away who do not know and never will know that you are acting on them or that they are being acted upon — they only feel that there is a force enabling them to do things and may very well suppose it is their own great energy and genius.

*

The fact that you don't feel a force does not prove that it is not there. The steam-engine does not feel a force moving it, but the force is there. A man is not a steam-engine? He is very little better, for he is conscious only of some bubbling on the surface which he calls himself and is absolutely unconscious of all the subconscient, subliminal, superconscient forces moving him. (This is a fact which is being more and more established by modern psychology though it has got hold only of the lower forces and not the higher, so you need not turn up your rational nose at it.) He twitters intellectually (= foolishly) about the surface results and attributes them all to his "noble self", ignoring the fact that his noble self is hidden far away from his own vision behind the veil of his dimly sparkling intellect and the reeking fog of his vital feelings, emotions, impulses, sensations and impressions. So your argument is utterly absurd and futile. Our aim is to bring the secret forces out and unwalled into the open so that instead of getting some shadows or lightnings of themselves out through the veil or being wholly obstructed, they may "pour down" and "flow in a river". But to expect that all at once is a presumptuous demand which shows an impatient ignorance and inexperience. If they begin to trickle at first, that is sufficient to justify the faith in a future downpour. You admit that you once or twice felt "a force coming down and delivering a poem out of me" (your opinion about its worth or worthlessness is not worth a cent, that is for others to pronounce). That is sufficient to blow the rest of your Jeremiad into smithereens; it proves that the force was and is there and at work and it is only your sweating Herculean labour that prevents you feeling it. Also it is the trickle that gives assurance of the possibility of the downpour. One has only to go on and by one's patience deserve the downpour or else, without deserving, stick on till one gets it. In Yoga itself the experience that is a promise and foretaste but gets shut off till the nature is ready for the fulfilment is a phenomenon familiar to every Yogin when he looks back on his past experience. Such were the brief visitations of Ananda you had some time before. It does not matter if you have not a leechlike tenacity — leeches are not the only type of Yogins. If you can stick anyhow or get stuck that is sufficient. The fact that you are not Sri Aurobindo (who said you were?) is an inept irrelevance. One needs only to be oneself in a reasonable way and shake off the hump when it is there or allow it to be shaken off without clinging to it with a "leechlike tenacity" worthy of a better cause.

The Divine Force Works under Conditions

The Divine Force, not using the supramental Power, can certainly throw back the forces of Death and that has been done many times. But the Divine Force works here under conditions imposed by the Divine Will and Law; it has to take up an immense mass of conflicting forces, conditions, habits and movements of Nature and out of it arrive at the result of a higher consciousness on earth and a higher state. If it were to act otherwise, then all would be done by a miracle or magic, no sadhana would be needed, no way beaten out for the process of spiritual evolution to follow; there would be no real transformation of consciousness, but only a temporary feat of force which having no basis in the substance of creation here would vanish as it came. Therefore conditions have to be satisfied, the work to be done has to be wrought out step by step. The powers that held the field up to now have to be given their chance to oppose, so that the problem may be solved and not evaded or turned into a sham fight or unreal game without significance. Therefore there is a sadhana to be done, there is a resistance to be overcome, a choice made between the higher and the lower state. The Divine Power does the work, gives a protection and a guidance; but it is not here to use an absolute force — except when that is sanctioned by the Divine Wisdom and in the light of that Wisdom justifiable. Then the decisive Power acts of itself and does what it has to do.

Writing about Spiritual Force

If I write about these questions [*of spiritual force*] from the Yogic point of view, even though on a logical basis, there is bound to be much that is in conflict with your own settled and perhaps cherished opinions, e.g. about "miracles", persons, the limits of judgment by sense data etc. I have avoided as much as possible writing about these subjects because I would have to propound things that cannot be understood except by reference to other data than those of the physical senses or of reason founded on these alone. I might have to speak of laws and forces not recognised by physical reason or science. In my public writings and my writings to sadhaks I have not dwelt on these because they go out of the range of ordinary knowledge and the understanding founded on it. These things are known to some, but they do not usually speak about it, while the public view of such of them as are known is either credulous or incredulous, but in both cases without experience or knowledge. So if the views founded on them are likely to upset, shock or bewilder, the better way is silence.

*

If I was annoyed, it was with myself for speaking of things which ought to be kept under a cover. I put the whole thing in a light form, no doubt, but the substance was perfectly serious, the intention being to point out that even in ordinary non-spiritual things the action of invisible or of subjective forces was open to doubt and discussion in which there could be no material certitude — while the spiritual force is invisible in itself and also invisible in its action. So it is idle to try to prove that such and such a result was the effect of spiritual force. Each must form his own idea about that — for if it is accepted it cannot be as a result of proof and argument, but only as a result of experience, of faith or of that insight in the heart or the deeper intelligence which looks behind appearances and sees what is behind them. Moreover it would not be seemly for me to appear to be making a claim for myself and pleading for recognition or acceptance — for the spiritual consciousness does not claim in that way, it can state the truth about itself but not fight for a personal acceptance. A general and impersonal statement about spiritual force is another matter, but I doubt whether the time has come for it or whether it could be understood by the mere reasoning intelligence.

Use and Misuse of the Divine Force

All power comes from the Divine but it is more usually misused than used spiritually or rightly.

*

The Divine Forces are meant to be used — the mistake of man individualised in the Ignorance is to use it for the ego and not for the Divine. It is that that has to be set right by the union with the Divine Consciousness and also by the widening of the individual being so that it can live consciously in the universal. Difficult it is owing to the fixed ego-habit, but it is not impossible.

The Action of the Divine Force

The action of the Force does not exclude tapasya, concentration and the need of sadhana. Its action rather comes as an answer or a help to these things. It is true that it sometimes acts without them; it very often wakes a response in those who have not prepared themselves and do not seem to be ready. But it does not always or usually act like that, nor is it a sort of magic that acts in the void or without any process. Nor is it a machine which acts in the same way on everybody or in all conditions and circumstances; it is not a physical but a spiritual Force and its action cannot be reduced to rules.

*

It [*the higher Force*] acts by awakening the inner consciousness gradually or swiftly, by replacing the principle of ego-service by the principle of service of the Divine, by making him watch his actions and see his own defects and pushing him to rectify them, by establishing a connection between his consciousness and the Mother's consciousness, by preparing his nature to be taken up more and more by the Mother's consciousness and force, by giving him experiences which make him ready for the major experiences of Yoga, by stimulating the growth of his psychic being, by opening him to the Mother as the Universal Being, etc. etc. Naturally it acts differently in different persons.

Allow the Divine Force to Act

It is quite true that, left to yourself, you can do nothing; that is why you have to be in contact with the Force which is there to do for you what you cannot do for yourself. The only thing *you* have to do is to allow the Force to act and put yourself on its side, which means to have faith in it, to rely upon it, not to trouble and harass yourself, to remember it quietly, to call upon it quietly, to let it act quietly. If you do that, all else will be done for you — not all at once, because there is much to clear away, but still it will be done steadily and more and more.

*

Passivity can be only to the Divine Force when it is felt at work, — there can be no passivity to other forces, for that would be dangerous in the extreme. Passivity does *not* mean a blank mind — it means allowing the Divine Force to work without interference of the mental preferences, vital desires or physical disinclinations. As for freedom from ego or desire, that is the

The Divine Force

general law of all Yoga, but it cannot be acquired by merely giving up work. The majority of Sannyasins are not at all free from desire or ego.

*

Always keep in touch with the Divine Force. The best thing for you is to do that simply and allow it to do its own work; wherever necessary, it will take hold of the inferior energies and purify them; at other times it will empty you of them and fill you with itself. But if you let your mind take the lead and discuss and decide what is to be done, you will lose touch with the Divine Force and the lower energies will begin to act for themselves and all go into confusion and a wrong movement.

*

One feels the Force only when one is in conscious contact with it.

*

It is a great progress, a decisive advance if, at the time the Force is acting behind the screen, you feel that it is there, that the help and support, the more enlightened consciousness is there still. This is the second stage in the sadhana. There is a third when there is no screen and the Force and all else are always felt whether actively working or pausing during a transition.

*

Remind yourself always that the Divine Force is there, that you have felt it and that, even if you seem to lose consciousness of it for a time or it seems something distant, still it is there and is sure to prevail. For those whom the Force has touched and taken up, belong thenceforth to the Divine.

Chapter Three

The Guru

Acceptance of the Guru

The Guru should be accepted in all ways — transcendent, impersonal, personal.

*

It has always been held in Indian yoga that the relation between Guru and disciple must be one of full confidence and full acceptance of the Guru by the Shishya. The latter was supposed to accept unquestioningly the guidance and to follow the instructions of the Guru without criticism or questioning; he was not supposed to criticise, to blame or to refuse adhesion or to follow in a questioning or grudging spirit: for that would stand in the way of his advance. The Indian disciple of those days would not have expected the Guru to suit his directions or instructions or ways of leading to the mental demands or vital ideas of the [*incomplete*]

*

There are three conditions for a disciple for profiting fully from his relation to a spiritual guide.
    1st: He must accept him entirely and him alone without submitting himself to any contrary or second influence.
    2nd: He must accept the indications given by the Guru and follow them firmly and with full faith and perseverance to the best of his own spiritual capacity.
    3rd: He must make himself open and receptive to the Guru for even more than what the Guru teaches to the mind of the disciple, it is what he spiritually is, the spiritual consciousness, the knowledge, the light, the power, the Divinity in him that helps the disciple to grow by his receiving that into himself and its being used within himself for the growth of his consciousness

and nature into its own divine possibility.

*

What the Guru can do for the sadhak depends upon the latter's receptivity — not upon any method or rule of sadhana. Certain psychological conditions or attitudes of the consciousness tend to increase the receptivity — e.g., humility towards the Guru, devotion, obedience, trust, a certain receptive passivity to his influence. The opposite things — independence, a critical attitude, questionings — go the other way and make it necessary for the Guru to help only indirectly or behind the veil. But the main thing is a kind of psychological openness in the consciousness which comes or increases of itself with the help of the will to receive and the right attitude. If there is that then it is not necessary to pull anything from the Guru, only to receive quietly. Pulling from him often draws untruly or things for which the consciousness is not ready to assimilate.

*

It is a deficiency of psychic perception and spiritual discrimination that makes people speak like that [*in a depreciatory way*] and ignore the importance of obedience. It is the mind wanting to follow its own way of thinking and the vital seeking freedom for its desires which argue in this manner. If you do not follow the rules laid down by the spiritual guide or obey one who is leading you to the Divine, then what or whom are you to follow? Only the ideas of the individual mind and the desires of the vital: but these things never lead to siddhi in Yoga. The rules are laid down in order to guard against certain influences and their dangers and to keep a right atmosphere in the Asram favourable to spiritual development; the obedience is necessary so as to get away from one's own mind and vital and learn to follow the Truth.

*

Yes, it [*obedience*] is difficult, but once achieved it is immensely fruitful.

*

You are putting the cart before the horse. It is not the right way to make the condition that if you get what you want you will be obedient and cheerful. But be always obedient and cheerful and then what you want will have a chance of coming to you.

*

Up to now no liberated man has objected to the Guruvada; it is usually only people who live in the mind or vital and have the pride of the mind or the arrogance of the vital that find it below their dignity to recognise a Guru.

*

One has to learn from the master and act according to his instructions because the master knows the subject and how it is to be learnt — just as in spiritual things one has to follow the Guru who has the knowledge and knows the way. If one learns all by oneself, the chances are that one will learn all wrong. What is the use of a freedom to learn wrongly? Of course if the pupil is more intelligent than the master, he will learn more than the master, just as a great spiritual capacity may arrive at realisations which the Guru has not — but even so, the control and discipline in the early stages is indispensable.

The Guru in the Supramental Yoga

The Guru is the Guide in the Yoga. When the Divine is accepted as the Guide, He is accepted as the Guru.

*

It is not usual to use the word Guru in the supramental Yoga, here everything comes from the Divine himself. But if anybody wants it he can use it for the time being.

*

The relation of Guru and disciple is only one of many relations which one can have with the Divine, and in this Yoga which aims at a supramental realisation, it is not usual to give it this name; rather, the Divine is regarded as the Source, the living Sun of Light and Knowledge and Consciousness and spiritual realisation and all that one receives is felt as coming from there and the whole being remoulded by the Divine Hand. This is a greater and more intimate relation than that of the human Guru and disciple, which is more of a limited mental ideal. Nevertheless, if the mind still needs the more familiar mental conception, it can be kept so long as it is needed; only do not let the soul be bound by it and do not let it limit the inflow of other relations with the Divine and larger forms of experience.

Surrender to the Guru

Because through it [*surrender to the Guru*][1] you surrender not only to the impersonal but to the personal, not only to the Divine in yourself but to the Divine outside you; you get a chance for the surpassing of ego not only by retreat into the Self where ego does not exist, but in the personal nature where it is the ruler. It is the sign of the will to complete surrender to the total Divine, *samagraṁ māṁ mānuṣīṁ tanum āśritam*. Of course it must be a genuine spiritual surrender for all this to be true.

*

When one takes sincerely to surrender, nothing must be concealed that is of any importance for the life of the sadhana. Confession helps to purge the consciousness of hampering elements and it clears the inner air and makes for a closer and more intimate and effective relation between the Guru and the disciple.

*

No [*surrender to the Divine and surrender to the Guru are not two different things*]. In surrendering to the Guru, it is to the Divine in him that one surrenders — if it were only to a human

---

[1] The correspondent asked, "What makes the surrender to the Guru so grand and glorious as to be called the surrender beyond all surrenders?" — Ed.

entity it would be ineffective. But it is the consciousness of the Divine Presence that makes the Guru a real Guru, so that even if the disciple surrenders to him thinking of the human being to whom he surrenders, that Presence would still make it effective.

*

Yes [*surrender to the formless Divine would leave parts of the being subject to the gunas and ego*] — because only the static parts would be free in formlessness, the active nature would be still in the play of the gunas. Many think they are free from ego because they get the sense of the formless Existence, they do not see that the egoistic element remains in their action just as before.

Other Gurus

All true Gurus are the same, the one Guru, because all are the one Divine. That is a fundamental and universal truth. But there is also a truth of difference; the Divine dwells in different personalities with different minds, teachings, influences so that He may lead different disciples with their special need, character, destiny by different ways to the realisation. Because all Gurus are the same Divine, it does not follow that the disciple does well if he leaves the one meant for him to follow another. Fidelity to the Guru is demanded of every disciple, according to the Indian tradition. "All are the same" is a spiritual truth, but you cannot convert it indiscriminately into action; you cannot deal with all persons in the same way because they are the one Brahman: if one did, the result pragmatically would be an awful mess. It is a rigid mental logic that makes the difficulty but in spiritual matters mental logic easily blunders; intuition, faith, a plastic spiritual reason are here the only guides.

*

To respect the spiritual attainment of X [*another spiritual teacher*] is all right, but it is a rule of this Yoga not to mix influences (and what he [*a sadhak*] has described is very much like undergoing an influence). Otherwise there may be harm done by two different methods getting mixed together — e.g. the vital being awakened to a Bhakti-Ananda influence on that plane before it is purified and ready.

The Guru's Help in Difficulty

I think this saying of Ramakrishna's[2] expresses a certain characteristic happening in sadhana and cannot be interpreted in a general and absolute sense; for in that sense it is hard for it to be true. All difficulties disappearing in a minute? Well, Vivekananda had the grace of Ramakrishna from the beginning, but I think his difficulty of doubt lasted for some time and to the end of his life the difficulty of the control of anger was there — making him say that all that was good in him was his Guru's gift but these things (anger etc.) were his own property. But what could be true is that the central difficulty may disappear by a certain touch between the Guru and the disciple. But what is meant by the *kṛpā*? If it is the general compassion and grace of the Guru, that, one would think, is always there on the disciple; his acceptance itself is an act of grace and the help is there for the disciple to receive. But the touch of grace, divine grace coming directly or through the Guru is a special phenomenon having two sides to it, — the grace of the Guru or the Divine, in fact both together, on one side and a "state of grace" in the disciple on the other. This "state of grace" is often prepared by a long tapasya or purification in which nothing decisive seems to happen, only touches or glimpses or passing experiences at the most, and it comes suddenly without warning. If this is what is spoken of in Ramakrishna's saying, then it is true that when it comes, the fundamental difficulties can in a moment and generally do disappear. Or at the very least something happens which makes the rest of the sadhana — however long it may take — sure and secure.

This decisive touch comes most easily to the "baby cat" people, those who have at some point between the psychic and

---

[2] *"With the Guru's grace all difficulties can disappear in a flash, even as agelong darkness does the moment you strike a match." — Ed.*

the emotional vital a quick and decisive movement of surrender to the Guru or the Divine. I have seen that when that is there and there is the conscious central dependence compelling the mind also and the rest of the vital, then the fundamental difficulty disappears. If others remain they are not felt as difficulties, but simply as things that have just to be done and need cause no worry. Sometimes no tapasya is necessary — one just refers things to the Power that one feels guiding or doing the sadhana and assents to its action, rejecting all that is contrary to it, and the Power removes what has to be removed or changes what has to be changed, quickly or slowly — but the quickness or slowness does not seem to matter since one is sure that it will be done. If tapasya is necessary, it is done with so much feeling of a strong support that there is nothing hard or austere in the tapasya.

For the others, the "baby monkey" type or those who are still more independent, following their own ideas, doing their own sadhana, asking only for some instruction or help, the grace of the Guru is there, but it acts according to the nature of the sadhak and waits upon his effort to a greater or less degree; it helps, succours in difficulty, saves in the time of danger, but the disciple is not always, is perhaps hardly at all aware of what is being done as he is absorbed in himself and his endeavour. In such cases the decisive psychological movement, the touch that makes all clear, may take longer to come.

But with all the *kṛpā* is there working in one way or another and it can only abandon the disciple if the disciple himself abandons or rejects it — by decisive and definitive revolt, by rejection of the Guru, by cutting the painter and declaring his independence, or by an act or course of betrayal that severs him from his own psychic being. Even then, except perhaps in the last case if it goes to an extreme, a return to grace is not impossible.

That is my own knowledge and experience of the matter. But as to what lay behind Ramakrishna's saying and whether he himself meant it to be a general and absolute statement — I do not pronounce.

*

All that is popular Yoga.[3] The Guru's touch or grace may open something, but the difficulties have always to be worked out still. What is true is that if there is complete surrender which implies the prominence of the psychic, these difficulties are no longer felt as a burden or obstacle but only as superficial imperfections which the working of the grace will remove.

*

It has always been said that to take disciples means to take upon yourself the difficulties of the disciples as well as your own. Of course, if the Guru does not identify himself with the disciple, does not take him into his own consciousness, keeps him outside and only gives him *upadeśa*, leaving him to do the rest himself, then the chance of these effects is much diminished, made practically nil.

The Knowledge Given by the Guru

I do not know what you mean by indirect knowledge. The knowledge given by the Guru, if that is what you mean, is in the nature of experience and becomes part and parcel of the experience. Mere instruction is not knowledge but only an intellectual indication of what must be realised by experience.

According to Yoga, as it is known in India, the mediation of the Guru is almost indispensable. It is not a crutch. It is a direct action of the Divine who is realised by the Guru. It is an opening of the consciousness to spiritual experience without which few can open at all or go very far. If they advance by themselves, they can fall into all sorts of perils and errors of which they have no knowledge and no idea how to guide themselves among these things.

All experience is direct — there is no such thing as an indirect spiritual experience. But after the consciousness is sufficiently opened and matured, a knowledge and guidance can

---

[3] *The correspondent wrote, "It is said that if a disciple receives his Guru's touch or grace, his main difficulties very often disappear." — Ed.*

come from within and above and the sadhana proceeds by Divine working within. But the sadhak has to be very careful, for he may easily mistake the guiding of his own mind, ego or vital or the guiding of some inferior Power that flatters his ego for the Divine guidance. It is by the inner experience and consciousness that one knows a spiritual result — one feels and sees it happening.

There are two kinds of knowledge — mental knowledge such as you describe here which is usually necessary as a mental preparation or for guidance and the real knowledge which is spiritual. One receives the mental knowledge from the Guru in the shape of instruction and guidance, but that is only a part of what he gives — for the man who gives only mental or what you call indirect knowledge is not a Guru but only a teacher, Acharya.

As for spiritual knowledge, it consists of two elements, experience and a direct knowledge which is not mental but is of the nature of a light showing the deeper truth of things, a direct vision and perception of the Truth.

The ordinary consciousness is not capable of receiving it as knowledge except in a fragmentary way because it belongs to a deeper consciousness within or a higher consciousness above the mind. The ordinary consciousness has therefore to open to the deeper and the higher consciousness. It has to receive the knowledge from within and above. It cannot do this if it does not open. There must, therefore, first necessarily be an opening, however small, before any direct knowledge can come. As the knowledge comes the opening also can widen and so admit a greater and greater direct knowledge and experience. In some, however, the opening comes first very wide and then the knowledge comes afterwards in a great stream, some light of the Truth and many experiences.

If one has merely a mental idea about the Divine, that is not knowledge. It is with the experiences and the inner light of knowledge that the realisation of the Divine begins. As for example, one may have the mental idea of the Divine Peace but that is nothing, only a mental conception. It is only when one has the feeling of the Divine Peace descending from above or in oneself or surrounding one that one begins to know what it is. That is what is called experience. Afterwards one begins to have a direct vision in knowledge of what the Peace is and what is its place in regard to the Divine Realisation; that is direct knowledge.

The Capacity of the Guru

One can have a guru inferior in spiritual capacity (to oneself or to other gurus) carrying in him many human imperfections, and yet, if you have the faith, the bhakti, the right spiritual stuff, contact the Divine through him, attain to spiritual experiences, to spiritual realisation, even before the guru himself. Mark the "if", — for that proviso is necessary; it isn't every disciple who can do that with every guru. From a humbug you can acquire nothing but humbuggery. The guru must have something in him which makes the contact with the Divine possible, something which works even if he is not himself in his outer mind quite conscious of its action. If there is nothing at all spiritual in him he is not a guru — only a pseudo. Undoubtedly, there can be considerable differences of spiritual realisation between one guru and the other; but much depends on the inner relation between guru and shishya. One can go to a very great spiritual man and get nothing or only a little from him; one can go to a man of less spiritual capacity and get all he has to give — and more. The causes of this disparity are various and subtle; I need not expand on them here. It differs with each man. I believe the guru is always ready to give what can be given, if the disciple can receive, or it may be when he is ready to receive. If he refuses to receive or behaves inwardly or outwardly in such a way as to make reception impossible or if he is not sincere or takes up the wrong attitude, then things become difficult. But if one is sincere and faithful and has the right attitude and if the guru is a true guru, then, after whatever time, it *will* come.

*

What X quotes about the limitation of the power of the Guru to that of a teacher who shows the way but cannot help or guide is the conception of certain paths of Yoga such as the pure Adwaitin and the Buddhist which say that you must rely upon yourself and no one can help you; but even the pure Adwaitin does in fact rely upon the Guru and the chief mantra of Buddhism insists on *śaraṇam* to Buddha. For other paths of sadhana, especially those which like the Gita accept the reality of the individual soul as an "eternal portion" of the Divine or which believe that Bhagavan and the bhakta are both real, the help of the Guru has always been relied upon as an indispensable aid.

I don't understand the objection to the validity of Vivekananda's experience; it was exactly the realisation which is described in the Upanishads as a supreme experience of the Self. It is not a fact that an experience gained in samadhi cannot be prolonged into the waking state.

*

Ramakrishna had the siddhi himself before he began giving to others — so had Buddha. I don't know about the others [*Vivekananda, Ramatirtha, Ramdas, Mahavir, Shankara*]. By perfection of course is meant siddhi in one's own path — realisation. Ramakrishna always put that as a rule that one should not become a teacher to others until one has the full authority.

The Bhakta and the Disciple

It does not strike me that Krishnaprem's letters are admirable as an *aperçu* of current thoughts and general tendencies; it was rather his power to withdraw so completely from these thoughts and tendencies and look from a (for him) new and an abiding source of knowledge that impressed me as admirable. If he had remained interested and in touch with these current human movements, I don't suppose he would have done better with them than Romain Rolland or another. But he has gone to the Yoga-view of them, the summit-view, and it is the readiness with which he has been able to do it that struck me.

I would explain his progressing so far not entirely by his own superiority in the sense of a general fitness for Yoga but by the quickness and completeness with which he has taken inwardly the attitude of the Bhakta and the disciple. That is a rare achievement for a modern mind, be he European or "educated" Indian; for the modern mind is analytic, dubitative, instinctively "independent" even when it wants to be otherwise; it holds itself back and hesitates in front of the Light and Influence that comes to it; it does not plunge into it with a simple directness, crying, "Here I am, ready to throw from me all that was myself or seemed to be, if so I can enter into Thee; remake my consciousness into the Truth in thy way, the way of the Divine." There is something in us that is ready for it, but there is this element that intervenes and makes a curtain of non-receptivity; I know by my own experience with myself and others how long it can make a road that could never perhaps, for us who seek the entire truth, have been short and easy, but still we might have been spared many wanderings and stand-stills and recoils and detours. All the more I admire the ease with which Krishnaprem seems to have surmounted this formidable obstacle.

I do not know if his Guru falls far short in any respect, but with the attitude he has taken, her deficiencies, if any, do not matter. It is not the human defects of the Guru that can stand in the way when there is the psychic opening, confidence and surrender. The Guru is the channel or the representative or the manifestation of the Divine, according to the measure of his personality or his attainment; but whatever he is, it is to the Divine that one opens in opening to him, and if something is determined by the power of the channel, more is determined by the inherent and intrinsic attitude of the receiving consciousness, an element that comes out in the surface mind as simple trust or direct unconditional self-giving, and once that is there, the essential things can be gained even from one who seems to others than the disciple an inferior spiritual source and the rest will grow up in the sadhak of itself by the Grace of the Divine, even if the human being in the Guru cannot give it. It is this that Krishnaprem appears to have done perhaps from the first; but in most nowadays this attitude seems to come with difficulty after much hesitation and delay and trouble. In my own case I owe the first decisive turn of my inner life to one who was infinitely inferior to me in intellect, education and capacity and by no means spiritually perfect or supreme; but, having seen a Power behind him and decided to turn there for help, I gave myself entirely into his hands and followed with an automatic passivity the guidance. He himself was astonished and said to others that he had never met anyone before who could surrender himself so absolutely and without reserve or question to the guidance of the helper. The result was a series of transmuting experiences of such a radical character that he was unable to follow and had to tell me to give myself up in future to the Guide within with the same completeness of surrender as I had shown to the human channel. I give this example to show how these things work; it is not in the calculated way the human reason wants to lay down, but by a more mysterious and greater law.

Part Two

The Synthetic Method of the Integral Yoga

Section One

A Yoga of Knowledge, Works, Bhakti and Self-Perfection

Chapter One

The Central Processes of the Sadhana

Four Necessary Processes

As regards X's question — this is not a Yoga of Bhakti alone; it is or at least it claims to be an integral Yoga, that is, a turning of all the being in all its parts to the Divine. It follows that there must be knowledge and works as well as Bhakti and, in addition, it includes a total change of the nature, a seeking for perfection, so that the nature also may become one with the nature of the Divine. It is not only the heart that has to turn to the Divine and change, but the mind also — so knowledge is necessary, and the will and power of action and creation also — so works too are necessary. In this Yoga the methods of other Yogas are taken up — like this of Purusha-Prakriti, but with a difference in the final object. Purusha separates from Prakriti, not in order to abandon her, but in order to know himself and her and to be no longer her plaything, but the knower, lord and upholder of the nature; but having become so or even in becoming so, one offers all that to the Divine. One may begin with knowledge or with works or with Bhakti or with Tapasya of self-purification for perfection (change of nature) and develop the rest as a subsequent movement or one may combine all in one movement. There is no single rule for all, it depends on the personality and the nature. Surrender is the main power of the Yoga, but the surrender is bound to be progressive; a complete surrender is not possible in the beginning, but only a will in the being for that completeness, — in fact it takes time; yet it is only when the surrender is complete that the full flood of the sadhana is possible. Till then there must be the personal effort with an increasing reality of surrender. One calls in the power of the Divine Shakti and once that begins to come into the being, it at first supports the personal endeavour, then progressively takes up the whole action, although the consent of the sadhak continues to be always necessary. As the Force works, it brings in the different processes that are necessary for the sadhak, processes of knowledge, of Bhakti, of spiritualised action, of transformation of the nature. The idea that they cannot be combined is an error.

*

The object of the sadhana is opening of the consciousness to the Divine and the change of the nature. Meditation or contemplation is one means to this but only one means; bhakti is another; work is another. Chittashuddhi was practised by the Yogis as a first means towards realisation and they got by it the saintliness of the saint and the quietude of the sage. But the transformation of the nature of which we speak is something more than that, and this transformation does not come by contemplation alone; works are necessary, Yoga in action is indispensable.

The Need for Plasticity

One must not treat human nature like a machine to be handled according to rigid mental rules — a great plasticity is needed in dealing with its complex motives.

*

Fundamentally the nature in all is the same and the methods of sadhana have the same principle — but the differences in detail and arrangement are very great.

*

You forget that men differ in nature and therefore each will approach the sadhana in his own way — one through work, one through bhakti, one through meditation and knowledge — and those who are capable of it through all together. You are perfectly justified in following your own way, whatever may be the theories of others — but let them follow theirs. In the end all can converge together towards the same goal.

Work, Meditation and Bhakti

There is no opposition between work and sadhana. Work itself done in the right spirit is sadhana. Meditation is not the only means of sadhana. Work is one means; love and worship and surrender are another.

*

It [*the value of work in sadhana*] depends more on the intensity of the spirit put into it than on the intensity of the work itself. As for the line on which most stress is laid, it depends on the nature. There are some people who are not cut out for meditation and it is only by work that they can prepare themselves; there are also those who are the opposite. As for the enormous development of egoism, that can come whatever one follows. I have seen it blossom in the *dhyānī* as well as in the worker; Krishnaprem says it does so in the bhakta. So it is evident that all soils are favourable to this Narcissus flower. As for "no need of sadhana", obviously one who does not do any sadhana cannot change or progress. Work, meditation, bhakti, all must be done as sadhana.

*

I have always said that work done as sadhana — done, that is to say, as an outflow of energy from the Divine offered to the Divine or work done for the sake of the Divine or work done in a spirit of devotion — is a powerful means of sadhana and that such work is especially necessary in this Yoga. Work, bhakti and meditation are three supports of Yoga. One can do with all three, or two or one. There are people who can't meditate in the set way that one calls meditation, but they progress through work or through bhakti or through the two together. By work and bhakti one can develop a consciousness in which eventually a natural meditation and realisation become possible.

*

The growth out of the ordinary mind into the spiritual consciousness can be effected either by meditation, dedicated work or bhakti for the Divine. In our Yoga, which seeks not only a static peace or absorption but a dynamic spiritual action, work is indispensable. As for the Supramental Truth, that is a different matter; it depends only on the descent of the Divine and the action of the Supreme Force and is not bound by any method or rule.

*

There are very few among the sadhaks here who at all concern themselves with the supermind or know anything about it except as something which the Mother and I will bring down some day and establish here. Most are seeking realisation through meditation, through love and worship or through activity and work. Meditation and silence are not necessary for everyone; there are some, even among those spoken of by you and others as the most advanced sadhaks, who do their sadhana not through meditation, for which they have no turn, but through activity, work or creation supported or founded on love and bhakti. It is not the credo but the person who matters. We impose no credo; it is sufficient if there is an established and heart-felt relation between ourselves and the disciple.

*

I was quite in earnest in speaking of the progress you had made by the psychic movement and the endeavour to detect and remove the ego. I had already written to you strongly approving of that way. It is in our Yoga the way to devotion and surrender — for it is the psychic movement that brings the constant and pure devotion and the removal of ego that makes it possible to surrender. The two things indeed go together.

The other way, which is the way to knowledge, is the meditation in the head by which there comes the opening above, the quietude or silence of the mind and the descent of peace etc. of the higher consciousness generally till it envelops the being and fills the body and begins to take up all the movements. But this involves a passage through silence, a certain emptiness of the ordinary activities — they being pushed out and done as a purely superficial action — and you strongly dislike silence and emptiness.

The third way which is one of the two ways towards Yoga by works is the separation of the Purusha from the Prakriti, the inner silent being from the outer active one, so that one has two consciousnesses or a double consciousness, one behind watching and observing and finally controlling and changing the other which is active in front. But this also means living in an inner peace and silence and dealing with the activities as if they were a thing of the surface. (The other way of beginning the Yoga of works is by doing them for the Divine, for the Mother, and not for oneself, consecrating and dedicating them till one concretely feels the Divine Force taking up the activities and doing them for one.)

If there is any secret or key of my Yoga which you say you have not found, it lies in these methods — and, in reality, there is nothing so mysterious, impossible or even new about them in themselves. It is only the farther development at a later stage and the aim of the Yoga that are new. But that one need not concern oneself with in the earlier stages unless one wishes to do so as a matter of mental knowledge.

*

Poetry by itself does not bring to the goal, but it can help as a means to express and deepen one's aspiration while it gives the vital an activity which can keep it from rusting and maintains its energy. Otherwise it may droop or go dry or sulk or non-cooperate. What will bring towards the goal is the growth of the psychic being, the increase in bhakti, psychic clarity of vision with regard to one's inner movements and the will to get rid of the vital ego, increase in pure self-giving. Meditation and the rest can bring only partial results or often no results until there has been a sufficient psychic preparation. Even with those who begin with a flood of experiences because of some mental or vital preparation in past lives whose results happen to be near the surface, these lead to nothing definite till the psychic preparation is made; they often have all their struggle still to go through and some sink with their bag of experiences on their head and a magnified ego on their back. It was this psychic growth that suddenly began in you. Don't let it stop; for through that lies your way. Once that is done, you can meditate and do everything else that may be needful.

*

Meditation is one means of the approach to the Divine and a great way, but it cannot be called a short cut — for most it is a long and difficult though very high ascent. It can by no means be short unless it brings a descent and even then it is only a foundation that is quickly laid — afterwards meditation has to build laboriously a big superstructure on that foundation. It is very indispensable, but there is nothing of the short cut about it.

Karma is a much simpler road — provided one's mind is not fixed on the karma to the exclusion of the Divine. The aim must be the Divine and the work can only be a means. The use of poetry etc. is to keep one in contact with one's inner being and that helps to prepare for the direct contact with the inmost, but one must not stop with that, one must go on to the real thing. If one thinks of being a "literary man", a poet, a painter as things worthwhile for their own sake, then it is no longer the Yogic spirit. That is why I have sometimes to say that our business is to be Yogis, not merely poets, painters etc.

Love, bhakti, surrender, the psychic opening are the only short cut to the Divine — or can be; for if the love and bhakti are too vital, then there is likely to be a seesaw between ecstatic expectation and *viraha, abhimāna,* despair, which will make it not a short cut but a long one, a zigzag, not a straight flight, a whirling round one's own ego instead of a running towards the Divine.

Surrender and Self-Giving

I may stress one point, however, that there need not be only one way to realisation of the Divine. If one does not succeed or has not yet succeeded in reaching him, feeling him or seeing him by the established process of meditation or by other processes like japa, yet one may have made progress towards it by the frequent welling up of bhakti in the heart or a constantly greater enlargement of it in the consciousness or by work for the Divine and dedication in service. You have certainly progressed in these two directions, increased in devotion and shown your capacity for service. You have also tried to get rid of obstacles in your vital nature and so effect a purification, not without success, in several difficult directions. The path of surrender is indeed difficult, but if one perseveres in it with sincerity, there is bound to be some success and a partial overcoming or diminution of the ego which may help greatly a farther advance upon the way. I can see no sufficient reason for the discouragement which so often overtakes you and sometimes makes you think that you are not cut out for the path; to indulge such a thought is always a mistake. A too ready proneness to discouragement and a consequent despondency is one of the weaknesses of your vital nature and to get rid of it would be a great help. One must learn to go forward on the path of Yoga, as the Gita insists, with a consciousness free from despondency — *anirviṇṇacetasā*. Even if one slips, one must rectify the posture; even if one falls, one has to rise and go undiscouraged on the divine way. The attitude must be, "The Divine has promised himself to me if I cleave to him always; that I will never cease to do whatever may come."

*

It is altogether unprofitable to enquire who or what class will arrive first or last at the goal. The spiritual path is not a field of competition or a race that this should matter. What matters is one's own aspiration for the Divine, one's own faith, surrender, selfless self-giving. Others can be left to the Divine who will lead each according to his nature. Meditation, work, bhakti are each means of preparative help towards fulfilment; all are included in this path. If one can dedicate oneself through work, that is one of the most powerful means towards the self-giving which is itself the most powerful and indispensable element of the sadhana.

To cleave to the path means to follow it without leaving it

or turning aside. It is a path of self-offering of the whole being in all its parts, the offering of the thinking mind and the heart, the will and actions, the inner and the outer instruments so that one may arrive at the experience of the Divine, the Presence within, the psychic and spiritual change. The more one gives of oneself in all ways, the better for the sadhana. But all cannot do it to the same extent, with the same rapidity, in the same way. How others do it or fail to do it should not be one's concern — how to do it faithfully oneself is the one thing important.

Aspiration and Will of Consecration

I have never put any ban on bhakti. Also I am not conscious of having banned meditation either at any time. I have stressed both bhakti and knowledge in my Yoga as well as works, even if I have not given any of them an exclusive importance like Shankara or Chaitanya.

The difficulty you feel or any sadhak feels about sadhana is not really a question of meditation versus bhakti versus works. It is a difficulty of the attitude to be taken, the approach or whatever you may like to call it.

If you can't as yet remember the Divine all the time you are working, it does not greatly matter. To remember and dedicate at the beginning and give thanks at the end ought to be enough for the present. Or at the most to remember too when there is a pause. Your method seems to me rather painful and difficult, — you seem to be trying to remember and work with one and the same part of the mind. I don't know if that is possible. When people remember all the time during work (it can be done), it is usually with the back of their minds or else there is created gradually a faculty of double thought or else a double consciousness — one in front that works, and one within that witnesses and remembers. There is also another way which was mine for a long time — a condition in which the work takes place automatically and without intervention of personal thought or mental action, while the consciousness remains silent in the Divine. The thing, however, does not come so much by trying as by a very simple constant aspiration and will of consecration — or else by a movement of the consciousness separating the inner from the instrumental being. Aspiration and will of consecration calling down a greater Force to do the work is a method which brings great results, even if in some it takes a long time about it. That is a great secret of sadhana, to know how to get things done by the Power behind or above instead of doing all by the mind's effort. I don't mean to say that the mind's effort is unnecessary or has no result — only if it tries to do everything by itself, that becomes a laborious effort for all except the spiritual athletes. Nor do I mean that the other method is the longed-for short cut; the result may, as I have said, take a long time. Patience and firm resolution are necessary in every method of sadhana.

Strength is all right for the strong — but aspiration and the Grace answering to it are not altogether myths; they are great realities of the spiritual life.

Sadhana, Tapasya, Aradhana, Dhyana

Sadhana is the practice of Yoga. Tapasya is the concentration of the will to get the results of sadhana and to conquer the lower nature. Aradhana is worship of the Divine, love, self-surrender, aspiration to the Divine, calling the name, prayer. Dhyana is inner concentration of the consciousness, meditation, going inside in Samadhi. Dhyana, tapasya and aradhana are all parts of sadhana.

Chapter Two
Combining Work, Meditation and Bhakti

The Place of Work in Sadhana

There is no stage of the sadhana in which works are impossible, no passage in the path where there is no foothold and action has to be renounced as incompatible with concentration on the Divine. The foothold is there always; the foothold is the reliance on the Divine, the opening of the being, the will, the energies to the Divine, the surrender to the Divine. All work done in that spirit can be made a means for the sadhana. It may be necessary for an individual here and there to plunge into meditation for a time and suspend work for that time or make it subordinate; but that can only be an individual case and a temporary retirement. Moreover, a complete cessation of work and entire withdrawal into oneself is seldom advisable; it may encourage a too one-sided and visionary condition in which one lives in a sort of midworld of purely subjective experiences without a firm hold on either external reality or on the highest Reality and without the right use of the subjective experience to create a firm link and then a unification between the highest Reality and the external realisation in life.

Work can be of two kinds — the work that is a field of experience used for the sadhana, for a progressive harmonisation and transformation of the being and its activities, and work that is a realised expression of the Divine. But the time for the latter can be only when the Realisation has been fully brought down into the earth-consciousness; till then all work must be a field of endeavour and a school of experience.

*

I do not mean by work action done in the ego and the ignorance, for the satisfaction of the ego and in the drive of rajasic desire. There can be no Karmayoga without the will to get rid of ego, rajas and desire, which are the seals of ignorance.

I do not mean philanthropy or the service of humanity or all the rest of the things — moral or idealistic — which the mind of man substitutes for the deeper truth of works.

I mean by work action done for the Divine and more and more in union with the Divine — for the Divine alone and nothing else. Naturally that is not easy at the beginning, any more than deep meditation and luminous knowledge are easy or even true love and bhakti are easy. But like the others it has to be begun in the right spirit and attitude, with the right will in you, then all the rest will come.

Works done in this spirit are quite as effective as bhakti or contemplation. One gets by the rejection of desire, rajas and ego a quietude and purity into which the Peace ineffable can descend; one gets by the dedication of one's will to the Divine, by the merging of one's will in the Divine Will the death of ego and the enlarging into the cosmic consciousness or else the uplifting into what is above the cosmic; one experiences the separation of Purusha from Prakriti and is liberated from the shackles of the outer nature; one becomes aware of one's inner being and feels the outer as an instrument; one feels the universal Force doing one's works and the Self or Purusha watching or witness but free; one feels all one's works taken from one and done by the universal or the supreme Mother or by the Divine Power controlling and acting from behind the heart. By constant reference of all one's will and works to the Divine, love and adoration grow, the psychic being comes forward. By the reference to the Power above we can come to feel it above and its descent and the opening to an increasing consciousness and knowledge. Finally works, bhakti and knowledge join together and self-perfection becomes possible — what we call the transformation of the nature.

These results certainly do not come all at once; they come more or less slowly, more or less completely according to the condition and growth of the being. There is no royal road to the divine realisation.

This is the Karmayoga as it is laid down in the Gita as I have developed it for the integral spiritual life. It is founded not on speculation and reasoning but on experience. It does not exclude meditation and it certainly does not exclude bhakti, for the self-offering to the Divine, the consecration of all oneself to the Divine which is the essence of this Karmayoga are essentially a movement of bhakti. Only it does exclude a life-fleeing exclusive meditation or an emotional bhakti shut up in its own inner dream taken as the whole movement of the Yoga. One may have hours of pure absorbed meditation or of the inner motionless adoration and ecstasy, but they are not the whole of the integral Yoga.

*

To say that one enters the stream of sadhana through work only is to say too much. One can enter it through meditation or bhakti also, but work is necessary to get into full stream and not drift away to one side and go circling there. Of course all work helps provided it is done in the right spirit.

*

Why argue from your personal experience great or little and turn it into a generalisation? A great many people (the majority perhaps) find it [sadhana through work] the easiest of all. Many find it easy to think of the Mother when working; but when they read or write, their mind goes off to the thing read or written and they forget everything else. I think that is the case with most. Physical work on the other hand can be done with the most external part of the mind, leaving the rest free to remember or to experience.

A Defence of Works

In spite of your disclaimer you practically come to the conclusion that all my nonsense about integral Yoga and karma being as much a way to realisation as jnana and bhakti is either a gleaming chimaera or practicable only by Avatars or else a sheer laborious superfluity — since one can bump straight into the Divine through the open door of Bhakti or sweep majestically in on him by the easy high road of meditation; so why this scramble through the jungle of karma by which nobody ever reached anywhere? The old Yogas are true, are they not? Then why a new-fangled, more difficult Yoga with unheard talk about the supramental and God knows what else? There can be no answer to that; for I can only answer by a repetition of the statement of my own knowledge and experience — that is what I have done in today's answer to X — and that amounts only to a perverse obstinacy in riding my gleaming and dazzling chimaera and forcing my nuisance of a superfluity on a world weary of itself and anxious to get a short easy cut to the Divine. Unfortunately, I don't believe in short cuts — at any rate none ever led me where I wanted to go. However, let it rest there.

I have never disputed the truth of the old Yogas — I have myself had the experience of Vaishnava Bhakti and of Nirvana in the Brahman; I recognise their truth in their own field and for their own purpose — the truth of their experience so far as it goes — though I am in no way bound to accept the truth of the mental philosophies founded on the experience. I similarly find that my Yoga is true in its own field — a larger field, as I think — and for its own purpose. The purpose of the old is to get away from life to the Divine — so, obviously, let us drop karma. The purpose of the new is to reach the Divine and bring the fullness of what is gained into life — for that, Yoga by works is indispensable. It seems to me that there is no mystery about that or anything to perplex anybody — it is rational and inevitable. Only you say that the thing is impossible; but that is what is said about everything before it is done.

I may point out that Karmayoga is not a new but a very old Yoga: the Gita was not written yesterday and Karmayoga existed before the Gita. Your idea that the only justification in the Gita for works is that it is an unavoidable nuisance, so better make the best of it, is rather summary and crude. If that were all, the Gita would be the production of an imbecile and I would hardly have been justified in writing two volumes on it or the world in admiring it as one of the greatest scriptures, especially for its treatment of the problem of the place of works in spiritual endeavour. There is surely more in it than that. Anyhow your doubt whether works can lead to realisation or rather your flat and sweeping denial of the possibility contradicts the experience of those who have achieved this supposed impossibility. You say that work lowers the consciousness, brings you out of the inner into the outer — yes, if you consent to externalise yourself in it instead of doing works from within; but that is just what one has to learn not to do. Thought and feeling can also externalise one in the same way; but it is a question of linking thought, feeling and act firmly to the inner consciousness by living there and making the rest an instrument. Difficult? Even bhakti is not easy and Nirvana is for most men more difficult than all.

You again try to floor me with Ramakrishna. But one thing puzzles me, as Shankara's stupendous activity of karma puzzles me in the apostle of inaction — you see you are not the only puzzled person in the world. Ramakrishna also gave the image of the jar which ceased gurgling when it was full. Well, but Ramakrishna spent the last years of his life in talking about the Divine and receiving disciples — that was not action, not work? Did Ramakrishna become a half-full jar after being a full one or was he never full? Did he get far away from God and so begin a work? Or had he reached a condition in which he was bound neither to rajasic work and mental prattling nor to inactivity and silence, but could do from the divine realisation the divine work and speak from the inner consciousness the divine word? If the last, perhaps in spite of his dictum, his example at least is rather in my favour.

I do not know why you drag in humanitarianism, activism, philanthropical *sevā* etc. None of these are part of my Yoga or in harmony with my definition of works, so they don't touch me. I never thought that politics or feeding the poor or writing beautiful poems would lead straight to Vaikuntha or the Absolute. If it were so, Romesh Dutt on one side and Baudelaire on the other would be the first to attain the Highest and welcome us there. It is not the form of the work itself or mere activity but the consciousness and Godward will behind it that are the essence of Karmayoga; the work is only the necessary instrumentation for the union with the Master of works, the transit to the pure Will and power of Light from the will and power of the Ignorance.

Finally, why suppose that I am against meditation or bhakti? I have not the slightest objection to your taking either or both as the means of approach to the Divine. Only I saw no reason why anyone should fall foul of works and deny the truth of those who have reached, as the Gita says, through works perfect realisation and oneness of nature with the Divine, *saṁsiddhim, sādharmyam*, as did "Janaka and others", simply because he himself cannot find or has not yet found their deeper secret — hence my defence of works.

Work and Meditation

Work by itself is only a preparation [*for spiritual life*], so is meditation by itself, but work done in the increasing Yogic consciousness is a means of realisation as much as meditation is.

I have not said, I hope, that work *only* prepares. Meditation also prepares for the direct contact. If we are to do work only as a preparation and then become motionless meditative ascetics, then all my spiritual teaching is false and there is no use for supramental realisation or anything else that has not been done in the past.

*

The including of the outer consciousness in the transformation is of supreme importance in this Yoga — meditation cannot do it. Meditation can deal only with the inner being. So work is of primary importance — only it must be done with the right attitude and in the right consciousness, then it is as fruitful as any meditation can be.

*

You need not have qualms about the time you give to action and creative work. Those who have an expansive creative vital or a vital made for action are usually at their best when the vital is not held back from its movement and they can develop faster by it than by introspective meditation. All that is needed is that the action should be dedicated, so that they may grow by it more and more prepared to feel and follow the Divine Force when it moves them. It is a mistake to think that to live in introspective meditation all the time is invariably the best or the only way of Yoga.

*

It is not meditation (thinking with the mind) but a concentration or turning of the consciousness that is important, — and that can happen in work, in writing, in any kind of action as well as in sitting down to contemplate.

*

It does not depend on sitting [*to meditate*]. Many don't sit. They become conscious by working.

*

There are some who cannot meditate and progress through work only. Each has his own nature. But to extend one method to all is always an error.

*

Meditation is best when it comes spontaneously. But there should be full concentration in the work if it is to take the place of meditation.

No Competition between Work and Meditation

There are several sadhaks who have advanced very far by work alone, work consecrated to the Mother or else by work mainly with very little time for meditation. Others have advanced far by meditation mainly, but work also. Those who tried to do meditation alone and became impatient of work (because they could not consecrate it to the Mother) have generally been failures like

X and Y. But one or two may succeed by meditation alone — if it is in their nature or if they have an intense and unshakable faith and bhakti. All depends on the nature of the sadhak.

As for the *purātana mānuṣa* I do not see that the workers have their external being less changed than others. There are some who are where they were or only a little progressive, there are others who have changed a good deal — none is transformed altogether, though some have found a sure and sound spiritual and psychic basis. But that applies equally to workers who do not spend time in meditation and to those who spend a long time in meditation.

Each sadhak must be left to himself and the Mother to find his right way which need not be that of his neighbour. There is in the Asram too much observation of each other by the sadhaks, criticism, discussion of persons, even baseless gossip about each other's character, ideas, sadhana, actions along sometimes with theories and (usually mistaken) advice. All that is not very consistent with the atmosphere of Yoga. People should keep all their energy for their own sadhana — unless of course they are commissioned by the Mother to speak or state anything about the Yoga.

*

The ignorance underlying this attitude [*that meditation is greater than work*] is in the assumption that one must necessarily do only work or only meditation. Either work is the means or meditation is the means, but both cannot be! I have never said, so far as I know, that meditation should not be done. To set up an open competition or a closed one between works and meditation is a trick of the dividing mind and belongs to the old Yoga. Please remember that I have been declaring all along an integral Yoga in which Knowledge, Bhakti, works — light of consciousness, Ananda and love, will and power in works — meditation, adoration, service of the Divine have all their place. Have I written seven volumes of the *Arya* all in vain? Meditation is not greater than Yoga of works nor works greater than Yoga by knowledge — both are equal.

Another thing — it is a mistake to argue from one's own very limited experience, ignoring that of others, and build on it large generalisations about Yoga. This is what many do, but the method has obvious demerits. You have no experience of major realisations through work, and you conclude that such realisations are impossible. But what of the many who have had them — elsewhere and here too in the Asram? That has no value? You kindly hint to me that I have failed to get anything by works? How do you know? I have not written the history of my sadhana — if I had, you would have seen that if I had not made action and work one of my chief means of realisation — well, there would have been no sadhana and no realisation except that, perhaps, of Nirvana.

I shall perhaps add something hereafter as to what works can do, but no time tonight.

Do not conclude however that I am exalting works as the sole means of realisation. I am only giving it its due place.

The Time Given to Work and Meditation

The work should not be diminished for that purpose [*meditation and japa*]. On the other hand it is not necessary for you to work all the time. If the work assigned to you is finished earlier, it does not matter about your not keeping the full office hours.

*

If this arrangement [*in work*] gives no time for meditation — no time for going inside and establishing there the peace, wideness and joy in which you can meet the Divine inside and in work — it seems defective. What I meant is that it is not necessary either to work all the time or to intoxicate the brain by unrelieved meditation as some do. The result of meditation can be obtained by work, but then you must be able or learn to live inwardly even in the work and to do all from within.

*

Half an hour's meditation in the day ought to be possible — if only to bring a concentrated habit into the consciousness which will help it, first to be less outward in work and, secondly, to develop a receptive tendency which can bear its fruits even in the work.

*

I have not suggested that you are to progress by *dhyāna* alone; but you have a great capacity for that and you cannot progress fully without it. In this Yoga some kind of action is necessary for all — though it need not take the form of some set labour. But for the moment progress through concentration and inner experience is the first necessity for you.

This [*stream of thoughts*] is what we call the activity of the mind, which always comes in the way of the concentration and tries to create doubt and dispersion of the energies. It can be got rid of in two ways, by rejecting it and pushing it out, till it remains as an outside force only — by bringing down the higher peace and light into the physical mind.

Concentration, Meditation and Prayer

What you felt before was in your mental being and consciousness; after coming here you have evidently come out into your external and physical consciousness, that is why you feel as if all you had before was gone. It is only covered over by the obscurity of the physical consciousness and not gone.

As for sadhana, I presume you mean by that some kind of exercise of concentration etc. For work also is sadhana, if done in the right attitude and spirit. The sadhana of inner concentration consists in:

(1) Fixing the consciousness in the heart and concentrating there on the idea, image or name of the Divine Mother, whichever comes easiest to you.

(2) A gradual and progressive quieting of the mind by this concentration in the heart.

(3) An aspiration for the Mother's presence in the heart and the control by her of mind, life and action.

But to quiet the mind and get the spiritual experience it is necessary first to purify and prepare the nature. This sometimes takes many years. Work done with the right attitude is the easiest means for that — i.e. work done without desire or ego, rejecting all movements of desire, demand or ego when they come, done as an offering to the Divine Mother, with the remembrance of her and prayer to her to manifest her force and take up the action so that there too and not only in inner silence you can feel her presence and working.

*

I don't think you understood very well what Mother was trying to tell you. First of all she did not say that prayers or meditation either were no good — how could she when both count for so much in Yoga? What she said was that the prayer must well up from the heart on a crest of emotion or aspiration, the Japa or meditation come in a live push carrying the joy or the light of the thing in it. If done mechanically and merely as a thing that ought to be done (stern grim duty!), it must tend towards want of interest and dryness and so be ineffective. It was what I meant when I said I thought you were doing Japa too much as a means for bringing about a result — I meant too much as a device, a process laid down for getting the thing done. That again was why I wanted the psychological conditions in you to develop, the psychic, the mental — for when the psychic is forward, there is no lack of life and joy in the prayer, the aspiration, the seeking, no difficulty in having the constant stream of bhakti and when the mind is quiet and inturned and upturned there is no difficulty or want of interest in meditation. Meditation by the way is a process leading towards knowledge and through knowledge, it is a thing of the head and not of the heart; so if you want dhyana, you can't have an aversion to knowledge. Concentration in the heart is not meditation, it is a call on the Divine, on the Beloved. This Yoga too is not a Yoga of knowledge alone — knowledge is one of its means, but its base being self-offering, surrender, bhakti, it is based on the heart and nothing can be eventually done without this base. There are plenty of people here who do or have done Japa and base themselves on bhakti, very few comparatively who have done the "head" meditation; love and bhakti and works are usually the base — how many can proceed by knowledge? Only the few.

Bhakti and Knowledge

To know about the sadhana with the mind is not indispensable. If one has bhakti and aspires in the heart's silence, if there is the true love for the Divine, then the nature will open of itself, there will be the true experience and the Mother's power working within you, and the necessary knowledge will come.

Section Two

Sadhana through Work

Chapter One

Work and Yoga

Work as Part of Sadhana

Work alone is not the object; work is a means of sadhana.

*

Certainly; work done in the right way and with the consciousness open to the Force is sadhana.

*

Without sadhana the object of Yoga cannot be attained. Work itself must be taken as part of sadhana. But naturally when you are working, you must think of the work, which you will learn to do from the Yogic consciousness as an instrument and with the memory of the Divine.

*

Sadhana and work done disinterestedly as part of the sadhana cannot be incompatible with each other — provided the work is attended to, sadhana can go on very well at the same time.

*

By disinterested work is usually meant work done for the sake of the work or for the sake of others without asking for return, reward or personal fruit or recompense; but in Yoga it means desireless work done for the Divine as an offering without condition or claim — only because it is the Divine's Will or out of love for the Divine.

*

Your object is not only to practise Yoga for your own internal progress and perfection, but also to do a work for the Divine.

*

This is not an Asram like others — the members are not Sannyasis; it is not *mokṣa* that is the sole aim of the Yoga here. What is being done here is a preparation for a work — a work which will be founded on Yogic consciousness and Yoga-Shakti, and can have no other foundation. Meanwhile every member here is expected to do some work in the Asram as part of his spiritual preparation.

*

Recommendation to X not to take you away but to let you realise the Divine first has no meaning. Must one realise the Divine before one can serve him or is not service of the Divine a step on the way to realisation and a help towards it? In any case, the service and the realisation are both necessary for a complete Yoga and one cannot fix an unalterable rule of precedence between the two.

*

X has to learn to consecrate his work and feel the Mother's power working through it. A purely sedentary subjective realisation is only a half realisation.

Work without Personal Motives

The only work that spiritually purifies is that which is done without personal motives, without desire for fame or public recognition or worldly greatness, without insistence on one's own mental motives or vital lusts and demands or physical preferences, without vanity or crude self-assertion or claim for position or prestige, done for the sake of the Divine alone and at the command of the Divine. All work done in an egoistic spirit, however good for people in the world of the Ignorance, is of no avail to the seeker of the Yoga.

*

It is the spirit and the consciousness in which it is done that makes an action Yogic — it is not the action itself.

*

Work and Yoga

To do anything for a reward is contrary to the rule of Yoga. One must do a thing because it is right or else do it for the Divine, not for a reward.

*

The difficulties will disappear when you have succeeded in consecrating yourself and your work and business entirely and without any internal division to the Divine.

Men usually work and carry on their affairs from the ordinary motives of the vital being, need, desire of wealth or success or position or power or fame or the push to activity and the pleasure of manifesting their capacities, and they succeed or fail according to their capability, power of work and the good or bad fortune which is the result of their nature and their Karma. When one takes up the Yoga and wishes to consecrate one's life to the Divine, these ordinary motives of the vital being have no longer their full and free play; they have to be replaced by another, a mainly psychic and spiritual motive, which will enable the sadhak to work with the same force as before, no longer for himself, but for the Divine. If the ordinary vital motives or vital force can no longer act freely and yet are not replaced by something else, then the push or force put into the work may decline or the power to command success may no longer be there. For the sincere sadhak the difficulty can only be temporary; but he has to see the defect in his consecration or his attitude and to remove it. Then the divine Power itself will act through him and use his capacity and vital force for its ends. In your case it is the psychic being and a part of the mind that have drawn you to the Yoga and were predisposed to it, but the vital nature or at least a large part of it has not yet put itself into line with the psychic movement. There is not as yet the full and undivided consecration of the active vital nature.

The signs of the consecration of the vital in action are these among others:

The feeling (not merely the idea or the aspiration) that all the life and the work are the Mother's and a strong joy of the vital nature in this consecration and surrender. A consequent calm content and disappearance of egoistic attachment to the work and its personal results, but at the same time a great joy in the work and in the use of the capacities for the divine purpose.

The feeling that the Divine Force is working behind one's actions and leading at every moment.

A persistent faith which no circumstance or event can break.

If difficulties occur, they raise not mental doubts or an inert acquiescence, but the firm belief that, with sincere consecration, the Divine Shakti will remove the difficulties, and with this belief a greater turning to her and dependence on her for that purpose. When there is full faith and consecration, there comes also a receptivity to the Force which makes one do the right thing and take the right means and then circumstances adapt themselves and the result is visible.

To arrive at this condition the important thing is a persistent aspiration, call and self-offering, and a will to reject all in oneself or around that stands in the way. Difficulties there will always be at the beginning and for as long a time as is necessary for the change; but they are bound to disappear if they are met by a settled faith, will and patience.

The Karmayoga of the Gita

I do not usually undertake the guidance of any except those who accept my own way of Yoga and show some signs of having a special call to it.

All I can suggest to him is to practise some kind of Karmayoga — remembering the Supreme in all his actions from the smallest to the greatest, doing them with a quiet mind and without ego-sense or attachment and offering them to Him as a sacrifice. He may also try or aspire to feel the presence of the Divine Shakti behind the world and its forces, distinguish between the lower nature of the Ignorance and the higher divine nature whose character is absolute calm, peace, power, Light and Bliss and aspire to be raised and led gradually from the lower to the higher.

If he can do this, he will become fit in time to dedicate

himself to the Divine and lead a wholly spiritual life.

*

The line that seems to be natural to him is the Karmayoga and he is therefore right in trying to live according to the teaching of the Gita; for the Gita is the great guide on this path. Purification from egoistic movements and from personal desire and the faithful following of the best light one has are a preliminary training for this path, and so far as he has followed these things he has been on the right way, but to ask for strength and light in one's action must not be regarded as an egoistic movement, for they are necessary in one's inner development.

Obviously, a more systematic and intensive sadhana is desirable or, in any case, a steady aspiration and a more constant preoccupation with the central aim could bring an established detachment even in the midst of outer things and outer activity and a continuous guidance. The completeness, the Siddhi of this way of Yoga — I speak of the separate path of Karma or spiritual action — begins when one is luminously aware of the Guide and the guidance and when one feels the Power working with oneself as the instrument and the participator in the divine work.

*

I gather from X's letter to you that he has been following a very sound method in his practice and has attained some good results. The first step in Karmayoga of this kind is to diminish and finally get rid of the ego-centric position in works, the lower vital reactions and the principle of desire. He must certainly go on on this road until he reaches something like its end. I would not wish to deflect him from that in any way.

What I had in view when I spoke [*in the preceding letter*] of a systematic sadhana was the adoption of a method which would generalise the whole attitude of the consciousness so as to embrace all its movements at a time instead of working only upon details — although that working is always necessary. I may cite as an example the practice of the separation of the Prakriti and the Purusha, the conscious being standing back detached from all the movements of Nature and observing them as witness and knower and finally as the giver (or refuser) of the sanction and at the highest stage of development, the Ishwara, the pure will, master of the whole nature.

By intensive sadhana I meant the endeavour to arrive at one of the great positive realisations which would be a firm base for the whole movement. I observe that he speaks of sometimes getting a glimpse of some wide calm when he feels the leading of Vyasa. A descent of this wide calm permanently into the consciousness is one of the realisations of which I was thinking. That he feels it at such times seems to indicate that he may have the capacity of receiving and retaining it. If that happened or if the Prakriti-Purusha realisation came, the whole sadhana would proceed on a strong permanent base with a new and entirely Yogic consciousness instead of the purely mental endeavour which is always difficult and slow. I do not however want to press these things upon him; they come in their own time and to press towards them prematurely does not always hasten their coming. Let him continue with his primary task of self-purification and self-preparation; I shall always be ready to give him what silent help I can.

*

I do not know that it is possible for me to give any guidance on the path you have chosen — it is at any rate difficult for me to say anything definite without more precise data than those contained in your letter.

There is no need for you to change the line of life and work you have chosen so long as you feel that to be the way of your nature (*svabhāva*) or dictated to you by your inner being or, for some reason, it is seen to be your proper dharma. These are the three tests and apart from that I do not know if there is any fixed line of conduct or way of work or life that can be laid down for the yoga of the Gita. It is the spirit or consciousness in which the work is done that matters most; the outer form can vary greatly for different natures. This, so long as one does not get the settled experience of the Divine Power taking up one's works and doing them; afterwards it is the Power which determines what is to be done or not done.

The overcoming of all attachments must necessarily be difficult and cannot come except as the fruit of a long *sādhanā* — unless there is a rapid general growth in the inner spiritual experience which is the substance of the Gita's teaching. The cessation of desire of the fruit, of the attachment to the work itself, the growth of equality to all beings, to all happenings, to good repute or ill repute, praise or blame, to good fortune or ill fortune, the dropping of the ego which are necessary for the loss of all attachments can come completely only when all work becomes a spontaneous sacrifice to the Divine, the heart is offered up to Him and one has the settled experience of the Divine in all things and all beings. This consciousness or experience must come in all parts and movements of the being, *sarvabhāvena*, not only in the mind and idea; then the falling away of all attachments becomes easy. I speak of the Gita's way of yoga, for in the ascetic life one obtains the same object differently, by cutting away from the objects of attachment and the consequent atrophy of the attachment itself through rejection and disuse.

*

If I have not written to you, it is because I could not add anything to what I had already written before to you. I cannot promise that within a given time you will have a result which will enable you either to go out into the world with a stronger spirit or succeed in the Yoga. For the Yoga you yourself say that you have not yet the whole mind for it and without the whole mind success is hardly possible in sadhana. For the other it is hardly the function of sadhana to prepare a man for ordinary life in the world. There is one thing only that could work in a direction which would help you to something which is not that, but still not the whole Yoga for which you intimate that you are not wholly ready. It is if you get the spirit of the Yoga of works as it is indicated in the Gita — forget yourself and your miseries in the aspiration to a larger consciousness, feel the greater Force working in the world and make yourself an instrument for a work to be done, however small it may be. But, whatever the way may be, you must accept it wholly and put your whole will into it — with a divided and wavering will you cannot hope for success in anything, neither in life nor in Yoga.

*

That is the ordinary Karmayoga in which the sadhak chooses his own work but offers it to the Divine — it is given to him in the sense that he is moved to it through some impulsion of his mind or heart or vital and feels that there is some cosmic power or *the* cosmic Power behind the impulsion and he tries to train himself to see the One Force behind all actions working out in him and others the cosmic Purpose.

Once he has the ideal of the direct surrender he has to find the direct moving or Guidance — that is why he rejects all that he sees to be merely mental, vital or physical impulsions coming from his own or universal Nature. Of course the full significance of the surrender comes out only when he is ready.

*

Any work can be done as a field for the practice of the spirit of the Gita.

*

The ordinary life consists in work for personal aim and satisfaction of desire under some mental or moral control, touched sometimes by a mental ideal. The Gita's Yoga consists in the offering of one's work as a sacrifice to the Divine, the conquest of desire, egoless and desireless action, bhakti for the Divine, an entering into the cosmic consciousness, the sense of unity with all creatures, oneness with the Divine. This Yoga adds the bringing down of the supramental Light and Force (its ultimate aim) and the transformation of the nature.

No Vital Demand in Work

The Mother had spoken to X, after receiving your letter, for arranging for the increase of your work. But now as you say you do not want the work and have given it up, there is nothing to be done. It is indeed unprofitable to do any work in this spirit of vital demand and unrest and impatience. I may add that the frown in Mother's eyes and her serious face existed only in the imagination of your restless and excited vital mind; the Mother's eyes and face could not have expressed something quite absent from her feelings or intention.

It is because you showed an intention of doing the sadhana in full earnest that we considered it necessary to point out to you that it could not be done without work or by mere solitary meditation, for that is the nature of this sadhana. We did not impose any work on you, but left it to you to choose. You yourself suggested the kitchen work and afterwards asked for an increase of it.

It is not possible to get peace of mind if you indulge in vital ego and the turbulent play of the vital mind, revolt, demand and impatience. Abhiman, revolt, violent insistence on the satisfaction of claims and wishes are foreign to the spirit of the Yoga, they can only bring disturbance and trouble. If you want peace of mind and true sadhana, the first thing you have to do is to cease regarding all these things as justified or justifiable or insisting on them. You must recognise that in allowing all this to rise in you, it is you yourself who have created your own trouble and you must resolutely separate yourself from these things and clear them out of you. Till you are firm in doing that, nothing can be done, — till then no spiritual progress or achievement is possible.

*

That is the most important thing to get over — ego, anger, personal dislikes, self-regarding sensitiveness etc. Work is not only for work's sake, but as a field of sadhana, for getting rid of the lower personality and its reactions and acquiring a full surrender to the Divine. As for the work itself it must be done according to the organisation arranged or sanctioned by the Mother. You must always remember that it is her work and not personally yours.

The Utility of Work

To keep up work helps to keep up the balance between the internal experience and the external development; otherwise one-sidedness and want of measure and balance may develop. Moreover, it is necessary to keep the sadhana of work for the Divine, because in the end that enables the sadhak to bring out the inner progress into the external nature and life and helps the integrality of the sadhana.

*

It is not at all a question of usefulness — although your work is very useful when you put yourself into it. Work is part of the sadhana, and in sadhana the question of usefulness does not arise, that is an outward practical measure of things, though even in the outward ordinary life utility is not the only measure. The question is of aspiration to the Divine, whether that is your central aim in life, your inner need or not. Sadhana for oneself is another matter — one can take it up or leave it. The real sadhana is for the Divine — it is the soul's need and one cannot give it up even if in moments of despondency one thinks one can.

*

Work here and work done in the world are of course not the same thing. The work there is not in any way a divine work in special — it is ordinary work in the world. But still one must take it as a training and do it in the spirit of karmayoga — what matters there is not the nature of the work in itself but the spirit in which it is done. It must be in the spirit of the Gita, without desire, with detachment, without repulsion, but doing it as perfectly as possible, not for the sake of the family or promotion or to please the superiors, but simply because it is the thing that has been given in the hand to do. It is a field of inner training, nothing more. One has to learn in it three things, equality, desirelessness, dedication. It is not the work as a thing for its own sake, but one's doing of it and one's way of doing it that one has to dedicate to the Divine. Done in that spirit it does not matter what the work is. If one trains oneself spiritually like that, then one will be ready to do in the true way whatever special work directly for the Divine (such as the Asram work) one may any day be given to do.

*

Yes, obviously, that is one great utility of work that it tests the nature and puts the sadhak in front of the defects of his outer being which might otherwise escape him.

*

It will be better to do the work as a sadhana for getting rid of the defects rather than accept the defects as a reason for not doing the work. Instead of accepting these reactions as if they were an unchangeable law of your nature, you should make up your mind that they must come no longer — calling down the aid of the Mother's force to purify the vital and eliminate them altogether. If you believe that the trouble in the body must come, naturally it will come; rather fix in your mind the idea and will that it must not come and will not come. If it tries to come reject it and throw it away from you.

*

The actions are of importance only as expressing what is in the nature. You have to be conscious of whatever in your actions is not in harmony with the Yoga and to get rid of it. But for that what is needed is your own consciousness, the psychic, observing from within and throwing off what is seen to be undesirable.

*

For the sadhak outward struggles, troubles, calamities are only a means of surmounting ego and rajasic desire and attaining to complete surrender. So long as one insists on success, one is doing the work partly at least for the ego; difficulties and outward failures come to warn one that it is so and to bring complete equality. This does not mean that the power of victory is not to be acquired; but it is not success in the immediate work that is all-important; it is the power to receive and transmit a greater and greater correct vision and inner Force that has to be developed and this must be done quite coolly and patiently without being elated or disturbed by immediate victory or failure.

Right Attitude in Work

The spiritual effectivity of work of course depends on the inner attitude. What is important is the spirit of offering put into the work. If one can in addition remember the Mother in the work or through a certain concentration feel the Mother's presence or force sustaining or doing the work, that carries the spiritual effectivity still farther. But even if one cannot in moments of clouding, depression or struggle do these things, yet there can be behind a love or bhakti which was the original motive power of the work and that can remain behind the cloud and reemerge like the sun after dark periods. All sadhana is like that and it is why one should not be discouraged by the dark moments, but realise that the original urge is there and that therefore the dark moments are only an episode in the journey which will lead to greater progress when they are once over.

*

As for the work, it is a means of preparation, it can also be a means of growing into the inner consciousness. But then it must be done not as work only but as an offering to the Mother, without insisting on the ego, with an aspiration to feel her Force working in one, her Presence presiding over the work, seeking to give all to her, not claiming anything for oneself. That is the spirit of work offered as a sacrifice; done like that, work becomes a sadhana and a Yoga.

*

What you have to realise is that your success or failure depends, first and always, on your keeping in the right attitude and in the true psychic and spiritual atmosphere and allowing the Mother's force to act through you.

If I can judge from your letters, you take its support too much for granted and lay the first stress on your own ideas and plans and words about the work; but these whether good or bad, right or mistaken, are bound to fail if they are not instruments of the true Force. You have to be always concentrated, always referring all difficulties for solution to the force that is being sent from here, always letting it act and not substituting your own mind and separate vital will or impulse.

Proceed with your work, never forgetting the condition of success. Do not lose yourself in the work or in your ideas or plans or forget to keep yourself in constant touch with the true source. Do not allow anybody's mind or vital influence or the influence of the surrounding atmosphere or the ordinary human mentality to come between you and the power and presence of the Mother.

*

You know what is the right thing to do — to take and keep the necessary inner attitude — when there is the openness to the Force and the strength, courage and power in action coming from it, outward circumstances can be met and turned in the right direction.

Equanimity in Work

Helpless acceptance [*of difficulties*] is no part of the Yoga of works — what is necessary is a calm equanimity in the face both of helpful and adverse, fortunate or unfortunate happenings, good or evil fortune, success or failure of effort. One must learn to bear without flinching and disturbance, without rajasic joy or grief, doing all that is necessary, but not dejected if difficulties or failure come — one still goes on doing what can be done, not sinking under the burden of life.

*

To keep this equanimity and absence of reactions and from that calm ground to direct the Yoga-force on things and persons (not for egoistic aims but for the work to be done) is the position of the Yogi.

*

This is the right inner attitude, of equality — to remain unmoved whatever may outwardly happen. But what is needed for success in the outward field (if you do not use human means, diplomacy or tactics) is the power to transmit calmly a Force that can change men's attitude and the circumstances and make any outward action taken at once the right thing to do and effective.

*

You have to make yourself an instrument of the invisible Force — to be able in a way to direct it to the required point and for the required purpose. But for that samata must be entire — for a calm and luminous use of the Force is necessary. Otherwise the use of the Force, if accompanied by ego-reactions, may raise a corresponding ego-resistance and a struggle.

*

The increase of samata is only a first condition [*for attacks by adverse forces to become impossible in one's work*]. It is when on the basis of samata an understanding Force can be used to make their attacks nugatory that the attacks will become impossible.

The Impersonal Worker

To be impersonal, generally, is not to be ego-centric, not to regard things from the point of view of how they affect oneself, — but to see what things are in themselves, to judge impartially, to do what is demanded by the purpose of things or by the will of the Master of things, not by one's own personal point of view or egoistic interest or ego-formed idea or feeling. In work it is to do what is best for the work, without regard to one's own prestige or convenience, not to regard the work as one's own but as the Mother's, to do it according to rule, discipline, impersonal arrangement, even if conditions are not favourable to do the best according to the conditions etc. etc. The impersonal worker puts his best capacity, zeal, industry into the work, but not his personal ambitions, vanity, passions. He has always something in view that is greater than his little personality and his devotion or obedience to that dictates his conduct.

*

Your difficulty in work is that you regard it too much as your work and from your personal point of view. So questions of personal convenience, ideas, way of doing things, prestige, demands take a big place — and the result is quarrels. You have to learn to be impersonal. Even in the world work cannot be well done without that. How much more necessary is it for a sadhak of Yoga!

Service of the Divine

There should be no straining after power, no ambition, no egoism of power. The power or powers that come should be considered not as one's own, but as gifts of the Divine for the Divine's purpose. Care should be taken that there should be no ambitious or selfish misuse, no pride or vanity, no sense of superiority, no claim or egoism of the instrument, only a simple and pure psychic instrumentation of the nature in any way in which it is fit for the service of the Divine.

*

To be free from all egoistic motive, careful of truth in speech and action, void of self-will and self-assertion, watchful in all things is the condition for being a flawless servant.

*

Yes, the use to which you have turned your vital capacities in Bengal and Bombay, — to turn them into instruments of service and the Divine Work, is certainly the best possible. Through such action and such use of the vital power, one can certainly progress in Yoga. Vital power is necessary for work and you have an exceptional amount of it. Of course, to make a full Yogic use of it and of its force for action, the ego must gradually fade out and vital attachments and impulses be replaced by the spiritual motive. Bhakti, devotion to the Divine, and the spirit of service to the Divine are among the most powerful means for this change.

*

Reading and study though they can be useful for preparing the mind, are not themselves the best means of entering the Yoga. It is self-dedication from within that is the means. It is with the consciousness of the Mother that you must unite, a sincere self-consecration in the mind and heart and the Will is the means for it. The work given by the Mother is always meant as field for that self-consecration, it has to be done as an offering to her so that through the self-offering one may come to feel her force acting and her presence.

*

If one went to the Himalayas, the likelihood is that one would make oneself fit for inactive meditation and quite unfit for life and the Mother's service — so in the next life the character would be like that. This is simply the influence of old ideas that have no application in this Yoga. It is here in the life near the Mother, in the work itself that one must become fit to be a perfect instrument of the Mother.

*

All acts are included in action, — work is action regulated towards a fixed end and methodically and constantly done, service is work done for the Mother's purpose and under her direction.

All Work Equal in the Eyes of the Spirit

Self-dedication does not depend on the particular work you do, but on the spirit in which all work, of whatever kind it may be, is done. Any work, done well and carefully as a sacrifice to the Divine, without desire or egoism, with equality of mind and calm tranquillity in good or bad fortune, for the sake of the Divine and not for the sake of any personal gain, reward or result, with the consciousness that it is the Divine Power to which all work belongs, is a means of self-dedication through Karma.

*

Like the vital disturbance the physical inertia with all its symptoms is an attack of the hostile forces intended to cut short and prevent the higher opening. The ideas that arise to justify it are of no value — it is not true that physical work is of an inferior value to mental culture, it is the arrogance of the intellect that makes the claim. All work done for the Divine is equally divine; manual labour done for the Divine is more divine than mental culture done for one's own development, fame or mental satisfaction.

This inertia, numbness, pain should be thrown off with the same resolution as the vital disturbances. The only peculiarity of it in your case is the persistent violence of the attack as in the case of the vital — otherwise it is what others get also; but each time they reject, call on the Mother and get free, after a little time if the attack is violent, at once if it is of a lesser character.

If there is temporary physical inability, one can take rest but solely for the purpose of recovering the physical energy. The idea of giving up physical work for mental self-development is a creation of the mental ego.

*

Of course the idea of bigness and smallness is quite foreign to the spiritual truth. Spiritually there is nothing big or small. Such ideas are like those of the literary people who think writing a poem is a high work and making shoes or cooking the dinner is a small and low one. But all is equal in the eyes of the Spirit — and it is only the spirit within with which it is done that matters. It is the same with a particular kind of work, there is nothing big or small.

*

In the wider consciousness one can deal with the small as well as the high things, but one comes to deal with them with a larger as well as a profounder, subtler and more accurate view coming from a more and more understanding and luminous consciousness so that the thoughts about small things also cease to be themselves small or trivial, being more and more part of a higher knowledge.

*

One must be able to do the same work always with enthusiasm and at the same time be ready to do something else or enlarge one's scope at a moment's notice.

*

The sadhak ought to be ready to do any work that is needed, not only the work he prefers.

*

It is not that you have to do what you dislike, but that you have to cease to dislike. To do only what you like is to indulge the vital and maintain its domination over the nature — for that is the very principle of the untransformed nature, to be governed by its likes and dislikes. To be able to do anything with equanimity is the principle of karmayoga and to do it with joy because it is done for the Mother is the true psychic and vital condition in this Yoga.

*

There are those who have done the lawyer's work with the Mother's force working in them and grown by it in inward consciousness. On the other hand religious work can be merely external and vital in its nature or influence.

*

I may say however that I do not regard business as something evil or tainted, any more than it was so regarded in ancient spiritual India. If I did, I would not be able to receive money from X or from those of our disciples who in Bombay trade with East Africa; nor could we then encourage them to go on with their work but would have to tell them to throw it up and attend to their spiritual progress alone. How are we to reconcile X's seeking after spiritual light and his mill? Ought I not to tell him to leave his mill to itself and to the devil and go into some Ashram to meditate? Even if I myself had had the command to do business as I had the command to do politics I would have done it without the least spiritual or moral compunction. All depends on the spirit in which a thing is done, the principle on which it is built and use to which it is turned. I have done politics and the most violent kind of revolutionary politics, *ghoraṁ karma*, and I have supported war and sent men to it, even though politics is not always or often a very clean occupation nor can war be called a spiritual line of action. But Krishna calls upon Arjuna to carry on war of the most terrible kind and by his example encourage men to do every kind of human work, *sarvakarmāṇi*. Do you contend that Krishna was an unspiritual man and that his advice to Arjuna was mistaken or wrong in principle? Krishna goes farther and declares that a man by doing in the right way and in the right spirit the work dictated to him by his fundamental nature, temperament and capacity and according to his and its dharma can move towards the Divine. He validates the function and dharma of the Vaishya as well as of the Brahmin and Kshatriya. It is in his view quite possible for a man to do business and make money and earn profits and yet be a spiritual man, practise Yoga, have an inner life. The Gita is constantly justifying works as a means of spiritual salvation and enjoining a Yoga of works as well as of Bhakti and Knowledge. Krishna, however, superimposes a higher law also that work must be done without desire, without attachment to any fruit or reward, without any egoistic attitude or motive, as an offering or sacrifice to the Divine. This is the traditional Indian attitude towards these things, that all work can be done if it is done according to the dharma and, if it is rightly done, it does not prevent the approach to the Divine or the access to spiritual knowledge and the spiritual life.

There is of course also the ascetic ideal which is necessary for many and has its place in the spiritual order. I would myself say that no man can be spiritually complete if he cannot live ascetically or follow a life as bare as the barest anchorite's. Obviously, greed for wealth and money-making has to be absent from his nature as much as greed for food or any other greed and all attachment to these things must be renounced from his consciousness. But I do not regard the ascetic way of living as indispensable to spiritual perfection or as identical with it. There is the way of spiritual self-mastery and the way of spiritual self-giving and surrender to the Divine, abandoning ego and desire even in the midst of action or of any kind of work or all kinds of work demanded from us by the Divine. If it were not so, there would not have been great spiritual men like Janaka or Vidura in India and even there would have been no Krishna or else Krishna would have been not the Lord of Brindavan and Mathura and Dwarka or a prince and warrior or the charioteer of Kurukshetra, but only one more great anchorite. The Indian scriptures and Indian tradition, in the Mahabharata and elsewhere, make room both for the spirituality of the renunciation of life and for the spiritual life of action. One cannot say that one only is the Indian tradition and that the acceptance of life and works of all kinds, *sarvakarmāṇi*, is un-Indian, European or Western and unspiritual.

Interest in Work

It [*absorption in work*] depends on a certain extension and intensifying of the consciousness by which all activity becomes interesting not for itself but because of the consciousness put into it and, through the intensity of the energy, there is a pleasure in the exercise of the energy, and in the perfect doing of the work, whatever the work may be.

*

As a rule, I mean in their unchanged condition, the lower parts get interested and enthusiastic [*about work*] when the ego mixes with the interest. But the pure enthusiasm can come into them as they get more and more converted and purified and they then become very indispensable forces for the realisation.

*

It is natural for the vital or even the mind to feel energised by something new — but for the physical plane the work always repeated is the foundation — so one has to be able at least to take a steady calm interest in it always.

*

There must be the rasa [*in the work*], but it comes when there is the dynamic descent of the Power.

Joy in Work

Part of the physical cannot do without work, another part (more material) finds it an infliction. What gives the force and joy of the work is however not physical but vital.

*

The vital delight in the work is a necessary element for the work itself. Work done without it is much less easy to do and much less easy to offer.

*

Most people do things because they have to, not out of the happiness they find in the things. It is only its hobbies and penchants that the nature finds some happiness in, not usually in work — unless of course the work itself is one's hobby or penchant and can be indulged in or dropped as one likes.

*

Joy and enthusiasm and buoyancy are good things, but it must be on a basis of calm and with the head clear for work.

The reason of the difference of result between the two moods in work is that the first mood is that of a vital joy, while the other is that of a psychic quiet. Vital joy, though it is a very helpful thing for the ordinary human life, is something excited, eager, mobile without a settled basis — that is why it soon gets tired and cannot continue. Vital joy has to be replaced by a quiet settled psychic gladness with the mind and vital very clear and very peaceful. When one works on this basis, then everything becomes glad and easy, in touch with the Mother's force and fatigue or depression do not come.

Loss of Inspiration in Work

What you find happening [*a loss of inspiration*] is a common experience in all work. Mother says it is due to the fact that in beginning the work there is an inspiration of what to do and the mind at first acts as a channel for it and all goes well. Afterwards the mind begins to be acting on its own account, without one's noticing it usually unless one is very conscious and accustomed to scrutinise oneself — and do the thing without the original inspiration by its ordinary means. This is felt very clearly in work like poetry and music — for there one feels the inspiration coming and feels it failing and getting mixed up with the ordinary mind. So long as it goes on, everything is done easily and well, but as soon as the mind begins to interfere or to work in its place, then the work is less well done. In work like cooking one does not directly and vividly feel the inspiration, only a brightness and perceptiveness and confidence perhaps — so also one does not notice when the physical mind becomes active. In a thing like poetry one can break off till the inspiration comes again, but in cooking one can't do that, the work has to be finished there and then. I suppose this can be remedied only by one's becoming more conscious within as one does in sadhana, till one can see and counteract the wrong movement of inferior mental activity by bringing down of one's will again the right inspiration and perception.

Thoughts of Sadhana during Work

Thoughts of sadhana can go on very well along with work. To combine the inner spiritual consciousness and its growth with a consecrated outer activity is part of the Yoga.

*

I don't think any attempt should be made [*to turn inwards or revert to thoughts of sadhana during work*]. If the thoughts of sadhana come of themselves or the turning inwards or a silent aspiration to sadhana, that is all right.

Chapter Two

Becoming Conscious in Work

Working from Within

You must learn to act always from within — from your inner being which is in contact with the Divine. The outer should be a mere instrument and should not be allowed at all to compel or dictate your speech, thought or action.

*

All should be done quietly from within — working, speaking, reading, writing as part of the real consciousness — not with the dispersed and unquiet movement of the ordinary consciousness.

*

One can work and remain quiet within. Quietude does not mean having an empty mind or doing no action at all.

*

When one is concentrated within, the body can go on doing its work by the Force acting within it. Even the external consciousness can work separately under the motion of the Force while the rest of the consciousness is in concentration.

*

It is a little difficult at first to combine the inward condition with the attention to the outward work and mingling with others, but a time comes when it is possible for the inner being to be in full union with the Mother while the action comes out of that concentrated union and is consciously guided in all its details so that some part of the consciousness can attend to everything outside, even be concentrated upon it and yet feel the inward concentration in the Mother.

*

It is a very good sign that even in spite of full work the inner working was felt behind and succeeded in establishing the silence. A time comes for the sadhak in the end when the consciousness and the deeper experience go on happening even in full work or in sleep, while speaking or in any kind of activity.

*

It is probably because at the time of the work the tendency of the consciousness to externalise itself is greater (that is always the case), so the pressure grows stronger in order to produce a contrary inward tendency. This produces some tendency to go inside in the way of a complete internalisation (going into a sort of samadhi); but what should happen during work is a going inside in a wakeful condition and becoming aware of the psychic within as you used to do under the pressure while the outer mind does the work. This is the condition that must eventually come.

*

The stress of the Power is all right, but there is really nothing incompatible between the inner silence and action. It is to that combination that the sadhana must move.

*

It [*concentration of the inner consciousness*] can happen in several forms. It can become concentrated in silence as the witness — it can become concentrated in the feeling of the Divine Force flowing through it, the work being a result — it can become concentrated in the feeling of the presence of the Divine or the Ananda or love of the Divine while the working goes on separately in front. All this becomes so habitual that it goes on of itself without the need of call or effort or even of the mind's attention — it simply *is* there. There are other possibilities besides those mentioned above, but these are perhaps the most common.

*

It is perfectly possible to do work in an entire emptiness

without any interference or activity of the lower parts of the consciousness.

Working with a Double Consciousness

One can both aspire and attend to the work and do many other things at the same time when the consciousness is developed by Yoga.

*

It [*peace and contact in work, but no aspiration*] is because the energy is put outward in the work. But as the peace and contact grow a double consciousness can develop — one engaged in the work, another behind silent and observing or turned towards the Divine — in this consciousness the aspiration can be maintained even while the external consciousness is turned towards the work.

*

That is how the consciousness must work when it lives in the Divine. One part of the Force in it works and offers the work to the Mother, another part lives in the experience of the Mother, the third hears what the others say and answers without losing the inner consciousness.

*

No — it is only if it [*turning inwards during work*] is an inner absorption that it would come in the way. But what I mean is a sort of stepping backward into something silent and observant within which is not involved in the action, yet sees and can shed its light upon it. There are then two parts of the being, one inner looking at and witnessing and knowing, the other executive and instrumental and doing. This gives not only freedom but power — and in this inner being one can get into touch with the Divine not through mental activity but through the substance of the being, by a certain inward touch, perception, reception, receiving also the right inspiration or intuition of the work.

*

If one feels a consciousness not limited by the work, a consciousness behind supporting that which works, then it is easier [*to keep higher thoughts during work*]. That usually comes either by the wideness and silence fixing and extending itself or by the consciousness of a Force not oneself working through the worker.

*

Before things become pucca in the consciousness, the doing of work does carry the consciousness outward unless one has made it a sadhana to feel the "Force greater than oneself" working through one. That I suppose is why the Shankarites considered work to be in its own nature an operation of the Ignorance and incompatible with a condition of realisation. But as a matter of fact there are three stages there: (I) in which the work brings you to a lower as well as outer consciousness so that you have afterwards to recover the realisation; (II) in which the work brings you out, but the realisation remains behind (or above), not felt while you work, but as soon as the work ceases you find it there just as it was; (III) in which the work makes no difference, for the realisation or spiritual condition remains through the work itself. You seem this time to have experienced No. II.

*

In action it is always more difficult [*to keep a higher state of consciousness*] because the consciousness goes out towards the work or else is at least not wholly held within — it is therefore difficult to remain in an inward state. There is no other obstacle. But if the inward state is strong and habitual, then it gains upon the action also and at first one always feels it behind and afterwards it occupies the whole consciousness, outer included, and the action takes place in it. This is for static states like peace, self-realisation etc. If one has the realisation of the dynamic Force, there is no difficulty — because that can take up the action at once.

Absorption in Work

It is the external mind that gets absorbed in the work and

covers what is behind. There must be a double consciousness, one acting, one behind observing, separate, free to continue the sadhana.

*

The absorption in work is not undesirable — but the difficulty in turning inwards can only be temporary. A certain plasticity in the physical consciousness which is sure to come makes it easy to turn from one concentration to another.

*

It [*meditative absorption during work*] depends on the plasticity of the consciousness. Some are like that, they get so absorbed they don't want to come out or do anything else. One has to keep a certain balance by which the fundamental consciousness remains able to turn from one concentration to another with ease.

*

This tendency [*to be possessed by work*] has its advantage and disadvantage. It gets things done, but it prevents plasticity in the work. One must get free from the "possession" by the urge of the energy, but keep the drive and be able to distribute it at will.

*

Absorption in work is inevitable. It is enough to offer it when beginning and ending and to encourage the attitude to grow = for You and by You.

*

It is a certain inertia in the physical consciousness which shuts it up in the groove of what it is doing so that it is fixed in that and not free to remember [*the Mother*].

Remembering the Presence in Work

It is not at first easy to remember the presence in work; but if one revives the sense of the presence immediately after the work is over it is all right. In time the sense of the presence will become automatic even in work.

*

All the difficulties you describe are quite natural things common to most people. It is easy for one, comparatively, to remember and be conscious when one sits quiet in meditation; it is difficult when one has to be busy with work. The remembrance and consciousness in work have to come by degrees, you must not expect to have it all at once; nobody can get it all at once. It comes in two ways, — first, if one practises remembering the Mother and offering the work to her each time one does something (not all the time one is doing, but at the beginning or whenever one can remember), then that slowly becomes easy and habitual to the nature. Secondly, by the meditation an inner consciousness begins to develop which, after a time, not at once or suddenly, becomes more and more automatically permanent. One feels this as a separate consciousness from that outer one which works. At first this separate consciousness is not felt when one is working, but as soon as the work stops one feels it was there all the time watching from behind; afterwards it begins to be felt during the work itself, as if there were two parts of oneself — one watching and supporting from behind and remembering the Mother and offering to her and the other doing the work. When this happens, then to work with the true consciousness becomes more and more easy.

It is the same with all the rest. It is by the development of the inner consciousness that all the things you speak of will be set right. For instance it is a part of the being that has *utsāha* for the work, another that feels the pressure of quietude and is not so disposed to work. Your mood depends on which comes up at the time — it is so with all people. To combine the two is difficult, but a time comes when they do get reconciled — one remains poised in an inner concentration while the other is supported by it in its push towards work. The transformation of the nature, the harmonising of all these discordant things in the being are the work of sadhana. Therefore you need not be discouraged by observing these things in you. There is hardly anybody who has not found these things in himself. All this can be arranged by the action of the inner Force with the constant consent and call of the sadhak. By himself he might not be able to do it, but with the Divine Force working within all can be done.

*

The resistance you speak of and the insufficient receptivity and the inability to continue in communion while doing work, must all be due to some part of the physical consciousness that is still not open to the Light — probably something in the vital physical and the material subconscient which stands in the way of the physical mind being in its mass free and responsive.

There is no harm in raising the aspiration from below to meet the power from above. All that you have to be careful about is not to raise up the difficulty from below before the descending Power is ready to remove it.

There is no necessity of losing consciousness when you meditate. It is the widening and change of the consciousness that is essential. If you mean going inside, you can do that without losing consciousness.

Inner Guidance about Work

It is good that you were able to observe yourself all the time and see the movements and that the intervention of the new consciousness was frequent and automatic. At a later stage you will no doubt get a guidance in the mind also as to how to do the things you want to get done. Evidently your mind was too active — as well as the minds of others also — and so you missed your objective, owing to the excessive multitude of witnesses! However —

*

If you want that [*to become conscious of whether an action is right or not*] very much and aspire for it, it may come in one of several ways —

(1) You may get the habit or faculty of watching your movements in such a way that you see the impulse to action coming and can see too its nature,

(2) a consciousness may come which feels uneasy at once if a wrong thought or impulse to action or feeling is there,

(3) something within you may warn and stop you when you are going to do the wrong action.

*

As for the feeling from within, it depends on being able to go inside. Sometimes it comes of itself with the deepening of the consciousness by bhakti or otherwise; sometimes it comes by practice — a sort of referring the matter and listening for the answer — listening is of course a metaphor but it is difficult to express it otherwise — it doesn't mean that the answer comes necessarily in the shape of words, spoken or unspoken, though it does sometimes or for some; it can take any shape. The main difficulty for many is *to be sure of the right answer*. For that it is necessary to be able to contact the consciousness of the Guru inwardly — that comes best by bhakti. Otherwise it may become a delicate and ticklish job. Obstacles, (1) normal habit of relying on outward means for everything, (2) ego, substituting its suggestions for the right answer, (3) mental activity, (4) intruder nuisances. I think you need not be eager for this, but rely on the growth of the inner consciousness. The above is only by way of general explanation.

*

A constant aspiration for that [*to be constantly governed by the Divine*] is the first thing — next a sort of stillness within and a drawing back from the outward action into the stillness and a sort of listening expectancy, not for a sound but for the spiritual feeling or direction of the consciousness that comes through the psychic.

*

Your difficulty is that you worry yourself and think you have made mistakes when you have made none. If you want to get the right guidance, you must have more confidence and not always think that what comes to you is wrong and your work is bad and ugly. You generally get things right. If you do make a mistake here and there, it does not matter; everybody makes some mistakes; but by making them one can learn better.

Another thing is that, as I have told you, a thing can be done in several ways, all of which are good — but your mind seems to go on the feeling that one thing is good or true and all the rest is bad or false and, as it were, is seeking for the one only good way and then in everything it does it feels dissatisfied. When you have found a way of doing the work, it is better to do it and not always be worrying yourself for something better.

*

It is always the restlessness that makes you lose touch. If you are not sure about the work, remain quiet and you will get in time the idea of what to do; if you worry and are restless, you get confused and disturbed and can no longer feel connection with the Force, though it is always there above you and supporting you. As to blind selfish feelings, they are still more confusing and disturbing; but here too the only thing is to remain quiet, detach yourself, disown and throw away the feeling. To get upset, disturbed and in despair, is no use; it only prolongs the confusion and unrest and prevents you from feeling the connection.

*

Openness in work means the same thing as openness in the consciousness. The same Force that works in your consciousness in meditation and clears away the cloud and confusion whenever you open to it, can also take up your action and not only make you aware of the defects in it but keep you conscious of what is to be done and guide your mind and hands to do it. If you open to it in your work, you will begin to feel this guidance more and more until behind all your activities you will be aware of the Force of the Mother.

*

Why should you try the same things as the others? What one feels inspired to do, is the best thing for one.

Knowing the Divine Will

There is a consciousness other than mind and vital — if there were not, there would be no use in doing sadhana. The true will belongs to that consciousness.

*

When the mind is pure and the psychic prominent, then one feels what is according to the Divine Will and what is against it.

*

For the actions to be psychic, the psychic must be in front. The observing Purusha can separate himself, but cannot change the Prakriti. But to be the observing Purusha is a first step. Afterwards there must be the action of the Purusha Will as an instrument of the Mother's force. This Will must be founded on a right consciousness which sees what is wrong, ignorant, selfish, egoistic, moved by desire in the nature and puts it right.

*

It needs a quiet mind [to *know the Divine Will*]. In the quiet mind turned towards the Divine the intuition (higher mind) comes of the Divine's Will and the right way to do it.

*

Once the mental silence is attained, then in that the mental thoughts can be replaced by some vision and intuition regarding the work.

*

The transcendental Will for us is the supramental Will. For that to act in you directly, it is necessary to grow upward into the consciousness above the ordinary mind and to bring down these higher ranges into the mind, life and body. Indirectly through the higher Mind and intuition the supramental Will is already acting on you, but naturally this indirect action does not bring the full power.

*

The true automatic action (full of consciousness and light) begins only when one gets into touch with the supermind. Till then aspiration and tapasya (concentration) are needed; otherwise there is a wrong automatism due to inert passivity in which wrong forces can act.

Freedom in Work

Do? why should he [*a certain Yogi*] want to do anything if he was in the eternal peace or Ananda or union with the Divine? If a man is spiritual and has gone beyond the vital and mind, he does not need to be always "doing" something. The self or spirit has the joy of its own existence. It is free to do nothing and free to do everything — but not because it is bound to action and unable to exist without it.

*

The passage[1] describes the state of consciousness when one is aloof from all things even when in their midst and all is felt to be unreal, an illusion. There are then no preferences or desires, because things are too unreal to desire or to prefer one to another. But at the same time one feels no necessity to flee the world or not to do any action, because being free from the illusion, action or living in the world does not weigh upon one, one is not bound or involved. Those who flee from the world or shun action (the Sannyasis) do so because they would be involved or bound; they believe the world to be unreal, but in fact it weighs on them as a reality so long as they are in it. When one is perfectly free from the illusion of the reality of things, then they cannot weigh on one or bind at all.

*

---

[1] *This passage is not available.* — Ed.

But the Jivanmukta feels no bondage [*in work*]. In all work and action, he feels perfectly free, because the work is not done by him personally (there is no sense of limited ego) but by the cosmic Force. The limitations of the work are those put by the cosmic Force itself on its own action. He himself lives in communion of oneness with the Transcendent which is above the cosmos and feels no limitation. That is at least how it is felt in the Overmind.

Chapter Three

The Divine Force in Work

Receiving the Divine Power or Force

To be able to receive the Divine Power and let it act through you in the things of the outward life, there are three necessary conditions:

1. Quietude, equality — not to be disturbed by anything that happens, to keep the mind still and firm, seeing the play of forces, but itself tranquil.

2. Absolute faith — faith that what is for the best will happen, but also that if one can make oneself a true instrument, the fruit will be that which one's will guided by the Divine Light sees as the thing to be done — *kartavyaṁ karma*.

3. Receptivity — the power to receive the Divine Force and to feel its presence and the presence of the Mother in it and allow it to work, guiding one's sight and will and action. If this power and presence can be felt and this plasticity made the habit of the consciousness in action, — but plasticity to the Divine Force alone without bringing in any foreign element, — the eventual result is sure.

*

What happened to you shows what are the conditions of that state in which the Divine Power takes the place of the ego and directs the action, making the mind, life and body an instrument. A receptive silence of the mind, an effacement of the mental ego and the reduction of the mental being to the position of a witness, a close contact with the Divine Power and an openness of the being to that one Influence and no other are the conditions for becoming an instrument of the Divine, moved by that and that only.

That there was no mental expectation was all to the good; if there had been an expectation, the mind might have been active and interfered and either prevented the experience or else stood in the way of its being pure and complete.

The silence of the mind does not of itself bring in the supramental consciousness; there are many states or planes or levels of consciousness between the human mind and the Supermind. The silence opens the mind and the rest of the being to greater things, sometimes to the cosmic consciousness, sometimes to the experience of the silent Self, sometimes to the presence or power of the Divine, sometimes to a higher consciousness than that of the human mind; the mind's silence is the most favourable condition for any of these things to happen. In this Yoga it is the most favourable condition (not the only one) for the Divine Power to descend first upon and then into the individual consciousness and there do its work to transform that consciousness, giving it the necessary experiences, altering all its outlook and movements, leading it from stage to stage till it is ready for the last (supramental) change.

*

What happened is a thing that often happens and — taking your account of it — it reproduced in your case the usual stages. First you sat down in prayer — that means a call to the Above, if I may so express it. Next came the necessary condition for the answer to the prayer to be effective — "little by little a sort of restfulness came", in other words, the quietude of the consciousness which is necessary before the Power that has to act can act. Then the rush of the Force or Power, "a flood of energy and sense of power and glow" and the natural concentration of the being in inspiration and expression, the action of the Power. This is the thing that used to happen daily to the physical workers in the Asram. Working with immense energy and enthusiasm, with a passion for the work they might after a time feel tired — then they would call the Mother and a sense of rest came into them and with or after it a flood of energy so that twice the amount of work could be done without the least fatigue or reaction. In many there was a spontaneous call of the vital for the Force, so that they felt the flood of energy as soon as they began the work and it continued so long as the work had to be done.

The vital is the means of effectuation on the physical plane, so its action and energy are necessary for all work — without it, if the mind only drives without the cooperation and instrumentation of the vital, there is hard and disagreeable labour and effort with results which are usually not at all of the best kind. The ideal state for work is when there is a natural concentration of the consciousness in the special energy, supported by an easeful rest and quiescence of the consciousness as a whole. Distraction of the mind by other activities disturbs this balance of ease and concentrated energy, — fatigue also disturbs or destroys it. The first thing therefore that has to be done is to bring back the supporting restfulness and this is ordinarily done by cessation of work and repose. In the experience you had that was replaced by a restfulness that came from above in answer to your station of prayer and an energy that also came from above. It is the same principle as in sadhana — the reason why we want people to make the consciousness quiet so that the higher peace may come in and on the basis of that peace a new Force from above.

It is not effort that brought the inspiration. Inspiration comes from above in answer to a state of concentration which is itself a call to it. Effort on the contrary fatigues the consciousness and therefore is not favourable to the best work; the only thing is that sometimes — by no means always — effort culminates in a pull for the inspiration which brings some answer, but it is not usually so good and effective an inspiration as that which comes when there is the easy and intense concentration of the energy in its work. Effort and expenditure of energy are not necessarily the same thing; the best expenditure of energy is that which flows easily without effort at all — when the Inspiration or Force (any Force) works of itself and the mind and vital and even body are glowing instruments and the Force flows out in an intense and happy working — an almost labourless labour.

The Working of the Force

When you have opened yourself to a higher Force, when you

have made yourself a channel for the energy of its work, it is quite natural that the Force should flow and act in the way that is wanted or the way that is needed and for the effect that is needed. Once the channel is made, the Force that acts is not necessarily bound by the personal limitations or disabilities of the instrument; it can disregard them and act in its own power. In doing so it may use the instrument simply as a medium and, as soon as the work is finished, leave him just what he was before, incapable in his ordinary moments of doing such good work, capable only when he is seized and used and illumined. But also it may by its power of transforming action set the instrument right, accustom it to the necessary intuitive knowledge and movement so that this living perfected instrument can at will call for and receive the action of the Force. In technique, there are two different things, — there is the intellectual knowledge which one has acquired and applies or thinks one is applying — there is the intuitive cognition which acts in its own right, even if it is not actually possessed by the worker so that he cannot give an adequate account of the modes of working or elements of what he has done. Many poets have a very summary theoretic knowledge of metrical or linguistic technique; they have its use but they would not be able to explain how they write or what are the qualities and constituent methods of their successful art, but they achieve all the same things that are perfect in the weaving of sounds and the skill of words, consummate in rhythm and language. Intellectual knowledge of technique is a help but a minor help; it can become a mere device or a rigid fetter. It is an intuitive divination of the right process that is more frequent and a more powerful action — or even it is an inspiration that puts the right sounds or right words without need of even any intuitive choice. This is especially true of poetry, for there are arts — those that work in a more material substance — where perfect work cannot be done without full technical knowledge, — painting, sculpture, architecture.

What the higher Force writes through you is your own in the sense that you have been an instrument of manifestation — as is indeed every artist or worker. When you put your name to it, it is the name of the instrumental creator; but for sadhana it is necessary to recognise that the real Power, the true Creator was not your surface self, you were simply the living harp on which the Musician played his tune.

The true Ananda of creation is not the pleasure of the ego in having personally done well and in being somebody, that is an extraneous element which attaches itself to the true joy of work and creation. The Ananda comes by the inrush of a larger Might and Delight, *āveśa*; there is the thrill of being possessed and used by a superpersonal Power, the exultation and exaltation of the uplifting of the consciousness, the joy of its illumination and its greatened and heightened action and the joy of the beauty, power or perfection that is being created. How far, how intensely one feels these things, depends on the condition of the consciousness at the time, the temperament, the activity of the vital, the mind's receptivity and response. The Yogi (or even certain strong and calm minds) is not carried away, as the mind and the vital often are, by the Ananda, — he holds and watches it and there is no mere excitement mixed with the divine flow of it through the conscious instrument and the body. There is a greater Ananda of *samarpaṇa*, of spiritual realisation or divine love, but in the spiritual consciousness and life the Ananda of creation has its place.

*

To observe whether it [*one's work*] is really well done or not and feel the Ananda of work done for the Mother [*is the right attitude*]. Get rid of the "I". If it is well done, it is the Force that did it and your only part was to be a good or a bad instrument.

*

It is a Force that comes and pushes to work and is as legitimately a part of the spiritual life as others. It is a special Energy that takes hold of the worker in the being and fulfils itself through him. To work with a full energy like this in one is quite salutary. The only thing is not to overdo it — that is to avoid any exhaustion or recoil to a fatigued inertia.

As for the dedication make the *saṅkalpa* always of offering it, remember and pray when you can (I mean in connection with the work). This is to fix a certain attitude. Afterwards, the Force can take advantage of this key to open the deeper dedication within.

*

I was not [*in using the phrase "allow the Force to work through you"*] speaking of the Force coming down from above, but of the Force from behind doing action through the mind and body as instruments. Very often when the mind and body are inert, their actions still go on by this push from behind.

*

You used the Force for the work, and it supported you so long as you preferred to stick to that work. What is of first importance is not the religious or non-religious character of the work done, but the inner attitude in which it is done. If the attitude is vital and not psychic, then one throws oneself out in the work and loses the inner contact. If it is psychic, the inner contact remains, the Force is felt supporting or doing the work and the sadhana progresses.

*

The Force from above is the Force of the Higher Consciousness. That from behind works as a mental, vital or physical force according to need. When the being is open to it and there is a certain passivity to its working, it takes the place of the personal activity and the Person is a witness of its action.

The Force and the Peace in Action

The dynamic action when it comes acts without disturbing the silence and peace. There is the vast peace and silence and in that the Force or the Will works to do what is necessary — in that also is the action of Agni or the psychic.

*

It is this quiet and spontaneous action that is the characteristic divine action. The aggressive action is only, as you say, when there is resistance and struggle. This does not mean that the quiet force cannot be intense. It can be more intense than the aggressive, but its intensity only increases the intensity of the peace.

*

When you feel the better condition, the peace and force at work, it is better to allow the force to work, keeping yourself still and quiet, and not try to do things by the mind.

When there is the confusion or wrong condition, then you have to call down the quiet, to try to get back to the true position, not listening to the wrong thoughts but rejecting them. If you cannot do that at once, still remain as quiet as possible and aspire and offer yourself. The Divine Force can always do more than the personal effort; so the one thing is to get quiet and call it down or back to the front — for it is always there behind or above you.

Drawing upon the Force for Energy

During the course of the sadhana one can learn to draw upon the universal Life-Force and replenish the energies from it. But usually the best way is to learn to open oneself to the Mother's Force and become conscious of it supporting and moving or pouring into the system and giving the energy needed for the work whether it be mental, vital or physical.

There is naturally a higher Energy above the present universal forces and it is that which will transform the nature and take up the mental, vital, physical energies and change them into its own likeness.

*

If you mean by failure the weakness of the body, it is due probably to your having unduly strained it in obedience to rajasic vital impulses, an effect which was increased by vital relapses into tamas and the struggle of the vital attacks you had. But also it often happens even in the ordinary course of Yoga that physical strength is replaced by a Yogic strength or Yogic life force which keeps up the body and makes it work, but in the absence of this force the body is denuded of power, inert and tamasic. This can only be remedied by the whole being opening to Yoga shakti in each of its planes — Yogic mind force, Yogic life force, Yogic body force.

*

When doing this work you had the Force in you and the right consciousness filling the vital and physical — afterwards with relaxation the ordinary physical consciousness came up and brought back the ordinary reactions — fatigue, sciatica etc.

*

With the right consciousness always there, there would be no fatigue.

*

It [*the cause of fatigue*] is probably some desire or vital preference — likes and dislikes in the vital. All work given you must be felt as the Mother's and done with joy, opening yourself for the Mother's force to work through you.

*

If there is the full surrender in the work and you feel it is the Mother's and that the Mother's force is working in you, then fatigue does not come.

*

The pain, burning, restlessness, weeping and inability to work which you feel, come when there is some difficulty or resistance in some part of the nature. When it comes call on the Mother and reject these things; turn to her for the peace and quietude to return to your mind and settle in the heart, so that there shall be no place for these other things.

Avoiding Overstrain

Yes, it is a mistake to overstrain as there is a reaction afterwards. If there is energy, all must not be spent, some must be stored up so as to increase the permanent strength of the system.

*

Overstraining brings inertia up. Everybody has inertia in his nature: the question is of its greater or lesser operation.

*

When you feel tired, don't overstrain yourself but rest — doing only your ordinary work; restlessly doing something or other all the time is not the way to cure it. To be quiet without and within is what is needed when there is this sense of fatigue. There is always a strength near you which you can call in and it will remove these things, but you must learn to be quiet in order to receive it.

*

If the physical is in this condition and the work creates such reactions in it, it is no use forcing it violently and putting an overstrain upon it. It is better to educate and train the external material being slowly by bringing calm and peace and light and strength persistently into the nervous system and cells of the body. A violent compulsion on the body may well defeat its own object. Probably your sadhana has been too exclusively internal and subjective; but if it is so, this cannot be remedied in a moment. It is better therefore for you not to do heavy physical work like the Bakery's at present.

*

Idleness must of course go — but sometimes I think you have pulled too much the other way. To be able to work with full energy is necessary — but to be able not to work is also necessary.

*

As for working, it depends on what you mean by the word. Desire often leads either to excess of effort, meaning often much labour and a limited fruit, with strain, exhaustion and in case of difficulty or failure despondence, disbelief or revolt; or else it leads to pulling down the force. That can be done, but except for the Yogically strong and experienced, it is not always safe, though it may be often very effective; not safe, first, because it may lead to violent reactions or bring down contrary or wrong or mixed forces which the sadhak is not experienced enough to distinguish from the true ones. Or else it may substitute the sadhak's own limited power of experience or mental and vital constructions for the free gift and the true leading of the Divine. Cases differ, each has his own way of sadhana. But for you what I would recommend is constant openness, a quiet steady aspiration, no over-eagerness, a cheerful trust and patience.

*

To work all the time is excessive, unless there is need — but the impulse to work in itself is good.

*

If too much work is done, the quality of the work often deteriorates in spite of the zest of the workers.

Chapter Four
Practical Concerns in Work

Order and Rhythm

There can be no physical life without an order and rhythm. When this order is changed it must be in obedience to an inner growth and not for the sake of external novelty. It is only a certain part of the surface lower vital nature which seeks always external change and novelty for its own sake.

It is by a constant inner growth that one can find a constant newness and unfailing interest in life. There is no other satisfying way.

*

In the most physical things you have to fix a programme in order to deal with them, otherwise all becomes a sea of confusion and haphazard. Fixed rules have also to be made for the management of material things so long as people are not sufficiently developed to deal with them in the right way without rules. But in matters of the inner development and the sadhana it is impossible to map out a plan fixed in every detail and say, "Every time you shall stop here, there, in this way, on that line and no other." Things would become so tied up and rigid that nothing could be done; there could be no true and effective movement.

*

Order, harmony and organisation in physical things is a necessary part of efficiency and perfection and make the instrument more fit for whatever work is given to it.

*

The impatience of things going wrong is the defect of a quality — an insistence on accuracy and order. The thing is to keep the quality and get rid of the defect.

Rules, Discipline, Regularity, Thoroughness

Rules are indispensable for the orderly management of work; for without order and arrangement nothing can be properly done, all becomes clash, confusion and disorder.

*

A rule that can be varied by everyone at his pleasure is no rule. In all countries in which organised work is successfully done, (India is not one of them), rules exist and nobody thinks of breaking them, for it is realised that work (or life either) without discipline would soon become a confusion and an anarchic failure. In the great days of India everything was put under rule, even art and poetry, even Yoga. Here in fact rules are much less rigid than in any European organisation. Personal discretion can even in a frame of rules have plenty of play — but discretion must be discreetly used, otherwise it becomes something arbitrary or chaotic.

*

In work there must be a rule and discipline and as much punctuality as possible in regard to time.

*

To be able to be regular is a great force, one becomes master of one's time and one's movements.

*

That is quite necessary for work; efficiency and discipline are indispensable. They can however only partly be maintained by outward means — it really depends, in ordinary life, on the personality of the superior, his influence on the subordinates, his firmness, tact, kindness in dealing with them. But the sadhak depends on a deeper force, that of his inner consciousness and the Force working through him.

*

[*Discipline*:] To act according to a standard of Truth or a rule or law of action (dharma) or in obedience to a superior authority or to the highest principles discovered by the reason and intelligent will and not according to one's own fancy, vital impulses and desires. In Yoga obedience to the Guru or to the Divine and the law of the Truth as declared by the Guru is the foundation of discipline.

*

What most want is that things should be done according to their desire without check or reference. The talk of perfection is humbug. Perfection does not consist in everybody being a law to himself. Perfection comes by renunciation of desires and surrender to a higher Will.

*

Thoroughness means to do whatever you do completely, thoroughly, so that it may be entire and perfect, not carelessly or partially done. It refers to internal things as well as to external.

Harmony

When all is in agreement with one Truth or an expression of it, that is harmony.

*

Wherever there is excessive sensitiveness or quickness of temper, occasions of clash and quarrel will arise, no matter with whom one works — and especially where there is the pressure of the sadhana, which requires that all such weaknesses should be overcome, occasions are likely to arise which will bring them to the surface. The only way is not to indulge them or act under their influence, but to face them and overcome.

*

The difficulty rises from a certain excess of sensitiveness in the vital nature which feels strongly any want of harmony or opposition in the work or any untoward happening and, when that comes, one is apt to feel it as if a personal opposition and on the other side also a similar feeling arises and so the difficulty becomes prolonged and leads to conflict. As a matter of fact the difficulty often arises from circumstances, e.g. the B. S. [*Building Service*] with its much reduced staff and a rush of work using up all its men may find it more difficult to accommodate you than before. Or it may arise from people acting according to their view of a matter which does not accord with yours. Or again it may come from the person following his own ideas, view of what is convenient and effective and thus coming up against yours. There need be no personal feeling in all that and it is best not to look for any and not to see it from that point of view. What is needed is always to take a calm view of the thing and a clear vision — not only from one's own standpoint which may be eventually right and yet need modification in detail, but with a vision that sees also the standpoint of others. This broad seeing, quiet and impersonal, is needed in the full Yogic consciousness. Having it one can insist on what has to be insisted on with firmness but at the same time with a consideration and understanding of the other that removes the chance of any clash of personal feeling. Naturally if the other is unreasonable, he may still resent, but then it will be his own fault entirely and it will fall back on him only. It is here that we see the necessity of some change. Loyalty, fidelity, capacity, strength of will and other qualities in the work you have in plenty — a full calm and equality not only in the inner being where it can exist already, but in the outer nervous parts is a thing you have to get completely.

Avoiding Harshness, Severity, Anger

There are always defects on both sides which lead to this disharmony. On your side you have a tendency to too harsh a judgment of others, a readiness to see and stress the faults, defects, weak side of others and not to see enough their good side. This prevents the kindliness of outlook which should be there and gives an impression of harshness and critical severity and creates a tendency to contrariety and revolt which even when it is not there in the minds of the others, acts through their subconscient and creates all these discordant movements. To take advantage of what is good in others, keeping one's eye always on that, and to deal tactfully with their mistakes, faults and defects is the best way; it does not exclude firmness and maintenance of discipline, even severity when severity is due; but the latter should be rare and the others should not feel it as if it were a permanent attitude.

*

The one thing you must try to do in your relations with your fellow-workers is to master your nerves and irritability and take care not to speak roughly, angrily or peevishly to them. It is that that is creating most of the difficulty now. If you have to be firm, you can be firm, but at the same time quiet and even gentle. If you take care on this point, things are likely to improve soon.

If you put yourself in the Mother's hand and reject these vital movements in her strength, there is no reason why you should not pass through all ordeals and progress in the Yoga.

*

In all such dealings with others,[1] you should see not only your own side of the question but the other side also. There should be no anger, vehement reproach or menace, for these things only raise anger and retort on the other side. I write this because you are trying to rise above yourself and dominate your vital and when one wants to do that, one cannot be too strict with oneself in these things. It is best even to be severe to one's own mistakes and charitable to the mistakes of others.

*

The experience of the difference between your inner feelings and your surface reactions shows that you are becoming aware of different parts of your nature which each have their own

---

[1] In this case the correspondent became angry when his request for help in his work was not promptly met. — Ed.

character. In fact each human being is composed of different personalities that feel and behave in a different way and his action is determined by the one that happens to be prominent at the time. The one that has no feelings against anyone is either the psychic being or the emotional being in the heart, the one that feels anger and is severe is a part of the external vital nature on the surface. This anger and severity is a wrong form of something that in itself has a value, a certain strength of will and force of action and control in the vital being, without which work cannot be done. What is necessary is to get rid of the anger and to keep the force and firm will along with a developed judgment as to what is the right thing to do in any circumstances. For instance, people can be allowed to do things in their own way when that does not spoil the work, when it is only their way of doing what is necessary to be done; when their way is opposed to the discipline of the work, then they have to be controlled, but it should be done quietly and kindly, not with anger. Very often, if one has developed a silent power of putting the Mother's force on the work with one's own will as instrument, that by itself may be sufficient without having to say anything as the person changes his way of himself as if by his own initiative.

*

To discourage anybody is wrong, but to give false encouragement or encouragement of anything wrong is not right. Severity has sometimes to be used (though not overused), when without it an obstinate persistence in what is wrong cannot be set right. Very often, if an inner communication has been established, a silent pressure is more effective than anything else. No absolute rule can be laid down; one has to judge and act for the best in each case.

Working with Subordinates and Superiors

It [*disciplining subordinates*] has to be done in the right spirit and the subordinates generally must be able to feel that it is so, that they are being dealt with in all uprightness and justice and by a man who has sympathy and insight and not only severity and energy. It is a question of vital tact and a strong and large vital finding always the right way to deal with the others.

*

To be able to see the viewpoint of others and make allowance for their nature — neither being too harsh, authoritative or exacting, nor too weak and accommodating or indulgent, but still, even when firm, combining firmness with tact and sympathy, — is very necessary for one who has to deal with others as his inferiors in position and subject to his authority. It is also necessary when the position is reversed so that there may not be unnecessary clash or friction with official superiors.

*

The root of the difficulty has been in the readiness of the superior officers to accept without examination the things that are said against you. A double action is needed, to destroy the ill-will of the inferiors and to change the mind of the superiors — an invisible action, for in the visible they seem to be too much under the control of the Forces of the Ignorance.

Overcoming the Instinct of Domination

We have been very glad to get your letters with the details which prove how great and rapid a progress you have made in sadhana. All that you write shows a clear consciousness and a new orientation in the lower vital. To have seen clearly the instinct of domination and the pride of the instrument there means that that part of the being is on the right way to change — these defects must now be replaced by their true counterparts — the power to act selflessly on others for the Truth and the Right and the power to be a strong and confident but egoless instrument of the Divine. It is clear also that the physical is effectively opening, but the instinctive physical and vital-physical motions in it, fear in the body, weakness, disposition to ill-health must go also. As to diet, a light quantity of food sufficient for strength and sustenance is the best for you — meat is not advisable.

Let the wide opening that has come in you develop and your whole being down to the material fill with the true consciousness and the true power.

*

That is true.[2] As things are, the vital falsehood seems to take a temporary advantage over the superior sattwic nature.

Avoiding Disturbance

Whenever anything untoward happens, it is essential not to allow any vibrations of disturbance or unrest in either the physical mind or the nerves. One must remain calm and open to the Light and Force, then one will be able to act in the right way.

*

From the point of view of sadhana — you must not allow yourself to be in the least disturbed by these things [*lack of sympathy and support in one's work*]. What you have to do, what is right to be done, should be done in perfect calmness with the support of the Divine Force. All that is necessary for a successful result, can be done — including the securing of the support of those who are able to help you. But if this outer support is not forthcoming, you have not to be disturbed but to proceed calmly on your way. If there is any difficulty or unsuccess anywhere not due to your own fault, you have not to be troubled. Strength, unmoved calm, quiet, straight and right dealing with all things you have to deal with must be the rule of your action.

*

Keep unmoved, unoffended, do your work without being discouraged, call on the Force to act for you. It is a field of trial for you — the inward result is more important than the outward.

*

---

[2] *The correspondent remarked that people full of vital ego often override, deceive and even injure people with less egoistic push but greater capacity.* — Ed.

As for the work, I have already told you that it is not by your going away that there will be harmony and peace. Wherever there are human beings working together, differences and disagreements and incompatibilities of temper will always be there. It is only if the human nature changes that it will be otherwise, but that cannot be done at once. One has to go on quietly and patiently doing the work for the Mother's sake until the change can be made in yourself and others.

Avoiding Restlessness, Worry and Anxiety

As for quietude and work, quietude is the proper basis for work — not restlessness. You speak as if quietude and being alive and working were not compatible! The Mother and myself do plenty of work, I suppose, and we are quite alive, but it is out of quietude that we do it. To worry and be restless and think always "I am not doing well my work" is not the way; you have to be quiet, conscious more and more of a greater Force than your own working in you: that Force will hereafter take up your work and do it for you.

*

The difficulty you find results very much from your always worrying with your mind about things, thinking "This is wrong, that is wrong in me or my work" and, as a result, "I am incompetent, I am bad, nothing can be done with me." Your embroidery work, your lampshades etc. have always been very good, and yet you are always thinking "This is bad work, that is wrong" and by doing so, confuse yourself and get into a muddle. Naturally, you make a mistake now and then, but more when you worry like that than when you do things simply and confidently.

It is better whether with work or with sadhana to go on quietly, allowing the Force to act and doing your best to let it work rightly, but without this self-tormenting and constant restless questioning at every point. Whatever defects there are would go much sooner, if you did not harp on them too much; for by dwelling on them so much you lose confidence in yourself and in your power of openness to the Force — which is there all the same — and put unnecessary difficulties in the way of its working.

*

There is nothing really wrong with your work; it is very well done. It is only your imagination that makes you always think it is defective here and defective there. There may be slight mistakes sometimes, but that is the case with everybody. You have only to work quietly, getting the best inspiration you can and, if there is any difficulty, to be quiet and the right thing will come. To be true to the inner feeling, remaining turned towards us for help is absolutely the right way; to trouble and doubt and fret is quite the wrong way.

*

Do not worry about mistakes in work. Often you imagine that things are badly done by you when really you have done them very well; but even if there are mistakes, it is nothing to be sad about. Let the consciousness grow — only in the divine consciousness is there an entire perfection. The more you surrender to the Divine, the more will there be the possibility of perfection in you.

*

Do not attach too much importance to such mistakes or get upset about them. It is the nature of the mind to make such mistakes. It is only a higher consciousness that can set them right — the mind can be sure only after a very long training in each particular action and even then it has only to be off-guard for something untoward to occur. Do as well as you can, and for the rest let the higher consciousness grow till it can enlighten all the movements of the physical mind.

*

Skill in works will come when there is the opening in the physical mind and the body. There is no need to be anxious about that now. Do your best and do not be anxious about it.

Compliments and Criticism

That is a great error of the human vital — to want compliments for their own sake and to be depressed by their absence and imagine that it means there is no capacity. In this world one starts with ignorance and imperfection in whatever one does — one has to find out one's mistakes and to learn, one has to commit errors and find out by correcting them the right way to do things. Nobody in the world has ever escaped from this law. So what one has to expect from others is not compliments all the time, but praise of what is right or well done and criticism of errors and mistakes. The more one can bear criticism and see one's mistakes, the more likely one is to arrive at the fullness of one's capacity. Especially when one is very young — before the age of maturity — one cannot easily do perfect work. What is called the juvenile work of poets and painters — work done in their early years — is always imperfect, it is a promise and has qualities — but the real perfection and full use of their powers comes afterwards. They themselves know that very well, but they go on writing or painting because they know also that by doing so they will develop their powers.

As for comparison with others, one ought not to do that. Each one has his own lesson to learn, his own work to do and he must concern himself with that, not with the superior or inferior progress of others in comparison with himself. If he is behind today, he can be in full capacity hereafter and it is for that future perfection of his powers that he must labour. You are young and have everything yet to learn — your capacities are yet only in bud, you must wait and work for them to be in full bloom — and you must not mind if it takes months and years even to arrive at something satisfying and perfect. It will come in its proper time, and the work you do now is always a step towards it.

But learn to welcome criticism and the pointing out of imperfections — the more you do so, the more rapidly you will advance.

*

Someone who is learning to paint or play music or write and does not like to have his mistakes pointed out by those who already know — how is he to learn at all or reach any perfection of technique?

Thinking about Work

Think of your work only when it is being done, not before and not after.

Do not let your mind go back on a work that is finished. It belongs to the past and all rehandling of it is a waste of power.

Do not let your mind labour in anticipation on a work that has to be done. The Power that acts in you will see to it at its own time.

These two habits of the mind belong to a past functioning that the transforming Force is pressing to remove and the physical mind's persistence in them is the cause of your strain and fatigue. If you can remember to let your mind work only when its action is needed, the strain will lessen and disappear. This is indeed the transitional movement before the supramental working takes possession of the physical mind and brings into it the spontaneous action of the Light.

Dealing with Physical Things

Material things are not to be despised — without them there can be no manifestation in the material world.

*

Physical things have a life and value of their own which does not depend upon their price. To respect physical things and make a careful and scrupulous use of them is a part of the Yoga, for without that the mastery over matter cannot come.

*

What you feel about physical things is true — there is a consciousness in them, a life which is not the life and consciousness of man and animal which we know, but still secret and real. That is why we must have a respect for physical things and use them rightly, not misuse and waste, ill-treat or handle with a careless roughness. This feeling of all being conscious or alive comes when our own physical consciousness — and not the mind only — awakes out of its obscurity and becomes aware of the One in all things, the Divine everywhere.

*

It is very true that physical things have a consciousness within them which feels and responds to care and is sensitive to careless touch and rough handling. To know or feel that and learn to be careful of them is a great progress in consciousness.

*

There is a consciousness in each physical thing with which one can communicate. Everything has an individuality of a certain kind, houses, cars, furniture etc. The ancient peoples knew that and so they saw a spirit or "genius" in every physical thing.

*

The rough handling and careless breaking or waste and misuse of physical things is a denial of the Yogic Consciousness and a great hindrance to the bringing down of the Divine Truth to the material plane.

*

Wanton waste, careless spoiling of physical things in an incredibly short time, loose disorder, misuse of service and materials due either to vital grasping or to tamasic inertia are baneful to prosperity and tend to drive away or discourage the Wealth-Power. These things have long been rampant in the society and, if that continues, an increase in our means might well mean a proportionate increase in the wastage and disorder and neutralise the material advantage. This must be remedied if there is to be any sound progress.

Asceticism for its own sake is not the ideal of this Yoga, but self-control in the vital and right order in the material are a very important part of it — and even an ascetic discipline is better for our purpose than a loose absence of true control. Mastery of the material does not mean having plenty and profusely throwing it out or spoiling it as fast as it comes or faster. Mastery implies in it the right and careful utilisation of things and also a self-control in their use.

Chapter Five

Creative Activity

The Arts and the Spiritual Life

There is no incompatibility between spirituality and creative activity — they can be united.

*

Any activity can be taken as part of the sadhana if it is offered to the Divine or done with the consciousness or faith that it is done by the Divine Power. That is the important point.

*

Literature, poetry, science and other studies can be a preparation of the consciousness for life. When one does Yoga they can become part of the sadhana only if done for the Divine or taken up by the Divine Force, but then one should not want to be a poet for the sake of being a poet only, or for fame, applause, etc.

*

The spiritual life and one's own inner psychic and spiritual change should be the first preoccupation of a sadhak — poetry or painting is something quite subordinate and even then it should be done not to be a great poet or artist but as a help to the inner sadhana. It is time that everyone got away from the vital view of things to the psychic and spiritual on which alone can stand Yoga and the spiritual life.

*

Every artist almost (there are rare exceptions) has got something of the "public" man in him, in his vital physical parts, the need of the stimulus of an audience, social applause, satisfied vanity or fame. That must go absolutely if he wants to be a Yogi and his art a service not of man or of his own ego but of the Divine.

*

Well, that [*acting as a great musician etc.*] is an almost universal human weakness, especially with artists, poets, musicians and the whole splendid tribe — I have known even great Yogis suffer from just a touch of it! If one can see mentally the humour of it, it will fall off in the end.

Literature

To be a literary man is not a spiritual aim; but to use literature as a means of spiritual expression is another matter. Even to make expression a vehicle of a superior power helps to open the consciousness. The harmonising rests on that principle.

*

A "literary man" is one who loves literature and literary activity for their own separate sake. A Yogi who writes is not a literary man for he writes only what the inner Will and Word wants him to express. He is a channel and an instrument of something greater than his own literary personality.

*

The use of your writing is to keep you in touch with the inner source of inspiration and intuition, so as to wear thin the crude external crust in the consciousness and encourage the growth of the inner being.

*

Mother does not disapprove of your writing the book — what she does not like is your being so lost in it that you can do nothing else. You must be master of what you do and not possessed by it. She quite agrees to your finishing and offering the book on your birthday if that can be done. But you must not be carried away — you must keep your full contact with higher things.

*

I repeat that we do not object to your writing — whether it be poetry or short stories or novels. What we felt was that this kind of total absorption and possession by it was not good for your spiritual condition and that it put a lesser thing in front, even occupying the *whole* front of the consciousness for most of the time instead of putting it in its proper place in a sound spiritual harmony.

*

You can try [*writing a novel*], if you like. The difficulty is that the subject matter of a novel belongs mostly to the outer consciousness, so that a lowering or externalising can easily come. This apart from the difficulty of keeping the inner poise when putting the mind into outer work. If you could get an established poise within, then it would be possible to do any work without disturbing or lowering the consciousness.

*

As for the French writing, you should not think so much of expressing things — it does not matter whether others have written the same things and done it better. What you should aim at is simply to learn to write French perfectly, to get full use of the French language as an instrument. If the Force wants to express anything through you hereafter or not, is a thing you should leave to the Divine Will; once you give yourself into its hands in the true consciousness, it will know what to do or not to do through you and will make full use of whatever instrumentation you can put at its disposal.

Painting

Painting also is sadhana; so it is perfectly possible to make them one. It is a matter of dedicating the painting and feeling the force that makes you paint as the Mother's force.

*

Of course everybody is here for Yoga and not for painting.

Painting or any other activity has to be made here a part of Yoga and cannot be pursued for its own sake. If it stands insuperably in the way, then it has to be given up; but there is no reason why it should if it be pursued in the proper spirit, as a field or aid for spiritual growth, or as a work done for the Mother.

*

You have painting and music in you and if you apply yourself they will develop in you. Only it is best to do it as an instrument of the Mother and as an offering to her, and not allow any personal desire for fame or appreciation by others or any personal pride to be the motives — for it is that that gives trouble. All work done as an offering is a great help and does not give trouble.

*

What do you mean by vital excitement [*while painting*]? There is an intensity and enthusiasm of the vital without which it would be difficult to do any poem, picture or music of a creative kind. That intensity is not harmful.

*

You have been progressing of course, but what Mother told you and tells everyone is true that to be a real artist needs hard work for years together. But your mistake is to put stress on these things and get discouraged by any check or difficulty in them. The one thing to be done is to open your consciousness to what is coming down, to let the change operate so that the consciousness becomes a consciousness of peace and light and power and joy full of the Divine Presence. When that is there, then what the Divine wants to get done through you or developed in you will be done or developed with a rapidity and perfection which at present is impossible. The one thing needful first, all the rest is only now a field of exercise for the development of the one thing needful.

Singing

What you write about the singing is perfectly correct. You sing your best only when you forget yourself and let it come out from within without thinking of the need of excellence or the impression it may make. The famous singer should indeed disappear into the past, — it is only so that the inner singer can take her place.

*

I meant exactly the same thing as when I wrote to you that the "famous singer" must disappear and the "inner singer" take her place. "The old psychological lines" means the mental and vital aesthetic source of the singing, the desire of fame or success, singing for an audience — the singing must come from the soul within and it must be for the Divine. . . .

As for your singing, I was not speaking of any new creation from the aesthetic point of view, but of the spiritual change — what form it takes must depend on what you find *within* you when the deeper basis is there.

I do not see any necessity for giving up singing altogether; I only meant, — it is the logical conclusion from what I have written to you not now only but before, — that the inner change must be the first consideration and the rest must arise out of that. If singing to an audience pulls you out of the inner condition, then you could postpone that and sing for yourself and the Divine until you are able, even in facing an audience, to forget the audience. If you are troubled by failure or exalted by success, that also you must overcome.

Section Three

Sadhana through Concentration, Meditation and Japa

Chapter One
Concentration and Meditation

The Meaning of Concentration and Meditation

Concentration, for our Yoga, means when the consciousness is fixed in a particular state (e.g. peace) or movement (e.g. aspiration, will, coming into contact with the Mother, taking the Mother's name); meditation is when the inner mind is looking at things to get the right knowledge.

*

Concentration means fixing the consciousness in one place or on one object and in a single condition. Meditation can be diffusive, e.g. thinking about the Divine, receiving impressions and discriminating, watching what goes on in the nature and acting upon it etc.

*

Concentration is a gathering together of the consciousness and either centralising at one point or turning on a single object, e.g. the Divine — there can also be a gathered condition throughout the whole being, not at a point. In meditation it is not indispensable to gather like this, one can simply remain with a quiet mind thinking of one subject or observing what comes in the consciousness and dealing with it.

*

Meditation means thinking on one subject in a concentrated way. In concentration proper there is not a series of thoughts, but the mind is silently fixed on one object, name, idea, place etc.
There are other kinds of concentration, e.g. concentrating the whole consciousness in one place, as between the eyebrows, in the heart, etc. One can also concentrate to get rid of thought altogether and remain in a complete silence.

The Role of Concentration and Meditation (Dhyana) in Sadhana

In the beginning for a long time concentration is necessary even by effort because the nature, the consciousness are not ready. Even then the more quiet and natural the concentration, the better. But when the consciousness and nature are ready, then concentration must become spontaneous and easily possible without effort at all times. Even at last it becomes the natural and permanent condition of the being — it is then no longer concentration, but the settled poise of the soul in the Divine.

It is true that to be concentrated and do an outward action at the same time is not at first possible. But that too becomes possible. Either the consciousness divides into two parts, one the inner poised in the Divine, the other the outer doing the outer work — or else the whole is so poised and the force does the work through the passive instrument.

*

Concentration is necessary. By dhyana you awake the inner being; by concentration in life, in work, in the outer consciousness you make the outer being also fit to receive the Divine Light and Force.

*

It is in the waking consciousness that all has to be realised. But that cannot be done without a full preparation in the inner being and it is this preparation that is being done for you in *dhyāna*.

*

You have not to remain in dhyana all the time, but to bring into the waking state the consciousness you get there and you have to live in that all the time.

*

It is very good, and by regular meditation you are sure to make much progress. But I do not think to spend all the night in meditation would be good. The body needs sleep also. One hour meditation daily is already a very good result and it can be increased slowly to two.

*

Certainly, if all one's life one did nothing but meditate, it would be a one-sided affair. But at times to give the first place or a lion's share to meditation may be necessary. It is especially when things are coming down and have to be fixed.

*

The ease and peace are felt very deep and far within because they are in the psychic and the psychic is very deep within us, covered over by the mind and vital. When you meditate you open to the psychic, become aware of your psychic consciousness deep within and feel these things. In order that this ease and peace and happiness may become strong and stable and felt in all the being and in the body, you have to go still deeper within and bring out the full force of the psychic into the physical. This can most easily be done by regular concentration and meditation with the aspiration for this true consciousness. It can be done by work also, by dedication, by doing the work for the Divine only without thought of self and keeping the idea of consecration to the Mother always in the heart. But this is not easy to do perfectly.

*

Sir, is the Presence [*of the Divine*] of a physical nature or a spiritual fact? And is the physical sense accustomed or able to see or feel spiritual things — a spiritual Presence, a non-material Form? To see the Brahman everywhere is not possible unless you develop the inner vision — so to do that you have to concentrate. To see non-material forms is indeed possible for a few, because they have the gift by nature, but most can't do it without developing the subtle sight. It is absurd to expect the Divine to manifest his Presence without your taking any trouble to see it, — you have to concentrate.

The Object of Meditation

What do you call meditation? Shutting the eyes and concentrating? It is only one method for calling down the true consciousness. To join with the true consciousness or feel its descent is the only thing important and if it comes without the orthodox method, as it always did with me, so much the better. Meditation is only a means or device, the true movement is when even walking, working or speaking one is still in sadhana.

*

What is most important [*in meditation*] is the change of consciousness of which this feeling of oneness is a part. The going deep in meditation is only a means and it is not always necessary if the great experiences come easily without it.

*

The best help for concentration is to receive the Mother's calm and peace into your mind. It is there above you — only the mind and its centres have to open to it. It is what the Mother is pushing upon you in the evening meditation.

*

The object of meditation is to open to the Mother and grow through many progressive experiences into a higher consciousness in union with the Divine.

*

To enter into a deeper or higher consciousness or for that deeper or higher consciousness to descend into you — that is the true success of meditation.

Meditation Not Necessary for All

One can have no fixed hours of meditation and yet be doing sadhana.

*

Meditation is not indispensable. There are some who do not meditate and yet progress.

*

Then how is it [*meditation*] necessary for all, if some are asked not to do it? Much meditation is for those who can meditate much. It does not follow that because such meditation is good, therefore nobody should do anything else.

Methods of Meditation and Concentration

The attitude of spiritual meditation is to concentrate so as to receive or attain the spiritual truth — what means one takes depends upon the way, the path, the person.

*

If the difficulty in meditation is that thoughts of all kinds come in, that is not due to hostile forces but to the ordinary nature of the human mind. All sadhaks have this difficulty and with many it lasts for a very long time. There are several ways of getting rid of it. One of them is to look at the thoughts and observe what is the nature of the human mind as they show it but not to give any sanction and to let them run down till they come to a standstill — this is a way recommended by Vivekananda in his *Rajayoga*. Another is to look at the thoughts as not one's own, to stand back as the witness Purusha and refuse the sanction — the thoughts are regarded as things coming from outside, from Prakriti, and they must be felt as if they were passers-by crossing the mind-space with whom one has no connection and in whom one takes no interest. In this way it usually happens that after a time the mind divides into two, a part which is the mental witness watching and perfectly undisturbed and quiet and a part which is the object of observation, the Prakriti part in which the thoughts cross or wander. Afterwards one can proceed to silence or quiet the Prakriti part also. There is a third, an active method by which one looks to see where the thoughts come from and finds they come not from oneself, but from outside the head as it were; if one can detect them coming, then, *before they enter*, they have to be thrown away altogether. This is perhaps the most difficult way and not all can do it, but if it can be done it is the shortest and most powerful road to silence.

*

If you try to apply everything you read, there will be no end to your new beginnings. One can stop thinking by rejecting the thoughts and in the silence discover oneself. One can do it by letting the thoughts run down while one detaches oneself from them. There are a number of other ways. This one related in Brunton's book seems to me the Adwaita-jnani method of separating oneself from body, vital, mind, by *viveka*, discrimination, "I am not the body, I am not the life, I am not the mind" till he gets to the self, separate from mind, life and body. That also is one way of doing it. There is also the separation of Purusha from Prakriti till one becomes the witness only and feels separate from all the activities as the Witness Consciousness. There are other methods also.

*

The method of gathering of the mind is not an easy one. It is better to watch and separate oneself from the thoughts till one becomes aware of a quiet space within into which they come from outside.

*

All thoughts really come from outside, but one is not conscious of their coming. You have become conscious of this movement. There are different ways of getting rid of them; one is to reject them one by one before they can come in; another is to look at them with detachment till they fade away.

*

It is of course because of the old habit of the mental consciousness that it goes on receiving the thoughts from outside in spite of its being a fatigue — not that it wants them, but that they are accustomed to come and the mind mechanically lets them in and attends to them by force of habit. This is always one of the chief difficulties in Yoga when the experiences have begun and the mind wants to be always either concentrated or quiet. Some do what you propose [*direct rejection of thoughts*] and after a time succeed in quieting the mind altogether or the silence comes down from above and does it. But often when one tries this, the thoughts become very active and resist the silencing process and that is very troublesome. Therefore many prefer to go on slowly letting the mind quiet down little by little, the quietness spreading and remaining for longer periods until the unwanted thoughts fall away or recede and the mind is left free for knowledge from within and above.

What you might do is to try and see what results — if the thoughts attack too much and trouble, you could stop — if the mind quiets down quickly or more and more, then continue.

*

The mind is always in activity, but we do not observe fully what it is doing, but allow ourselves to be carried away in the stream of continual thinking. When we try to concentrate, this stream of self-moved mechanical thinking becomes prominent to our observation. It is the first normal obstacle (the other is sleep during meditation) to the effort towards Yoga.

The first thing to do is to realise that this thought-flow is not yourself, it is not you who are thinking, but thought that is going on in the mind. It is Prakriti with its thought-energy that is raising all this whirl of thought in you, imposing it on the Purusha. You as the Purusha must stand back as the witness observing the action, but refusing to identify yourself with it. The next thing is to exercise a control and reject the thoughts — though sometimes by the very act of detachment the thought-habit falls away or diminishes during the meditation and there is a sufficient silence or at any rate a quietude which makes it easy to reject the thoughts that come and fix oneself on the object of meditation. If one becomes aware of the thoughts as coming from outside, from the universal Nature, then one can throw them away before they reach the mind; in that way the mind finally falls silent. If neither of these things happens, a persistent practice of rejection becomes necessary — there should be no struggle or wrestling with the thoughts, but only a quiet self-separation and refusal. Success does not come at first, but if consent is constantly withheld, the mechanical whirl eventually lessens and begins to die away and one can then have at will an inner quietude or silence.

It should be noted that the result of the Yogic processes is not, except in rare cases, immediate and one must apply them with patience till they give a result which is sometimes long in coming if there is much resistance in the outer nature.

How can you fix the mind on the higher Self so long as you have no consciousness or experience of it? You can only concentrate on the idea of the Self. Or else one can concentrate on the idea of the Divine or the Divine Mother or on an image or on the feeling of devotion, calling the presence in the heart or the Force to work in the mind and heart and body and liberate the consciousness and give the self-realisation. If you concentrate on the idea of the Self, it must be with the conception of the Self as something different from mind and its thoughts, the vital and its feelings, the body and its actions — something standing back from all these, something that you can come to feel concretely as an Existence or Consciousness, separate from all that yet freely pervading all without being involved in these things.

*

You have to separate yourself from the mind also. You have to feel yourself even in the mental, vital, physical levels (not only above) a consciousness that is neither mind, life, nor body.

*

For the buzz of the physical mind, reject it quietly, without getting disturbed, till it feels discouraged and retires shaking its head and saying, "This fellow is too calm and strong for me." There are always two things that can rise up and assail the silence, — vital suggestions, the physical mind's mechanical recurrences. Calm rejection for both is the cure. There is a Purusha within who can dictate to the nature what it shall admit or exclude, but its will is a strong, quiet will; if one gets perturbed or agitated over the difficulties, then the will of the Purusha cannot act effectively as it would otherwise.

The dynamic realisation will probably take place when the higher consciousness comes fully down into the vital. When it comes into the mental it brings the peace of the Purusha and liberation and it may bring also knowledge. It is when it comes into the vital that the dynamic realisation becomes present and living.

Concentration on the Idea

If one concentrates on a thought or a word, one has to dwell on the essential idea contained in the word with the aspiration to feel the thing which it expresses.

*

I have not the original chapter before me just now; but from the sentences quoted[1] it seems to be the essential mental Idea. As for instance in the method of Vedantic knowledge one concentrates on the idea of Brahman omnipresent — one looks at a tree or other surrounding objects with the idea that Brahman is there and the tree or object is only a form. After a time if the concentration is of the right kind, one begins to become aware of a presence, an existence, the physical tree form becomes a shell and that presence or existence is felt to be the only reality. The idea then drops, it is a direct vision of the thing that takes its place — there is no longer any necessity of concentrating on the

---

[1] *The correspondent sent to Sri Aurobindo a passage from* The Synthesis of Yoga: *"This concentration proceeds by the Idea . . . ; for it is through the Idea that the mental being rises beyond all expression to that which is expressed, to that of which the Idea itself is only the instrument. By concentration upon the Idea the mental existence which at present we are breaks open the barrier of our mentality and arrives at the state of consciousness, the state of being, the state of power of conscious-being and bliss of conscious-being to which the Idea corresponds and of which it is the symbol, movement and rhythm."* THE COMPLETE WORKS OF SRI AUROBINDO, *vol. 23, p. 321.*

idea, one sees with a deeper consciousness, *sa paśyati*. It should be noted that this concentration on the idea is not mere thinking, *mananam* — it is an inner dwelling on the essence of the Idea.

Centres for Concentration

The nature of the meditation depends on the part of the being in which one is centred at the time. In the body (rather the subtle body than the physical, but connected with the corresponding parts in the gross physical body also) there are centres proper to each level of the being. There is a centre at the top of the head and above it which is that of the above-mind or higher consciousness; a centre in the forehead between the eyebrows which is that of the thinking mind, mental will, mental vision; a centre in the throat which is that of the expressive or externalising mind: these are the mental centres. Below comes the vital — the heart (emotional), the navel (the dynamic life-centre), another below the navel in the abdomen which is the lower or sensational vital centre. Finally, at the bottom of the spine is the Muladhara or physical centre. Behind the heart is the psychic centre. If one concentrates in the head as many do it is a mental-spiritual meditation one seeks for, if in the heart it is a psychic meditation; these are the usual places where one concentrates. But what rises up first or opens first may not be the mental or psychic, but the emotional or the vital; that depends on the nature — for whatever is easiest to open in it, is likely to open first. If it is in the vital, then the meditation tends to project the consciousness into the vital plane and its experiences. But from that one can get to the psychic by drawing more and more inwards, not getting absorbed into the vital experiences but separating oneself and looking at them with detachment as if one were deep inside and observing things outside oneself. Similarly one can get the mental experiences by concentrating in the thought and by it bringing a corresponding experience, e.g. the thought of all being the Brahman, or one can draw back from the thought also and observe one's own thoughts as outside things until one enters into the silence and the pure spiritual experience.

*

One can concentrate in any of the three centres which is easiest to the sadhak or gives most result. The power of the concentration in the heart-centre is to open that centre and by the power of aspiration, love, bhakti, surrender remove the veil which covers and conceals the soul and bring forward the soul or psychic being to govern the mind, life and body and turn and open them all — fully — to the Divine, removing all that is opposed to that turning and opening.

This is what is called in this Yoga the psychic transformation. The power of concentration above the head is to bring peace, silence, liberation from the body sense, the identification with mind and life and open the way for the lower (mental-vital-physical) consciousness to rise up to meet the higher Consciousness above and for the powers of the higher (spiritual or divine) Consciousness to descend into mind, life and body. This is what is called in this Yoga the spiritual transformation. If one begins with this movement, then the Power from above has in its descent to open all the centres (including the lowest centre) and to bring out the psychic being; for until that is done there is likely to be much difficulty and struggle of the lower consciousness obstructing, mixing with or even refusing the Divine Action from above. If the psychic being is once active this struggle and these difficulties can be greatly minimised.

The power of concentration in the eyebrows is to open the centre there, liberate the inner mind and vision and the inner or Yogic consciousness and its experiences and powers. From here also one can open upwards and act also in the lower centres; but the danger of this process is that one may get shut up in one's mental spiritual formations and not come out of them into the free and integral spiritual experience and knowledge and integral change of the being and nature.

*

I was very glad to get your letter and especially to know that you are more at peace. That is what is first needed, the settling down of a natural peace and quiet in the nature — the spiritual peace is a bigger thing that can come afterwards.

Then as to concentration. Ordinarily the consciousness is spread out everywhere, dispersed, running in this or that direction, after this subject and that object in multitude. When anything has to be done of a sustained nature, the first thing one does is to draw back all this dispersed consciousness and concentrate. It is then, if one looks closely, found to be concentrated in one place and on one occupation, subject or object — as when you are composing a poem or a botanist is studying a flower. The place is usually somewhere in the brain, if it is the thought, in the heart if it is the feeling in which one is concentrated. The Yogic concentration is simply an extension and intensification of the same thing. It may be on an object as when one does tratak on a shining point — then one has to concentrate so that one sees only that point and has no other thought but that. It may be on an idea or a word or a name, the idea of the Divine, the word OM, the name Krishna, or a combination of idea and word or idea and name. But, farther, in Yoga one also concentrates in a particular place. There is the famous rule of concentrating between the eyebrows — the centre of the inner mind, of occult vision, of the will is there. What you do is to think firmly from there on whatever you make the object of your concentration or else try to see the image of it from there. If you succeed in this, then after a time you feel that your whole consciousness is centred there in that place — of course for the time being. After doing it for some time and often, it becomes easy and normal.

I hope this is clear. Well, in this Yoga, you do the same, not necessarily at that particular spot between the eyebrows, but anywhere in the head or at the centre of the chest where the physiologists have fixed the cardiac centre. Instead of concentrating on an object, you concentrate in the head in a will, a call for the descent of the peace from above or, as some do, an opening of the unseen lid and an ascent of the consciousness above. In the heart-centre one concentrates in an aspiration, for an opening, for the presence or living image of the Divine there or whatever else is the object. There may be japa of a name but, if so, there must also be a concentration on it and the name must repeat itself there in the heart-centre.

It may be asked what becomes of the rest of the consciousness when there is this local concentration? Well, it either falls silent as in any concentration or, if it does not, then thoughts or other things may move about, as if outside, but the concentrated part does not attend to them or notice. That is when the concentration is reasonably successful.

One has not to fatigue oneself at first by long concentration if one is not accustomed, for then in a jaded mind it loses its power or value. One can "relax" and meditate instead of concentrating. It is only as the concentration becomes normal that one can go on for a longer and longer time.

*

There is no harm in concentrating sometimes in the heart and sometimes above the head. But concentration in either place does not mean keeping the attention fixed on a particular spot; you have to take your station of consciousness in either place and concentrate there not on the place, but on the Divine. This can be done with eyes shut or with eyes open, according as it best suits you.

You can concentrate on the sun, but to concentrate on the Divine is better than to concentrate on the sun.

*

You can concentrate the consciousness anywhere in any centre. You have only to think of yourself as centrally there and try to fix and keep that. A strain or any effort to do so is not necessary but a quiet and steady dwelling in the idea.

Most people associate consciousness with the brain or mind because that is the centre for intellectual thought and mental vision, but consciousness is not limited to that kind of thought or vision. It is everywhere in the system and there are several centres of it, e.g., the centre for inner concentration is not in the brain but in the heart, — the originating centre of vital desire is still lower down.

The two main places where one can centre the consciousness for Yoga are in the head and in the heart — the mind-centre and the soul-centre.

*

One has to open through concentration in the heart centre or above the head, in the former case to the psychic, in the latter to the higher Truth. But without the psychic preparation or at least a thorough purification of the being, the latter course is not safe.

*

It may be better to concentrate in the heart rather than in the mind, offer yourself from there and call the Mother into the heart leaving the thoughts to fall silent of themselves. Otherwise with the present method you have simply to persevere till the present brief and imperfect stillings of the mind become longer and deeper.

*

The concentration in the heart is what brings about the opening of the psychic which is your principal need. If the concentration has brought about a feeling which makes you judge clearly all the other movements and see their nature, then the psychic is already in action. For this is the psychic feeling which brings with it a clear insight into the nature of all movements that come and makes it easy to reject what has to be rejected and keep the right attitude and perception. It does not matter about the image of the Mother. It is her presence whether in form or not that has to be felt always and this the psychic opening will surely bring.

*

It [*concentration in the heart*] is the best to "start with" — but as you have already started with success on the two higher centres, there is no reason why you should discontinue that. The other you may try from time to time when you find a sufficient quietude. Concentration there leads — or should lead — to the psychic opening.

*

Concentration in the heart is best aided if possible by the power and light descending from above the head.

*

At the top of the head or above it is the right place for Yogic concentration in reading or thinking.

*

Brain concentration is always a tapasya and necessarily brings a strain. It is only if one is lifted out of the brain mind altogether that the strain of mental concentration disappears.

Postures for Concentration or Meditation

The sitting motionless posture is the natural posture for concentrated meditation — walking and standing are active conditions suited for the dispense of energy and the activity of the mind. It is only when one has gained the enduring rest and passivity of the consciousness that it is easy to concentrate and receive when walking or doing anything. A fundamental passive condition of the consciousness gathered into itself is the proper poise for concentration and a seated gathered immobility in the body is the best for that. It can be done also lying down, but that position is too passive, tending to be inert rather than gathered. This is the reason why Yogis always sit in an asana. One can accustom oneself to meditate walking, standing, lying, but sitting is the first natural position.

*

One can meditate very well when walking.

*

It is as each finds convenient. Some meditate better walking, some sitting.

*

The rigidity [*of the body during meditation*] comes very often when there is the descent of the higher consciousness into the body.

Regularity, Length and Other Conditions

If it is possible to keep a fixed period for meditation and stick to it, it would certainly be desirable.

*

To keep the consciousness awake you must set apart a certain time every day for concentration and remembering the Mother and keeping yourself in contact with us. What is gained is not lost by interruption, but it goes behind and may take time to come out again — so the thread should not be cut.

*

It is not the length of the meditations that makes the difference [*in making one vitally and physically strong*]. It is a concentration of the will that is needed.

*

It is better to make the deeper concentration when you are alone or quiet. Outward sounds ought not to disturb you.

*

In external things all men of action have to do that [*shift their concentration quickly from one thing to another*] — otherwise they would not be able to cope with their work. In respect to inner concentration, it is not so easy because people bring other vibrations which interfere with the poise of the consciousness — a mere mental interruption ought not to be difficult to recover from; but if the consciousness itself gets invaded or else drawn out, it takes time to get back. In the end a condition develops in which the inner consciousness is always concentrated and in a poise, *samāhitaḥ*, and outside things take place only on the outermost surface. Then it becomes easy.

*

It is quite natural that at first there should be the condition of calm and peace only when you sit for concentration. What is important is that there should be this condition whenever you sit and the pressure for it always there. But at other times the result is at first only a certain mental quiet and freedom from thoughts. Afterwards when the condition of peace is quite settled in the inner being — for it is the inner into which you enter whenever you concentrate — then it begins to come out and control the outer, so that the calm and peace remain even when working, mixing with others, talking or other occupations. For then whatever the outer consciousness is doing, one feels the inner being calm within — indeed one feels the inner being as one's real self while the outer is something superficial through which the inner acts on life.

*

The gaze should not be fixed for a long time as it overstrains the eyes (unless one has a long practice in Tratak). The fixing of the eyes is not necessary — a natural gaze is sufficient and it should be varied by meditation with closed eyes.

*

When the meditation is done with the photo, it is better done with open eyes.

Coming out of Concentration or Meditation

You enter into a condition of deep inwardness and quiet. But if one comes too suddenly out of it into the ordinary consciousness, then there may be a slight nervous shock or a beating of the heart such as you describe, for a short time. It is always best to remain quiet for a few moments before opening the eyes and coming out of this inwardness.

*

It is certainly much better to remain silent and collected for a time after the meditation. It is a mistake to take the meditation lightly — by doing that one fails to receive or spills what is received or most of it.

*

Your meditation is all right, as Mother saw — but when you came out of it, you fell into the ordinary consciousness, that is the difficulty. You must try to keep the true consciousness always, even in activity — then the sadhana will begin to be there all the time and your difficulty will disappear.

The Difficulty of the Mechanical Mind

That [*the constant recurrence of trivial thoughts*] is the nature of the mechanical mind — it is not due to any sensitiveness in it. Only as the other parts of the mind are more silent and under control, this activity looks more prominent and takes more space. It usually wears itself out, if one goes on rejecting it.

*

It was rather that the active mind became more quiet so that the movements of the mechanical mind became more evident — that is what often happens. What has to be done in that case is to detach oneself from these movements and concentrate without farther attention to them. They are then likely to sink into quietude or fall away.

*

To be able to detach oneself from the action of the mechanical mind is the first necessity so that it may be like a noise in the street which passes and which one can ignore. It is easier then for the quiet and peace of the mind to remain undisturbed by this action even if it occurs.

If the peace and silence continue to come down, they usually become so intense as to seize the physical mind also after a time.

*

You are probably paying too much attention to them [*mechanical thoughts*]. It is quite possible to concentrate and let the mechanical activity pass unnoticed.

*

The more the psychic spreads in the outer being, the more all these things [*the mechanical activities of the subconscious mind*] fall quiet. That is the best way. Direct efforts to still the mind are a difficult method.

Surface Thoughts and Imaginations

That [*a state in which the outer being responds to surface thoughts while the inner being is "engrossed in meditation"*] is not called meditation — it is a divided state of consciousness. Unless the consciousness is really engrossed and the surface thoughts are only things that come across and touch and pass, it can hardly be called meditation (dhyana). I don't see how the inner being can be "engrossed" while thoughts and imaginations of another kind are rampaging about in the consciousness. One can remain separate and see the thoughts and imaginations pass without being affected, but that is not being plunged or engrossed in meditation.

Straining and Concentration

Straining and concentration are not the same thing. Straining implies an over-eagerness and violence of effort, while concentration is in its nature quiet and steady. If there is restlessness or over-eagerness, then that is not concentration.

*

Effort means straining endeavour. There can be an action with a will in it in which there is no strain of effort.

*

It was by your personal efforts without guidance that you got into difficulties and into a heated condition in which you could not meditate etc. I asked you to drop the effort and remain quiet and you did so. My intention was that by your remaining quiet, it would be possible for the Mother's Force to work in you and establish a better starting-point and a course of initial experiences. It was what was beginning to come; but if your mind again becomes active and tries to arrange the sadhana for itself, then disturbances are likely to come. The Divine Guidance works best when the psychic is open and in front (yours was beginning to open), but it can also work even when the sadhak is either not conscious of it or else knows it only by its results. As for Nirvikalpa Samadhi, even if one wants it, it is only the result of a long sadhana in a consciousness prepared for it — it is no use thinking of it when the inner consciousness is only just beginning to open to Yogic experience.

Relaxation and Concentration

There are two different states, that which the consciousness takes in concentration and that which it takes in relaxation — the latter is the ordinary consciousness (ordinary for the sadhak, though not perhaps the ordinary consciousness of the average man), the former is what he is attaining to by tapas of concentration in sadhana. To go into the Akshara and witness experiences from there is easy for the sadhak who has got so far. He can also concentrate and maintain the unification of the main aspects of his being, although with more difficulty — but a relaxation there brings him back to the relaxed "ordinary" consciousness. It is only when what is gained by sadhana becomes normal to the ordinary consciousness that this can be avoided. In proportion as this is done, it becomes possible not only to experience the truth subjectively, but make it manifest in action.

Passive Meditation and Concentration

What happened in the beginning of his sadhana must have been that he made the mistake of entering into a passive meditation instead of into a concentration proper. This kind of passive meditation can bring a great peace and quiet and joy. The Light also may come and other spiritual experiences. But it leaves the vital and body passive and without defence against inertia, illness etc. instead of bringing it either a dynamic force or a strong self-contained peace. The consciousness instead of being concentrated gets widely diffused and loosely extended. From the passivity came the weakness and disinclination for the worldly duties; from the diffusion the play of activity in the mind which prevented sleep and could not be controlled in a tendency also for the subtle being to go out of the body in the waking condition instead of through sleep as it ordinarily does, whence the beating of the heart and the cold feet. Concentration must in the earlier stages be active and dynamic with the consciousness gathered and capable of turning the will in any direction.

The concentration in this Yoga must be in the head or in the heart-centre, not in the centre at the base of the spinal cord — that can only come afterwards when all the other centres have been opened.

It is sometimes a little difficult to correct the effects of a wrong start. At any rate he may try the effects of an active concentration in either the head (forehead centre) or heart. The latter may be safer so as to avoid the return of the heating of the head which came from that first concentration. If there are any disturbing results, the concentration should not be continued and all should be turned towards a purification of the being such as he speaks of having practised and only when this is sufficiently advanced, should the concentration be resumed.

Inertia, Laziness, Tiredness in Meditation

It is not a fact that when there is obscurity or inertia, one cannot concentrate or meditate. If one has in the inner being the steady will to do it, it can be done.

*

It is quite natural to want to meditate while reading Yogic literature — that is not the laziness.
The laziness of the mind consists in not meditating when the consciousness wants to do so.

*

Ego, I suppose, or inertia [*hinders the feeling of satisfied peace or quiet release in meditation*]. If higher meditation or being above keeps you dull and without any kind of satisfaction or peace in sadhana, these are the only two reasons I can think of.

*

If the mind gets tired, naturally it is difficult to concentrate — unless you have become separated from the mind.

*

Naturally one does not get tired if the meditation has become natural. But if the capacity is not there yet, then many cannot go on without a strain which brings fatigue.

*

Concentration is very helpful and necessary — the more one concentrates (of course in the limits of the body's capacity without straining it), the more the force of the Yoga grows. But you must be prepared for the meditation being sometimes not successful and not get upset by it — for that variability of the meditations happens to everybody. There are different causes for it. But it is mostly something physical that interferes, either the need of the body to take time to assimilate what has come or been done or sometimes inertia or dullness due to causes such as those you mention or others. The best thing is to remain quiet and not get nervous or dejected — till the force acts again.

Meditation, Sleep and Samadhi

When one tries to meditate, there is a pressure to go inside, lose the waking consciousness and wake inside, in a deep inner consciousness. But at first the mind takes it for a pressure to go to sleep, since sleep is the only kind of inner consciousness to which it has been accustomed. In Yoga by meditation sleep is therefore often the first difficulty — but if one perseveres then gradually the sleep changes to an inner conscious state.

*

I think the sleepiness is a stage which everybody goes through — a sort of mechanical reaction of the physical to the pressure for including it in the concentration of the sadhana. It is best not to mind it; it will go of itself as the consciousness increases and takes the physical into its poise. It is better to let us know about any physical troubles.

*

The sleep does come like that when one tries to meditate. It has to be dealt with, where that is possible, by turning it into a conscious inner and indrawn state and, where not, by remaining in a quietly concentrated wakefulness open (without effort) to receive.

*

This tendency to sit and be perfectly quiet and this pressure of sleep are not at all due to laziness. You must put that idea out of your head. It is due to the tendency to quiet, peace, going inside; when the sadhana begins with some intensity, it is most often like that for a time. Afterwards there is a more even balance between the inner and the outer consciousness or rather the outer begins to change and become of one piece with the inner. So do not let this trouble you.

*

When the pressure gives a tendency to insideness (samadhi), the physical being, not being accustomed to go inside except in the way of sleep, translates this into a sense of sleepiness.

*

It [*the tendency to fall asleep during meditation*] is a common obstacle with all who practise Yoga at the beginning. This sleep disappears gradually in two ways — (1) by the intensifying of the force of concentration — (2) by the sleep itself becoming a kind of swapna samadhi in which one is conscious of inner experiences that are not dreams (i.e. the waking consciousness is lost for the time, but it is replaced not by sleep but by an inward conscious state in which one moves in the supraphysical of the mental or vital being).

*

The Yogic sleep is good only when it is Yogic enough to contain something, to be an inner consciousness or an experience of other planes. The *jāgarti* is important — to be conscious in the sleep, an inner waking. But when the mind is not accustomed, it tends to respond to the impulse towards this "going inside" into an inner consciousness caused by meditation by simply falling into the usual sleep to which it is accustomed. *Nidrā* is one of the recognised difficulties of Yoga — *nidrā* refusing to turn into samadhi, whether *svapna-samādhi* or *suṣupti*. So the force is necessary and I will try to send it. I only wish people would give me more time for this inner work both for myself and them! but that seems past hoping for.

*

It is probably that [*in meditation*] you go inside into a sort of samadhi but are not yet conscious there (hence the idea of sleep). X is not asleep, but he has when he goes inside no control of his body. Many Yogis have this difficulty and use a contrivance which is put under the chin to hold up the head and with it the body during this inward-going concentration.

*

There is no harm in the deep sleep that comes — as I have told you, it is the tendency to go deep inside that brings it and it is necessary to go deep inside in order to establish the full connection between the psychic and the rest of the nature.

Chapter Two

Mantra and Japa

The Word

The word is a sound expressive of the idea. In the supra-physical plane when an idea has to be realised, one can by repeating the word-expression of it, produce vibrations which prepare the mind for the realisation of the idea. That is the principle of the Mantra and of japa. One repeats the name of the Divine and the vibrations created in the consciousness prepare the realisation of the Divine. It is the same idea that is expressed in the Bible, "God said, Let there be Light, and there was Light." It is creation by the Word.

*

The Word has power — even the ordinary written word has a power. If it is an inspired word it has still more power. What kind of power or power for what depends on the nature of the inspiration and the theme and the part of the being it touches. If it is the Word itself, — as in certain utterances of the great Scriptures — Veda, Upanishads, Gita, — it may well have a power to awaken a spiritual impulse, an uplifting, even certain kinds of realisation. To say that it cannot contradicts spiritual experience.

The Vedic poets regarded their poetry as *mantras*, they were the vehicles of their own realisations and could become vehicles of realisation for others. Naturally, these mostly would be illuminations, not the settled and permanent realisation that is the goal of Yoga — but they could be steps on the way or at least lights on the way. Many have such illuminations, even initial realisations while meditating on verses of the Upanishads or the Gita. Anything that carries the Word, the Light in it, spoken or written, can light this fire within, open a sky, as it were, bring the effective vision of which the Word is the body. In all ages spiritual seekers have expressed their aspirations or their experiences in poetry or inspired language and it has helped themselves and others. Therefore there is nothing absurd in my assigning to such poetry a spiritual or psychic value and effectiveness to poetry of a psychic or spiritual character.

Mantras

Mantras come to many people in meditation. The Rishis say in the Veda that they had the Truth by vision and inspiration, "truth-hearing seers", *kavayaḥ satyaśrutaḥ* — Veda is *śruti* got by inner hearing.

*

When one repeats a mantra regularly, very often it begins to repeat itself within, which means that it is taken up by the inner being. In that way it is more effective.

*

It [*the effect of japa*] depends on the way in which the japa is done.
    If rightly done, the mantra is a means of opening to the light and knowledge etc. from above and it ceases as soon as that is done.

*

I do not believe a mantra can change the physical consciousness. What it does, if it is effective, is to open the consciousness and to bring into it the power of that which the mantra represents.

*

There is such a thing as mantra-shakti; but it acts only on certain conditions.

The Mantra OM

OM is the mantra, the expressive sound-symbol of the Brahman Consciousness in its four domains from the Turiya to the external or material plane. The function of a mantra is to create vibrations in the inner consciousness that will prepare it for the realisation of what the mantra symbolises and is supposed indeed to carry within itself. The mantra OM should therefore lead towards the opening of the consciousness to the sight and feeling of the One Consciousness in all material things, in the inner being and in the supraphysical worlds, in the causal plane above now superconscient to us and, finally, the supreme liberated transcendence above all cosmic existence. The last is usually the main preoccupation with those who use the mantra.

In this Yoga there is no fixed mantra, no stress is laid on mantras, although sadhaks can use one if they find it helpful or so long as they find it helpful. The stress is rather on an aspiration in the consciousness and a concentration of the mind, heart, will, all the being. If a mantra is found helpful for that, one uses it. OM if rightly used (not mechanically) might very well help the opening upwards and outwards (cosmic consciousness) as well as the descent.

*

It [*Pranava japa*] is supposed to have a force of its own although that force cannot fully work without the meditation on the meaning. But my experience is that in these things there is no invariable rule and that most depends on the consciousness or the power of response in the sadhak. With some it has no effect, with some it has a rapid and powerful effect even without meditation — for others the meditation is necessary for any effect to come.

The Mantra *So'ham*

A divine Name or a Mantra (like the *So'ham*) can enter the adhara and move in the breathing as in your experience. When it does so, that is not the opening of which I speak in the sentence you quote, but it may come to make the aspiration effective by helping in the opening — by removing something that prevents the opening and by leading to the experience it carries in it.

The experience to which the *So'ham* mantra leads is the

realisation of one Being everywhere, all as the Divine, oneself and all as essentially one with that Divine. It is an experience in which one's separate personal existence shut up in the body ceases to be the normal thing; one feels the body as a point or small thing in a vast existence, consciousness or Ananda that is the Divine and oneself as spread out in that vast consciousness — as if the world were within us and not we inside the world or as if the world were one with us and one with the Divine. It is the "cosmic consciousness" that comes by this mantra. For our Yoga this is a beginning only, not the end as it is in the ordinary Yoga, — a liberation, not the Siddhi.

The Gayatri Mantra

The power of the Gayatri is the Light of the divine Truth. It is a mantra of Knowledge.

*

The Gayatri mantra is the mantra for bringing the light of Truth into all the planes of the being. The other [*Sri Aurobindo Mira*] has a general power.

*

It is not necessary to give up Gayatri Japa or the process which you are following at present. Concentration in the heart is one method, concentration in the head (or above) is another; both are included in this Yoga and one has to do whichever one finds easiest and most natural. The object of the concentration in the heart is to open the centre there (heart-lotus), to feel the presence of the Divine Mother in the heart and to become aware of one's soul or psychic being which is a portion of the Divine. The object of the concentration in the head is to rise to the Divine Consciousness and bring down the Light of the Mother or her Force or Ananda into all the centres. This movement of ascent and descent is implied in the process of your japa and it is not therefore necessary to renounce it.

There is a level corresponding to the Satya Loka in the head but the consciousness has at a certain stage to rise above the head freely to meet the same level in the universal Consciousness above.

Mantras in the Integral Yoga

The idea of your friend that it is necessary to receive a mantra from here and for that he must come is altogether wrong. There is no mantra given in this Yoga. It is the opening of the consciousness to the Mother from within that is the true initiation and that can only come by aspiration and rejection of restlessness in the mind and vital.

*

We do not usually give any mantra. Those who repeat something in meditation call on the Mother.

*

As a rule the only mantra used in this sadhana is that of the Mother or of my name and the Mother. The concentration in the heart and the concentration in the head can both be used — each has its own result. The first opens up the psychic being and brings bhakti, love and union with the Mother, her presence within the heart and the action of her Force in the nature. The other opens the mind to self-realisation, to the consciousness of what is above mind, to the ascent of the consciousness out of the body and the descent of the higher consciousness into the body.

*

There is not necessarily any difference of Force.[1] Usually the Mother's name has the full power in it; but in certain states of consciousness the double Name may have a special effect.

---

[1] *The correspondent asked whether there is any difference of Force when one repeats only the Mother's name and when one repeats both the names of Sri Aurobindo and the Mother together. — Ed.*

Namajapa or Repetition of the Name

The name of the Divine is usually called in for protection, for adoration, for increase of bhakti, for the opening up of the inner consciousness, for the realisation of the Divine in that aspect. As far as it is necessary to work in the subconscious for that, the Name must be effective there.

*

It [*the effectiveness of namajapa*] depends on the person and how he does it. The Name of the Divine is in itself a power, if it is taken with the right faith and in the right attitude.

*

Namajapa has a great power in it.

*

Namochcharana has power but only if it comes from the heart and the soul; mere repetition with the mind is not enough.

*

Whatever name is called the Power that answers is the Mother. Each name indicates a certain aspect of the Divine and is limited by that aspect; the Mother's Power is universal.

*

Naturally, whatever name one concentrates on [*while awake*] will repeat itself [*in sleep*], if any does. But the calling of Mother in sleep is not necessarily a repetition — it is the inner being that often calls to her in difficulty or in need.

*

I did not encourage the name with the breathing because that seemed like pranayam. Pranayam is a very powerful thing, but if done haphazardly it may lead to the raising of obstructions and even in extreme cases illness in the body.

Verses of the Gita Used as Japa

Verses of the Gita can be used as japa, if the object is to realise the Truth that the verses contain in them. If X's father has taken the salient verses containing the heart of the teaching for that purpose, then it is all right. Everything depends on the selection of the verses. A coherent summary of the Gita's teaching cannot easily be put together by putting together some verses, but that is not necessary for a purpose of this kind which could only be to put the key truths together — not for intellectual exposition but for grasping in realisation which is the object of japa.

Success in Japa

I am sorry the old reaction to the japa has recurred. Perhaps the mind is doing it too much as a means for a result. The japa is usually successful only on one of two conditions, — if it is repeated with a sense of its significance, a dwelling of something in the mind on the nature, power, beauty, attraction of the Godhead it signifies and is to bring into the consciousness, that is the mental way, — or if it comes up from the heart or rings in it with a certain sense or feeling of bhakti making it alive, that is the emotional way. Either the mind or the vital has to give it support or sustenance. But if it makes the mind dry and the vital restless, it must be missing that support and sustenance. There is of course a third way, the reliance on the power of the mantra or name in itself, but then one has to go on till that power has sufficiently impressed its vibrations on the inner being to make it at a given moment suddenly open to the Presence or the Touch. But if there is a struggling or insistence for the result, then this effect which needs a quiet receptivity in the mind is impeded. That is why I insisted so much on mental quietude and on not too much straining or effort — to give time to allow the psychic and the mind to develop the necessary condition of receptivity — a receptivity as natural as when one receives an inspiration for poetry and music. It is also why I do not want you to discontinue your poetry — it helps and does not hinder the preparation because it is a means of developing the right position of receptivity and bringing out the bhakti which is there in the inner being. To spend all the energy on japa or meditation is a strain which even those who are accustomed to successful meditation find it difficult to do — unless in periods when there is an uninterrupted flow of experiences from above.

*

It is very good news that you got rid of the attack and it was the japa that helped you to do it. This and past experience also shows that if you can overcome the old association of the japa with sterility and sorrow, it can do its natural function of creating the right consciousness — for that is what the japa is intended to do. It first changes the vibrations of the consciousness, brings into it the right state and the right responses and then brings in the power or the presence of the Deity. Several times before you wrote to me that by doing japa you got rid of the old impulse and recovered calm and the right turn of the consciousness and now it has helped you to get rid of the invasion of sorrow and despondency. Let us hope that this last will also soon lose its strength like the impulse and calm and serenity begin to establish itself in the whole nature.

Section Four

Sadhana through Love and Devotion

Chapter One
Divine Love, Psychic Love and Human Love

Divine Love and Its Manifestation

To bring the Divine Love and Beauty and Ananda into the world is, indeed, the whole crown and essence of our Yoga. But it has always seemed to me impossible unless there comes as its support and foundation and guard the Divine Truth — what I call the Supramental — and its Divine Power. Otherwise Love itself blinded by the confusions of this present consciousness may stumble in its human receptacles and, even otherwise, may find itself unrecognised, rejected or rapidly degenerating and lost in the frailty of man's inferior nature. But when it comes in the Divine Truth and Power, Divine Love descends first as something transcendent and universal and out of that transcendence and universality it applies itself to persons according to the Divine Truth and Will, creating a vaster, greater, purer personal love than any the human mind or heart can now imagine. It is when one has felt this descent that one can be really an instrument for the birth and action of the Divine Love in the world.

*

It [*the Divine Truth*] can come solely as knowledge or as knowledge + calm and peace or knowledge with power. It is not always accompanied by Ananda.

What was meant [*in the preceding letter*] was that it is possible to have some kind of Ananda on all the planes, vital, mental, physical; but if one wants to live securely in the highest divine Ananda it can only be done by bringing down the (supramental) Truth and living first in the supramental Light. But this is the eventual aim of the Yoga; it does not debar one from accepting whatever Ananda comes on the way. Only, mere pleasure or vital excitement and gratification must not be mistaken for Ananda.

*

The human form is naturally unable to bear the Divine Love or contain it, because it is itself a creation of the ignorance, weak and impure. It must be transformed in order to be capable of that; it must become strong and pure. First of all, it must have the strength to love the Divine alone and turn away from all other ties. But besides that a new consciousness must be created in it — first a consciousness of pure and purifying Divine Peace from above which must take hold of all down to the most physical — then in that peace an increasing inner strength pure and unegoistic — then the Divine Light and Knowledge transforming all the consciousness and movements. When this has been done, then the human form can contain the Divine Love and Ananda. Till then the touches of the Divine Love and Ananda are usually momentary or brief, they cannot remain. In an impure consciousness the Divine Love if it came in would create a perturbation and possibly be attacked by a mixture which would make it impossible for it to stay. It is therefore that touches only can come.

*

I understand that it is the physical consciousness which has come up forcibly with the old vital human movements and feelings and this has clouded for the moment the sense of higher things and the aspiration for Truth and Purity that is their atmosphere. The Divine Love may not be able yet to manifest on the physical plane, humanity being what it is, as fully and freely as it would otherwise do, but that does not make it less close or intense than the human. It is there waiting to be understood and accepted and meanwhile giving all the help you can receive to raise and widen you into the consciousness in which it will be no longer possible for these difficulties and these misunderstandings to recur — the state in which there is possible the full and perfect union.

*

It [*the Divine Love*] exists in itself and does not depend on outer contact or outer expression. Whether it shall express itself outwardly or how it will express itself outwardly depends on the spiritual truth that has to be manifested.

*

There is the one divine Love secret in all things, but the manifestation [*of it in matter and in forms of life*] depends upon the state of consciousness and its organisation.

*

I do not exactly know what you mean by the Divine Love being established down to the subconscious. What love? the soul's love for the Divine? or the principle of the Divine Love and Ananda which is the highest thing that can be reached? To establish the latter down to the subconscient is a thing which would mean the entire transformation of the whole being and it cannot be done except as the result of the supramental change which is as yet far away. The other may be established even now in principle, but to make it living and complete in the whole being would mean the psychic transformation completed with the spiritual also well under way already.

*

The Intuitive or Overmind are more open to the truth of Divine Love and more capable of universalising love than the mind ordinarily is — love there is also more calm in its intensity, less ego-bound than in the mental parts. But the mind can also approach their quality of love, if the love in it grows psychic and spiritual.

*

By becoming divine in nature [*one can love divinely*]; there is no other way.

Divine Love and Psychic Love

The Divine's love is that which comes from above poured down from the Divine Oneness and its Ananda on the being — psychic love is a form taken by divine love in the human being according to the needs and possibilities of the human consciousness.

*

If love is psychic in its nature, it always brings the sense of oneness or at least of an inner intimate closeness of being. The Divine Love is based upon oneness and the psychic derives from the Divine Love.

*

The psychic love is pure and full of self-giving without egoistic demand, but it is human and can err and suffer. The Divine Love is something much vaster and deeper and full of light and ananda.

Psychic Love

When there is no demand or desire, only love and self-giving, that is the psychic love.

*

Psychic love is quite satisfying, and it can change even the vital love into something great and beautiful.

*

Why do you want something remarkable? The love of the soul is the true thing, simple and absolute — the rest is good only if it is a means of manifestation of the soul's love.

*

The soul's love and joy come from within from the psychic being. What comes from above is the Ananda of the higher consciousness.

*

The love that belongs to the spiritual planes is of a different kind — the psychic has its own more personal love, bhakti, surrender. Love in the higher or spiritual mind is more universal and impersonal. The two must join together to make the highest divine love.

*

The psychic realisation is one of diversity in unity (the portion and the whole); it is not one of dissolving like a drop of water in the sea — for then no love or devotion is possible unless it is love of oneself, devotion to oneself.

Universal Love and Psychic Love

Universal love is always universal — psychic love can individualise itself.

*

Cosmic love depends on the realisation of oneness of self with all. Psychic love or feeling for all can exist without this realisation.

*

The oneness with all in its basis is something self-existent and self-content which does not *need* expression. When it does express itself as love, it is something wide and universal, untroubled and firm even when it is intense. This is in the basic cosmic oneness. There is also the surface cosmic consciousness which is an awareness of the play of cosmic forces — here anything may rise, sex also. It is this part that needs the perfect psychisation, otherwise one cannot even hold, contain and deal with it in the proper way.

*

I do not quite understand X's question. Does he mean to ask whether one can become conscious of the Divine's Love for all creatures before one is oneself filled with the universal love for others? If that is the meaning, then one can certainly become conscious of the Divine's Love before one has oneself the universal love — one can become conscious of it by contact with the Divine in oneself. Naturally the consciousness of it should lead to the development of a universal love for all. But if he means a love that is divine, not tainted by the lower movements, then it is true that until there comes the peace, purity, freedom from ego, wideness, light of the universal consciousness which is the basis of the universal love, it is difficult to have a love that is free from all the defects, limitations, taints of ordinary human love. The more one has of the universality the more one tends to be freed from these things.

Love for the Divine

The love which is turned towards the Divine ought not to be the usual vital feeling which men call by that name; for that is not love, but only a vital desire, an instinct of appropriation, the impulse to possess and monopolise. Not only is this not the divine Love, but it ought not to be allowed to mix in the least degree in the Yoga. The true love for the Divine is a self-giving, free of demand, full of submission and surrender; it makes no claim, imposes no condition, strikes no bargain, indulges in no violences of jealousy or pride or anger — for these things are not in its composition. In return the Divine Mother also gives herself, but freely — and this represents itself in an inner giving — her presence in your mind, your vital, your physical consciousness, her power re-creating you in the divine nature, taking up all the movements of your being and directing them towards perfection and fulfilment, her love enveloping you and carrying you in its arms Godwards. It is this that you must aspire to feel and possess in all your parts down to the very material, and here there is no limitation either of time or of completeness. If one truly aspires and gets it, there ought to be no room for any other claim or for any disappointed desire. And if one truly aspires, one does unfailingly get it, more and more as the purification proceeds and the nature undergoes its needed change.

Keep your love pure of all selfish claim and desire; you will find that you are getting all the love that you can bear and absorb in answer.

Realise also that the Realisation must come first, the work to be done, not the satisfaction of claim and desire. It is only when the Divine Consciousness in its supramental Light and Power has descended and transformed the physical that other things can be given a prominent place — and then too it will not be the satisfaction of desire, but the fulfilment of the Divine Truth in each and all and in the new life that is to express it. In the divine life all is for the sake of the Divine and not for the sake of the ego.

I should perhaps add one or two things to avoid misapprehensions. First, the love for the Divine of which I speak is not a psychic love only; it is the love of all the being, the vital and vital-physical included, — all are capable of the same self-giving. It is a mistake to believe that if the vital loves, it must be a love that demands and imposes the satisfaction of its desire; it is a mistake to think that it must be either that or else the vital, in order to escape from its "attachment", must draw away altogether from the object of its love. The vital can be as absolute in its unquestioning self-giving as any other part of the nature; nothing can be more generous than its movement when it forgets self for the Beloved. The vital and physical should both give themselves in the true way — the way of true love, not of ego-desire.

*

I suppose "love" expresses something more intense than *bhālobāshā* which can include mere liking or affection. But whether love or *bhālobāshā*, the human feeling is always either based on or strongly mixed with ego, — that is why it cannot be pure. It is said in the Upanishad, "One does not love the wife for the sake of the wife" or the child or friend etc. as the case may be "but for one's self's sake one loves the wife". There is usually a hope of return, of benefit or advantage of some kind, or of certain pleasures and satisfactions, mental, vital or physical, that the person loved can give. Remove these things and the love very soon sinks, diminishes or disappears or turns into anger, reproach, indifference or even hatred. But there is also an element of habit, something that makes the presence of the person loved a sort of necessity because it has always been there — and this is sometimes so strong that even in spite of entire incompatibility of temper, fierce antagonism, something like hatred, it lasts and even these gulfs of discord are not enough to make the persons part; in other cases this feeling is more tepid and after a time one gets accustomed to separation or accepts a substitute. There is again often the element of some kind of spontaneous attraction or affinity, mental, vital or physical, which gives a stronger cohesion to the love. Lastly, there is in the highest or deepest kind of love the psychic element, which comes from the inmost heart and soul, a kind of inner union or self-giving or at least a seeking for that, a tie or an urge independent of other conditions or elements, existing for its own sake and not for any mental, vital or physical pleasure, satisfaction, interest or habit. But usually the psychic element in human love, even where it is present, is so much mixed, overloaded and hidden under the others that it has little chance of fulfilling itself or achieving its own natural purity and fullness. What is called love is therefore sometimes one thing, sometimes another, most often a confused mixture, and it is impossible to give a general answer to the questions you put as to what is meant by love in such and such a phrase. It depends on the persons and the circumstances.

When the love goes towards the Divine, there is still this ordinary human element in it. There is the call for a return and if the return does not seem to come, the love may sink; there is the self-interest, the demand for the Divine as a giver of all that the human being wants and, if the demands are not acceded to, abhimana against the Divine, loss of faith, loss of fervour. Etc. etc. But the true love for the Divine is in its fundamental nature not of this kind, but psychic and spiritual. The psychic element is the need of the inmost being for self-giving, love, adoration, union which can only be fully satisfied by the Divine. The spiritual element is the need of the being for contact, merging, union with its own highest and whole self and source of being and consciousness and bliss, the Divine. These two are two sides of the same thing. The mind, vital, physical can be the supports and recipients of this love, but they can be fully that only when they become remoulded into harmony with the psychic and spiritual elements of the being and no longer bring in the lower insistences of the ego.

*

Love for the Divine must be there in all the being — not only in the spirit and the psychic heart, but in the vital and the physical consciousness also.

*

The influence of the love for the Divine when it takes hold of any part is to turn it towards the Divine — as you describe it "concentration on the Mother" — and in the end all is gathered and harmonised around this central turn of the being. The difficulty is with the mechanical parts of the being in which the old thoughts go on recurring by habit. If the concentration continues to grow, this becomes a thing of little importance at the circumference of the mind and in the end drops away to be replaced by things that belong to the new consciousness.

Human Love in the Sadhana

And first about human love in the sadhana. The soul's turning through love to the Divine must be through a love that is essentially divine, but as the instrument of expression at first is a human nature, it takes the forms of human love and bhakti. It is only as the consciousness deepens, heightens and changes that that greater eternal love can grow in it and openly transform the human into the divine. But in human love itself there are several kinds of motive-forces. There is a psychic human love which rises from deep within and is the result of the meeting of the inner being with that which calls it towards a divine joy and union; it is, once it becomes aware of itself, something lasting, self-existent, not dependent upon external satisfactions, not capable of diminution by external causes, not self-regarding, not prone to demand or bargain but giving itself simply and spontaneously, not moved to or broken by misunderstandings, disappointments, strife and anger, but pressing always straight towards the inner union. It is this psychic love that is closest to the divine and it is therefore the right and best way of love and bhakti. But that does not mean that the other parts of the being, the vital and physical included, are not to be used as means of expression or that they are not to share in the full play and the whole meaning of love, even of divine love. On the contrary, they are a means and can be a great part of the complete expression of divine love, — provided they have the right and not the wrong movement. There are in the vital itself two kinds of love, — one full of joy and confidence and abandon, generous, unbargaining, ungrudging and very absolute in its dedication and this is akin to the psychic and well-fitted to be its complement and a means of expression of the divine love. And neither does the psychic love or the divine love despise a physical means of expression wherever that is pure and right and possible: it does not depend upon that, it does not diminish, revolt or go out like a snuffed candle when it is deprived of any such means; but when it can use it, it does so with joy and gratitude. Physical means can be and are used in the approach to divine love and worship; they have not been allowed merely as a concession to human weakness, nor is it the fact that in the psychic way there is no place for such things. On the contrary they are one means of approaching the Divine and receiving the Light and materialising the psychic contact, and so long as it is done in the right spirit and they are used for the true purpose they have their place. It is only if they are misused or the approach is not right because tainted by indifference and inertia, or revolt or hostility, or some gross desire, that they are out of place and can have a contrary effect.

    But there is another way of vital love which is more usually the way of human nature and that is a way of ego and desire. It is full of vital craving, desire and demand; its continuance depends upon the satisfaction of its demands; if it does not get what it craves, or even imagines that it is not being treated as it deserves — for it is full of imaginations, misunderstandings, jealousies, misinterpretations — it at once turns to sorrow, wounded feeling, revolt, pride, anger, all kinds of disorder, finally cessation and departure. A love of this kind is in its very nature ephemeral and unreliable and it cannot be made a foundation for divine love. There has been too much of this kind in the relations of the sadhaks with the Mother — approaching her, I suppose, as a human mother with all the reactions of the lower vital nature. For a long time it was perforce tolerated — and this was the concession made to human weakness — even accepted in the beginning as a thing too prominent in the human being not to be there to some extent but to be transformed by degrees; but too often, it has refused to transform itself and has made itself a source of confusion, disorder, *asiddhi*, sometimes complete disaster. It is for this reason that we discourage this lower vital way of human love and would like people to reject and eliminate these elements as soon as may be from their nature. Love should be a flowering of joy and union and confidence and self-giving and Ananda, — but this lower vital way is only a source of suffering, trouble, disappointment, disillusion and disunion. Even a slight element of it shakes the foundations of peace and replaces the movement towards Ananda by a fall towards sorrow, discontent and Nirananda.

In your own case you often write in your wrong moods as if human love, even with some of these lower ingredients, were the only thing possible to you. But that is not so at all, for it contradicts your own deepest experiences. Always what your inner being has asked is Love, Bhakti, Ananda and whenever it comes to the surface it is, even if only in a first elementary form, the divine love which it brings with it. A basis of deep and intense calm and stillness, a great intensity of emotion and Bhakti, an inrush of Ananda, this is in these moments your repeated experience. On the other hand when you insist too much on the love which exists by external cravings, what comes is the other movement — fits of despondency, sorrow, Nirananda. In stressing on the psychic basis, in wishing you to conquer this other movement, I am only pointing you to the true way of your own nature — of which the psychic bhakti, the true vital love are the real moving forces, and the other is only a superficial immixture.

Human Love and Divine Love

May I put in a plea for my poor Supramental against which you seem to have something like a grudge? I should like to say that the Supramental is not something cold, distant and remote; on the contrary, when it descends into the physical, it will mean the full outflow and full completeness and expression of love on the vital and physical as well as on every other plane. And it is because I know it means this and many other desirable things that I am so insistent on bringing it down as soon as possible.

And let me say also that, as regards human love and divine love, I admitted the first as that from which we have to proceed and to arrive at the other, intensifying and transforming into it, not eliminating, human love. Divine Love, in my view of it, is again not something ethereal, cold and far, but a love absolutely intense, intimate and full of unity, closeness and rapture using all the nature for its expression. Certainly, it is without the confusions and disorders of the present lower vital nature which it will change into something entirely warm, deep and intense; but that is no reason for supposing that it will lose anything that is true and happy in the elements of love.

*

Love cannot be cold — for there is no such thing as cold love, but the love of which the Mother speaks in that passage[1] is something very pure, fixed and constant; it does not leap like fire and sink for want of fuel, but is steady and all-embracing

---

[1] "*It* [the being] *knows that this active state of love should be constant and impersonal, that is, absolutely independent of circumstances and persons, since it cannot and must not be concentrated upon any one thing in particular. . . .*" The Mother, Prayers and Meditations, (Pondicherry: Sri Aurobindo Ashram, 2003), Collected Works of the Mother (second edition), vol. 1, p. 335.

and self-existent like the light of the sun. There is also a divine love that is personal, but it is not like the ordinary personal human love dependent on any return from the person — it is personal but not egoistic, — it goes from the real being in the one to the real being in the other. But to find that, liberation from the ordinary human way of approach is necessary.

*

The Divine Love, unlike the human, is deep and vast and silent; one must become quiet and wide to be aware of it and reply to it. X must make it his whole object to be surrendered so that he may become a vessel and instrument — leaving it to the Divine Wisdom and Love to fill him with what is needed. Let him also fix this in the mind not to insist that in a given time he must progress, develop, get realisation; whatever time it takes, he must be prepared to wait and persevere and make his whole life an aspiration and an opening for the one thing only, the Divine. To give oneself is the secret of sadhana, not to demand and acquire. The more one gives oneself, the more the power to receive will grow. But for that all impatience and revolt must go; all suggestions of not getting, not being helped, not being loved, going away, of abandoning life or the spiritual endeavour must be rejected.

*

The Mother did not tell you that love is not an emotion, but that Divine Love is not an emotion, — a very different thing to say. Human love is made up of emotion, passion and desire, — all of them vital movements, therefore bound to the disabilities of the human vital nature. Emotion is an excellent and indispensable thing in human nature, in spite of all its shortcomings and dangers, — just as mental ideas are excellent and indispensable things in their own field in the human stage. But our aim is to go beyond mental ideas into the light of the supramental Truth, which exists not by ideative thought but by direct vision and identity. In the same way our aim is to go beyond emotion to the height and depth and intensity of the Divine Love and there feel through the inner psychic heart an inexhaustible oneness with the Divine which the spasmodic leapings of the vital emotions cannot reach or experience.

As supramental Truth is not merely a sublimation of our mental ideas, so Divine Love is not merely a sublimation of human emotions; it is a different consciousness, with a different quality, movement and substance.

*

Human love is mostly vital and physical with a mental support — it can take an unselfish, noble and pure form and expression only if it is touched by the psychic. It is true, as you say, that it is more usually a mixture of ignorance, attachment, passion and desire. But whatever it may be, one who wishes to reach the Divine must not burden himself with human loves and attachments, for they form so many fetters and hamper his steps, turning him away besides from the concentration of his emotions on the one supreme object of love.

There is such a thing as psychic love, pure, without demand, sincere in self-giving, but it is not usually left pure in the attraction of human beings to one another. One must also be on one's guard against the profession of psychic love when one is doing sadhana, — for that is most often a cloak and justification for yielding to a vital attraction or attachment.

Universal love is the spiritual founded on the sense of the One and the Divine everywhere and the change of the personal into a wide universal consciousness, free from attachment and ignorance.

Divine love is of two kinds — the Divine love for the creation and the souls that are part of itself and the love of the seeker and love for the Divine Beloved; it has both a personal and impersonal element, but the personal is free here from all lower elements or bondage to the vital and physical instincts.

*

If I am to take some expressions in one of your letters at their face value you seem to put forward — at least as a poet

— three notions about spiritual seeking which are somewhat extraordinary.
    1. "It is the *same* love which is addressed towards a 'carnal prize' and towards the Divine." I should imagine that one who approached the Divine with a "carnal" or an untransformed vital love would embrace something of the vital world but certainly get nowhere near the Divine.
    2. The Divine in itself is something cold and empty and dark — only human love gives it some warmth and attraction. I always thought that the Divine was the supreme ineffable Ananda of which human love and delight is only a clouded and fallen ray — most often hardly even that — compared with the empyrean of ethereal fire. How can the luminous eternal Ananda be something cold and dark, I should like to know?
    3. Or perhaps you only mean that the Divine Infinite which the calm sages seek is by the very fact of their calm and wisdom something cold, dark, empty, gloomy. Has it not occurred to you that if they really sought for something cold, dark and gloomy as the supreme good, they would not be sages but asses? The sages sought after the Divine as the supreme existence, consciousness and Bliss, the Light beyond lights by which all this shineth, the joy beyond all other joys. Even the seekers of the Absolute Indefinable find in it the peace that passeth all understanding and that is nothing cold, dark or gloomy. The Nihilistic Buddhists? But they did not believe in the Divine or in Eternity, only in Non-existence and what they sought was not the supreme good, but self-extinction and the end of suffering — an intelligible aim, but something quite different from the stress towards the Eternal.

The Vital and Love for the Divine

When the vital joins in the love for the Divine, it brings into it heroism, enthusiasm, intensity, absoluteness, exclusiveness, the spirit of self-sacrifice, the total and passionate self-giving of all the nature. It is the vital passion for the Divine that creates the spiritual heroes, conquerors or martyrs.

*

I have never said that the vital is to have no part in the love for the Divine, only that it must purify and ennoble itself in the light of the psychic being. The results of self-loving love between human beings are so poor and contrary in the end — that is what I mean by the ordinary vital love — that I want something purer and nobler and higher in the vital also for the movement towards the Divine.

*

The outer being has to learn to love in the psychic way without ego. If it loves in the egoistic vital way, then it only creates difficulties for itself and for the sadhana and for the Mother.

*

Yes, that is the nature of vital love. It is based on desire and the sense of claim or sense of possession; psychic love is based on self-giving.

*

If the love is absolute and complete and there has never been any vital demand connected with it, then suggestions of revolt cannot come.

*

Formerly whenever the opening of the heart came you began to associate it with vital enjoyment and turned it upon others instead of turning the love towards the Divine and keeping its essential purity — so also the higher consciousness when it came down was being dispersed in mental movements. This time they were both coming in a purer form, but the danger of the mental and vital forces catching hold of them is still there and then both are likely to stop or break down. So you must be careful to allow no vital deviation this time.

*

Your difficulty is that the vital has not yet arrived at the secret of the self-existent Ananda of love, the Ananda of love's own pure truth, the inner beauty of it for its own sake, the secret of the inner abiding ecstasy; it cannot yet believe that the thing exists. But it is travelling towards it and this feeling was probably a stage — a groping after a purer vital emotion on the way to the purest of all which is one with the Divine.

*

What he describes[2] is a vital demand of the ego for emotional self-satisfaction; it *is* Maya. It is not true love, for true love seeks for union and self-giving and that is the love one must bring to the Divine. This vital (so-called) love brings only suffering and disappointment; it does not bring happiness; it never gets satisfied and, even if it is granted something that it asks for, it is never satisfied with it.

It is perfectly possible to get rid of this Maya of the vital demand, if one wishes to do it, — but the will to do it must be sincere. If he is sincere in his will, he will certainly get help and protection.

*

Generally when people speak of vital intimacy they mean something very external which does not need to be brought down since it is common in human life. If it is the inner vital intimacy with the Divine, then of course that makes the union more complete, provided it is based on the psychic.

---

[2] *The correspondent wrote, "I want a heart that can respond to all my moods, that can understand me, that can do me justice, that can love me intensely and exclusively." Sri Aurobindo's reply was written to his secretary, who answered the enquirer. — Ed.*

Chapter Two
Bhakti, Devotion, Worship

Turning the Emotions towards the Divine

It is no part of this Yoga to dry up the heart; but the emotions must be turned towards the Divine. There may be short periods in which the heart is quiescent, turned away from the ordinary feelings and waiting for the inflow from above; but such states are not states of dryness but of silence and peace. The heart in this Yoga should in fact be the main centre of concentration until the consciousness rises above.

*

Emotion is a good element in Yoga; but emotional *desire* becomes easily a cause of perturbation and an obstacle.

Turn your emotions towards the Divine, aspire for their purification; they will then become a help on the way and no longer a cause of suffering.

Not to kill emotion, but to turn it towards the Divine is the right way of the Yoga.

But it must become pure, founded upon spiritual peace and joy, capable of being transmuted into Ananda. Equality and calm in the mind and vital parts, an intense psychic emotion in the heart can perfectly go together.

Awake by your aspiration the psychic fire in the heart that burns steadily towards the Divine — that is the one way to liberate and fulfil the emotional nature.

*

Emotion is necessary in the Yoga and it is only the excessive emotional sensitiveness which makes one enter into despondency over small things that has to be overcome. The very basis of this Yoga is bhakti and if one kills one's emotional being there can be no bhakti. So there can be no possibility of emotion being excluded from the Yoga.

*

It is only the ordinary vital emotions, which waste the energy and disturb the concentration and peace, that have to be discouraged. Emotion itself is not a bad thing; it is a necessary part of the nature, and psychic emotion is one of the most powerful helps to the sadhana. Psychic emotion, bringing tears of love for the Divine or tears of ananda, ought not to be suppressed: it is only a vital mixture that brings disturbance in the sadhana.

*

It is quite true that by going above one can get out of all problems, for they no longer exist, but the problems are there below and it is difficult to be always above with so much unsolved and calling for solution. But just as one can go high above, so one can go deep within and it is this going deep within that is needed. What happened was at the surface of the emotional being and if one simply stays there the difficulties of the emotional can come, but what has to be done is not to stay on the surface but go deep within. For the psychic is there behind the emotional surface, deep behind the heart centre. Once one reaches it, these things can no longer touch; what will be there is the inner peace and happiness, the untroubled aspiration, the presence or nearness of the Mother.

*

To indulge in the emotions, love, grief, sorrow, despair, emotional joy etc. for their own sake with a sort of mental-vital over-emphasis on them is what is called sentimentalism. There should be even in deep feeling a calm, a control, a purifying restraint and measure. One should not be at the mercy of one's feelings and sentiments, but master of oneself always.

*

When the consciousness indulges in these things [*joy and sorrow*] and wallows in the excitement of emotional joy or suffering, that is called sentimentalism. There is another kind in which the mind enjoys its perceptions of emotion, love and suffering etc. and plays with them, but that is a less violent and more superficial sentimentalism.

Bhakti or Devotion

Bhakti is not an experience, it is a state of the heart and soul. It is a state which comes when the psychic being is awake and prominent.

*

The very object of Yoga is a change of consciousness — it is by getting a new consciousness or by unveiling the hidden consciousness of the true being within and progressively manifesting and perfecting it that one gets first the contact and then the union with the Divine. Ananda and bhakti are part of that deeper consciousness, and it is only when one lives in it and grows in it that ananda and bhakti can be permanent. Till then, one can only get experiences of ananda and bhakti, but not the constant and permanent state. But the state of bhakti and constantly growing surrender does not come to all at an early stage of the sadhana; many, most indeed, have a long journey of purification and tapasya to go through before it opens, and experiences of this kind, at first rare and interspaced, afterwards frequent, are the landmarks of their progress. It depends on certain conditions, which have nothing to do with superior or inferior Yoga capacity, but rather with a predisposition in the heart to open, as you say, to the Sun of the divine Influence.

*

You are no doubt right about asking for the bhakti, for I suppose it is the master-claim of your nature: for that matter, it is the strongest motive force that sadhana can have and the best means for all else that has to come. It is why I said that it is through the heart that spiritual experience must come to you. The loyalty and the rest that you have for me and the Mother may not, as you say, be part of the bhakti itself, but they could not be there were not the bhakti deep inside. It is its coming out in full force into the surface consciousness that is to be brought about and it seems to me that it is inevitable that it should come as the outer coverings fall off. What is within must surely make its way to the surface.

*

You believe in traditional ideas of Yoga — well, according to traditional ideas also, the one easiest method is that of bhakti, reliance, self-giving, *bhakti, nirbhara, samarpaṇa*. What still stands in your way — for it was and is growing towards that in you, is an old confusion in mind and vital. The heart says, "I want bhakti", the mind says, "No, no, let us reason", the vital says, "Nonsense, I can't surrender." What you need is to quiet down that confusion created by the mind's past sanskaras and either fix on the one thing or harmonise. Bhakti as the basic force, knowledge, strength and joy in the Divine as the result — that is the harmony proposed in this Yoga. But in either way, if either is done, then peace becomes easily possible.

*

What I meant by the change was the great improvement in your mental and vital attitude and reactions to outward things and to life which was very evident in your letters and account of happenings and gave them quite a new atmosphere warm and clear and psychic. Naturally the change is not yet absolute and integral, but it does seem to be fundamental. Moreover, it is certainly due to a growing bhakti within, especially an acceptance of bhakti as your path and of the implications of that acceptance. The mind has taken a new poise less intellectual and more psychic. What prevents you from seeing the growth of bhakti (sometimes you have seen it and written about it) is a continuance of the physical mind which sets going with a constant repetitionary whirl of its fixed ideas whenever there is any touch of depression. One of these ideas is that you don't progress, will not progress and can never progress, the old thing that used to say, "Yoga is not for the likes of me" etc. The activity of the physical mind (next to the wrong activity of the vital) is what most keeps one's consciousness on the surface and prevents it from being conscious within and of what goes on within; it can see something of what happens on the surface of the nature, the results of the inner movement but not the cause of the happenings, which is the inner movement itself. That is one reason why I like to see the physical mind occupied in poetry and music etc. and other salubrious activities which help the inner growth and in which the inner bhakti can express itself, for that keeps the physical mind busy, unoccupied with the mechanical rotatory movement and allows and helps the inner growth. The rotatory movement is less than it was before and I expect it one of these days to get tired of itself and give up altogether.

*

What you felt about replacement is quite true. The transformation proceeds to a large extent by a taking away or throwing out of the old superficial self and its movements and replacing them by a new deeper self and its true action.

It does not matter if the higher feelings, devotion etc. seem to you sometimes like an influence or colouring. It looks like that when you feel yourself in the external physical or outer vital or outer mind. These feelings really are those of your inmost self, your soul, the psychic in you and when you are in the psychic consciousness, they become normal and natural. But when your consciousness shifts and becomes more external, then these workings of the soul or of the divine consciousness are felt as themselves external, as merely an influence. All the same, you have to open yourself to them constantly and they will then more and more either soak in steadily or come in successive waves or floods and go on till they have filled the mind, the vital, the body. You will then feel them always as not only normal but as part of your very self and the true substance of your nature.

*

The flow of devotion and love is a thing which the more it repeats or awakens is bound to overflow to all the parts of being and have its effect on them.

*

If it is the way of *ahaitukī bhakti* that you want to follow, that can be no obstacle; for there can be none better. For in that way everything can be made a means — poetry and music for instance become not merely poetry and music and not merely even an expression of bhakti, but themselves a means of bringing the experience of love and bhakti. Meditation itself becomes not an effort of mental concentration, but a flow of love and adoration and worship. If simply and sincerely followed, the way of *ahaitukī bhakti* can lead as far as any other.

*

There can be no such thing as a mechanical and artificial devotion — there is either devotion or there is not. Devotion may be intense or not intense, complete or incomplete, sometimes manifest and sometimes veiled, but mechanical or artificial devotion is a contradiction in terms.

*

These [*arguments against external bhakti*] are the exaggerations made by the mind taking one side of Truth and ignoring the other sides.[1] The inner bhakti is the main thing and without it the external becomes a form and mere ritual, but the external has its place and use when it is straightforward and sincere.

*

Bhakti should be for the Divine only — the sadhaks are sadhaks, trying to reach the Divine, but still full of faults and struggles.

*

A "bhakti" which claims everything from the Divine and does not give itself is not real bhakti.

---

[1] *The correspondent had been asked by a fellow-sadhak, "Why do you want to meditate on a photograph of Sri Aurobindo? If you can meditate within, this external form of bhakti is not necessary." — Ed.*

Bhakti and Love

The nature of bhakti is adoration, worship, self-offering to what is greater than oneself — the nature of love is a feeling or seeking for closeness and union. Self-giving is the character of both; both are necessary in the Yoga and each gets its full force when supported by the other.

*

Love is not a name of the Divine, it is a power of his consciousness and being. Bhakti and love are not quite the same thing, but love is one of the elements of bhakti. There are different kinds of bhakti and that which is of the nature of love is the strongest and is considered the highest, most intense and ecstatic of all. Also in love itself that form of it which is made of self-giving; surrender, absolute adoration, urge towards a selfless union is the true kind of bhakti that is love. "Conquering love" or "Love the victor"[2] means love prevailing over all that stands in the way of its reign, over ignorance, falsehood, selfishness, ego, passion and lust, outward or self-regarding desires and all else till it reigns alone and victorious, bringing down all the other gifts of the Divine Consciousness. It is by force of love and selflessness and self-giving that the sadhak can help Love to conquer.

*

I suppose it [*premabhakti*] is bhakti with love as its basis; there can be bhakti of worship, submission, reverence, obedience etc. but without love.

*

Selflessness, self-giving, entire faith and confidence, absence of demand and desire, surrender to the Divine Will, love concentrated on the Divine — are some of the main signs [*of true love and bhakti*].

---

[2] *These are probably the names of two roses named by the Mother according to their significance. — Ed.*

Emotional Bhakti

It is a misunderstanding to suppose that I am against Bhakti or against emotional Bhakti — which comes to the same thing, since without emotion there can be no Bhakti. It is rather the fact that in my writings on Yoga I have given Bhakti the highest place. All that I have said at any time which could account for this misunderstanding was against an *unpurified* emotionalism which, according to my experience, leads to want of balance, agitated and disharmonious expression or even contrary reactions and, at its extreme, nervous disorder. But the insistence on purification does not mean that I condemn true feeling and emotion any more than the insistence on a purified mind or will means that I condemn thought and will. On the contrary, the deeper the emotion, the more intense the Bhakti, the greater is the force for realisation and transformation. It is oftenest through intensity of emotion that the psychic being awakes and there is an opening of the inner doors to the Divine.

*

If one does not encourage the devotion of the emotional being merely because the lower vital is not yet under control and acts differently, then how is the devotion to grow and how is the lower vital to change? Until the final clarification and harmonising of the nature there are always contradictions in the being, but that is not a reason for in any way suppressing the play of the better movements — on the contrary it is these that should be cultivated and made to increase.

*

It [*emotion*] has its place, only it must not be always thrown outward but pressed inward so as to open fully the psychic doors.

*

The emotional [*devotion*] is more outward than the psychic [*devotion*] — it tends towards outward expression. The psychic is inward and gives the direction to the whole inner and outer life. The emotional can be intense, but is neither so sure in its basis nor powerful enough to change the whole direction of the life.

Vital Bhakti

Vital bhakti is usually full of desires and demands, — it expects a return for what it gives; it loves the Divine more for its own sake than for the sake of the Divine. If it does not get what it wants, it is capable of revolting or turning elsewhere. It is often pursued by jealousy, misunderstanding, unfaithfulness, anger etc., — the usual imperfections of human love, and can turn these against its object of bhakti. On the other hand, if there is vital bhakti governed by the psychic, these defects disappear and the vital gives an ardour and enthusiasm to the love and bhakti which gives it a greater push for effectuation in action and life. The vital should always be the instrument of the soul for self-expression in life and not act on its own account (ego, desire) or on its own separate impulse.

*

The vital bhakti is egoistic, usually full of claims and demands on the Divine and revolting when they are not satisfied. The mental is simply a worship in the thought and idea without love in the heart.

*

It [*an inner state of dryness*] is because it is the analysing mind that is active — that always brings a certain dryness; the higher mind or the intuition bring a much more spontaneous and complete knowledge — the beginning of the real Jnana without this effect. The bhakti which you feel is psychic, but with a strong vital tinge; and it is the mind and the vital between them that bring in the opposition between the bhakti and the Jnana. The vital concerned only with emotion finds the mental knowledge dry and without rasa, the mind finds the bhakti to be a blind emotion fully interesting only when its character has been analysed and understood. There is no such opposition when the psychic and the higher plane knowledge act together predominantly — the psychic welcomes knowledge that supports its emotion, the higher thought consciousness rejoices in the bhakti.

*

It is a mistake to think that a constant absence of *vyākulatā* is a sign that the aspiration or will for the Divine is not true. It is only in certain exclusive forms of Bhakti Yoga that a constant *vyākulatā* or weeping or *hāhākāra* (the latter is more often vital than psychic) is the rule. Here though the psychic yearning may come sometimes or often in intense waves, what comes as the basis is a quietude of the being and in that quietude a more and more steady perception of the truth and seeking for the Divine and need of the Divine so that all is turned towards that more and more. It is into this that the experience and growing realisation come. Because the opening is growing in you, you are getting this *ābhāsa* of the presence (beyond form) of the Mother. It is as the inner realisation grows that the presence in the physical form takes its full value.

Viraha or Pangs of Separation

Viraha is a transitional experience on the plane of the vital seeking for the Spirit — there is no reason why it should not be possible at a quite early stage. It is the realisations without any uneasiness, realisations in pure Ananda that belong to the more developed sadhana.

*

The pure feeling of *viraha* is psychic — but if rajasic or tamasic movements come in (such as depression, complaint, revolt etc.) then it becomes tamasic or rajasic.

*

Pangs of separation belong to the vital, not to the psychic; the psychic having no pangs need not express them. The psychic is always turned towards the Divine in faith, joy and confidence

— whatever aspiration it has is full of trust and hope.

Enmity to the Divine

I have not had time yet to write about the enmity theory. I will do so more fully in two or three days. But I may say at once that the idea does not seem to me at all true that by enmity to the Divine one can reach the Divine and that too more quickly than by bhakti. The idea is contrary to the spiritual truth of things, to reason, to nature and to experience.

*

As regards your defence of X, they sound like X's own ideas and very queer ideas they are. If they are right, we should have to come to the following conclusions —

1. Sattwa is not the best passage towards realisation, Rajas is the best way to become spiritual. It is the rajasic man with his fierce ego and violent passions who is the true sadhak of the Divine.

2. The Asura is the best bhakta. The Gita is quite wrong in holding up the Deva nature as the condition of realisation and the Asura nature as contrary to it. It is the other way round.

3. Ravana, Hiranyakashipu, Shishupala were the greatest devotees of the Divine because they were capable of hostility to the Divine and so were liberated in a few lives — compared with them the great Rishis and Bhaktas were very poor spiritual vessels. I am aware of the paradox about Ravana in the Purana, but let me point out that these Asuras and Rakshasas did not pretend to be disciples or worshippers of Rama or Krishna or Vishnu or use their position as disciples to get moksha by revolt — they got it by being enemies and getting killed and absorbed into the Godhead.

4. Obedience to the Guru, worship of the Divine are all tommy rot and fit only for sheep, not men. To turn round furiously on the Guru or the Divine, abuse him, express contempt, challenge his sincerity, declare his actions to be wrong, foolish or a trick — to assert oneself as right at every point and his

judgment as mistaken, prejudiced, absurd, false, a support of devils etc. etc. is the best way of devotion and the true relation between Guru and Shishya. Disobedience is the highest respect to the Guru, anger and revolt are the noblest worship one can give to the Divine.

5. One who takes the blows of Mahakali with joy as a means of discovering his faults and increasing in light and strength and purity is a sheep and unworthy of disciplehood — one who responds to the quietest pressure to change by revolt and persisting in his errors is a strong man and a mighty adhar and a noble disciple on the way to perfection.

I could go on multiplying the consequences, but I have no time. Do you really believe all these things? They are the natural consequences of X's theory or of this theory of revolt as the way to perfection. If you accept the premiss, you have to accept the logical consequences. That is what X did — only he called his errors Truth and the way prescribed by me was falsehood explicable only by the fact that I was a "Master who had forgotten his higher self". And the consequences led to his departure, not willed by us, but by his own choice — and under such circumstances that he has made it a practical impossibility for me to let him come back unless he undergoes a change which the experience of the past does not warrant me in thinking possible.

Contact with the Divine

Aspiration and devotion are the natural and easy means for getting the contact. The other way by effort is laborious, slow and not sure. The mind must open, but it will open best by the power of devotion and aspiration.

*

The more the calm, peace, joy and happiness descend and take possession, the stronger the foundation. It is the sign of the contact.

The other thing needed is the descent of the consciousness which you felt in the heart and breast. That will come of itself, if this devotion and sole dependence on the Light continues.

*

The psychic contact does not bring mental knowledge, but it brings true perception and true feeling and it can bring down also, if you aspire from the psychic centre, a knowledge higher and truer than intellectual knowledge.

*

Quietude and surrender are the first things to be established. In that must come the full contact. By that contact, if well established, will come a steady progressive sadhana, not the old confused sadhana.

*

When you fall from the contact, the first and only thing you have to do is to reestablish it — to remain quiet and open yourself. Everything else you must detach yourself from and reject. It is because you listen to ideas and suggestions of all kinds and still attach value to the old kind of "experiences", that you cannot reestablish the contact.

*

As for not having it [contact] always, it is because there are parts of the being that are still unconscious or perhaps states of unconsciousness come. For instance, people write letters to each other, but they are quite unconscious that they are exchanging forces in doing so. You have become conscious of it, because of the development of your inner consciousness by Yoga — and yet there are likely to be times when you still write from the external awareness only, and then you will see the words only without being aware of what is behind. So owing to the development of the inner consciousness, you are able to understand what contacts are and get the true contact, but at times the external consciousness may be stronger than the inner one, then you are no longer (for the time being) able to get the contact.

*

The photograph is a vehicle only³ — but if you have the right consciousness, then you can bring something of the living being into it or become aware of the being for which it stands and can make it a means of contact. It is like the *prāṇapratiṣṭhā* in the image in the temple.

Contact and Union with the Divine

Seeing is of many kinds. There is a superficial seeing which only erects or receives momentarily or for some time an image of the Being seen; that brings no change, unless the inner bhakti makes it a means for change. There is also the reception of the *living* image of the Divine in one of his forms into oneself, — say, in the heart, — that can have an immediate effect or initiate a period of spiritual growth. There is also the seeing outside oneself in a more or less objective and subtle physical or physical way.

As for *milana*, the abiding union is within and that can be there at all times; the outer *milana* or contact is not usually abiding. There are some who often or almost invariably have the contact whenever they worship; the Deity may become living to them in the picture or other image they worship, may move and act through it; others may *feel* him always present, outwardly, subtle-physically, abiding with them where they live or in the very room; but sometimes this is only for a period. Or they may feel the Presence with them, see it frequently in a body (but not materially except sometimes), feel its touch or embrace, converse with it constantly, — that is also one kind of *milana*. The greatest *milana* is one in which one is constantly aware of the Deity constantly abiding in oneself, in everything in the world, holding all the world in him, identical with existence and yet supremely beyond the world — but in the world too one sees, hears, feels nothing but him, so that the very senses bear witness to him alone — and this does *not* exclude such specific personal manifestations as those vouchsafed to Krishnaprem

---

³ *While looking at a photograph of Sri Aurobindo, the correspondent felt that he was looking at a living being with eyes "as living as real eyes".* — Ed.

and his guru. The more ways there are of the union, the better.

*

Adesh and darshan are elements of a stage of sadhana in which there is still much distance from the closer state of union. The mind and vital seek the contact through darshan and the guidance through Adesh. What we aim at in our Yoga is the constant union and presence and control of the Divine at every moment. But on the mental and vital level this usually remains imperfect and there is much chance of error. It is by the supramentalisation that the perfect Truth of this Divine Union in action can come.

Outer Worship

There is no restriction in this Yoga to inward worship and meditation only. As it is a Yoga for the whole being, not for the inner being only, no such restriction could be intended. Old forms of the different religions may fall away, but absence of all forms is not the rule of the sadhana.

*

I was thinking [*in writing "Old forms ... may fall away"*] not of Pranam etc. which have a living value, but of old forms which persist although they have no longer any value — e.g. Sraddha for the dead. Also here forms which have no relation to this Yoga — for instance Christians who cling to the Christian forms or Mahomedans to the Namaz or Hindus to the Sandhyavandana in the old way may soon find them either falling off or else an obstacle to the free development of their sadhana.

*

What is meant by *bāhyapūjā*? If it is purely external, then of course it is the lowest form; but if done with the true consciousness inside, it can bring the greatest completeness of the adoration by allowing the body and the most external consciousness to share in the spirit and act of worship.

*

What you say is no doubt true, but it is better not to take away the support that may still be there for the faith of those who need such supports. These visions and images and ceremonies are meant for that. It is a spiritual principle not to take away any faith or support of faith unless the persons who have it are able to replace it by something larger and more complete.

If the *prāṇapratiṣṭhā* brings down a powerful Presence [*into an image*], that may remain there long after the one who has brought it has left his body. Usually it is maintained by the bhakti of the officiant and the sincerity of belief and worship of those who come to the temple for adoration. If these fail there is likely to be a withdrawal of the Presence.

*

The "scientific" explanation [*for the disappearance of food offered to a deity in a temple*] would be that somebody, a servant perhaps, disregarding prohibitions got secretly in and polished off the food of offering when there was nobody to see! That however assumes that occult manifestations are impossible, which is not the case; it is besides only a probable inference or theory. Occultists, or some of them, hold that the food offered to unseen beings is sometimes (but not by any means always) taken in its subtle elements, leaving the outward body of the food as it was. The actual taking of the food, physically, is rare, but instances are believed to have happened where the bhakti was very strong.

Prayer

Prayer and aspiration are a part of the spiritual life and do not conflict with surrender, provided one is not disturbed in either way by the fulfilment or unfulfilment of the prayer and keeps one's faith and quietude all the same. In the ordinary life prayer is one of the chief elements of human relation with the Divine and is often but not always answered; when it is not answered the religious man keeps his faith in the Divine and either understands that to answer was not the Divine Will or else he prays more fervently till his prayer is heard — that depends on the man and the circumstances. A sadhak can intercede internally for others in their affairs, provided he remains unattached and equal-minded, but he is not bound to intervene.

*

Of course all prayer is not heard — the world would be a still more disastrous affair than it is, if everybody's prayers were heard, however sincere. Even the Godward prayer is not always heard — at once, even as faith is not always justified at once. Both prayer and faith are powers towards realisation which have been given to man to aid him in his struggle — without them, without aspiration and will and faith (for aspiration is a prayer) it would be difficult for him to get anywhere. But all these things are merely means for setting the Divine Force in action — and it sometimes takes long, very long even, before the forces come into action or at least before they are seen to be in action or bear their result. The ecstasist is not altogether wrong even when he overstates his case. Even the overstatements sometimes help to convince the Cosmic Power, so that it says "Oh well, if it is like that all right — ".

*

As for prayer, no hard and fast rule can be laid down. Some prayers are answered, all are not. You may ask, why should not then all prayers be answered? But why should they be? It is not a machinery: put a prayer in the slot and get your asking. Besides, considering all the contradictory things mankind is praying for at the same moment, God would be in a rather awkward hole if he had to grant all of them; it wouldn't do.

*

If one lives in the world one can offer such prayers [*for help in resolving worldly problems*]; but one must not expect that the Divine shall fulfil all those prayers or think that he is bound to do so. When one is a sadhak the prayer should be for the inner things belonging to the sadhana and for outer things only so far as they are necessary for that and for the divine work.

*

What you say about prayer is correct. That [*impersonal prayer*] is the highest kind of prayer, but the other kind also (i.e. the more personal) is permissible and even desirable. All prayer rightly offered brings us closer to the Divine and establishes a right relation with Him.

*

As for the prayers, the fact of praying and the attitude it brings, especially unselfish prayer for others, itself opens you to the higher Power, even if there is no corresponding result in the person prayed for. Nothing can be positively said about that, for the result must necessarily depend on the persons, whether they are open or receptive or something in them can respond to any Force the prayer brings down.

*

Prayers should be full of confidence and without sorrow or lamenting.

Part Three

The Integral Yoga and Other Spiritual Paths

Section One

A Yoga of Transformation

Chapter One
Distinctive Features of the Integral Yoga

The Meaning of Purna Yoga

Purna Yoga means (1) that instead of approaching the Divine through the mind alone (Jnana) or the heart alone (Bhakti) or through will and works alone (Karma Yoga), one seeks the Divine with all the parts and powers of the consciousness and the being, uniting these three ways and many others in a single Yoga (way of union with the Divine) and receives the Divine in His presence, consciousness, force, light and bliss in all the consciousness and the being.

(2) That one seeks not only the realisation of the Divine in the soul and self but also in the whole nature (that means the transformation of this lower human into the Divine spiritual nature).

(3) That one seeks the Divine not only beyond life (by the cessation of birth) but for life, so that life also may become a realisation of the Divine and a manifestation of the Divine Nature.

*

As for the book itself,[1] I am unfortunately ignorant of the Telugu language and cannot read the original, but from the account given in English I have formed some idea of the substance. I gather that it is in the main a statement and justification of the Purna Yoga and of my message; I believe you have rightly stated the two main elements of it, — first, the acceptance of the world as a manifestation of the Divine Power, not its rejection as a mistake or an illusion, and, secondly, the character of this manifestation as a spiritual evolution with Yoga as a means for

---

[1] *A book by a disciple living outside the Ashram.* — Ed.

the transformation of mind, life and body into the instruments of a spiritual and supramental perfection. The universe is not only a material but a spiritual fact, life not only a play of forces or a mental experience, but a field for the evolution of the concealed spirit. Human life will receive its fulfilment and transformation into something beyond itself only when this truth is seized and made the motive force of our existence and the means of its effective realisation discovered. The means of realisation is to be found in an integral Yoga, a union in all the parts of our being with the Divine and a consequent transmutation of all their now jarring elements into the harmony of a higher divine consciousness and existence.

This-Worldliness and Other-Worldliness

One thing I feel I must say in connection with your remark about the soul of India and X's observation about "this stress on this-worldliness to the exclusion of other-worldliness". I do not quite understand in what connection his remark was made or what he meant by this-worldliness, but I feel it necessary to state my own position in the matter. My own life and my Yoga have always been, since my coming to India, both this-worldly and other-worldly without any exclusiveness on either side. All human interests are, I suppose, this-worldly and most of them have entered into my mental field and some, like politics, into my life, but at the same time, since I set foot on Indian soil on the Apollo Bunder in Bombay, I began to have spiritual experiences, but these were not divorced from this world but had an inner and intimate bearing on it, such as a feeling of the Infinite pervading material space and the Immanent inhabiting material objects and bodies. At the same time I found myself entering supraphysical worlds and planes with influences and an effect from them upon the material plane, so I could make no sharp divorce or irreconcilable opposition between what I have called the two ends of existence and all that lies between them. For me all is the Brahman and I find the Divine everywhere. Everyone has the right to throw away this-worldliness and choose other-worldliness only and if he finds peace by that choice he is greatly blessed. I, personally, have not found it necessary to do this in order to have peace. In my Yoga also I found myself moved to include both worlds in my purview, the spiritual and the material, and to try to establish the divine Consciousness and the divine Power in men's hearts and in earthly life, not for personal salvation only but for a life divine here. This seems to me as spiritual an aim as any and the fact of this life taking up earthly pursuits and earthly things into its scope cannot, I believe, tarnish its spirituality or alter its Indian character. This at least has always been my view and experience of the reality and nature of the world and things and the Divine: it seemed to me as nearly as possible the integral truth about them and I have therefore spoken of the pursuit of it as the integral Yoga. Everyone is, of course, free to reject and disbelieve in this kind of integrality or to believe in the spiritual necessity of an entire other-worldliness excluding any kind of this-worldliness altogether, but that would make the exercise of my Yoga impossible. My Yoga can include indeed a full experience of the other worlds, the plane of the supreme Spirit and the other planes in between and their possible effects upon our life and material world; but it will be quite possible to insist only on the realisation of the supreme Being or Ishwara even in one aspect, Shiva, Krishna as Lord of the world and Master of ourselves and our works or else the universal Sachchidananda, and attain to the essential results of this Yoga and afterwards to proceed from them to the integral results if one accepted the ideal of the divine life and this material world conquered by the Spirit. It is this view and experience of things and of the truth of existence that enabled me to write *The Life Divine* and *Savitri*. The realisation of the Supreme, the Ishwara, is certainly the essential thing; but to approach him with love and devotion and bhakti, to serve him with one's works and to know him, not necessarily by the intellectual cognition, but in a spiritual experience, is also essential in the path of the integral Yoga.

The Importance of Descent in the Yoga

I meant by it [*the phrase "a far greater Truth"*] the descent of the supramental Consciousness upon earth; all truths below the supramental (even that of the highest spiritual on the mental plane, which is the highest that has yet manifested) are either partial or relative or otherwise deficient and unable to transform the earthly life, they can only at most modify and influence it. The supermind is the vast Truth-consciousness of which the ancient seers spoke; there have been glimpses of it till now, sometimes an indirect influence or pressure, but it has not been brought down into the consciousness of the earth and fixed there. To so bring it down is the aim of our Yoga.

But it is better not to enter into sterile intellectual discussions. The intellectual mind cannot even realise what the supermind is; what use, then, can there be in allowing it to discuss what it does not know? It is not by reasoning, but by constant experience, growth of consciousness and widening into the Light that one can reach those higher levels of consciousness above the intellect from which one can begin to look up to the Divine Gnosis. Those levels are not yet the supermind, but they can receive something of its knowledge.

The Vedic Rishis never attained to the supermind for the earth or perhaps did not even make the attempt. They tried to rise individually to the supramental plane, but they did not bring it down and make it a permanent part of the earth-consciousness. Even there are verses of the Upanishad in which it is hinted that it is impossible to pass through the gates of the Sun (the symbol of the supermind) and yet retain an earthly body. It was because of this failure that the spiritual effort of India culminated in Mayavada. Our Yoga is a double movement of ascent and descent; one rises to higher and higher levels of consciousness, but at the same time one brings down their power not only into mind and life, but in the end even into the body. And the highest of these levels, the one at which it aims is the supermind. Only when that can be brought down is a divine transformation possible in the earth-consciousness.

*

I never heard of silence descending in other Yogas — the mind goes into silence. Since however I have been writing of ascent and descent, I have been told from several quarters that there is nothing new in this Yoga — so I am wondering whether people were not getting ascents and descents without knowing it! or at least without noticing the process. It is like the rising above the head and taking the station there — which I and others have experienced in this Yoga. When I spoke of it first, people stared and thought I was talking nonsense. Wideness must have been felt in the old Yogas because otherwise one could not feel the universe in oneself or be free from the body consciousness or unite with the Anantam Brahman. But generally as in Tantrik Yoga one spoke of the consciousness rising to the Brahmarandhra, top of the head, as the summit. Rajayoga of course lays stress on Samadhi as the means of the highest experience. But obviously if one has not the Brahmi sthiti in the waking state, there is no completeness in the realisation. The Gita distinctly speaks of being *samāhita* (which is equivalent to being in samadhi) and the Brahmi sthiti as a waking state in which one lives and does all actions.

*

It happens that people may get the descent without noticing that it is a descent because they feel the result only. The ordinary Yoga does not go beyond the spiritual mind — people feel at the top of the head the joining with the Brahman, but they are not aware of a consciousness above the head. In the same way in the ordinary Yoga one feels the ascent of the awakened inner consciousness (Kundalini) to the *brahmarandhra* where the Prakriti joins the Brahman-consciousness, but they do not feel the descent. Some may have had these things, but I don't know that they understood their nature, principle or place in a complete sadhana. At least I never heard of these things from others before I found them out in my own experience. The reason is that the old Yogins when they went above the spiritual mind passed into samadhi, which means that they did not attempt to be conscious in these higher planes — their aim being to pass away into the

Superconscient and not to bring the Superconscient into the waking consciousness, which is that of my Yoga.

*

I explain this absence of the descent experiences myself by the old Yogas having been mainly confined to the psycho-spiritual-occult range of experience — in which the higher experiences come into the still mind or the concentrated heart by a sort of filtration or reflection — the field of this experience being from the Brahmarandhra downward. People went above this only in samadhi or in a condition of static mukti without any dynamic descent. All that was dynamic took place in the region of the spiritualised mental and vital-physical consciousness. In this Yoga the consciousness (after the lower field has been prepared by a certain amount of psycho-spiritual-occult experience) is drawn upwards above the Brahmarandhra to ranges above belonging to the spiritual consciousness proper and instead of merely receiving from there has to live there and from there change the lower consciousness altogether. For there is a dynamism proper to the spiritual consciousness whose nature is Light, Power, Ananda, Peace, Knowledge, infinite Wideness and that must be possessed and descend into the whole being. Otherwise one can get mukti but not perfection or transformation (except a relative psycho-spiritual change). But if I say that, there will be a general howl against the unpardonable presumption of claiming to have a knowledge not possessed by the ancient saints and sages and pretending to transcend them. In that connection I may say that in the Upanishads (notably the Taittiriya) there are some indications of these higher planes and their nature and the possibility of gathering up the whole consciousness and rising into them. But this was forgotten afterwards and people spoke only of the buddhi as the highest thing with the Purusha or Self just above, but there was no clear idea of these higher planes. Ergo, ascent possibly to unknown and ineffable heavenly regions in samadhi, but no descent possible — therefore no resource, no possibility of transformation here, only escape from life and mukti in Goloka, Brahmaloka, Shivaloka or the Absolute.

*

Perhaps you are of the opinion of Ramana Maharshi, "The Divine is here, how can he descend from anywhere?" The Divine may be here, but if he has covered here his Light with darkness of Ignorance and his Ananda with suffering, that, I should think, makes a big difference to the plane and, even if one enters into that sealed Light etc., it makes a difference to the Consciousness but very little to the Energy at work in this plane which remains of a dark or mixed character.

The Inclusiveness of the Yoga

I don't know why it [*a comparison between Sri Aurobindo's Yoga and someone else's*] should be disparaging to my Yoga. My Yoga takes up all the Yoga of the past and goes beyond.

*

One can feel the experiences of any sadhana as a part of this one.

Chapter Two
Asceticism and the Integral Yoga

Not an Ascetic Path

It is not indispensable to be an ascetic — it is enough if one can learn to live within in the inner being instead of on the surface, discover the soul or true individuality which is veiled by the surface mind and life forces and open the being to the superconscient Reality. But in this one cannot succeed unless one is wholly sincere and one-pointed in the effort.

As to the second question, participation in Sri Aurobindo's[1] mission depends on capacity to do a difficult Yoga or on a call to devote oneself to that ideal without thought of the claims of the ego or the vital desires. Otherwise it is better not to think of it.

*

It is good that you have decided to concentrate on the true object of your coming here, but while absorption in mental work and social contacts is not favourable for Yoga, excessive seclusion has also its spiritual disadvantage. An inner concentration supported by a limitation of external contacts is sufficient. Some kind of activity and service to the Divine is also a very necessary element in the integral spiritual life.

*

To be by oneself very much needs a certain force of inner life. It may be better to vary solitude with some sort of its opposite. But each has its advantages and disadvantages and it is only by being vigilant and keeping an inner poise that one can avoid the latter.

*

---

[1] *In this letter to an enquirer living outside the Ashram, Sri Aurobindo refers to himself in the third person.* — Ed.

I think there is still a misunderstanding in your mind about the demands of the Yoga. The Divine does *not* demand a complete solitude, aloof and lonely — it is only a few whose nature needs such concentration within to find themselves who have to do that and even for them a complete segregation is not likely to be helpful except perhaps for a time. All that is necessary is a total turning of the life to the Divine and it can be done by degrees without too much forcing of the nature. Literature, poetry, music can be as much a part of Yoga as anything else.

One can meet the Divine in speaking as well as in silence, in action as well as in physical solitude and quietude. An entire retirement can only be a personal case — and as a condition for an inward or outward work, but it is no general rule indispensable for the sadhana. In many cases, most indeed, it would do more harm than good as has been seen in many cases where it has been unduly attempted. A cheerful and sunny life is as good an atmosphere for Yoga as any the Himalayas can give.

Why then this depression and despair?

*

I may say that I am not responsible for your loss of zest in the vital. This vairagya, or loss of zest, as you have yourself said, began before you came here. I have indeed laid some stress on the conquest of sex, for obvious reasons; but I have hardly laid a compulsory stress on anything else. Certainly, I have not encouraged you to lose joy in vital creativeness; I have only held up the ideal of turning it towards the Divine and away from the ego. To keep the vital full of life and energy and to trust mainly to the inner growth and the descent of a higher consciousness for a change, using the will too but for self-mastery, not for suppression, but for subordination of the lower to the higher, has been my teaching. The turn to vairagya, to tapasya of an ascetic kind was the impulse of something in your own nature; it insisted on its necessity just as a part of the vital insisted on its opposite: even it condemned my suggestion of something less grim and strenuous as an easy-going absence of aspiration etc. I do not say that vairagya and tapasya are not ways to reach the Divine, but done like that they are painful ways and long; if one takes them, one must be determined and go through. For one part to push all zest out of the vital and for the other to regret and say, why did I ever do it, will never do. And it is in this kind of tapasya that perfection or at least perfect purification is demanded before there can be any realisation. I have never said that for my Yoga; the only thing I insist upon is some faith, inner surrender and opening of oneself to receive, — not absolute, but just sufficient. Experience has to begin long before perfect purification and from experience to experience one comes to realisation and through realisation to more and more perfection; anything that can be called real perfection can only come at the end. But there is something in you that is impatient of gradualness, of small mercies; its motto seems to be all or nothing.

*

I am rather aghast as I stare at the detailed proposals made by you! Fastings? I don't believe in them, though I have done them myself. You would only eat like an ogre afterwards. Shaved head! Great heavens! have you realised the consequences? I pass over the aesthetic shock to myself from which I might not recover — but the row that would arise from Cape Comorin to the Himalayas! You would be famous in a new way which would cast all your previous Glories into the shade. And just when you are turning away from fame and all the things of the ego! No, no — too dangerous by half. Sleep without the mosquito net? That would mean no sleep which is as bad as no eating. Not only your eyes would become weak, but yourself also — and to boot gloomy, grey and gruesome, more gruesome than the Supramental of your worst apprehensions. No and no again. As for the rest, I placed some of them before the Mother and she eyed them without favour.

After all real asceticism is hardly possible except in a hut or on the Himalayas. The heart of asceticism, besides, is having no desires or attachment, being indifferent, able to do without things, satisfied with whatever comes. If you asceticise outwardly it becomes a rule of life and you keep it up because it is a rule, for the principle of the thing or for the *kudos* of it or as a point of honour. But I have noticed about the ascetics by rule that when you remove the curb they become just like others — with a few exceptions, of course, — which proves that the transformation was not real. A more subtle method used by some is to give up for a time, then try the object of desire again and so go on till you have thoroughly tested yourself! E.g. you give up your potatoes and eat only Asram food for a time — if a call comes for the potatoes or from them, then you are not cured; if no call comes, still you cannot be sure till you have tried the potatoes again and seen whether the desire, attachment or sense of need revives. If it does not and the potatoes fall away from you of themselves, then there is some hope that the thing is done!

However, all this will make you think that I am hardly fit to be a guru in the path of asceticism and you will probably be right. You see, I have such a strong penchant for the inner working and am so persuaded that if you give the psychic a chance, it will get rid of the vital bonds without all this sternness and trouble.

*

Rules like these [*not reading newspapers, eating a fixed diet, keeping only a few things*] are intended to help the vital and physical to come under the discipline of sadhana and not get dispersed in fancies, impulses, self-indulgences; but they must be done simply, not with any sense of superiority or ascetic pride, but as a mere matter of course. It is true also that they can be made the occasion of a too great mental rigidity — as if they were things of supreme importance *in themselves* and not only a means. Put in their right place and done in the right spirit, they can be very helpful for their purpose.

Asceticism and Detachment

This is a feeling (the unimportance of things in Time) that the ascetic discipline sometimes uses in order to get rid of attachment to the world — but it is not good for any positive or dynamic spiritual purpose.

*

Sannyasa does not take away attachment — it amounts only to running away from the object of attachment which may help but cannot by itself alone be the radical cure.

*

After realisation whatever the Higher Will demands is the best — but first detachment is the rule. To reach the Freedom without the discipline and detachment is given to few.

Two Methods of Living in the Supreme

There are always two methods of living in the Supreme. One is to draw away the participation of the consciousness from things altogether and go so much inwards as to be separated from existence and live in contact with that which is beyond it. The other is to get to that which is the true Essence of all things, not allowing oneself to be absorbed and entangled by the external forms. Desire, attachment, slavery to the attractions of the external sense are the chief obstacles to this movement — so in either way they have to be got rid of. But it is quite possible to see the Supreme before the attraction of external sense is gone — only one cannot live securely in It if there is desire and external attachment because that is always taking one away from the inner poise.

*

This Yoga does not mean a rejection of the powers of Life, but an inner transformation and a change of the spirit in the life and the use of the powers. These powers are now used in an egoistic spirit and for undivine ends; they have to be used in a spirit of surrender to the Divine and for the purposes of the divine Work. That is what is meant by conquering them back for the Mother. If anyone feels himself too weak to resist the clutch of the egoistic money-force he need not make the endeavour.

The Human Approach to the Divine

I send you the promised letter today;[2] you will see that it is less a reply to the exact terms of your letter than a "Defence of the gospel of divinisation of life" against the strictures and the incomprehensions of the mentality (or more often the vitality) that either misunderstands or shrinks from it — or perhaps misunderstands because it shrinks, and shrinks too because it misunderstands both my method and my object. It is not a complete defence, but only raises or answers a main point here and there. The rest will come hereafter.

But all language is open to misunderstanding; so I had better in sending on the letter make or try to make certain things clear.

1. Although I have laid stress on things divine in answer to an excessive (because contrary) insistence on things human, it must not be understood that I reject everything human, — human love or worship or any helpful form of human approach as part of the Yoga. I have never done so, otherwise the Asram could not be in existence. The sadhaks who enter the Yoga are human beings, and if they were not allowed a human approach at the beginning and long after, they would not be able to start the Yoga or would not be able to continue it. The discussion arises only because the word "human" is used in practice, not only as identical with the human vital (and the outward mind), but with certain forms of the human vital ego-nature. But the human vital has many other things in it and is full of excellent material. All that is asked by the Yoga is that this material should be utilised in the right way and with the right spiritual attitude and, also, that the human approach to the Divine should not be constantly turned into a human revolt and reproach against it. And that too we ask only for the sake of the success of the approach itself and of the human being who is making it.

2. Divinisation itself does not mean the destruction of the human elements; it means taking them up, showing them the way to their own perfection, raising them by purification and

---

[2] *See the letter beginning "Even if things" on pages 475–83.* — Ed.

perfection to their full power and Ananda. And that means the raising of the whole of earthly life to its full power and Ananda.

3. If there were not a resistance in vital human nature, a pressure of forces adverse to the change, forces which delight in imperfection and even in perversion, this change would effect itself without difficulty by a natural and painless flowering — as, for example, your own powers of poetry and music have flowered out here with rapidity and ease under the light and rain of a spiritual and psychic influence — because everything in you desired that change and your vital was willing to recognise imperfections, to throw away any wrong attitude — e.g., the desire for mere fame — and to be dedicated and perfect. Divinisation of life means, in fact, a greater art of life; for the present art of life produced by ego and ignorance is something comparatively mean, crude and imperfect (like the lower forms of art, music and literature which are yet more attractive to the ordinary human mind and vital), and it is by a spiritual and psychic opening and refinement that it has to reach its true perfection. This can only be done by its being steeped in the divine Light and Flame in which its material will be stripped of all heavy dross and turned into the true metal.

4. Unfortunately, there *is* the resistance, a very obscure and obstinate resistance. That necessitates a "negative" element in the Yoga, an element of rejection of things that stand in the way and of pressure upon those forms that are crude and useless to disappear, on those that are useful but imperfect or have been perverted to attain or to recover their true movement. To the vital this pressure is very painful, first, because it is obscure and does not understand and, secondly, because there are parts of it that want to be left to their crude motions and not to change. That is why the intervention of a psychic attitude is so helpful. For the psychic has the happy confidence, the ready understanding and response, the spontaneous surrender; it knows that the touch of the Guru is meant to help and not to hurt, or, like Radha in the poem, that whatever the Beloved does is meant to lead to the Divine Rapture.

5. At the same time, it is not from the negative part of the

movement that you have to judge the Yoga, but from its positive side; for the negative part is temporary and transitional and will disappear, the positive alone counts for the ideal and for the future. If you take conditions which belong to the negative side and to a transitional movement as the law of the future and the indication of the character of the Yoga, you will commit a serious misjudgment, a grave mistake. This Yoga is not a rejection of life or of closeness and intimacy between the Divine and the sadhaks. Its ideal aims at the greatest closeness and unity on the physical as well as the other planes, at the most divine largeness and fullness and joy of life.

Vairagya

Vairagya means a positive detachment from things of this life — but it does not *immediately* carry with it a luminous aspiration except for a few fortunate people. For the positive detachment is often a pulling away by the soul while the vital clings and is gloomy and reluctant.

*

Vairagya is certainly one way of progressing towards the goal — the traditional way and a drastic if painful one. To lose the desire for human vital enjoyments, to lose the passion for literary or other success, praise, fame, to lose even the insistence on spiritual success, the inner bhoga of Yoga, have always been recognised as steps towards the goal — provided one keeps the one insistence on the Divine. I prefer myself the calmer way of equality, the way pointed out by Krishna, than the more painful one of Vairagya. But if the compulsion in one's nature — or the compulsion of one's inner being forcing its way by that means through the difficulties of the nature — is on that line, it must be recognised as a valid line. What has to be got rid of in that case is the note of despair in the vital which responds to the cry you speak of — that it will never gain the Divine because it has not yet got the Divine or that there has been no progress. There has certainly been a progress, the greater push of the psychic, this very detachment itself always growing somewhere in you. The thing is to hold on, not to cut the cord which is pulling you up because it hurts the hands. To keep the one insistence if all the others fall away from you.

It is evident that something in you, perhaps continuing the unfinished curve of a past life, is pushing you on this path of vairagya and the more stormy way of bhakti — in spite of our preference for a less painful one and yours also — something that is determined to be drastic with the outer nature so as to make itself free to fulfil its secret aspiration. But do not listen to these suggestions of the voice that says, "You shall not succeed and it is no use trying." That is a thing that need never be said in the Way of the Spirit, however difficult it may seem at the moment to be. Keep through all the aspiration which you express so beautifully in your poem; for it is certainly there and comes out from the depths, and if it is the cause of suffering — as great aspirations usually are in a world and nature where there is so much to oppose them — it is also the promise and surety of emergence and victory in the future.

*

I quite acknowledge the utility of a temporary state of vairagya as an antidote to the too strong pull of the vital. But vairagya always tends to a turning away from life and a tamasic element in vairagya, despair, depression etc., often dilapidates the force of the being and may even lead in some cases to falling between two stools so that one loses earth and misses heaven. I therefore prefer to replace vairagya by a firm and quiet rejection of what has to be rejected, sex, vanity, ego-centrism, attachment, etc. etc.; but that does not include rejection of the activities and powers that can be made instruments of the sadhana and the divine work, such as art, music, poetry etc. — Yoga can be done without the rejection of life, without killing or impairing the life-joy and the vital force.

*

I have objected in the past to vairagya of the ascetic kind and the tamasic kind — and by the tamasic kind I mean that spirit which comes defeated from life, not because it is really disgusted with life but because it could not cope with it or conquer its prizes; for it comes to Yoga as a kind of asylum for the maimed or weak and to the Divine as a consolation prize for the failed boys in the world-class. The vairagya of one who has tasted the world's gifts or prizes but found them insufficient or, finally, tasteless and turns away towards a higher and more beautiful ideal or the vairagya of one who has done his part in life's battles but seen that something greater is demanded of the soul, is perfectly helpful and a good gate to the Yoga. Also the sattwic vairagya which has learned what life is and turns to what is above and behind life. By the ascetic vairagya I mean that which denies life and world altogether and wants to disappear into the Indefinite — and I object to it for those who come to this Yoga because it is incompatible with my aim which is to bring the Divine into life. But if one is satisfied with life as it is, then there is no reason to seek to bring the Divine into life, — so vairagya in the sense of dissatisfaction with life as it is is perfectly admissible and even in a certain sense indispensable for my Yoga.

*

There is the sattwic vairagya — but many people have the rajasic or tamasic kind. The rajasic is carried by a revolt against the conditions of one's own life, the tamasic arises from dissatisfaction, disappointment, a feeling of inability to succeed or face life, a crushing under the grips and pains of life. These bring a sense of the vanity of existence, a desire to seek something less miserable, more sure and happy or else to seek a liberation from existence here, but they do not bring immediately a luminous aspiration or pure aspiration with peace and joy for the spiritual attainment.

*

No, I didn't say that you chose the rajasic or tamasic vairagya. I only explained how it came, of itself, as a result of a movement of the vital in place of the sattwic vairagya which is supposed to precede and cause or accompany or result from a turning away from the world to seek the Divine. The tamasic vairagya comes from the recoil of the vital when it feels that it has to give up the joy of life and becomes listless and joyless; the rajasic comes when the vital begins to lose the joy of life but complains that it is getting nothing in its place. Nobody chooses such movements; they come independently of the mind as habitual reactions of the human nature. To replace these things by detachment, an increasing quiet aspiration, a pure bhakti, an ardent surrender to the Divine, was what I suggested as the true forward movement.

Chapter Three
A Realistic Adwaita

The World Not an Illusion

I do not agree with the view that the world is an illusion, *mithyā*. The Brahman is here as well as in the supracosmic Absolute. The thing to be overcome is the Ignorance which makes us blind and prevents us from realising Brahman in the world as well as beyond it and the true nature of existence.

Shankara, Buddhism, Evolution

I don't know that I can help you very much with an answer to your friend's questions. I can only state my own position with regard to these matters.

1. Shankara's explanation of the universe.

It is rather difficult to say nowadays what really was Shankara's philosophy: there are numberless exponents and none of them agrees with any of the others. I have read accounts given by some scores of his exegetes and each followed his own line. We are even told by some that he was no Mayavadin at all although he has always been famed as the greatest exponent of the theory of Maya, but rather, the greatest Realist in philosophical history. One eminent follower of Shankara even declared that my philosophy and Shankara's were identical, a statement which rather took my breath away. One used to think that Shankara's philosophy was this that the Supreme Reality is a spaceless and timeless Absolute (Parabrahman) which is beyond all feature or quality, beyond all action or creation, and that the world is a creation of Maya, not absolutely unreal but real only in time and while one lives in time; once we get into a knowledge of the Reality we perceive that Maya and world and all in it have no abiding or true existence. It is, if not non-existent, yet false, *jagan mithyā*; it is a mistake of the consciousness, it is and it is not; it is an irrational and inexplicable mystery in its origin, though we can see its process or at least how it keeps itself imposed on the consciousness. Brahman is seen in Maya as Ishwara upholding the works of Maya and the apparently individual soul is really nothing but Brahman itself. In the end, however, all this seems to be a myth of Maya, *mithyā*, and not anything really true. If that is Shankara's philosophy, it is to me unacceptable and incredible, however brilliantly ingenious it may be and however boldly and incisively reasoned; it does not satisfy my reason and it does not agree with my experience.

I don't know exactly what is meant by this *yuktivāda*. If it is meant that it is merely for the sake of arguing down opponents, then this part of the philosophy has no fundamental validity; Shankara's theory destroys itself. Either he meant it as a sufficient explanation of the universe or he did not. If he did, it is no use dismissing it as *yuktivāda*. I can understand that thoroughgoing Mayavadin's declaration that the whole question is illegitimate, because Maya and the world do not really exist; in fact the problem how the world came into existence is only a part of Maya, is like Maya unreal and does not truly arise; but if an explanation is to be given it must be a real and valid satisfying explanation. If there are two planes and in putting the question we are confusing the two planes, that argument can only be of value if both planes have some kind of existence and the reasoning and explanation are true in the lower plane but cease to have any meaning for a consciousness which has passed out of it.

2. Adwaita.

People are apt to speak of the Adwaita as if it were identical with Mayavada monism, just as they speak of Vedanta as if it were identical with Adwaita only; that is not the case. There are several forms of Indian philosophy which base themselves upon the One Reality, but they admit also the reality of the world, the reality of the Many, the reality of the differences of the Many as well as the sameness of the One (*bhedābheda*). But the Many exist in the One and by the One, the differences are variations in manifestation of that which is fundamentally ever the same. This we actually see as the universal law of existence where oneness is always the basis with an endless multiplicity and difference in the oneness; as for instance there is one mankind but many kinds of man, one thing called leaf or flower but many forms, patterns, colours of leaf and flower. Through this we can look back into one of the fundamental secrets of existence, the secret which is contained in the one Reality itself. The oneness of the Infinite is not something limited, fettered to its unity; it is capable of an infinite multiplicity. The Supreme Reality is an Absolute not limited by either oneness or multiplicity but simultaneously capable of both; for both are its aspects, although the oneness is fundamental and the multiplicity depends upon the oneness.

There is possible a realistic as well as an illusionist Adwaita. The philosophy of *The Life Divine* is such a realistic Adwaita. The world is a manifestation of the Real and therefore is itself real. The reality is the infinite and eternal Divine, infinite and eternal Being, Consciousness-Force and Bliss. This Divine by his power has created the world or rather manifested it in his own infinite Being. But here in the material world or at its basis he has hidden himself in what seem to be his opposites, Non-Being, Inconscience and Insentience. This is what we nowadays call the Inconscient which seems to have created the material universe by its inconscient Energy; but this is only an appearance, for we find in the end that all the dispositions of the world can only have been arranged by the working of a supreme secret intelligence. The Being which is hidden in what seems to be an inconscient void emerges in the world first in Matter, then in Life, then in Mind and finally as the Spirit. The apparently inconscient Energy which creates is in fact the Consciousness-Force of the Divine and its aspect of consciousness, secret in Matter, begins to emerge in Life, finds something more of itself in Mind and finds its true self in a spiritual consciousness and finally a supramental consciousness through which we become aware of the Reality, enter into it and unite ourselves with it. This is what we call evolution which is an evolution of consciousness and an evolution of the Spirit in things and only outwardly an evolution of species. Thus also, the delight of existence emerges from the original insentience first in the contrary forms of pleasure and pain and then has to find itself in the bliss of the Spirit or as it is called in the Upanishads, the bliss of the Brahman. That is the central idea in the explanation of the universe put forward in *The Life Divine*.

3. Nirguna and Saguna.

In a realistic Adwaita there is no need to regard the Saguna as a creation from the Nirguna or even secondary or subordinate to it: both are equal aspects of the one Reality, its position of silent status and rest and its position of action and dynamic force; a silence of eternal rest and peace supports an eternal action and movement. The one Reality, the Divine Being is bound by neither since it is in no way limited; it possesses both. There is no incompatibility between the two, as there is none between the Many and the One, the sameness and the difference. They are all eternal aspects of the universe which could not exist if either of them were eliminated, and it is reasonable to suppose that they both came from the Reality which has manifested the universe and are both real. We can only get rid of the apparent contradiction — which is not really a contradiction but only a natural concomitance — by treating one or the other as an illusion. But it is hardly reasonable to suppose that the eternal Reality allows the existence of an eternal illusion with which it has nothing to do or that it supports and enforces on being a vain cosmic illusion and has no power for any other and real action. The force of the Divine is always there in silence as in action, inactive in silence, active in the manifestation. It is hardly possible to suppose that the Divine Reality has no power or force or that its only power is to create a universal falsehood, a cosmic lie — *mithyā*.

4. Compounds and Disintegration.

No doubt all compounds, being not integral things in themselves but integrations, can disintegrate. Also it is true of life, though not a physical compound, that it has a curve of birth or integration and, after it reaches a certain point, of disintegration, decay and death. But these ideas or this rule of existence cannot be safely applied to things in themselves. The soul is not a compound but an integer, a thing in itself; it does not disintegrate, but at most enters into manifestation and goes out of manifestation. That is true even of forms other than constructed physical or constructed life-forms; they do not disintegrate but appear and disappear or at most fade out of manifestation. Mind itself as opposed to particular thoughts is something essential and permanent; it is a power of the Divine Consciousness. So is life, as opposed to constructed living bodies; so I think is what we call material energy which is really the force of essential substance in motion, a power of the Spirit. Thoughts, lives, material objects are formations of these energies, constructed or simply manifested according to the habit of the play of the particular energy. As for the elements, what is the pure natural condition of an element? According to modern Science what used to be called elements turn out to be compounds and the pure natural condition, if any, must be a condition of pure energy; it is that pure condition into which compounds including what we call elements must go when they pass by disintegration into Nirvana.

5. Nirvana.

What then is Nirvana? In orthodox Buddhism it does mean a disintegration, not of the soul — for that does not exist — but of a mental compound or stream of associations or *saṁskāras* which we mistake for ourself. In illusionist Vedanta it means not a disintegration but a disappearance of a false and unreal individual self into the one real self or Brahman; it is the idea and experience of individuality that so disappears and ceases, — we may say a false light that is extinguished (*nirvāṇa*) in the true Light. In spiritual experience it is sometimes the loss of all sense of individuality in a boundless cosmic consciousness; what was the individual remains only as a centre or a channel for the flow of a cosmic consciousness and a cosmic force and action. Or it may be the experience of the loss of individuality in a transcendent being and consciousness in which the sense of cosmos as well as the individual disappears. Or again, it may be in a transcendence which is aware of and supports the cosmic action. But what do we mean by the individual? What we usually call by that name is a natural ego, a device of Nature which holds together her action in the mind and body. This ego has to be extinguished, otherwise there is no complete liberation possible; but the individual self or soul is not this ego. The individual soul is the spiritual being which is sometimes described as an eternal portion of the Divine but can also be described as the Divine himself supporting his manifestation as the Many. This is the true spiritual individual which appears in its complete truth when we get rid of the ego and our false separative sense of individuality, realise our oneness with the transcendent and cosmic Divine and with all beings. It is this which makes possible the Divine Life. Nirvana is a step towards it; the disappearance of the false separative individuality is a necessary condition for our realising and living in our true eternal being, living divinely in the Divine. But this we can do in the world and in life.

6. Rebirth.

If evolution is a truth and is not only a physical evolution of species, but an evolution of consciousness, it must be a spiritual and not only a physical fact. In that case, it is the individual who evolves and grows into a more and more developed and perfect consciousness and obviously that cannot be done in the course of a brief single human life. If there is the evolution of a conscious individual, then there must be rebirth. Rebirth is a logical necessity and a spiritual fact of which we can have the experience. Proofs of rebirth, sometimes of an overwhelmingly convincing nature, are not lacking, but as yet they have not been carefully registered and brought together.

7. Evolution.

In my explanation of the universe I have put forward this cardinal fact of a spiritual evolution as the meaning of our existence here. It is a series of ascents from the physical being and consciousness to the vital, the being dominated by the life-self, thence to the mental being realised in the fully developed man and thence into the perfect consciousness which is beyond the mental, into the Supramental consciousness and the Supramental being, the Truth-Consciousness which is the integral consciousness of the spiritual being. Mind cannot be our last conscious expression because mind is fundamentally an ignorance seeking for knowledge; it is only the Supramental Truth-Consciousness that can bring us the true and whole Self-Knowledge and world-Knowledge; it is through that only that we can get to our true being and the fulfilment of our spiritual evolution.

Chapter Four
Transformation in the Integral Yoga

The Meaning of Transformation

By transformation I do not mean some change of the nature — I do not mean for instance sainthood or ethical perfection or Yogic siddhis (like the Tantrik's) or a transcendental (*cinmaya*) body. I use transformation in a special sense, a change of consciousness radical and complete and of a certain specific kind which is so conceived as to bring about a strong and assured step forward in the spiritual evolution of the being, an advance of a greater and higher kind and of a larger sweep and completeness than that smaller though decisive achievement of the emerging Consciousness when a mentalised being first appeared in a vital and material animal world. If anything short of that takes place or at least if a real beginning is not made on that basis, a fundamental progress towards this fulfilment, then my object is not accomplished. A partial realisation, something mixed and inconclusive, does not meet the demand I make on life and Yoga.

Light of realisation is not the same thing as Descent. Realisation by itself does not necessarily transform the being as a whole; it may bring only an opening or heightening or widening of the consciousness at the top so as to realise something in the Purusha part without any radical change in the parts of Prakriti. One may have some light of realisation at the spiritual summit of the consciousness but the parts below remain what they were. I have seen any number of instances of that. There must be a descent of the light not merely into the mind or part of it but into all the being down to the physical and below before a real and total transformation can take place. A light in the mind may spiritualise or otherwise change the mind or part of it in one way or another, but it need not change the vital nature; a light in the vital may purify and enlarge the vital movements or else silence and immobilise the vital being, but leave the body and the physical consciousness as it was, or even leave it inert or shake its balance. And the descent of Light is not enough, it must be the descent of the whole higher consciousness, its Peace, Power, Knowledge, Love, Ananda. Moreover, the descent may be enough to liberate, but not to perfect, or it may be enough to make a great change in the inner being, while the outer remains an imperfect instrument, clumsy, sick or unexpressive. Finally, the transformation effected by the sadhana cannot be complete unless it is a supramentalisation of the being. Psychisation is not enough, it is only a beginning; spiritualisation and the descent of the higher consciousness is not enough, it is only a middle term; the ultimate achievement needs the action of the supramental Consciousness and Force. Something less than that may very well be considered enough by the individual, but it is not enough for the earth-consciousness to take the definitive stride forward it must take at one time or another.

I have never said that my Yoga was something brand new in all its elements. I have called it the integral Yoga and that means that it takes up the essence and many processes of the old Yogas — its newness is in its aim, standpoint and the totality of its method. In the earlier stages which is all I deal with in books like the *Riddle* or the *Lights*[1] there is nothing in it that distinguishes it from the old Yogas except the aim underlying its comprehensiveness, the spirit in its movements and the ultimate significance it keeps before it — also the scheme of its psychology and its working, but as that was not and could not be developed systematically or schematically in these letters, it has not been grasped by those who are not already acquainted with it by mental familiarity or some amount of practice. The detail or method of the later stages of the Yoga which go into little known or untrodden regions, I have not made public and I do not at present intend to do so.

I know very well also that there have been seemingly allied ideals and anticipations — the perfectibility of the race, certain

---

[1] The Riddle of This World *and* Lights on Yoga, *two small books of letters published in 1933 and 1935 respectively. A third such book,* Bases of Yoga, *was published in 1936.* — Ed.

Tantric sadhanas, the effort after a complete physical siddhi by certain schools of Yoga, etc. etc. I have alluded to these things myself and have put forth the view that the spiritual past of the race has been a preparation of Nature not merely for attaining to the Divine beyond this world, but also for this very step forward which the evolution of the earth-consciousness has still to make. I do not therefore care in the least, — even though these ideals were, up to some extent parallel, yet not identical with mine, — whether this Yoga and its aim and method are accepted as new or not; that is in itself a trifling matter. That it should be recognised as true in itself by those who can accept or practise it and should make itself true by achievement, is the one thing important; it does not matter if it is called new or a repetition or revival of the old which was forgotten. I laid emphasis on it as new in a letter to certain sadhaks so as to explain to them that a repetition of the aim and idea of the old Yogas was not enough in my eyes, that I was putting forward a thing to be achieved that has not yet been achieved, not yet clearly visualised, even though it is one natural but still secret destined outcome of all the past spiritual endeavour.

It is new as compared with the old Yogas:

(1) Because it aims not at a departure out of world and life into a Heaven or a Nirvana, but at a change of life and existence, not as something subordinate or incidental, but as a distinct and central object. If there is a descent in other Yogas, yet it is only an incident on the way or resulting from the ascent — the ascent is the real thing. Here the ascent is indispensable, but what is decisive, what is finally aimed at is the resulting descent. It is the descent of the new consciousness attained by the ascent that is the stamp and seal of the sadhana. Even Tantra and Vaishnavism end in the release from life; here the object is the divine fulfilment of life.

(2) Because the object sought after is not an individual achievement of divine realisation for the sole sake of the individual, but something to be gained for the earth-consciousness here, a cosmic, not solely a supra-cosmic achievement. The thing to be gained also is the bringing in of a Power of consciousness

(the supramental) not yet organised or active directly in earth-nature, even in the spiritual life, but yet to be organised and made directly active.

(3) Because a method has been preconised for achieving this purpose which is as total and integral as the aim set before it, viz. the total and integral change of the consciousness and nature, taking up old methods but only as a part action and passing on to others that are distinctive. I have not found this method (as a whole) or anything like it in its totality proposed or realised in the old Yogas. If I had I should not have wasted my time in hewing out a road and in thirty years of search and inner creation when I could have hastened home safely to my goal in an easy canter over paths already blazed out, laid down, perfectly mapped, macadamised, made secure and public. Our Yoga is not a retreading of old walks, but a spiritual adventure.

Towards a Transformation of Earth Life

I believe Krishnaprem's comment was on a passage in which I wrote that this Yoga was not like the old ones in that it aimed not at an ascent or passing beyond life but at a descent of the divine consciousness into life. Its aim is double — two movements fusing themselves into one — an ascending into divine consciousness and a transformation of earth life by the divine consciousness coming down here. All the old Yogas put the emphasis on going to Nirvana or to heaven, Vaikuntha, Goloka, Brahmaloka etc. for good and so getting rid of rebirth. My emphasis is on life here and its transformation and I put that as the aim at once of my Yoga and of the terrestrial manifestation. I am quite unaware that any of the old Yogas hold this as the aim before them. Even Vaishnavism and Tantra are in the end other-worldly; mukti is the aim of their efforts and anything else could be only incidental and secondary or a result on the way. If my view is correct, then my statement was not an error.

I have not denied that the ideal of a change on earth is of old standing. It is there vaguely in the human mind perhaps since the beginning, though more often perfection is put in some golden age of the past and deterioration and a cataclysm is the law of the future. Christianity foresees a descent of Christ and his rule on earth, but this is figured as an outward event, not as a change produced by an inward power and process or by Yoga. A reign of the saints is also foreshadowed in some Hindu scriptures, but that equally is something different from my conception. As for sainthood itself or the siddhis of Yoga including a siddha body, that too is not what I mean by transformation — it is a radical change of consciousness and nature itself that I envisage. I do not know also that these things were sought by the process of descent — the Tamil Shaiva saints for instance sought for the siddha body by tremendous austerities; the siddhis they sought were all there in the sukshma mental and vital worlds and by a stupendous effort and mastery of the body they brought them down into the physical instrument. I have always said that these things and these methods are out of my scope and eschewed by me in my Yoga. I tried some of these but after achieving some initial results I saw it was a bypath and I left it.

To get rid of or mastery over *kāma-krodha* is not the transformation, it is at best a preliminary step towards it provided it is done not in the moral way by mental self-control but in the spiritual way. Sainthood is not my object. I do not know how far Ramakrishna had gone towards the transformation as I conceive it; the metaphors you quote contain nothing precise with which I can compare my own experience or my own intuitions about the change. According to certain accounts there was a descent of Kali into his body which made it luminous, but he repressed it as something contrary to what he was seeking after. If there is something anywhere in the past which coincides with the aim and conceived process of my Yoga I shall be glad to know of it; for that would certainly be an aid to me. I put no value on the newness of what I am doing or trying to do. If the path was already there open and complete, it is a great pity that I should have wasted all my life clearing it out anew with much difficulty and peril when I could just have walked on a clear and safe avenue towards the goal of my endeavour. But the nearest I could get to it were some things in the Veda and Upanishads (secret words, veiled hints) which seemed to coincide with or point towards certain things in my own knowledge and experience. But after incorporating certain parts of the Vedic method as far as I could interpret or recover it, I found it was insufficient and I had to seek farther.

*

Transformation is a word that I have brought in myself (like supermind) to express certain spiritual concepts and spiritual facts of the integral Yoga. People are now taking them up and using them in senses which have nothing to do with the significance which I put into them. Purification of the nature by the "influence" of the Spirit is not what I mean by transformation; purification is only part of a psychic change or a psycho-spiritual change — the word besides has many senses and is very often given a moral or ethical meaning which is foreign to my purpose. What I mean by the spiritual transformation is something dynamic (not merely liberation of the self, or realisation of the One which can very well be attained without any descent). It is a putting on of the spiritual consciousness dynamic as well as static in every part of the being down to the subconscient. That cannot be done by the influence of the Self leaving the consciousness fundamentally as it is with only purification, enlightenment of the mind and heart and quiescence of the vital. It means a bringing down of Divine Consciousness static and dynamic into all these parts and the entire replacement of the present consciousness by that. This we find unveiled and unmixed above mind, life and body and not in mind, life and body. It is a matter of the undeniable experience of many that this can descend and it is my experience that nothing short of its *full* descent can thoroughly remove the veil and mixture and effect the full spiritual transformation. No metaphysical or logical reasoning in the void as to what the Atman "must" do or can do or needs or needs not to do is relevant here or of any value. I may add that transformation is not the central object of other paths as it is of this Yoga — only so much purification and change is demanded by them as will lead to liberation and the beyond-life. The influence of the Atman can no doubt do that — a full descent of a new Consciousness into the whole nature from top to bottom to transform life here is not needed at all for the spiritual escape from life.

*

It is not a hope but a certitude that the complete transformation of the nature will take place.

Spiritualisation and Transformation

Spiritualisation means the descent of the higher peace, force, light, knowledge, purity, Ananda etc. which belong to any of the higher planes from Higher Mind to Overmind, for in any of these the Self can be realised. It brings about a subjective transformation; the instrumental Nature is only so far transformed that it becomes an instrument for the Cosmic Divine to get some work done while the self within remains calm and free and united to the Divine. But this is an incomplete individual transformation — the full transformation of the instrumental Nature can only come when the Supramental change takes place. Till then the nature remains full of many imperfections, but the self in the higher planes does not mind them, as it is itself free and unaffected. The inner being down to the inner physical can also become free and unaffected. The Overmind is subject to limitations in the working of the effective Knowledge, limitations in the working of the Power, subjection to a partial and limited Truth, etc. It is only in the supermind that the full Truth consciousness comes into being.

*

There are many planes above man's mind — the supramental is not the only one, and on all of them the self can be realised, — for they are all spiritual planes.

Mind, vital and physical are inextricably mixed together only in the surface consciousness — the inner mind, inner vital, inner physical are separate from each other. Those who seek the self by the old Yogas separate themselves from mind, life and body and realise the self apart from these things. It is perfectly easy to separate mind, vital and physical from each other without the need of supermind. It is done by the ordinary Yogas.

The difference between this and the old Yogas is not that they are incompetent and cannot do these things — they can do them perfectly well — but that they proceed from realisation of self to Nirvana or some Heaven and abandon life, while this does not abandon life. The supramental is necessary for the transformation of terrestrial life and being, not for reaching the self. One must realise self first — only afterwards can one realise the supermind.

*

In the former Yogas it was the experience of the spirit which is always free and one with the Divine that was sought. The nature had to change only enough to prevent its being an obstacle to that knowledge and experience. The complete change down to the physical was only sought for by a few and then more as a "siddhi" than anything else, not as the manifestation of a new Nature in the earth consciousness.

*

I do not know that any except a very few great Yogis have really changed their outer nature. In all the Asrams I have seen people were just as others except for certain specific moral controls put on certain kinds of outer action (food, sex etc.), but the general nature was the human nature (as in the story of Narad and Janaka). It is even a theory of the old Yogas that the *prārabdha karma* and therefore necessarily the permanent elements of external character do not change — only one gets the inner realisation and separates oneself from it so that it drops off at death like a soiled robe and leaves the spirit free to enter into Nirvana. Our object is a spiritual change and not merely an ethical control, but this can only come first by a spiritual rejection from within and then by a supramental descent from above.

*

Sri Aurobindo[2] has no remarks to make on Huxley's comments with which he is in entire agreement. But in the phrase "to its heights we can always reach" very obviously "we" does not refer to humanity in general but to those who have a sufficiently developed inner spiritual life.[3] It is probable that Sri Aurobindo was thinking of his own experience. After three years of spiritual effort with only minor results he was shown by a Yogi the way to silence his mind. This he succeeded in doing entirely in two or three days by following the method shown. There was an entire silence of thought and feeling and all the ordinary movements of consciousness except the perception and recognition of things around without any accompanying concept or other reaction. The sense of ego disappeared and the movements of the ordinary life as well as speech and action were carried on by some habitual activity of Prakriti alone which was not felt as belonging to oneself. But the perception which remained saw all things as utterly unreal; this sense of unreality was overwhelming and universal. Only some undefinable Reality was perceived as true which was beyond space and time and unconnected with any cosmic activity but yet was met wherever one turned. This condition remained unimpaired for several months and even when the sense of unreality disappeared and there was a return to participation in the world-consciousness, the inner peace and freedom which resulted from this realisation remained permanently behind all surface movements and the essence of the realisation itself was not lost. At the same time an experience intervened; something else than himself took up his dynamic activity and spoke and acted through him but without any personal

---

[2] *In this letter to a disciple living outside the Ashram, Sri Aurobindo refers to himself in the third person.* — Ed.
[3] *In his book* The Perennial Philosophy *(London: Chatto and Windus, 1946, p. 74), Aldous Huxley quoted and commented on the following passage by Sri Aurobindo: "The touch of Earth is always reinvigorating to the son of Earth, even when he seeks a supraphysical Knowledge. It may even be said that the supraphysical can only be really mastered in its fullness — to its heights we can always reach — when we keep our feet firmly on the physical. 'Earth is His footing,' says the Upanishad whenever it images the Self that manifests in the universe." The Life Divine, volume 21 of* THE COMPLETE WORKS OF SRI AUROBINDO, *pp. 13-14.* — Ed.

thought or initiative. What this was remained unknown until Sri Aurobindo came to realise the dynamic side of the Brahman, the Ishwara, and felt himself moved by that in all his sadhana and action. These realisations and others which followed upon them, such as that of the Self in all and all in the Self and all as the Self, the Divine in all and all in the Divine, are the heights to which Sri Aurobindo refers and to which he says we can always rise; for they presented to him no long or obstinate difficulty. The only real difficulty which took decades of spiritual effort to carry out towards completeness was to apply the spiritual knowledge utterly to the world and to the surface psychological and outer life and to effect its transformation both on the higher levels of Nature and on the ordinary mental, vital and physical levels down to the subconscience and the basic Inconscience and up to the supreme Truth-consciousness or Supermind in which alone the dynamic transformation could be entirely integral and absolute.

The Attempt at Physical Transformation

Sri Krishna never set out to arrive at any physical transformation, so anything of the kind could not be expected in his case.

Neither Buddha nor Shankara nor Ramakrishna had any idea of transforming the body. Their aim was spiritual mukti and nothing else. Krishna taught Arjuna to do liberated works, but he never spoke of any physical transformation.

I do not know that we can take this [*Yudhisthira's entry into the heavenly kingdom in his mortal body*] as a historical fact. Swarga is not somewhere in the Himalayas, it is another world in another plane of consciousness and substance. Whatever the story may mean, therefore, it has nothing to do with the question of physical transformation on earth.

*

Ramakrishna himself never thought of transformation or tried for it. All he wanted was bhakti for the Mother and along with that he received whatever knowledge she gave him and did whatever she made him do. He was intuitive and psychic from the beginning and only became more and more so as he went on. There was no need in him for the transformation which we seek; for although he spoke of the divine man (Ishwarakoti) coming down the stairs as well as ascending, he had not the idea of a new consciousness and a new race and the divine manifestation in the earth-nature.

*

Whatever may have happened to Chaitanya or Ramalingam, whatever physical transformation they may have gone through is quite irrelevant to the aim of the supramentalisation of the body. Their new body was either a non-physical or subtle physical body not adapted for life on the earth. If it were not so, they would not have disappeared. The object of supramentalisation is a body fitted to embody and express the physical consciousness on earth so long as one remains in the physical life. It is a step in the spiritual evolution on the earth, not a step in the passage towards a supraphysical world. The supramentalisation is the most difficult part of the change arrived at by the supramental Yoga, and all depends on whether a sufficient change can be achieved in the consciousness at present to make such a step possible, but the nature of the step is different from that aimed at by other Yogas. There is not therefore much utility in these discussions — one has first of all to supramentalise sufficiently the mind and vital and physical consciousness generally — afterwards one can think of supramentalisation of the body. The psychic and spiritual transformation must come first, only afterwards would it be practical or useful to discuss the supramentalisation of the whole being down to the body.

Section Two

Other Spiritual Paths and the Integral Yoga

Chapter One
The Newness of the Integral Yoga

Old and New Truth

Well, I don't suppose the new race can be created by or according to logic or that any race has been. But why should the idea of the creation of a new race be illogical? It is not only my ideas that baffle reason, but Adhar Das's also! he must really be a superman, — self-made of course, outside the laboratory. As for the past seers, they don't trouble me. If going beyond the experiences of the past seers and sages is so shocking, each new seer and sage in turn has done that shocking thing — Buddha, Shankara, Chaitanya etc. all did that wicked act. If not, what was the necessity of their starting new philosophies, religions, schools of Yoga? If they were merely verifying and meekly repeating the lives and experiences of past seers and sages without bringing the world some new thing, why all that stir and pother? Of course, you may say they were simply explaining the old truth but in the right way — but this would mean that nobody had explained or understood it rightly before — which is again "giving the lie etc." Or you may say that all the new sages (they were not among X's cherished past ones in their day), e.g. Shankara, Ramanuja, Madhwa, were each merely repeating the same blessed thing as all the past seers and sages had repeated with an unwearied monotony before them. Well, well, but why repeat it in such a way that each "gives the lie" to the others? Truly, this shocked reverence for the past is a wonderful and fearful thing! After all, the Divine is infinite and the unrolling of the Truth may be an infinite process or at least, if not quite so much, yet with some room for new discovery and new statement, even perhaps new achievement, not a thing in a nutshell cracked and its contents exhausted once for all by the first seer or sage, while the others must religiously crack the same nutshell all over again, each tremblingly careful not to give the lie to the "past" seers and sages.

Spiritual Realisation and the Supramental Transformation

This Yoga aims at the conscious union with the Divine in the supermind and the transformation of the nature. The ordinary Yogas go straight from Mind into some featureless condition of the cosmic Silence and through it try to disappear upward into the Highest. The object of this Yoga is to transcend mind and enter into the Divine Truth of Sachchidananda which is not only static but dynamic and raise the whole being into that Truth.

*

The Divine can be realised on any plane according to the capacity of that plane, as the Divine is everywhere. The Yogis and saints realise the Divine on the spiritualised mind plane, that does not mean they become supramental.

*

But why should they [*Yogis of the traditional schools*] feel any pressure [*of the supramental descent*] when they are satisfied with the realisation they have? They live in the spiritual mind and the nature of the mind is to separate — here to separate some high aspect or state of the Divine and seek that to the exclusion of all else. All the spiritual philosophies and schools of Yoga do that. If they go beyond, it is to the Absolute and mind cannot conceive of the Absolute except as something inconceivable, *neti neti*. Moreover for getting samadhi they concentrate on one single idea and what they reach is that which is represented by that idea — the samadhi is in its nature an exclusive concentration on that. So why should it open them to anything else? There are only a few who are sufficiently plastic to escape from this self-limitation of the sadhana — what they experience is that there is no end to the realisation, when you get to one peak, you find another beyond it. In order to see more than this one has to get into conscious waking touch with the supramental or at least get a glimpse of it — and that means passing beyond spiritual mind.

*

Certainly, the realisation of the Spirit comes long before the development of Overmind or Supermind; hundreds of sadhaks in all times have had the realisation of the Atman on the higher mental plane, *buddheḥ paratah*, but the supramental realisation was not theirs. One can get *partial* realisations of the Self or Spirit or the Divine on any plane, mental, vital, physical even, and when one rises above the ordinary mental plane of man into a higher and larger mind, the Self begins to appear in all its conscious wideness. It is by full entry into this wideness of the Self that cessation of mental activity becomes possible; one gets the inner Silence. After that this inner Silence can remain even when there is activity of any kind; the being remains silent within, the action goes on in the instruments and one receives all the necessary indications and execution of action whether mental, vital or physical from a higher source without the fundamental peace and calm of the Spirit being troubled.

The Overmind and Supermind states are something yet higher than this; but before one can understand them, one must first have the self-realisation, the full action of the spiritualised mind and heart, the psychic awakening, the liberation of the imprisoned consciousness, the purification and entire opening of the *ādhāra*. Do not think now of those ultimate things (Overmind, Supermind), but get first these foundations in the liberated nature.

*

By divine realisation is meant the spiritual realisation — the realisation of Self, Bhagavan or Brahman on the mental-spiritual plane or else the overmental plane. That is a thing (at any rate the mental-spiritual) which thousands have done. So it is obviously easier to do than the supramental. Also nobody can have the supramental realisation who has not had the spiritual.

It is true that neither can be got in any effective way unless the whole being is turned towards it — unless there is a real and very serious spirit and dynamic reality of sadhana.

It is true that I want the supramental not for myself but for the earth and souls born on the earth, and certainly therefore

I cannot object if anybody wants the supramental. But there are the conditions. He must want the Divine Will first and the soul's surrender and spiritual realisation (through works, bhakti, knowledge, self-perfection) on the way.

The central sincerity is the first thing and sufficient for an aspiration to be entertained — a total sincerity is needed for the aspiration to be fulfilled.

*

There are different statuses (*avasthā*) of the Divine Consciousness. There are also different statuses of transformation. First is the psychic transformation, in which all is in contact with the Divine through the psychic consciousness. Next is the spiritual transformation in which all is merged in the Divine in the cosmic consciousness. Third is the supramental transformation in which all becomes supramentalised in the divine gnostic consciousness. It is only with the last that there can begin the *complete* transformation of mind, life and body — in my sense of completeness.

*

You are mistaken in two respects. First, the endeavour towards this achievement [*the transformation of mind, life and body*] is not new and some Yogis have achieved it, I believe — but not in the way I want it. They achieved it as a personal siddhi maintained by Yoga-siddhi — not a dharma of the nature. Secondly, the supramental transformation is not the same as the spiritual-mental. It is a change of mind, life and body which the mental or overmental-spiritual cannot achieve. All whom you mention were spirituals, but in different ways. Krishna's mind, for instance, was overmentalised, Ramakrishna's intuitive, Chaitanya's spiritual-psychic, Buddha's illumined higher mental. I don't know about B. G. [*Bijoy Goswami*] — he seems to have been brilliant but rather chaotic. All that is different from the supramental. Then take the vital of the Paramhansas. It is said their vital behaves either like a child (Ramakrishna) or like a madman or like a demon or like something inert (cf.

Jadabharata). Well, there is nothing supramental in all that. So?
One can be a fit instrument for the Divine in any of the transformations. The question is, an instrument for what?

*

Your Guru's teaching and that of this Yoga are essentially the same; what he called *cittaśuddhi* is what we mean by the psychic change. The teaching here is more developed because it includes the Supramental means of creating a divine life. Also the getting of the truth is different, since here it is put in such a way as to initiate men of all castes, races, creeds and cultures without distinction to share in the Truth and the Divine Life. But it is no use trying to draw those who received the earlier teaching, for their sight is still circumscribed by past forms and feelings and cannot extend itself beyond them. It is good that you have freed yourself from the desire to do so and taken an impersonal position — if any have to come they will come. Our concentration must be on all preparing themselves so that what was foreseen by your Guru may be fulfilled this time and here.

Depreciation of the Old Yogas

As for the depreciation of all the old Yogas as something quite easy, unimportant and worthless, and the consequent depreciation of Buddha and Yajnavalkya and other great spiritual figures of the past, is it not evidently absurd on the face of it?

*

It [*self-realisation*] is not a long process? The whole life and several lives more are often not enough to achieve it. Ramakrishna's guru took 30 years to arrive and even then he was not satisfied that he had realised it.

*

Wonderful! The realisation of the Self which includes the liberation from ego, the consciousness of the One in all, the established and consummated transcendence out of the universal

Ignorance, the fixity of the consciousness in the union with the Highest, the Infinite and Eternal is not anything worth doing or recommending to anybody — is "not a very difficult stage"!

Nothing new? Why should there be anything new? The object of spiritual seeking is to find out what is eternally true, not what is new in Time.

From where did you get this singular attitude towards the old Yogas and Yogis? Is the wisdom of the Vedanta and Tantra a small and trifling thing? Have then the sadhaks of this Asram attained to self-realisation and are they liberated Jivan-muktas, free from ego and ignorance? If not, why then do you say, "it is not a very difficult stage", "their goal is not high", "is it such a long process?"

I have said that this Yoga was "new" because it aims at the integrality of the Divine in this world and not only beyond it and at a supramental realisation. But how does that justify a superior contempt for the spiritual realisation which is as much the aim of this Yoga as of any other?

The Old Lines and This Line

Plenty of people, I suppose, would go on with the old lines[1] — for it is not likely that all would be able to take this line. As for the Darshanas most of them have fallen into disuse already except as a battlefield for Pandits. It is only the Vedanta and Patanjali and the later Bhakti Yoga that are still alive, not so much as darshanas but as traditional systems of Yoga.

---

[1] *The correspondent asked, "Is it not likely that the Darshanas and Upanishads will be forgotten in the next hundred years as the New Yoga establishes itself in the world? If it is possible to get the necessary things from your writings and the Mother's, who would care to read the enigmatic sutras and concealed formulas of the Darshanas, Upanishads and Vedas?" — Ed.*

Chapter Two
The Veda and the Upanishads

The Vedic Rishis

It is not I only who have done what the Vedic Rishis did not do. Chaitanya and others developed an intensity of Bhakti which is absent in the Veda and many other instances can be given. Why should the past be the limit of spiritual experience?

*

I can't say whether any of them [*the Vedic Rishis*] attained the supramental plane, but the ascent to it was their object. Swar is evidently the illumined regions of Mind, between the supramental and the human intelligence formed by the rays of the Sun. According to the Upanishads those who ascend into the rays of the Sun return, but those who ascend into the Sun itself do not come back. That is because the ascent to supermind was envisaged, but the descent and organisation of the supermind here (as apart from the descent of the Rays) was not. We need not bother about the rebirth of the Rishis — they will come along if they are needed, I suppose.

*

I don't know of any [*Vedic Rishis*] that have taken birth this time. According to the Puranic stories there must have been many Rishis who were far from being *jitendriya, jitakrodha*. But also there are many Yogis who are satisfied with having the inner experience of the Self but allow movements of a rajasic or tamasic nature on the surface, holding that these will fall off with the body.

*

The Vedic Rishis were mystics of the ancient type who everywhere, in India, Greece, Egypt and elsewhere, held the secret truths and methods of which they were in possession as very sacred and secret things not to be disclosed to the unfit who would misunderstand, misapply, misuse and degrade the knowledge. Their writings were therefore so couched as only to be intelligible in their secret meaning to the initiated, *niṇyā vacāṁsi nivacanāni kavaye* — secret words that carry their significance only to the seer. They were equipped with an apparent meaning exoteric and religious for the people, esoteric, occult and spiritual for the initiates. That the people should not find out the real Truth was their intention; they wanted them only to know the outward truths for which they were fit.

*

This picture of Vedic society [*a completely pastoral life, without priests or warriors*] could easily be challenged. The householder may have lit daily the fire on the household altar, but when he wanted to offer a sacrifice he did it with the aid of sacrificial priests who knew the ritual. Sometimes the Rishi himself performed the sacrifice for the householder. He was not a priest by profession, however, for he might have any occupation in the society. Besides, in a large sacrifice there were many versed in the Vedic rites who performed different functions. In the very first verse of the Rig Veda Agni is described as being himself the Purohit, the priest representative of the householder sacrificer, Yajamana, as the Ritwik, the one who saw to the arrangement of the rites, the Hota who invoked the Gods and gave the offering, and in other hymns he is spoken of as the priest of the purification, the priest of the lustration etc. All this has obviously an esoteric sense but it testifies to the habitual presence of a number of priests at any large sacrifice. So we cannot say that there were no priests in the Vedic age. There does not seem to have been any priestly caste until later times when the four castes came definitely into being. But the Brahmins were not predominantly priests but rather scholars and intellectuals with a religious authority derived from birth and from knowledge of the scriptures and the books of the social law, Shastra. The function of priesthood has never been highly honoured in India and it would therefore be incorrect to speak of priestcraft or any rule by priests or ecclesiastics at any time in Indian history.

As for the warriors, there are in the Rig Veda two or three hymns describing a great battle which the scholars declare to have been the fight of one king against ten allied kings, and besides that, the hymns are full of images of war and battle. These too have an esoteric meaning, but they indicate a state of things in which war and battle must have been frequent; so we cannot say that there were no warriors.

Again, your description seems to indicate that all the householders were initiated in the knowledge held by the Rishis. But this was a secret knowledge imparted by the Rishi to his family and to disciples whom he found to be fit, it was not given to everyone. The language of the Veda was also veiled and mystic, "secret words of seer-wisdom which yielded their meaning to the seer" as one of the Rishis described them, but understood in an outward sense by the ordinary uninitiated man. This principle of secrecy was common to all the mysteries in every country and it was maintained also in ancient India. The religious worship practised by the common man and any communion it might bring with the gods was only a preliminary preparation and not the deeper knowledge.

It was always held in ancient India that religion, life and society should be so arranged that every man should have the opportunity to grow spiritually by whatever means is suitable to his capacity, *adhikāra*. Everywhere there was a system of gradations by which this purpose could be served. It provided for a continual contact of man at every step with what was behind and beyond the material life. In Vedic times meditation, worship and sacrifice were the means by which this connection with the Unseen was sought to be established and maintained. The sacrifice was symbolic in its ritual and the symbols were supposed to have an occult power to create a relation between the unseen powers worshipped and the worshipper; by it they were called in to preside over and help all the action and life of the human being. Worship was for establishing a more inner relation and meditation the means of spiritual experience, development and knowledge. The institutions which grew up in later Vedic times, such as the four Asramas and the four Varnas, the fourfold arrangement of society originally had the same intention and are so recognised in the Gita. So trained a man could develop until he was ready for a deeper knowledge and receive the initiation. In the Vedic times this deeper knowledge was the mystic doctrine and practice of the Vedic Rishis; it was that that afterwards developed on a hundred branching lines into the later systems of Yoga.

The Veda and the Greeks

As to the Eleusinian mysteries, about which he has asked an explanation, they were connected with the same mystic knowledge as was held in India by the Vedic Rishis. Demeter and Persephone were goddesses worshipped by the Greeks; Demeter is the Earth-Mother and Persephone was the goddess of the Harvest, but in the mystic symbols Persephone represented the earth consciousness buried in the Ignorance and emerging into the Divine Light. The Eleusinian mysteries were instituted as an outward symbol of this secret knowledge.

*

The Soma wine was the symbol of the divine or spiritual Ananda. This wine was however symbolic and cannot be exactly equated with the nectar or ambrosia of the Greeks which were the food and drink of the gods and sustained their immortality; but outwardly there is some resemblance.

No Incarnation of the Vedic Gods

In the Veda there is no idea or experience of a personal emanation or incarnation of any of the Vedic gods. When the Rishis speak of Indra or Agni or Soma in men, they are speaking of the god in his cosmic presence, power or function. This is evident from the very language when they speak of Agni as the immortal in mortals, the immortal Light in man, the inner Warrior, the

Guest in human beings. It is the same with Indra or Soma. The building of the gods in man means a creation of the divine Powers, Indra the Power of the Light, Soma the Power of the Ananda in the human nature.

No doubt, the Rishis felt the actual presence of the gods above, near, around or in them, but this was a common experience of all, not special and personal, not an emanation or incarnation. One may see or feel the presence of the Divine or a divine Power above the head or in the heart or in any or all of the centres, feel the presence, see the form living there; one may be governed in all one's actions, thoughts and feelings by it; one may lose one's separate personality in it, may identify and merge. But all that does not constitute an incarnation or emanation of the Divine or of the Power. These things are universal experiences to which any Yogin may arrive; to reach this condition with relation to the Divine is indeed a common object of Yoga.

An incarnation is something more, something special and individual to the individual being. It is the substitution of the Person of a divine being for the human person and an infiltration of it into all the movements so that there is a dynamic personal change in all of them and in the whole nature; not merely a change of the character of the consciousness or a general surrender into its hands, but a subtle intimate personal change. Even when there is an incarnation from the birth, the human elements have to be taken up, but when there is a descent, there is a total conscious substitution.

This is a long, subtle and persistent process. The incarnating Person first overshadows as an influence, then enters into the centres one after the other, sometimes in the same form, sometimes in different forms, then takes up all the nature and its actions. What you describe does not correspond to this process; it seems to be an endeavour to build the gods in yourself in the Vedic sense and the Vedic manner. That can bring, if it succeeds, their powers and a sense of their presence; it cannot bring about an incarnation. An incarnation is destined, is chosen for you; the human person cannot choose or create an incarnation for himself by his own personal will. To attempt it is to invite a spiritual disaster.

One thing must be said — that an incarnation is not the object of this Yoga; it is only a condition or means towards the object. The one and only aim we have before us is to bring down the supramental consciousness and the supramental Truth into the world; the Truth and nothing but the Truth is our aim, and if we cannot embody this Truth, a hundred incarnations do not matter. But to bring down the true supramental and nothing but the true supramental, to escape from all mental mixture is not an easy matter. The mere descent of the suns into the centres, even of all the seven suns into all the seven centres is only the seed; it is not the thing itself done and finished. One may feel the descent of suns, one may have the attempt, the beginning of an incarnation, and yet in the end one may fail if there is a flaw in the nature or a failure to pass through all the ordeals and satisfy all the hard conditions of the perfect spiritual success. Not only the whole mental, vital and physical nature of the ignorant human being has to be overcome and transformed, but also the three states of mental consciousness which intervene between the human and the supramental and like all mind are capable of admitting great and capital errors. Till then there may be descents of supramental influence, light, power, Ananda, but the supramental Truth cannot be possessed, organised, put in possession of the whole nature. One must not think before that that one possesses the supermind; for that is a delusion which would prevent the fulfilment.

One thing more. The more intense the experiences that come, the higher the forces that descend, the greater become the possibilities of deviation and error. For the very intensity and the very height of the force excites and aggrandises the movements of the lower nature and raises up in it all the opposing elements in their full force, but often in the disguise of truth, wearing a mask of plausible justification. There is needed a great patience, calm, sobriety, balance, an impersonal detachment and sincerity free from all taint of ego or personal human desire. There must be no attachment to any idea of one's own, to any experience, to any kind of imagination, mental building or vital demand; the light of discrimination must always play to detect these things, however fair or plausible they may seem. Otherwise the Truth will have no chance of establishing itself in its purity in the nature.

Terms and Verses of the Upanishads

It is quite impossible to say to what they [*the seers of the Upanishads*] were referring in those days.[1] We have no longer a clue to their symbolism. But it is meant that the lower worlds are in the higher worlds even as the higher worlds are in the lower worlds — they penetrate each other. E.g. in our system there is a vital mental, several layers of the vital itself, a physical vital and so on in each realm. Everything contains everything else, as it were.

*

It is quite probable that the sloka [*Katha Upanishad 2.3.4*] refers to a going up into higher worlds of felicity and light and this can be called a liberation or release. In later times the idea grew strong that from all these higher worlds return is inevitable and it is only release from all cosmic existence that gives mukti. The Vedic Rishis seem to have looked to an ascent into a divine luminous world or state above the falsehood and ignorance. In the Upanishad the sun is the symbol of the supramental Truth and it is said that those who pass into it may return but those who pass through the gates of the Sun itself do not; possibly this means that an ascent into the supermind itself above the golden lid of overmind was the definitive liberation. The Veda speaks of the Truth hidden by a Truth where the Sun looses his horses from his car and there all the myriad rays are drawn together into One and that was considered the goal. The Isha Upanishad also speaks of the golden lid hiding the face of the Truth by removing which the Law of the Truth is seen and the highest

---

[1] *The correspondent asked for an explanation of certain terms in a passage (3.6.1) from the Brihadaranyaka Upanishad. — Ed.*

knowledge in which the One Purusha is known (*so'ham asmi*) is described as the *kalyāṇatama* form of the Sun. All this seems to refer to the supramental states of which the Sun is the symbol.

*

The mental realisation [*of the one self*] does not bring this result [*the ending of delusion* (moha) *and grief* (śoka)], the spiritual does.[2] In the Vedantic experience "seeing" means also becoming, one is that one self, identified, — all action of Nature seems to one a movement in that one self which is itself not touched by it. Therefore there is no *moha* or *śoka*. That is, when one can keep the experience and when it is complete. Even if one has the experience only as something within while the movements of the vital continue on the surface, yet these movements are felt as external and superficial, not really belonging to oneself — the self within remains untouched, calm, griefless, at peace. If the vital also is transformed into this consciousness, then even on the surface grief becomes impossible.

*

Perception is not enough to transform the nature. *Paśyataḥ*[3] in the spiritual language does not mean only perception. Perception is of the mind and a mental perception is not enough — a substantial and dynamic realisation in all the being is necessary. Otherwise one of three things may happen. (1) The mind perceives oneness but the vital is not affected, it goes on with its impulses, for the vital is governed not by thought or reason but by tendency, impulse, desire-force — it uses reason only as a justification for its tendencies. Or even the vital may say, "All is one so it does not matter what I do. Why should not I seek oneness with others in my own way?" (2) If the mind has a realisation, but the vital does not share in it or distorts it, then also the vital can insist on its own way or even carry the mind

---

[2] *The correspondent asked for a clarification of verse 7 of the Isha Upanishad, which ends, "... how shall he be deluded, whence shall he have grief who sees everywhere oneness?" — Ed.*

[3] *This term appears in verse 7 of the Isha Upanishad. — Ed.*

along with it. As the Gita says, the senses (vital) carry away the mind even of the sage who sees, as the wind carries away a ship on a stormy sea. (3) The inner being may have the realisation strongly and live in the oneness, calm, peace, but the interior parts of the outer may feel the reactions of desire etc. In this case the reactions are more superficial; but even so rejection is needed till they cease. When all the being lives in the solid realisation of calm, peace, liberation, oneness, then the desires fall away and the necessity of rejection ceases, because there is nothing to reject any longer.

*

It [*the identification of* buddhi *with the* vijñānamaya kośa] is the error that came with the excessive intellectualism of the philosophers and commentators. I don't think *buddhi* includes intuition as something separate in kind from intellect — the intellectualists considered intuition to be only a rapid process of intellectual thought — and they still think that. In the Taittiriya Upanishad the sense of *vijñāna* is very clear — its essence is *ṛtam*, the spiritual Truth; but afterwards the identification with *buddhi* became general.

*

I do not suppose they [*the commentators*] mean expressly intuition [*by buddhi*]; they regard *buddhi* as the means of knowledge, so they include all knowledge in it, and as the *vijñānamaya kośa* is the Knowledge sheath, they think it must mean *buddhi*. Obviously it doesn't. The description you have quoted[4] evidently means something much higher than *buddhi*. It is the *satyam ṛtam bṛhat* of the Upanishad — the truth-consciousness of the Veda.

The Vedantin

No, certainly I did not mean that the Vedantin who sees a greater working behind the appearances of the world is living

---

[4] *From the Taittiriya Upanishad 2.4.1.* — Ed.

in a different world from this material one — if I had meant that, all that I had written would be without point or sense. I meant a Vedantin who lives in this world with all its suffering and ignorance and ugliness and evil and has had a full measure of these things, betrayal and abandonment by friends, failure of outward objects and desires in life, attack and persecution, accumulated illnesses, constant difficulty, struggles, stumblings in his Yoga. It is not that he lives in a different world, but he has a different way of meeting its ordeals, blows and dangers. He takes them as the nature of this world and the result of the ego-consciousness in which it lives. He tries therefore to grow into another consciousness in which he feels what is behind the outward appearance, and as he grows into that larger consciousness he begins to feel more and more a working behind which is helping him to grow in the spirit and leading him toward mastery and freedom from ego and ignorance and he sees that all has been used for that purpose. Till he reaches this consciousness with its larger knowledge of things, he has to walk by faith and his faith may sometimes fail him, but it returns and carries him through all the difficulties. Everybody is not bound to accept this faith and this consciousness, but there is something great and true behind it for the spiritual life.

*

I doubt whether the condition of which you speak is that of the realised Vedantin[5] — except of course the loss of the sense of personality and the non-identification with desire and the movements of Prakriti. Still perhaps the condition of the *jaḍavat* Paramhansa (like Jada Bharata) may resemble it. The theory of *prārabdha karma* goes farther than that — it assumes that even if there are vital movements, that is also only the continuance of the machine of Prakriti and will drop off at death. They may, perhaps. I don't base the gospel of the transformation of Nature

---

[5] *The correspondent wrote that he felt dull, sleepy and mechanical, with no sense of desire or personality; therefore he could easily imagine why the realised Vedantin could say that with the static realisation of Brahman one's past karma would fall off at death.* — Ed.

on an impossibility of taking a static release as final — the static release is necessary, but I don't consider that to take it as final is the object of coming into world-existence. I hold that the static release is only a beginning, a first step in the Divine. If anyone is satisfied with the first step as all that is possible for him, I have no objection to his taking it like that.

Chapter Three
Jainism and Buddhism

Jainism

The Jain philosophy is concerned with individual perfection. Our effort is quite different. We want to bring down the Supermind as a new faculty. Just as the mind is now a permanent state of consciousness in humanity, so also we want to create a race in which the Supermind will be a permanent state of consciousness.

*

Why cannot one love or experience [*the Cosmic Divine or the Transcendent Divine*] concretely? many have done it. And why assume that He is immobile, silent and aloof? The Cosmic Divine can be as close to one as one's own self and the Transcendent as intimate as the closest friend or lover. It is only in the physical consciousness that there is some difficulty in realising it.

The Jain realisation of an individual godhead is all right so far as it goes — its defect is that it is too individual and isolated.

Buddhism

Buddhist teaching does not recognise any inner self or soul — there is only a stream of consciousness from moment to moment — the consciousness itself is only a bundle of associations — it is kept moving by the wheel of Karma. If the associations are untied and thrown away (they are called sanskaras), then it dissolves; the idea of self or a persistent person ceases; the stream flows no longer, the wheel stops. There is left, according to some, Sunya, a mysterious Nothing from which all comes; according to others a mysterious Permanent in which there is no individual existence. This is Nirvana. Buddha himself always refused to say what there was beyond cosmic existence; he spoke neither of God nor Self nor Brahman. He said there was no utility in discussing that — all that was necessary was to know the causes of this unhappy temporal existence and the way to dissolve it.

*

Buddha, it must be remembered, refused always to discuss what was beyond the world. But from the little he said it would appear that he was aware of a Permanent beyond equivalent to the Vedantic Para-Brahman, but which he was quite unwilling to describe. The denial of anything beyond the world except a negative state of Nirvana was a later teaching, not Buddha's.

*

If Buddha really combated and denied all Vedantic conceptions of the Self then it can be no longer true that Buddha refrained from all metaphysical speculations or distinct pronouncements as to the nature of the ultimate Reality. The view you take of his conception of Nirvana seems to concur with the Mahayanist interpretation and its conception of the Permanent, *dhruvam*, which could be objected to as a later development like the opposite Nihilistic conception of the Shunyam. What Buddha very certainly taught was that the world is not-Self and that the individual has no true existence since what does exist in the world is a stream of impermanent consciousness from moment to moment and the individual person is fictitiously constituted by a bundle of sanskaras and can be dissolved by dissolving the bundle. This is in conformity with the Vedantic Monistic view that there is no true individual. As to the other Vedantic view of the one Self, impersonal and universal and transcendent, it does not seem that Buddha made any distinct and unmistakable pronouncements on abstract metaphysical questions; but if the world or all in the world is not-Self, *anātman*, there can be no more room for a universal Self, only at most for a transcendent Real Being. His conception of Nirvana was of something transcendent of the universe, but he did not define what it was because he was not concerned with any abstract metaphysical speculations about the Reality; he must have thought them unnecessary and irrelevant and any indulgence in them likely to divert from the true object. His explanation of things was psychological and not metaphysical and his methods were all psychological, the breaking up of the false associations of consciousness which cause the continuance of desire and suffering, so getting rid of the stream of birth and death in a purely phenomenal (not an unreal) world; the method of life by which this liberation could be effected was also a psychological method, the eightfold path developing right understanding and right action. His object was pragmatic and severely practical and so were his methods; metaphysical speculations would only draw the mind away from the one thing needful.

As to Buddha's attitude towards life, I do not quite see how service to mankind or any ideal of improvement of the world-existence can have been part of his aim, since to pass out of life into a transcendence was his object. His eightfold path was the means towards that end and not an aim in itself or indeed in any way an aim. Obviously if right understanding and right action became the common rule of life, there would be a great improvement in the world, but for Buddha's purpose that could be an incidental result and not at all part of his central object. You say, "Buddha himself urged the necessity to serve mankind: his ideal was to achieve a consciousness of inner eternity and then be a source of radiant influence and action." But where and when did Buddha say these things, use these terms or express these ideas? "The service of mankind" sounds like a very modern and European conception; it reminds me of some European interpretations of the Gita as merely teaching the disinterested performance of duty or the pronouncement that the whole idea of the Gita is service. The exclusive stress or overstress on mankind or humanity is also European. Mahayanist Buddhism laid stress on compassion, fellow-feeling with all, *vasudhaiva kuṭumbakam*, just as the Gita speaks of the feeling of oneness with all beings and preoccupation with the good of all beings, *sarvabhūtahite ratāḥ*, but this does not mean humanity only but all beings and *vasudhā* means all earth-life. Are there any sayings of Buddha which would justify the statement that the object or one object of attaining to Nirvana was to become a source of radiant influence and action? The consciousness of inner eternity may have that result, but can we really say that that was Buddha's ideal, the object which he held in view or for which he came?

*

Buddhism is the turning away from *duḥkha* and its causes to the peace of Nirvana. The *duḥkhavāda* did not exist in India, except in the theory of the Vaishnava *viraha*; otherwise it was not considered as a means or even a stage in the sadhana. But that does not mean that *duḥkha* does not come in the sadhana — it comes and has to be rejected and overcome, overpassed — excepting the psychic sorrow which does not disturb or depress but rather liberates the vital. To make a *vāda* or gospel of sorrow is dangerous because sorrow if indulged becomes a habit, sticks and few things, if once they stick, can be more sticky.

Buddhist Nirvana

The Buddhist Nirvana and the Adwaitin's Moksha are the same thing. It corresponds to a realisation in which one does not feel oneself any longer as an individual with such a name or such a form, but an infinite eternal Self spaceless (even when in space), timeless (even when in time). Note that one can perfectly well do actions in that condition and it is not to be gained only by Samadhi.

*

It [*the Nirvana of Buddha*] is the same [*as the Nirvana of the Gita*]. Only the Gita describes it as Nirvana in the Brahman while Buddha preferred not to give any name or say anything about that into which the nirvana took place. Some later schools of Buddhists described it as Sunya, the equivalent of the Chinese Tao, described as the Nothing which is everything.

*

The feeling of the Self as a vast peaceful Void, a liberation from existence as we know it, is one that one can always have, Buddhist or no Buddhist. It is the negative aspect of Nirvana — it is quite natural for the mind, if it follows the negative movement of withdrawal, to get that first, and if you lay hold on that and refuse to go farther, being satisfied with this liberated Non-Existence, then you will naturally philosophise like the Buddhists that Sunya is the eternal truth. Lao Tse was more perspicacious when he spoke of it as the Nothing that is All. Many of course have the positive experience of the Atman first, not as a void but as pure unrelated Existence like the Adwaitins (Shankara) or as the one Existent.

*

They [*those who have had the experience of Nirvana*] do not feel as if they had any existence at all. In the Buddhistic Nirvana they feel as if there were no such thing at all, only an infinite zero without form. In the Adwaita Nirvana there is felt only one vast existence, no separate being is discernible anywhere. There are forms of course but they are only forms, not separate beings. Mind is silent, thought has ceased, — desires, passions, vital movements there are none. There is consciousness but only a formless elemental consciousness without limits. The body moves and acts, but the sense of body is not there. Sometimes there is only the consciousness of pure existence, sometimes only pure consciousness, sometimes all that exists is only a ceaseless limitless Ananda. Whether all else is really dissolved or only covered up is a debatable point, but at any rate it is an experience as if of their dissolution.

*

I don't think I have written, but I said once that souls which have passed into Nirvana may (not "must") return to complete the larger upward curve. I have written somewhere, I think, that for this Yoga (it might also be added, in the natural complete order of the manifestation) the experience of Nirvana can only be a stage or passage to the complete realisation. I have said also that there are many doors by which one can pass into the realisation of the Absolute (Parabrahman) and Nirvana is one of them, but by no means the only one. You may remember Ramakrishna's saying that the Jivakoti can ascend the stairs, but not return, while the Ishwarakoti can ascend and descend at will. If that is so, the Jivakoti might be those who describe only the curve from Matter through Mind into the silent Brahman and the Ishwarakoti those who get to the integral Reality and can therefore combine the Ascent with the Descent and contain the "two ends" of existence in their single being.

*

The realisation of this Yoga is not lower but higher than Nirvana or Nirvikalpa Samadhi.

*

In our Yoga the Nirvana is the beginning of the higher Truth, as it is the passage from the Ignorance to the higher Truth. The Ignorance has to be extinguished in order that the Truth may manifest.

Different Kinds of Buddhism

Buddhism is of many kinds and the entirely nihilistic kind is only one variety. Most Buddhism admits a Permanent as beyond the creation of Karma and Sanskaras. Even the Sunya of the Sunyapanthis is described like the Tao of Lao Tse as a Nothing which is All. So as a higher "above mental" state is admitted which one tries to reach by a strong discipline of the consciousness, it may be called spirituality.

*

There are elements in most Yogas which enter into this one, so it is not surprising if there is something in Buddhism also. But such notions as a Higher Evolution beyond Nirvana seem to me not genuinely Buddhistic, unless of course there is some offshoot of Buddhism which developed something so interpreted by the author. I never heard of it as part of Buddha's teachings

— he always spoke of Nirvana as the goal and refused to discuss metaphysically what it might be.

*

About the One [*of the Buddhists*] there are different versions. I just read somewhere that the Buddhist One is a Superbuddha from whom all Buddhas come — but it seemed to me a rehash of Buddhism in Vedantic terms born of a modern mind. The Permanent of Buddhism has always been supposed to be Supracosmic and Ineffable — that is why Buddha never tried to explain what it was; for, logically, how can one talk about the Ineffable? It has really nothing to do with the Cosmos which is a thing of sanskaras and Karma.

*

There is no reason why the passage about Buddhism [*in an essay of the correspondent*] should be omitted. It gives one side of the Buddhistic teaching which is not much known or is usually ignored, for that teaching is by most rendered as Nirvana (Sunyavada) and a spiritualised humanitarianism. The difficulty is that it is these sides that have been stressed especially in the modern interpretations of Buddhism and any strictures I may have passed were in view of these interpretations and that one-sided stress. I am aware of course of the opposite tendencies in the Mahayana and the Japanese cult of Amitabha Buddha which is a cult of bhakti. It is now being said even of Shankara that there was another side of his doctrine — but his followers have made him stand solely for the Great Illusion, the inferiority of bhakti, the uselessness of Karma — *jagan mithyā*.

Buddhism and Vedanta

The impressions in the approach to Infinity or the entry into it are not always quite the same; much depends on the way in which the mind approaches it. It is felt first by some as an infinity above, by others as an infinity around into which the mind disappears (as an energy) by losing its limits. Some feel not the absorption of the mind energy into the infinite, but a falling entirely inactive; others feel it as a lapse or disappearance of energy into pure Existence. Some first feel the infinity as a vast existence into which all sinks or disappears, others, as you describe it, as an infinite ocean of Light above, others as an infinite ocean of Power above. A certain school of Buddhists felt it in their experience as a limitless Sunya, the Vedantists on the contrary see it as a positive Self-Existence featureless and absolute. No doubt the various experiences were erected into various philosophies, each putting its conception as definitive; but behind each conception there was such an experience. What you describe as a completely emptied mind substance devoid of energy or light, completely inert, is the condition of neutral peace and empty stillness which is or can be a stage of the liberation. But it can afterwards feel itself filled with infinite existence, consciousness (carrying energy in it) and finally Ananda.

*

The universe is only a partial manifestation and Brahman as its foundation is the Sat. But there is also that which is not manifested and beyond manifestation and is not contained in the basis of manifestation. The Buddhists and others get from that the conception of Asat as the ultimate thing.

Another meaning given is: Sat = the Eternal, Asat = the Temporary and Unreal.

*

The ego and its continuity, they [*the Buddhists*] say, are an illusion, the result of the continuous flowing of energies and ideas in a determined current. There is no real formation of an ego. As to the liberation, it is in order to get free from *duḥkha* etc., — it is a painful flow of energies and to get free from the pain they must break up their continuity. That is all right, but how it started, why it should end at all and how anybody is benefited by the liberation, since there is nobody there, only a mass of idea and action — these things are insoluble mysteries. But is there not the same difficulty with the Mayavadin also, since there is no Jiva really, only Brahman and Brahman is by nature free and unbound for ever? So how did the whole absurd affair of Maya come into existence and who is liberated? That is what the old sages said at last: "There is none bound, none freed, none seeking to be free." It was all a mistake (a rather long-standing one though). The Buddhists, I suppose, could say that also.

Chapter Four
Sankhya and Yoga

Sankhya

In the spiritual thought of India during the time of the Rishis and even before, the Sankhya and Vedanta elements were always combined. The Sankhya account of the constitution of the being (Purusha, Prakriti, the elements, Indriyas, Buddhi etc.) was universally accepted and Kapila was mentioned with veneration everywhere. In the Gita he is mentioned among the great Vibhutis; Krishna says, "I am Kapila among the sages."

Patanjali's Yoga

Divine union [*was the aim of Yoga in Patanjali's day*], yes — but for the ascetic schools it was union with the featureless Brahman, the Unknowable beyond existence or, if with the Ishwara, still it was the Ishwara in a supracosmic consciousness. From that point of view Patanjali's aphorism[1] is sound enough. When he says Yoga, he means the process of Yoga, the object which has to be kept in view in the process — for by the cessation of *cittavṛtti* one gets into *samādhi* and *samādhi* is the only way of uniting solely and completely with the Brahman beyond existence.

*

Stopping the movements of the chitta [*is what is meant by* cittavṛttinirodha]. In our Yoga it is more necessary to transform these movements than to stop them altogether, but the power to stop them is necessary — it is usually done by the mind falling into silence and then imposing the same silence on the vital nature.

*

---

[1] Yogaścittavṛttinirodhaḥ (Yogasūtra *1.2*). — *Ed.*

Chit is the pure consciousness — as in Sat Chit Ananda.

Chitta is the stuff of mixed mental-vital-physical consciousness out of which arise the movements of thought, emotion, sensation, impulse etc. It is these that in Patanjali's system have to be stilled altogether so that the consciousness may be immobile and go into samadhi.

It [*stopping the movements of the chitta*] has a different function [*in this Yoga*]. The movements of the ordinary consciousness have to be quieted and into the quietude there has to be brought down a higher consciousness and its powers which will transform the nature.

*

If you suppress [*the* cittavṛttis], you will have no movements of the chitta at all; all will be immobile until you remove the suppression or will be so immobile that there cannot be anything else than immobility.

If you still, the chitta will be quiet; whatever movements there are will not disturb the quietude.

If you control or master, then the chitta will be immobile when you want, active when you want, and its action will be such that what you wish to get rid of will go, only what you accept as true and useful will come.

*

Some people do get disgusted with the body for its uncleanness, but I should say it is very few.

The suggestion of Patanjali[2] supposes that the mind is everything, so if I get the idea that the body is an unclean thing, all my feelings will harmonise with that idea. But it is not so — there are other parts which do not care for the idea or knowledge in the mind and are not affected by it but are led by their own instincts and desires. It is only those who have already the turn to vairagya who can make use of Patanjali's suggestion to help

---

[2] *The suggestion that disgust for one's body arises from the idea of cleanliness. In his letter the correspondent quoted Patanjali's aphorism,* Śaucāt svāṅga-jugupsā (Yogasūtra 2.40). — Ed.

their already existing vairagya. The medical man for instance holds his knowledge of the composition of the body as a matter of fact of science, he keeps it separate there in the scientific compartment of his mind and it does not in the least affect his other ideas, feelings or activities.

The Yoga-Vasishtha

I have not myself read the Yoga-Vasishtha, but from what I have read about it, it must be a book written by somebody with a remarkable occult knowledge.

Asanas and Pranayama

No use doing asanas and pranayam. It is not necessary to burn with passion. What is needed is a patient increasing of the power of concentration and steady aspiration so that the silence you speak of may fix in the heart and spread to the other members. Then the physical mind and subconscient can be cleared and quieted.

*

The asanas are one means for control of the body, as is Pranayam for the life-forces, but neither is indispensable.

*

Mother thinks that the shirshasan is not safe for your eyes. While some of these asanas are simple and safe, others are not so; they require a training of the body or practice under the eye of an expert. It might not be prudent for you to take them up in an amateur fashion.

*

Pranayam is safe only if one knows how to do it and is on guard against its possible dangers: (1) danger to health by mistakes in the method, (2) rising of the vital forces, especially lust, egoism and wrongly directed strength and force, (3) the awakening of concealed sanskaras of the physical nature or latent karma from past lives.

*

Tell him it is not safe to do Pranayam without guidance by one who is expert in Rajayoga or Hathayoga. Pranayam is not a part of the sadhana here.

*

You can write to him that it is not safe to do Pranayam except under the directions of a guru who is siddha in either Rajayoga or Hathayoga. Gasping is obviously a sign of something wrong — for the breathing in Pranayam must be perfectly unimpeded and regular. It is better either to stop the Pranayam or to find out somebody who is practised in the method and take instructions from him what to do.

*

Your experience is correct. The true breathing is not merely the inspiration and expiration from the lungs which is merely the mechanism of it, but a drawing in of the universal energy of Prana into every cell of the body.

Chapter Five
The Yoga of the Bhagavad Gita

The Teaching of the Gita

This world *is* as the Gita describes it, *anityam asukham*, so long as we live in the present world-consciousness; it is only by turning from that to the Divine and entering into the Divine Consciousness that one can possess, through the world also, the Eternal.

*

The Gita cannot be described as exclusively a gospel of love. What it sets forth is a Yoga of knowledge, devotion and works based on a spiritual consciousness and realisation of oneness with the Divine and of the oneness of all beings in the Divine. Bhakti, devotion and love of God carrying with it unity with all beings and love for all beings is given a high place but always in connection with knowledge and works.

Apparent Contradictions in the Gita

The language of the Gita in many matters seems sometimes contradictory because it admits two apparently opposite truths and tries to reconcile them. It admits the ideal of departure from sansara into the Brahman as one possibility; also it affirms the possibility of living free in the Divine (in Me, it says) and acting in the world as the Jivanmukta. It is this latter kind of salvation on which it lays the greatest emphasis. So Ramakrishna put the "divine souls" (Ishwarakoti) who can descend the ladder as well as ascend it higher than the ordinary Jivas (Jivakoti) who, once having ascended, have not the strength to descend again for divine work. The full truth lies in the supramental consciousness and the power to work from there on life and matter.

*

There is no real contradiction; the two passages[1] indicate in the Gita's system two different movements of its Yoga, the complete surrender being the crowning movement. One has first to conquer the lower nature, deliver the self involved in the lower movement by means of the higher Self which rises into the divine nature; at the same time one offers all one's actions including the inner action of the Yoga as a sacrifice to the Purushottama, the transcendent and immanent Divine. When one has risen into the higher Self, has the knowledge and is free, one makes the complete surrender to the Divine, abandoning all other dharmas, living only by the divine Consciousness, the divine Will and Force, the divine Ananda.

Our Yoga is not identical with the Yoga of the Gita although it contains all that is essential in the Gita's Yoga. In our Yoga we begin with the idea, the will, the aspiration of the complete surrender; but at the same time we have to reject the lower nature, deliver our consciousness from it, deliver the self involved in the lower nature by the self rising to freedom in the higher nature. If we do not do this double movement, we are in danger of making a tamasic and therefore unreal surrender, making no effort, no tapas and therefore no progress; or else we may make a rajasic surrender not to the Divine but to some self-made false idea or image of the Divine which masks our rajasic ego or something still worse.

*

It was not your account of the inconsistencies of the Gita, but those that have been urged against the combining of sadhanas of which the Gita is the finest example that I was speaking of. Your objection to Krishna's pouring contradictory sadhanas on Arjuna was, I said, akin to these and not more sustainable.

All the other side questions I consider irrelevant and of no importance. The setting of the Gita is poetic and legendary and I consider it an admirable setting, but if you consider it a bad

---

[1] *The correspondent asked how to reconcile two passages in the Gita: "Deliver the self by means of the Self" and "Abandon all dharmas, take refuge in Me alone" (Gita 6.5 and 18.66). — Ed.*

one, that does not matter. It makes no difference, even if you are right, to the spiritual excellence of the Gita. I care nothing whether Sanjaya and Krishna and Arjuna of the Mahabharat were myths or real persons. The only thing that is important is that the sadhana of the Gita is a real thing and can be lived and that if spiritually lived, its so-called inconsistencies are no inconsistencies but many well-related aspects of a single Divine Truth — the vision seen by Arjuna included. The rest is a matter of opinion and, as I say, of no spiritual importance.

*

The Gita was *not* meant by the writer to be an allegory — you can say, if you like, that now we should dismiss the ancient war element by interpreting it as if it were an allegory. The Gita is Yoga, spiritual truth applied to external life and action — but it may be *any* action and not necessarily an action *resembling* that of the Gita. The *principle* of the spiritual consciousness applied to action has to be kept; the particular example used by the Gita may be treated as a thing belonging to a past world.

The Gita, the Divine Mother and the Purushottama

The Gita does not speak expressly of the Divine Mother; it speaks always of surrender to the Purushottama — it mentions her only as the Para Prakriti who becomes the Jiva, i.e., who manifests the Divine in the multiplicity and through whom all these worlds are created by the Supreme and he himself descends as the Avatar. The Gita follows the Vedantic tradition which leans entirely on the Ishwara aspect of the Divine and speaks little of the Divine Mother because its object is to draw back from world-nature and arrive at the supreme realisation beyond it; the Tantrik tradition leans on the Shakti or Ishwari aspect and makes all depend on the Divine Mother, because its object is to possess and dominate the world-nature and arrive at the supreme realisation through it. This Yoga insists on both the aspects; the surrender to the Divine Mother is essential, for without it there is no fulfilment of the object of the Yoga.

In regard to the Purushottama the Divine Mother is the supreme divine Consciousness and Power above the worlds, Adya Shakti; she carries the Supreme in herself and manifests the Divine in the worlds through the Akshara and the Kshara. In regard to the Akshara she is the same Para Shakti holding the Purusha immobile in herself and also herself immobile in him at the back of all creation. In regard to the Kshara she is the mobile cosmic Energy manifesting all beings and forces.

*

I do not know that there is anything like a Purushottama consciousness which the human being can attain or realise *for himself*, — for, in the Gita, the Purushottama is the Supreme Lord, the Supreme Being who is beyond the Immutable and the Mutable and contains both the One and the Many. Man, says the Gita, can attain the Brahmic consciousness, realise himself as an eternal portion of the Purushottama and live in the Purushottama. The Purushottama consciousness is the consciousness of the Supreme Being and man by loss of ego and realisation of his true essence can *live in* it.

The Gita and the Integral Yoga

It is not a fact that the Gita gives the whole base of Sri Aurobindo's message; for the Gita seems to admit the cessation of birth in the world as the ultimate aim or at least the ultimate culmination of Yoga; it does not bring forward the idea of spiritual evolution or the idea of the higher planes and the supramental Truth-Consciousness and the bringing down of that consciousness as the means of the complete transformation of earthly life.

The idea of the supermind, the Truth-Consciousness is there in the Rig Veda according to Sri Aurobindo's interpretation and in one or two passages of the Upanishads, but in the Upanishads it is there only in seed in the conception of the being of knowledge, *vijñānamaya puruṣa*, exceeding the mental, vital and physical being; in the Rig Veda the idea is there but in principle only, it is not developed and even the principle of it has disappeared from the Hindu tradition.

It is these things among others that constitute the novelty of Sri Aurobindo's message as compared with the Hindu tradition, — the idea that the world is not either a creation of Maya or only a play, *līlā*, of the Divine, or a cycle of births in the ignorance from which we have to escape, but a field of manifestation in which there is a progressive evolution of the soul and the nature in Matter and from Matter through Life and Mind to what is beyond Mind till it reaches the complete revelation of Sachchidananda in life. It is this that is the basis of the Yoga and gives a new sense to life.

*

To the question in your last letter there can be no reply except that it is only either a single-minded faith or a fixed will that can give you the open road to the Yoga. It is because your ideas and your will are in a constant state of flux or of oscillation that you do not succeed. Even with a deficient faith, a fixed mind and will can carry one on and bring the experiences by which an uncertain faith is changed into certitude.

It is the reason why it is difficult for me to answer your questions about the different alternatives. I may say that the way of the Gita is itself a part of the Yoga here and those who have followed it, to begin with or as a first stage, have a stronger basis than others for this Yoga. To look down on it therefore as something separate and inferior is not a right standpoint. But whatever it is, you must yourself choose, nobody can do it for you. Those who go and come, can do so profitably only if or because they have made the decision and keep to it; when they are here, it is for the Yoga that they come, when they are elsewhere, the will for the Yoga remains with them there. You have to get rid of your constant reasonings and see whether you can do without the impulse towards Yoga or not — if you cannot, then it is useless thinking of the ordinary life without Yoga — your nature will compel you to seek after it even if you have to seek all your life with a small result. But the small result is mainly due to the mind which always came in the way and the vital weakness which gives it its support for its reasonings. If you fixed your will irrevocably, that would give you a chance — and whether you followed it here or elsewhere would make only a minor difference.

    I suggested the Gita method for you because the opening which is necessary for the Yoga here seems to be too difficult for you. If you made a less strenuous demand upon yourself, there might be a greater chance. In any case, if you cannot return to the ordinary life, it seems, in the absence of an opening to the Power that is here, the only course for you.

Chapter Six

The Adwaita of Shankaracharya

Shankara's Mayavada

If Shankara's conception of the undifferentiated pure Consciousness as the Brahman is your view of it, then it is not the path of this Yoga that you should choose; for here the realisation of pure Consciousness and Being is only a first step and not the goal. But an inner creative urge from within can have no place in an undifferentiated Consciousness — all action and creation must necessarily be foreign to it.

I do not base my Yoga on the insufficient ground that the Self (not soul) is eternally free. That affirmation leads to nothing beyond itself, or, if used as a starting-point, it could equally well lead to the conclusion that action and creation have no significance or value. The question is not that but of the meaning of creation, whether there is a Supreme who is not merely a pure undifferentiated Consciousness and Being, but the source and support also of the dynamic energy of creation and whether the cosmic existence has for It a significance and a value. That is a question which cannot be settled by metaphysical logic which deals in words and ideas, but by a spiritual experience which goes beyond Mind and enters into spiritual realities. Each mind is satisfied with its own reasoning, but for spiritual purposes that satisfaction has no validity, except as an indication of how far and on what line each one is prepared to go in the field of spiritual experience. If your reasoning leads you towards the Shankara idea of the Supreme, that might be an indication that the Vedanta Adwaita (Mayavada) is your way of advance.

This Yoga accepts the value of cosmic existence and holds it to be a reality; its object is to enter into a higher Truth-Consciousness or Divine Supramental Consciousness in which action and creation are the expression not of ignorance and imperfection, but of the Truth, the Light, the Divine Ananda.

But for that, surrender of the mortal mind, life and body to that Higher Consciousness is indispensable, since it is too difficult for the mortal human being to pass by its own effort beyond mind to a supramental consciousness in which the dynamism is no longer mental but of quite another power. Only those who can accept the call to such a change should enter into this Yoga.

*

The Shankara knowledge is, as your Guru pointed out, only one side of the Truth; it is the knowledge of the Supreme as realised by the spiritual Mind through the static silence of the pure Existence. It was because he went by this side only that Shankara was unable to accept or explain the origin of the universe except as illusion, a creation of Maya. Unless one realises the Supreme on the dynamic as well as the static side, one cannot experience the true origin of things and the equal reality of the active Brahman. The Shakti or Power of the Eternal becomes then a power of illusion only and the world becomes incomprehensible, a mystery of cosmic madness, an eternal delirium of the Eternal. Whatever verbal or ideative logic one may bring to support it, this way of seeing the universe explains nothing; it only erects a mental formula of the inexplicable. It is only if you approach the Supreme through his double aspect of Sat and Chit-Shakti, double but inseparable, that the total truth of things can become manifest to the inner experience. The other side was developed by the Shakta Tantrics. The two together, the Vedantic and the Tantric truth unified, can arrive at the integral knowledge.

But philosophically this is what your Guru's teaching comes to and it is obviously a completer truth and a wider knowledge than that given by the Shankara formula. It is already indicated in the Gita's teaching of the Purushottama and the Parashakti (Adya Shakti) who becomes the Jiva and upholds the universe. It is evident that Purushottama and Parashakti are both eternal and are inseparable and one in being; the Parashakti manifests the universe, manifests too the Divine in the universe as the Ishwara and herself appears at his side as the Ishwari Shakti. Or, one may say, it is the Supreme Consciousness-Power of the

Supreme that manifests or puts forth itself as Ishwara Ishwari, Atma Atmashakti, Purusha Prakriti, Jiva Jagat. That is the truth in its completeness as far as the mind can formulate it. In the Supermind these questions do not even arise — for it is the mind that creates the problem by erecting oppositions between aspects of the Divine which are not really opposed to each other but are one and inseparable.

This supramental knowledge has not yet been attained, because the supermind itself has not been attained, but the reflection of it in intuitive spiritual consciousness is there and that was what was evidently realised in experience by your Guru and what he was expressing in mental terms in the quoted passage. It is possible to go towards this knowledge by beginning with the experience of dissolution in the One, but on condition that you do not stop there, taking it as the highest Truth, but proceed to realise the same One as the supreme Mother, the Consciousness Force of the Eternal. If on the other hand you approach through the supreme Mother, she will give you the liberation in the silent One also as well as the realisation of the dynamic One and from that it is easier to arrive at the Truth in which both are one and inseparable. At the same time the gulf created by Mind between the Supreme and his Manifestation is bridged and there is no longer a fissure in the truth which makes all incomprehensible. If in the light of this you examine what your Guru taught, you will see that it is the same thing in less metaphysical language.

*

They [*two philosophers*] want to show that Shankara was not so savagely illusionist as he is represented — that he gave a certain temporary reality to the world, admitted Shakti etc. But these (supposing he made them) are concessions inconsistent with the logic of his own philosophy which is that only the Brahman exists and the rest is ignorance and illusion. The rest has only a temporary and therefore an illusory reality in Maya. He farther maintained that Brahman could not be reached by works. If that was not his philosophy, I should like to know what was his philosophy. At any rate that was how his philosophy has been understood by people. Now that the general turn is away from the rigorous Illusionism, many of the Adwaitins seem to want to hedge and make Shankara hedge with them.

Vivekananda accepted Shankara's philosophy with modifications, the chief of them being Daridra-Narayan-seva which is a mixture of Buddhist compassion and modern philanthropy.

*

I believe according to the Adwaitins God is only the reflection of Brahman in Maya — just as Brahman is seen outwardly as the world which has only a practical not a real reality, so subjectively Brahman is seen as God, Bhagavan, Ishwara, and that also would be a practical not a real reality — which is and can be only the relationless Brahman all by itself in a worldless eternity. At least that is what I have read — I don't know whether Shankara himself says that. One is always being told by modern Adwaitins that Shankara did not mean what people say he meant — so one has to be careful in attributing any opinion to him.

*

Of course Shankara must have meant Mayavada. It is hardly possible that everybody should have misunderstood his ideas (which were not in the least veiled or enigmatic) till his modern apologists discovered what they really were.

*

Shankara surely stands or falls by the Mayavada. Even the *Bhaja Govindam* poem is Mayavadic in spirit. I am not well-acquainted with these other writings[1] — so it is difficult for me to say anything about that side of the question.

*

Chittashuddhi belongs to Rajayoga. In the pure Adwaita the method is rather to detach oneself by vichara and viveka and

---

[1] *Writings attributed to Shankara such as* Prabodhasudhākara. *The correspondent asked whether Shankara changed his view from Mayavada to Lilavada later in his life.* — Ed.

realise "I am not the mind, not the life, etc. etc." In that case, no shuddhi would be necessary — the self would separate from the nature good or bad and regard it as a machinery which having no more the support of the egoless man would fall away of itself along with the body. Of course chittashuddhi can be resorted to also, but for cessation of the chittavrittis, not for their better dynamism as an instrument of the Divine. Shankara insists that all karma must fall off before one can be liberated — the soul must realise itself as *akartā*, there is no salvation in or by works in the pure Yoga of knowledge. So how could Shankara recognise dynamism? Even if he recognises chittashuddhi as necessary, it must be as a preparation for getting rid of karma, not for anything else.

Mayavada and Nirvana

About Nirvana:

When I wrote in the *Arya*, I was setting forth an overmind view of things to the mind and putting it in mental terms, that was why I had sometimes to use logic. For in such a work — mediating between the intellect and the supra-intellectual — logic has a place, though it cannot have the chief place it occupies in purely mental philosophies. The Mayavadin himself labours to establish his point of view or his experience by a rigorous logical reasoning. Only, when it comes to an explanation of Maya he, like the scientist dealing with Nature, can do no more than arrange and organise his ideas of the process of this universal mystification; he cannot explain how or why his illusionary mystifying Maya came into existence. He can only say, "Well, but it is there."

Of course, it is there. But the question is, first, "What is it? is it really an illusionary Power and nothing else, or is the Mayavadin's idea of it a mistaken first view, a mental imperfect reading, even perhaps itself an illusion?" And next, "Is illusion the sole or the highest Power which the Divine Consciousness or Superconsciousness possesses?" The Absolute is an absolute Truth free from Maya, otherwise liberation would not be possible. Has then the supreme and absolute Truth no other active Power than a power of falsehood and with it, no doubt, for the two go together, a power of dissolving or disowning the falsehood, — which is yet there for ever? I suggested that this sounded a little queer. But queer or not, if it is so, it is so — for as you point out, the Ineffable cannot be subjected to the laws of logic.

But who is to decide whether it is so? You will say, those who get there. But get where? To the Perfect and the Highest, *pūrṇam param*. Is the Mayavadin's featureless Brahman that Perfect, that Complete — is it the very Highest? Is there not or can there not be a higher than that highest, *parātparam*? That is not a question of logic, it is a question of spiritual fact, of a supreme and complete experience. The solution of the matter must rest not upon logic, but upon a growing, ever heightening, widening spiritual experience — an experience which must of course include or have passed through that of Nirvana and Maya, otherwise it would not be complete and would have no decisive value.

Now to reach Nirvana was the first radical result of my own Yoga. It threw me suddenly into a condition above and without thought, unstained by any mental or vital movement; there was no ego, no real world — only when one looked through the immobile senses, something perceived or bore upon its sheer silence a world of empty forms, materialised shadows without true substance. There was no One or many even, only just absolutely That, featureless, relationless, sheer, indescribable, unthinkable, absolute, yet supremely real and solely real. This was no mental realisation nor something glimpsed somewhere above, — no abstraction — it was positive, the only positive reality — although not a spatial physical world, pervading, occupying or rather flooding and drowning this semblance of a physical world, leaving no room or space for any reality but itself, allowing nothing else to seem at all actual, positive or substantial. I cannot say there was anything exhilarating or rapturous in the experience, as it then came to me, — the ineffable Ananda I had years afterwards, — but what it brought was an inexpressible Peace, a stupendous silence, an infinity of release and freedom. I lived in that Nirvana day and night before it began to admit other things into itself or modify itself at all, and the inner heart of experience, a constant memory of it and its power to return remained until in the end it began to disappear into a greater Superconsciousness from above. But meanwhile realisation added itself to realisation and fused itself with this original experience. At an early stage the aspect of an illusionary world gave place to one in which illusion[2] is only a small surface phenomenon with an immense Divine Reality behind it and a supreme Divine Reality above it and an intense Divine Reality in the heart of everything that had seemed at first only a cinematic shape or shadow. And this was no reimprisonment in the senses, no diminution or fall from supreme experience, it came rather as a constant heightening and widening of the Truth; it was the spirit that saw objects, not the senses, and the Peace, the Silence, the freedom in Infinity remained always with the world or all worlds only as a continuous incident in the timeless eternity of the Divine.

Now that is the whole trouble in my approach to Mayavada. Nirvana in my liberated consciousness turned out to be the beginning of my realisation, a first step towards the complete thing, not the sole true attainment possible or even a culminating finale. It came unasked, unsought for, though quite welcome. I had no least idea about it before, no aspiration towards it, in fact my aspiration was towards just the opposite, spiritual power to help the world and do my work in it, yet it came — without even a "May I come in" or a "By your leave". It just happened and settled in as if for all eternity or as if it had been really there always. And then it slowly grew into something not less but greater than its first self! How then could I accept Mayavada or persuade myself to pit against the Truth imposed on me from above the logic of Shankara?

But I do not insist on everybody passing through my experience or following the Truth that is its consequence. I have

---

[2] In fact it is not an illusion in the sense of an imposition of something baseless and unreal on the consciousness, but a misinterpretation by the conscious mind and sense and a falsifying misuse of manifested existence.

no objection to anybody accepting Mayavada as his soul's truth or his mind's truth or their way out of the cosmic difficulty. I object to it only if somebody tries to push it down my throat or the world's throat as the sole possible, satisfying and all-comprehensive explanation of things. For it is not that at all. There are many other possible explanations; it is not at all satisfactory, for in the end it explains nothing; and it is — and must be unless it departs from its own logic — all-exclusive, not in the least all-comprehensive. But that does not matter. A theory may be wrong or at least one-sided and imperfect and yet extremely practical and useful. That has been amply shown by the history of science. In fact a theory whether philosophical or scientific is nothing else than a support for the mind, a practical device to help it to deal with its object, a staff to uphold it and make it walk more confidently and get along on its difficult journey. The very exclusiveness and one-sidedness of the Mayavada make it a strong staff or a forceful stimulus for a spiritual endeavour which means to be one-sided, radical and exclusive. It supports the effort of the Mind to get away from itself and from Life by a short cut into superconscience. Or rather it is the Purusha in Mind that wants to get away from the limitations of Mind and Life into the superconscient Infinite. Theoretically, the most radical way for that is for the mind to deny all its perceptions and all the preoccupations of the vital and see and treat them as illusions. Practically, when the mind draws back from itself, it enters easily into a relationless peace in which nothing matters — for in its absoluteness there are no mental or vital values — and from which the mind can rapidly move towards that great short cut to the Superconscient, mindless trance, *suṣupti*. In proportion to the thoroughness of that movement all the perceptions it had once accepted become unreal to it — illusion, Maya. It is on its road towards immergence.

Mayavada, therefore, with its sole stress on Nirvana, quite apart from its defects as a mental theory of things, serves a great spiritual end and, as a path, can lead very high and far. Even, if the Mind were the last word and there were nothing beyond it except the pure Spirit, I would not be averse to accepting it as the only way out. For what the mind with its perceptions and the vital with its desires have made of life in this world, is a very bad mess, and if there were nothing better to be hoped for, the shortest cut to an exit would be the best. But my experience is that there is something beyond Mind; Mind is not the last word here of the Spirit. Mind is an ignorance-consciousness and its perceptions cannot be anything else than either false, mixed or imperfect — even when "true", a partial reflection of the Truth and not the very body of Truth herself. But there is a Truth-Consciousness, not static only and self-introspective, but also dynamic and creative, and I prefer to get at that and see what it says about things and can do rather than take the short cut away from things offered as its own end by the Ignorance.

Still, I would have no objection, if your attraction towards Nirvana were not merely a mood of the mind and vital but an indication of the mind's true road and the soul's issue. But it seems to me that it is only the vital recoiling from its own disappointed desires in an extreme dissatisfaction, not the soul leaping gladly to its true path. This vairagya is itself a vital movement; vital vairagya is the reverse side of vital desire — though the mind of course is there to give reasons and say ditto. Even this vairagya, if it is one-pointed and exclusive, can lead or can point towards Nirvana. But you have many sides to your personality or rather many personalities in you; it is indeed their discordant movements each getting in the way of the other, as happens when they are expressed through the external mind, that have stood much in the way of your sadhana. There is the vital personality which was turned towards success and enjoyment and got it and wanted to go on with it but could not get the rest of the being to follow. There is the vital personality that wanted enjoyment of a deeper kind and suggested to the other that it could very well give up these unsatisfactory things if it got an equivalent in some faeryland of a higher joy. There is the psycho-vital personality that is the Vaishnava within you and wanted the Divine Krishna and bhakti and Ananda. There is the personality which is the poet and musician and a seeker of beauty through these things. There is the mental-vital personality which when it saw the vital standing in the way insisted on a grim struggle of Tapasya, and it is no doubt that also which approves vairagya and Nirvana. There is the physical-mental personality which is the Russellite, extrovert, doubter. There is another mental-emotional personality all whose ideas are for belief in the Divine, Yoga, bhakti, Guruvada. There is the psychic being also which has pushed you into the sadhana and is waiting for its hour of emergence.

What are you going to do with all these people? If you want Nirvana, you have either to expel them or stifle them or beat them into coma. All authorities assure us that this exclusive Nirvana business is a most difficult job (*duḥkhaṁ dehavadbhiḥ* says the Gita), and your own fatal attempt at suppressing the others was not encouraging, — according to your own account it left you as dry and desperate as a sucked orange, no juice left anywhere. If the desert is your way to the promised land, that does not matter. But —

Well, if it is not, then there is another way — it is what we call the integration, the harmonisation of the being. That cannot be done from outside, it cannot be done by the mind and vital being — they are sure to bungle their affair. It can be done only from within by the soul, the Spirit which is the centraliser, itself the centre of these radii. In all of them there is a truth that can harmonise with the true truth of the others. For there is a truth in Nirvana — Nirvana is nothing but the peace and freedom of the Spirit which can exist in itself, be there world or no world, world-order or world-disorder. Bhakti and the heart's call for the Divine have a truth — it is the truth of the divine Love and Ananda. The will for Tapasya has in it a truth — it is the truth of the Spirit's mastery over its members. The musician and poet stand for a truth, it is the truth of the expression of the Spirit through beauty. There is a truth behind the mental Affirmer; even there is a truth behind the mental doubter, the Russellian, though far behind him — the truth of the denial of false forms. Even behind the two vital personalities there is a truth, the truth of the possession of the inner and outer worlds — not by the ego but by the Divine. That is the harmonisation for which our Yoga stands — but it cannot be achieved by any outward arrangement, it can only be achieved by going inside and looking, willing and acting from the psychic and from the spiritual centre. For the truth of the being is there and the secret of Harmony also is there.

The Illusionist Metaphors

The illusionist metaphors all fail when you drive them home — they are themselves an illusion. Identification with the body is an error, not an illusion. We are not the body, but the body is still something of ourselves. With realisation the erroneous identification ceases — in certain experiences the existence of the body is not felt at all. In the full realisation the body is within us, not we in it, it is an instrumental formation in our wider being — our consciousness exceeds but also pervades it; it can be dissolved without our ceasing to be the self. That is about all.

*

Your objection is correct. The snake-rope image cannot be used to illustrate the non-existence of the world, it would only mean that our seeing of the world is not that of the world as it really is. The idea of complete illusion would better be illustrated by the juggler's rope-climbing trick, where there is no rope and no climber, and yet one is persuaded that they are there.

Laya

According to both Buddha and Shankara liberation means *laya* of the individual in some transcendent Permanence that is not individualised — so logically a belief in the individual soul must prevent liberation while the sense of misery in the world leads to the attempt to escape.

*

The impulse towards laya is a creation of the mind, it is not the sole possible destiny of the soul. When the mind tries to abolish its own Ignorance, it finds no escape from it except laya, because it supposes that there is no higher principle of cosmic existence beyond itself — beyond itself is only the pure Spirit, the absolute impersonal Divine. Those who go through the heart (love, bhakti) do not accept laya, they believe in a state beyond of eternal companionship with the Divine or dwelling in the Divine without laya. All this quite apart from supramentalisation. What then becomes of your starting point that laya is the inevitable destiny of the soul and it is only the personal descent of the Avatar that saves it from inevitable laya?

*

There were two points of error [*in the correspondent's remarks about laya*]. (1) That the soul formerly had no other possibility once it reached the Divine than laya. There were other possibilities, e.g. passing into a higher plane, living in the Divine or in the presence of the Divine. Both imply the refusal of birth and leaving the Lila on earth. (2) That it was only for the sake of living with the incarnate Divine and by reason of this descent that the soul consented to give up laya. The capital point is the supramentalisation of the being which is the Divine intention in the evolution on earth and cannot fail to come; the descent or incarnation is only an instrumentation for bringing that about. Your statement therefore became wrong by incompleteness.

*

It is the Vedantic Adwaita experience of laya. It is only one phase of experience — not the whole or the highest Truth of the Divine.

Chapter Seven
Tantra

Tantra and the Integral Yoga

Veda and Vedanta are one side of the one Truth; Tantra with its emphasis on Shakti is another. In this Yoga all sides of the Truth are taken up, not in the systematic forms given them formerly, but in their essence and carried to the fullest and highest significance. But Vedanta deals more with the principles and essentials of the divine knowledge and therefore much of its spiritual knowledge and experience has been taken bodily into the *Arya*. Tantra deals more with forms and processes and organised powers — all these could not be taken as they were, for the integral Yoga needs to develop its own forms and processes, but the ascent of the consciousness through the centres and other Tantrik knowledge are there behind the process of transformation to which so much importance is given by me — also the truth that nothing can be done except through the force of the Mother.

*

The ascension and descent of the Force in this Yoga accomplishes itself in its own way without any necessary reproduction of the details laid down in the books [*on Tantra*]. Many become conscious of the centres, but others simply feel the ascent or descent in a general way or from level to level rather than from centre to centre, that is to say, the Force descending first to the head, then to the heart, then to the navel and still below. It is not at all necessary to become aware of the deities in the centres according to the Tantrik description, but some feel the Mother in the different centres. In these things our sadhana does not cleave to the knowledge given in the books, but only keeps to the central truth behind and realises it independently without any subjection to the old forms and symbols. The centres themselves have a different interpretation here from that given in the books of the Tantriks.

Kundalini, the Chakras and the Integral Yoga

The process of the Kundalini awakened rising through the centres as also the purification of the centres is a Tantrik knowledge. In our Yoga there is no willed process of the purification and opening of the centres, no raising up of the Kundalini by a set process either. Another method is used, but still there is the ascent of the consciousness from and through the different levels to join the higher consciousness above; there is the opening of the centres and of the planes (mental, vital, physical) which these centres command; there is also the descent which is the main key of the spiritual transformation. Therefore there is, I have said, a Tantrik knowledge behind the process of transformation in this Yoga.

*

There is [*in the Integral Yoga*] no willed opening of the chakras, they open of themselves by the descent of the Force. In the Tantrik discipline they open from down upwards, the Muladhara first — in our Yoga, they open from up downward. But the ascent of the force from the Muladhara does take place.

*

The ascent of the Kundalini — not its descent, so far as I know — is a recognised phenomenon; there is one that corresponds in our Yoga, the feeling of the consciousness ascending from the vital or physical to meet the higher consciousness. This is not necessarily through the chakras but is often felt in the whole body. Similarly the descent of the higher consciousness is not felt necessarily or usually through the chakras but as occupying the whole head, neck, chest, abdomen, body.

*

In the Tantra the centres are opened and Kundalini is awakened by a special process, its action of ascent is felt through the spine. Here it is the pressure of the Force from above that awakens it and opens the centres. There is an ascension of the consciousness going up till it joins the higher consciousness above. This repeats itself (sometimes a descent also is felt) until all the centres are open and the consciousness rises above the body. At a later stage it remains above and widens out into the cosmic consciousness and the universal Self. This is a usual course, but sometimes the process is more rapid and there is a sudden and definite opening above.

*

It [*a force in the navel region rising upward in a coiling, pulsating movement*] is what is meant by the Kundalini rising towards the Brahmarandhra — not the whole of it, but something of it is released coiling or circling upward with vibrations (*spandana*) from the Muladhara. It is not always felt like that. Sometimes one simply feels currents or a Force of some kind rising up or just an ascending movement of consciousness. But in all cases it is the release of the Yogic consciousness which is shut up in the chakras and its ascent to meet the Divine Consciousness above. It is this and the corresponding descent from above that make Yogic experiences and realisations possible.

*

It [*the Kundalini*] is the Yogic force asleep in the Muladhara and covered up in the other centres by the ordinary consciousness. When it is liberated, it rises up to join the Brahmic (Divine) consciousness above passing through the centres on its way.

*

There is no Kundalini Shakti above the head. Above the head is the universal or Divine Consciousness and Force. The Kundalini is the latent power asleep in the chakras.

*

The Energy in the Kundalini is the Mother's.

*

I am afraid the attempt to apply scientific analogies to spiritual or Yogic things leads more often to confusion than to anything else, — just as it creates confusion if thrust upon philosophy also. Kundalini coiled in the Muladhara is asleep, plunged in the inconscience, supporting the play of the Ignorance. Naturally if she heaves up from there, there may be a disturbance or disruption of the states of the Ignorance, but that would be rather a salutary upheaval and helpful to the purpose of Yoga. Kundalini becoming conscious rises up to meet the Brahman in the thousand-petalled lotus. A mere ejection from her uniting with the higher consciousness would hardly lead to a radical change. Of course she need not abandon connection with the physical centre altogether; but she is no longer coiled there: if she were, the great occult force residing there would not be liberated. The usual image of her risen and awake is, I believe, that of a serpent standing erect, the tail touching the lowest centre, the head the highest at the Brahmarandhra. Thus with all the centres open and active she unites the two poles, superior and inferior, of the being, the spirit with Matter.

*

Sri Aurobindo[1] cannot undertake to guide you as your Guru, for the reason that he takes as disciples only those who follow his special path of Yoga; your experiences follow a different line. In his Yoga there may be an occasional current in the spine as in other nerve channels or different parts of the body, but no awakening of the Kundalini in this particular and powerful fashion. There is only a quiet uprising of the consciousness from the lower centres to join the spiritual consciousness above and a descent of the Divine Force from above which does its own work in the mind and body — the manner and stages varying in each sadhak. A perfect confidence in the Divine Mother and a vigilance to repel all wrong suggestions and influences is the main law of this Yoga. Your opening having once been so powerful on

---

[1] *This letter was written by Sri Aurobindo in the third person and sent to the enquirer through his secretary. — Ed.*

the more usual Tantric lines (even without your own will intervening), it is hardly probable that it could now change easily to other lines — any such effort might create a serious disturbance. In speaking of a competent Guru Sri Aurobindo meant one who had himself practised this opening of the centres and become siddha in that line of Yoga. It should not be impossible to find one — when one has the call for the Guru, the Guru sooner or later comes. Meanwhile to put away fear and have confidence in the Divine working is indispensable — but no effort should be made to force the pace by concentrated meditation unless you have a guide whom you can trust — a clear guidance from within or a guide from without. The inspiration about the Ida nadi and the subsequent waking of the Shakti show that there was an intervention at a critical moment and that the call to it whenever needed is likely to be effective.

In the experiences proper related in your first letter there is absolutely nothing that should have disturbed you — all was quite normal, the usual experiences of the Yogin at such a juncture and very good and powerful, such as do not come except by the grace of the Divine. Probably the opening came after slow invisible preparation as a result of the meditation on the lotus at the top of the head; for that is always an invitation to the Kundalini to awake or for the lower consciousness to rise and meet the higher. The disturbing factor came with the feeling of discomfort in the heart due to some resistance in the physical being which is very often felt and can be overcome by the working of the Force itself and the fear that came afterwards in the seats of the vital Nature, heart, navel etc. But that was no part of the experience, it was an interference by a wrong reaction from the lower or exterior consciousness. If you had not allowed yourself to be disturbed, probably nothing untoward would have disturbed the process. One must not get frightened by unusual states or movements or experiences, the Yogi must be fearless, *abhīḥ*; it is absurd to have a fear because one can control one's states; that is a power very much to be desired and welcomed in Yoga.

The crisis related in the second letter would hardly have

come, if there had not been this reaction; but in any case there was the intervention and setting right of the trouble. However these reactions and the fact that the disturbance came show that something in the exterior consciousness is not altogether prepared; it is better to wait and seek for a guide so that ignorant steps or reactions may not bring again a serious trouble or danger. This is all that Sri Aurobindo can say by way of enlightenment and advice. He does not usually intervene with anyone not his disciple, but as your case was an unusual one and your call urgent, he has given you what light he can on your experience.

Levels of Speech (Vak)

The Tantriks locate these forms of speech in different chakras. Speech may be internal or external, either may have the stamp of the same power. But if it is to be measured by withdrawal from externality, then Para ought to mean something of the causal realm beyond mind.

*

Pashyanti is evidently speech with the vision of Truth in it — Para is probably the revelatory and inspired speech. I am not certain about the exact nature of the others [*Vaikhari and Madhyama*].

Chapter Eight
Bhakti Yoga and Vaishnavism

The Vaishnava Theory and Sadhana

They [*the Vaishnavas*] accept the world as a Lila, but the true Lila is elsewhere in the eternal Brindavan. All the religions which believe in the personal Godhead accept the universe as a reality, a Lila or a creation made by the will of God, but temporal and not eternal. The aim is the eternal status above.

*

The idea of a temporary Kingdom of heaven on earth is contained in the Puranas and conceived by some Vaishnava saints or poets; but it is a devotional idea, no philosophical basis is given for the expectation. I think the Tantric overcoming of imperfection is more individual, not collective.

*

It is the Vaishnava theory — that if you only repeat the name of Hari it is enough — nothing else needed. Even if you do it by accident, you will go posthaste to Heaven. It has always seemed to be the apotheosis of laziness and incompetence. There are plenty of people who have a little Bhakti for Krishna but I don't find them revelling in all the fruits of tapasya.

*

If you can feel the Name bringing you peace, it should be able to bring everything else, bhakti, joy, the revelation of the Power and the Presence and the full feeling and consciousness of it to you. That is indeed the process of the Vaishnava sadhana and the power of the Name in it. Only, keep your poise and persevere.

*

The Supramental is something in which the basis is absolute calm and however intense a Divine Love there is in it it does not disturb the calm but increases its depth. Chaitanya's experience was not that of Supermind, but of a Love and Ananda brought from above into the vital — the response of the vital is an extreme passion and exultation of Godward love and Ananda, the result of which is these *vikāras*. Chaitanya claimed this supremacy for the Radha experience because Ananda is higher than the experiences of the spiritual mind, Ananda being according to the Upanishads the supreme plane of experience. But this is a logical conclusion which cannot be accepted wholly — one must pass through the supermind to arrive to the highest Ananda and in the supermind there is a unification and harmonisation of all the divine Powers (Knowledge, etc. as well as Love and Ananda). Different sadhanas emphasise one aspect or another as the highest, but it is this union of all that must be the true base of the highest realisation and experience.

Vaishnava Bhakti and the Integral Yoga

It is not necessary to repeat past forms [*of Bhakti Yoga*] — to bring out the bhakti of the psychic being and give it whatever forms come naturally in the development is the proper way for our sadhana.

*

What three signs [*of the Paramhansa*]? If you refer to the four conditions (child, madman, demon, inert), it is not Ramakrishna who invented that. It is an old Sanskrit sloka, *bālonmādapiśācajaḍavat*, describing the Paramhansa or rather the various forms of Paramhansahood. The Paramhansa is a particular grade of realisation, there are others supposed to be lower or higher.

I have no objection to them [*vital manifestations of love and bhakti*] in their own place. But I must remind you that in my Yoga all vital movements must come under the control of the psychic and of the spiritual calm, knowledge and peace. If they conflict with the psychic or the spiritual control, they upset the balance and prevent the forming of the base of transformation.

If unbalance is good for other paths, that is the business of those who follow them. It does not suit mine.

*

Everybody must be made to understand clearly that this is not a sadhana of emotional and egoistic *bhakti*, but of surrender. One who makes demands and threatens to commit suicide if his demands are not complied with, is not meant for this Yoga....

This Yoga is not a Yoga of emotional egoistic vital bhakti full of demands and desires. There is no room in it for *ābdār* of any kind. It is only for those who surrender to the Divine and obey implicitly the directions given to them by Sri Aurobindo and the Mother.

The True Vaishnava Attitude

Your whole-hearted acceptance of the Vaishnava idea and bhakti becomes rather bewildering when it is coupled with an insistence that love cannot be given to the Divine until one has experience of the Divine. For what is more common in the Vaishnava attitude than the joy of bhakti for its own sake? "Give me bhakti," it cries, "whatever else you may keep from me. Even if it is long before I can meet you, even if you delay to manifest yourself, let my bhakti, my seeking for you, my cry, my love, my adoration be always there." How constantly the Bhakta has sung, "All my life I have been seeking you and still you are not there, but still I seek and cannot cease to seek and love and adore." If it were really impossible to love God unless you first experience him, how could this be? In fact your mind seems to be putting the cart before the horse. One seeks after God first, with persistence or with passion, one finds him afterwards, some sooner than others, but most after a long seeking. One does not find him first, then seek after him. Even a glimpse only comes after long or fervent seeking. One has the love of God or at any rate some heart's desire for him and afterwards one becomes aware of God's love, its reply to the heart's desire, its response of the supreme joy and Ananda. One does not say to God, "Show your love for me first, shower on me the experience of yourself, satisfy my demand, then I will see whether I can love you so long as you deserve it." It is surely the seeker who must seek and love first, follow the quest, become impassioned for the Sought — then only does the veil move aside and the Light be seen and the Face manifest that alone can satisfy the soul after its long sojourn in the desert.

Then again you may say, "Yes, but whether I love or not, I want, I have always wanted and now I want more and more, but I get nothing." Yes, but wanting is not all. As you now begin to see, there are conditions that have to be met — like the purification of the heart. Your thesis was, "Once I want God, God must manifest to me, come to me, at least give glimpses of himself to me, the real solid concrete experiences, not mere vague things which I can't understand or value. God's Grace must answer my call for it, whether I yet deserve it or not — or else there is no Grace." God's Grace may indeed do that in certain cases, but where does the "must" come in? If God must do it, it is no longer God's Grace, but God's duty or an obligation or a contract or a treaty. The Divine looks into the heart and removes the veil at the moment which he knows to be the right moment to do it. You have laid stress on the bhakti theory that one has only to call his name and he must reply, he must at once be there. Perhaps, but for whom is this true? For a certain kind of Bhakta surely who feels the power of the Name, who has the passion of the Name and puts it into his cry. If one is like that, then there may be the immediate reply — if not, one has to become like that, then there will be the reply. But some go on using the Name for years, before there is an answer. Ramakrishna himself got it after a few months, but what months! and what a condition he had to pass through before he got it! Still he succeeded quickly because he had a pure heart already — and that divine passion in it.

It is not surely the Bhakta but the man of knowledge who demands experience first. He can say, "How can I know without experience?", but even he goes on seeking like Tota Puri even though for thirty years, striving for the decisive realisation. It is really the man of intellect, the rationalist who says, "Let God, if he exists, prove himself to me first, then I will believe, then I will make some serious and prolonged effort to explore him and see what he is like."

All this does not mean that experience is irrelevant to sadhana — I certainly cannot have said such a stupid thing. What I have said is that the love and seeking of the Divine can be and ordinarily is there before the experience comes — it is an instinct, an inherent longing in the soul and it comes up as soon as certain coverings of the soul disappear or begin to disappear. The next thing I have said is that it is better to get the nature ready first (the purified heart and all that) before the "experiences" begin rather than the other way round and I base that on the many cases there have been of the danger of experiences before the heart and vital are ready for the true experience. Of course in many cases there is a true experience first, a touch of the Grace, but it is not something that lasts and is always there, but rather something that touches and withdraws and waits for the nature to get ready. But this is not so in every case, not even in many cases, I believe. One has to begin with the soul's inherent longing, then the struggle with the nature to get the temple ready, then the unveiling of the Image, the permanent Presence in the sanctuary.

P.S. All this is of course only an answer couched in mental terms to your one objection or inability to conceive how one can love God without having first known Him or had experience of Him. But mental reasoning by itself leads to nothing — it is something in yourself that has to see and then there is no difficulty. Fortunately, you are moving near to that. Nor would I trouble at all about this point, if you did not make of it a support for depression and despair. Otherwise it would have no importance, since with one idea or with the other one can arrive at the goal because the soul drives towards it.

The Sunlit Way of Yoga

Peace was the very first thing that the Yogins and seekers of old asked for and it was a quiet and silent mind — and that always brings peace — that they declared to be the best condition for realising the Divine. A cheerful and sunlit heart is the fit vessel for the Ananda and who shall say that Ananda or what prepares it is an obstacle to the Divine union? As for despondency, it is surely a terrible burden to carry on the way. One has to pass through it sometimes, like Christian of *The Pilgrim's Progress* through the Slough of Despond, but its constant reiteration cannot be anything but an obstacle. The Gita specially says, "Practise the Yoga with an undespondent heart", *anirviṇṇacetasā*.

I know perfectly well that pain and suffering and struggle and excesses of despair are natural — though not inevitable — on the way, — not because they are helps, but because they are imposed on us by the darkness of this human nature out of which we have to struggle into the Light. I do not suppose Ramakrishna or Vivekananda would have recommended the incidents you allude to as an example for others to follow — they would surely have said that faith, fortitude, perseverance were the better way. That after all was what they stuck to in the end in spite of these bad moments and they would never have dreamed of giving up the Yoga or the aspiration for the Divine on the ground that they were unfit and not meant for the realisation.

At any rate Ramakrishna told the story of Narada and the ascetic Yogi and the Vaishnava Bhakta with approval of its moral. I put it in my own language but keep the substance. Narada on his way to Vaikuntha met a Yogi practising hard tapasya on the hills. "O Narada," cried the Yogi, "you are going to Vaikuntha and will see Vishnu. I have been practising terrific austerities all my life and yet I have not even now attained to Him. Ask Him at least for me when I shall reach Him." Then Narada met a Vaishnava, a Bhakta who was singing songs to Hari and dancing to his own singing, and he cried also, "O Narada, you will see my Lord, Hari. Ask my Lord when I shall reach Him and see His face." On his way back Narada came first to the Yogi. "I have asked Vishnu; you will realise Him after six more lives." The Yogi raised a cry of loud lamentation,

"What, so many austerities! such gigantic endeavours! and my reward is realisation after six long lives! O how hard to me is the Lord Vishnu." Next Narada met again the Bhakta and said to him, "I have no good news for you. You will see the Lord, but only after a lakh of lives." But the Bhakta leapt up with a great cry of rapture, "Oh, I shall see my Lord Hari! after a lakh of lives I shall see my Lord Hari! How great is the grace of the Lord." And he began dancing and singing in a renewed ecstasy. Then Narada said, "Thou hast attained. Today thou shalt see the Lord!" Well, you may say, "What an extravagant story and how contrary to human nature!" Not so contrary as all that and in any case hardly more extravagant than the stories of Harishchandra and Shivi. Still I do not hold up the Bhakta as an example, for I myself insist on the realisation in this life and not after six or a lakh of births more. But the point of these stories is in the moral and surely when Ramakrishna told it, he was not ignorant that there was a sunlit path of Yoga! He even seems to say that it is the quicker way as well as the better! You are quite mistaken in thinking that the possibility of the sunlit path is a discovery or original invention of mine. The very first books on Yoga I read more than thirty years ago spoke of the dark and sunlit way and emphasised the superiority of the second over the other.

It is not either because I have myself trod the sunlit way or flinched from difficulty and suffering and danger. I have had my full share of these things and the Mother has had ten times her full share. But that was because the finders of the Way had to face these things in order to conquer. No difficulty that can come on the sadhak but has faced us on the path; against many we have had to struggle hundreds of times (in fact that is an understatement) before we could overcome; many still remain protesting that they have a right until the perfect perfection is there. But we have never consented to admit their inevitable necessity for others. It is in fact to ensure an easier path to others hereafter that we have borne that burden. It was with that object that the Mother once prayed to the Divine that whatever difficulties, dangers, sufferings were necessary for the path might be laid on her rather than on others. It has been so far heard that as a result of daily and terrible struggles for years those who put an entire and sincere confidence in her *are* able to follow the sunlit path and even those who cannot, yet when they do put the trust find their path suddenly easy and, if it becomes difficult again, it is only when distrust, revolt, abhiman, or other darknesses come upon them. The sunlit path is not altogether a fable.

But you will ask what of those who cannot? Well, it is for them I am putting forth all my efforts to bring down the supramental Force within a measurable time. I know that it will descend but I am seeking its near descent and, with whatever dark obstruction of the earth-nature or furious inroads of the Asuric forces seeking to prevent it, it is approaching the terrestrial soil. The supramental is not, as you imagine, something cold, hard and rocklike. It bears within it the presence of the Divine Love as well as the Divine Truth and its reign here means for those who accept it the straight and thornless path on which there is no wall or obstacle of which the ancient Rishis saw the far-off promise.

The dark path is there and there are many who make like the Christians a gospel of spiritual suffering; many hold it to be the unavoidable price of victory. It may be so under certain circumstances, as it has been in so many lives at least at the beginning, or one may choose to make it so. But then the price has to be paid with resignation, fortitude or a tenacious resilience. I admit that if borne in that way the attacks of the Dark Forces or the ordeals they impose have a meaning. After each victory gained over them, there is then a sensible advance; often they seem to show us the difficulties in ourselves which we have to overcome and to say, "Here you must conquer us and here." But all the same it is a too dark and difficult way which nobody should follow on whom the necessity does not lie.

In any case one thing can never help and that is to despond always and say, "I am unfit; I am not meant for the Yoga." And worse still are these perilous mental formations such as you are always accepting that you must fare like *X* (one whose difficulty of exaggerated ambition was quite different from yours) and that you have only six years etc. These are clear formations of the Dark Forces seeking not only to sterilise your aspiration but to lead you away and so prevent your sharing in the fruit of the victory hereafter. I do not know what Krishnaprem has said but his injunction, if you have rightly understood it, is one that cannot stand as valid, since so many have done Yoga relying on tapasya or anything else but not confident of any divine Grace. It is not that, but the soul's demand for a higher Truth or a higher life that is indispensable. Where that is, the Divine Grace whether believed in or not, will intervene. If you believe, that hastens and facilitates things; if you cannot yet believe, still the soul's aspiration will justify itself with whatever difficulty and struggle.

*

Prāyopaveśana would be quite the wrong movement, it would be a sort of Satyagraha against the Divine. In essence it is an attempt to force the Divine to do what one wants instead of trusting to him to do what is best according to his own divine will and wisdom; it is a culminating act of vital impatience and disappointed desire, while the true movement is a pure aspiration and an ardent surrender.

After all, one has not a *right* to call on the Divine to manifest himself; it can come only as a response to a spiritual or psychic state of consciousness or to a long course of sadhana rightly done; or, if it comes before that or without any apparent reason, it is a grace; but one cannot demand or compel grace; grace is something spontaneous which wells out from the Divine Consciousness as a free flower of its being. The bhakta looks for it, but he is ready to wait in perfect reliance, even if need be all his life, knowing that it will come, never varying in his love and surrender because it does not come now or soon. That is the spirit of so many songs of the devotees, which you have sung yourself; I heard one such song from you in a record some time ago and a very beautiful song it was and beautifully sung — "Even if I have not won thee, O Lord, still I adore."

What prevents you from having that, is the restless element

of vital impatience and ever recurring or persisting disappointment at not having what you want from the Divine. It is the idea, "I wish so much for it, surely I ought to have it; why is it withheld from me?" But wanting, however strongly, is not a passport to getting; there is something more to it than that. Our experience is that too much vital eagerness and insistence often blocks the way, it makes a sort of obstructing mass or a whirl of restlessness and disturbance which leaves no quiet space for the Divine to get in or for the thing wished for to come. Often it does come, but when the impatience has been definitely renounced and one waits, quietly open, for whatever may be (or for the time not be) given. But so often when you are preparing for a greater progress in the true devotion the habit of this vital element stands up and takes hold and interrupts the progress made.

The joylessness also comes from the vital. It is partly due to the disappointment but not solely, for it is a very common phenomenon when there is a pressure from the mind and soul on the vital to give up its attachments and its full unpurified acceptance of the outward life; it often gets a rajasic or tamasic vairagya instead of the sattwic kind, refuses to take a joy in anything, becomes dry, listless or unhappy, or it says, "Well, I have given up, I am giving up, but in exchange I must have the realisation you promise me; why don't I get it, I can't wait." To get rid of that, it is best, even while observing it, not to identify oneself with it; if the mind or some part of the mind sanctions or justifies, it will persist or recur. If sorrow there must be, the other kind you described in the previous letter is preferable, the sadness that has a sweetness in it, no revolt, no despair, only the psychic longing for the true thing to come.

It is not by *prāyopaveśana* or anything of the kind that it must come, but by the increase of the pure and true bhakti. You have been constantly told so by us and lately be Krishnaprem and his guru; remember that she told you that the presence of Krishna during your singing was a sure sign that it would come, — not necessarily today or tomorrow or the day after, but that it would surely come. We can't be all of us wrong and your vital impatience only in the right. For heaven's sake, get rid of it and settle down to quiet aspiration and an ever growing devotion and surrender leaving it to Krishna to do what he is sure to do in his own way and time.

Ordinary Life, Vaishnava Traditions and the Supramental Yoga

Even if things were as bad as you say, I don't see how going away would help you in the least — (it would certainly not make you non-human); some have tried before this device of progress by departure and it has never succeeded, they have had to come back and face their difficulty. Why do you always come back to this notion of going away or entertain it at all? It is quite meaningless from any rational point of view; it only encourages the adverse Force which wants to take you away from the path to return to the attack, and it prevents the speedy conversion of that dissatisfied part of your vital which is always kicking against the pricks — the pricks of your soul and of your spiritual destiny. However sad the prospect may seem to this dissatisfied vital fragment, your destiny is to be a Yogi and the sooner it reconciles itself to the prospect the better for it and for all the other personalities in you. Your alleged or inferred unfitness is a delusion, an imagination of this vital part; it doesn't exist. If persistence of difficulties is a proof of unfitness, then there is nobody in this Asram who is fit for the Yoga. We would all have to pack up our belongings or give them away and start either to get back to the ordinary world or en route for the Himalayas.

You describe the rich human egoistic life you might have lived and you say "not altogether a wretched life, you will admit". On paper, it sounds even very glowing and satisfactory, as you describe it. But there is no real or final satisfaction in it, except for those who are too common or trivial to seek anything else, and even they are not really satisfied or happy, — and in the end, it tires and palls. Sorrow and illness, clash and strife, disappointment, disillusionment and all kinds of human suffering come and beat its glow to pieces — and then decay and death.

That is the vital egoistic life as man has found it throughout the ages, and yet it is that which this part of your vital regrets? How do you fail to see, when you lay so much stress on the desirability of a merely human consciousness, that suffering is its badge? When the vital resists the change from the human into the divine consciousness, what it is defending is its right to sorrow and suffering and all the rest of it, varied and relieved no doubt by some vital or mental pleasures and satisfactions, but very partially relieved by them and only for a time. In your own case, it was already beginning to pall on you and that was why you turned from it. No doubt, there were the joys of the intellect and of artistic creation, but a man cannot be an artist alone; there is the outer quite human lower vital part and, in all but a few, it is the most clamorous and insistent part. But what was dissatisfied in you? It was the soul within, first of all, and through it the higher mind and the higher vital. Why then find fault with the Divine for misleading you when it turned you to the Yoga or brought you here? It was simply answering to the demand of your own inner being and the higher parts of your nature. If you have so much difficulty and become restless, it is because you are still divided and something in your lower vital still regrets what it has lost or, as a price for its adhesion or a compensation — a price to be *immediately* paid down to it, — asks for something similar and equivalent in the spiritual life. It refuses to believe that there is a greater compensation, a larger vital life waiting for it in which there shall not be the old inadequacy and unrest and final dissatisfaction. The foolishness is not in the Divine guidance, but in the irrational and obstinate resistance of this confused and obscure part of you to the demand, made not only by this Yoga, but by all Yoga — to the necessary conditions for the satisfaction of the aspiration of your own soul and higher nature.

The "human" vital consciousness has moved always between these two poles, the ordinary vital life which cannot satisfy and the recoil from it to the ascetic solution. India has gone fully through that see-saw; now Europe is beginning once more after a full trial to feel the failure of the mere vital egoistic life.

The traditional Yogas — to which you appeal — are founded upon the movement between these two poles. On one side are Shankara and Buddha and most go, if not by the same road, yet in that direction; on the other are Vaishnava or Tantric lines which try to combine asceticism with some sublimation of the vital impulse. And where did these lines end? They fell back to the other pole, to a vital invasion, even corruption and a loss of their spirit. At the present day the general movement is towards an attempt at reconciliation, and you have alluded sometimes to some of the protagonists of this attempt and asked me my opinion about them, yours being unfavourable. But these men are not mere charlatans, and if there is anything wrong with them (on which I do not pronounce), it can only be because they are unable to resist the magnetic pull of this lower pole of the egoistic vital desire-nature. And if they are unable to resist, it is because they have not found the true force which will not only neutralise that pull and prevent deterioration and downward lapse, but transform and utilise and satisfy in their own deeper truth, instead of destroying or throwing away, the life-force and the embodiment in matter; for that can only be done by the supermind power and by no other.

You appeal to the Vaishnava-Tantric traditions, to Chaitanya, Ramprasad, Ramakrishna. I know something about them and, if I did not try to repeat them, it is because I do not find in them the solution, the reconciliation I am seeking. Your quotation from Ramprasad does not assist me in the least — and it does not support your thesis either. Ramprasad is not speaking of an embodied, but of a bodiless and invisible Divine — or visible only in a subtle form to the inner experience. When he speaks of maintaining his claim or case against the Mother until she lifts him into her lap, he is not speaking of any outer vital or physical contact, but of an inner psychic experience; precisely, he is protesting against her keeping him in the external vital and physical nature and insists on her taking him on the psychospiritual plane into *spiritual* union with her. All that is very good and very beautiful, but it is not enough; the union has indeed to be realised in the inner psycho-spiritual experience first, because without that nothing sound or lasting can be done; but also there must be a realisation of the Divine in the outer consciousness and life, in the vital and physical planes on their own essential lines. It is that which, without your mind understanding it or how it is to be done, you are asking for, and I too; only I see the necessity of a vital transformation, while you seem to think and to demand that it should be done without any radical transformation, leaving the vital as it is. In the beginning, before I discovered the secret of the supermind, I myself tried to seek the reconciliation through an association of the spiritual consciousness with the vital, but my experience and all experience shows that this leads to nothing definite and final, — it ends where it began, midway between the two poles of human nature. An association is not enough, a transformation is indispensable.

The tradition of later Vaishnava bhakti is an attempt to sublimate the vital impulses through love by turning human love towards the Divine. It made a strong and intense effort and had many rich and beautiful experiences; but its weakness was just there, that it remained valid only as an inner experience turned towards the inner Divine, but it stopped at that point. Chaitanya's *prema* was nothing but a psychic divine love with a strong sublimated vital manifestation. But the moment Vaishnavism before or after him made an attempt at greater externalisation, we know what happened — a vitalistic deterioration, much corruption and decline. You cannot appeal to Chaitanya's example as against psychic or divine love; it was not something merely vital-human; in its essence, though not in its form, it was very much the first step in the transformation, which we ask of the sadhaks, to make their love psychic and use the vital not for its own sake, but as an expression of the soul's realisation. It is the first step and perhaps for some it may be sufficient, for we are not asking everybody to become supramental; but for any *full* manifestation on the physical plane the supramental is indispensable.

In this later Vaishnava tradition the sadhana takes the form of an application of human vital love in all its principal turns to the Divine; *viraha, abhimāna*, even complete separation (like the departure of Krishna to Mathura) are made prominent elements of this Yoga. But all that was only meant — in the sadhana itself, not in the Vaishnava poems — as a passage of which the end is *milana* or complete union; but the stress laid on the untoward elements by some would almost seem to make strife, separation, *abhimāna*, the whole means if not the very object of this kind of *prema-yoga*. Again, this method was only applied to the inner, not to a physically embodied Divine and had a reference to certain states and reactions of the inner consciousness in its seeking after the Divine. In the relations with the embodied Divine manifestation, or, I may add, of the disciple with the Guru, such things might rise as a result of human imperfection, but they were not made part of the theory of the relations. I do not think they formed a regular and authorised part of the relations of the bhaktas to Chaitanya or of the disciples at Dakshineshwar towards Ramakrishna! On the contrary, the relation of the disciple to the Guru in the Guruvada is supposed always to be that of worship, respect, complete happy confidence, unquestioning acceptance of the guidance. The application of the unchanged vital relations to the embodied Divine or the Guru may lead and has led to movements which are not conducive to the progress of the Yoga.

Ramakrishna's Yoga was also turned only to an inner realisation of the inner Divine, — nothing less but also nothing more. I believe his sentence about the claim of the sadhak on the Divine for whom one has sacrificed everything was the assertion of an inner and not an outer claim, on the inner rather than on any physically embodied Divine: it was a claim for the full spiritual union, the God-lover seeking the Divine, but the Divine also giving himself and meeting the God-lover. There can be no objection to that; such a claim all seekers of the Divine have; but as to the modalities of this Divine meeting, it does not carry us much farther. In any case, my object is a realisation on the physical plane and I cannot consent merely to repeat Ramakrishna. I seem to remember too that for a long time he was withdrawn into himself, all his life was not spent with his disciples! He got his siddhi first in retirement and when he came out and received everyone — well, a few years of it wore out his body. To that, I suppose, he had no objection; he even pronounced a theory, when Keshav Chandra was dying, that spiritual experience *ought* to wear out the body! But at the same time, when asked why he got his illness in the throat, he answered that it was the sins of his disciples which they threw upon him and he had to swallow! Not being satisfied, as he was, with an inner liberation alone, I cannot accept these ideas or these results, for it does not sound to me like a successful meeting of the Divine and the sadhak *on the physical plane*, however successful it might have been for the inner life. Krishna did great things and was very clearly a manifestation of the Divine. But I remember a passage of the Mahabharata in which he complains of the unquiet life his followers and adorers gave him, their constant demands, reproaches, their throwing of their unregenerate vital nature upon him. And in the Gita he speaks of this human world as a transient and sorrowful affair and, in spite of his gospel of divine action, seems almost to admit that to leave it is after all the last solution! The traditions of the past are very great in their own place, — in the past; but I do not see why we should merely repeat them and not go farther. In the spiritual development of the consciousness upon earth the great past ought to be followed by a greater future.

There is the rub that you seem all to ignore entirely, the difficulties of the physical embodiment and the divine realisation on the physical plane. For most, it seems to be a simple alternative; either the Divine comes down in full power and the thing is done — no difficulty, no necessary conditions, no law or process, only miracle and magic, or else, well, this can't be the Divine! Again you all (or almost all) insist on the Divine becoming human, remaining in the human consciousness and you protest against any attempt to make the human divine; on the other hand there is an outcry of disappointment, bewilderment, distrust, perhaps indignation, if there are human difficulties, if there is strain in the body, a swaying struggle with adverse forces, obstacles, checks, illness, and some begin to say, "Oh, there is nothing divine here!" — as if one could remain, vitally and physically, in the untransformed undivinised human consciousness, in unchanged contact with it, satisfying its demands, and yet be immune under all circumstances and in all conditions against strain and struggle and illness. If I want to divinise the human consciousness, to bring down the supramental, the Truth-Consciousness, the Light, the Force into the physical to transform it, to create there a great fullness of Truth and Light and Power and Bliss and Love, and make these other things impossible, the response is repulsion, or fear, or unwillingness — or a doubt whether it is possible. On one side there is the claim that illness and the rest should be impossible, on the other a violent rejection of the only condition under which these things can become impossible. I know that this is the natural inconsistency of the human vital mind wanting two inconsistent and incompatible things together; but that is one reason why it is necessary to transform the human and put something a little more luminous in its place.

But is the Divine then something so terrible, horrible or repellent that the idea of its entry into the physical, its divinising of the human should create this shrinking, refusal, revolt or fear? I can understand that the unregenerate vital attached to its own petty sufferings and pleasures, to the brief ignorant drama of life, should shrink from what will change it. But why should a God-lover, a God-seeker, a sadhak fear the divinisation of the consciousness! Why should he object to becoming one in nature with what he seeks, why should he recoil from *sādṛśya-mukti*? Behind this fear there are usually two causes: first, there is the feeling of the vital that it will have to cease to be obscure, crude, muddy, egoistic, unrefined (spiritually), full of stimulating desires and small pleasures and interesting sufferings (for it shrinks even from the Ananda which will replace them); next, there is some vague ignorant idea of the mind, due, I suppose, to the ascetic tradition, that the divine nature is something cold, bare, empty, austere, aloof, without the glorious riches of the egoistic human vital life. As if there were not a divine vital and as if that divine vital is not itself and, when it gets the means to manifest, will not make the life on earth also infinitely more full of beauty, love, radiance, warmth, fire, intensity and divine passion and capacity for bliss than the present impotent, suffering, pettily and transiently excited and soon tired vitality of the still so imperfect human creation!

But you will say that it is not the Divine from which you recoil, rather you accept and ask for it (provided that it is not too divine), but what you object to is the supramental — grand, aloof, incomprehensible, unapproachable, a sort of austere Nirakara Brahman. The supramental so described is a bogey created by this part of your vital mind in order to frighten itself and justify its attitude. Behind this strange description there seems to be an idea that the supramental is a new version of the Vedantic featureless and incommunicable Parabrahman, vast, grand, cold, empty, remote, devastating, overwhelming; it is not quite that, of course, since it can come down, but for all practical purposes it is just as bad! It is curious that you admit your ignorance of what the supramental can be, and yet you in these moods not only pronounce categorically what it is like, but reject emphatically my experience about it as of no practical validity or not valid for anybody but myself! I have not insisted, I have answered only casually because I am not asking you now to be non-human or divine, much less to be supramental; but as you are always returning to this point when you have these attacks and making it the pivot — or at least a main support — of your depression, I am obliged to answer. The supramental is *not* grand, aloof, cold and austere; it is not something opposed to or inconsistent with a full vital and physical manifestation; on the contrary, it carries in it the only possibility of the full fullness of the vital force and the physical life on earth. It is because it is so, because it was so revealed to me and for no other reason that I have followed after it and persevered till I came into contact with it and was able to draw down some power of it and its influence. I am concerned with the earth and not with worlds beyond for their own sake; it is a terrestrial realisation that I seek and not a flight to distant summits. All other Yogas regard this life as an illusion or a passing phase; the supramental Yoga alone regards it as a thing created by the Divine for a progressive manifestation and takes the fulfilment of the life and the body for its object. The supramental is simply the Truth-Consciousness and what it brings in its descent is the full truth of life, the full truth of consciousness in Matter. One has indeed to rise to high summits to reach it, but the more one rises, the more one can bring down below. No doubt, life and body have not to remain the ignorant, imperfect, impotent things they are now; but why should a change to fuller life-power, fuller body-power be considered something aloof, cold and undesirable? The utmost Ananda the body and life are now capable of is a brief excitement of the vital mind or the nerves or the cells which is limited, imperfect and soon passes; with the supramental change all the cells, nerves, vital forces, embodied mental forces can become filled with a thousandfold Ananda, capable of an intensity of bliss which passes description and which need not fade away. How aloof, repellent and undesirable! The supramental love means an intense unity of soul with soul, mind with mind, life with life, and an entire flooding of the body consciousness with the physical experience of oneness, the presence of the Beloved in every part, in every cell of the body. Is that too something aloof and grand but undesirable? With the supramental change, the very thing on which you insist, the possibility of the free physical meeting of the embodied Divine with the sadhak without conflict of forces and without undesirable reactions becomes possible, assured and free. That too is, I suppose, something aloof and undesirable? I could go on — for pages, but this is enough for the moment.

Different Approaches through Love and Bhakti

It seems to me that these differences of valuation come from the mind laying stress on one side or another of the approach to the Divine or exalting one aspect of realisation over another. When there is the approach through the heart, through Love and Bhakti, its highest culmination is in a transcendent Ananda, an unspeakable Bliss or Beatitude of union with the Divine through Love. The school of Chaitanya laid especial and indeed sole emphasis on this way and made this the whole reality of

Krishna consciousness. But the transcendent Ananda is there at the origin and end of all existence and this is not and cannot be the sole way to it. One can arrive at it also through the Vasudeva consciousness, which is a wider, more mentalised approach — as in the method of the Gita where knowledge, works, bhakti are all centred in Krishna, the One, the Supreme, the All and arrive through the cosmic consciousness to the luminous transcendence. There is the way too described in the Taittiriya Upanishad, the Vedanta's Gospel of Bliss. These are certainly wider methods, for they take up the whole existence through all its parts and ways of being to the Divine. If less intense at their starting point, a vaster and slower movement, there is no reason to suppose that they are less intense on their summits of arrival. It is the same transcendence to which all arrive, either with a large movement gathering up everything spiritual in us to take it there in a vast sublimation, or in a single intense uplifting from one point, a single exaltation leaving all the rest aside. But who shall say which is profounder of the two? Concentrated love has a profundity of its own which cannot be measured; concentrated wisdom has a wider profundity but one cannot say that it is deeper.

Cosmic values are only reflections of the truth of the Transcendence in a lesser truth of time experience which is separative and sees diversely a thousand aspects of the One. As one rises through the mind or any part of the manifested being, any one or more of these aspects can become more and more sublimated and tend towards its supreme transcendental intensity, and whatever aspect is so experienced is declared by the spiritualised mental consciousness to be the supreme thing. But when one goes beyond mind all tends not only to sublimate but to fuse together until the separated aspects recover their original unity, indivisible in the absoluteness of all made one. Mind can conceive and have experience of existence without consciousness or Ananda and this receives its utmost expression in the inconscience attributed to Matter. So also it can conceive of Ananda or Love as a separate principle; it even feels consciousness and existence losing themselves in a trance or swoon of

Love or Ananda. So too the limited personal loses itself in the illimitable Person, the lover in the supreme Beloved, or else the personal in the Impersonal, — the lover feels himself immersed, losing himself in the transcendental reality of Love or Ananda. The personal and the impersonal are themselves posited and experienced by mind as separate realities — and one or other is declared and seen as supreme, so that the personal can have *laya* in the Impersonal or on the contrary the impersonal disappear into the absolute reality of the supreme and divine Person; the impersonal in that view is only an attribute or power of the personal Divine. But at the summit of spiritual experience passing beyond mind one begins to feel the fusion of all these things into one. Consciousness, Existence, Ananda return to their indivisible unity, Sachchidananda. The personal and the impersonal become irrevocably one, so that to posit one as against the other appears as an act of ignorance. This tendency of unification is the basis of the supramental consciousness and experience; for cosmic or creative purposes the supermind can put forward one aspect prominently where that is needed, but it is aware of all the rest behind it or contained in it and does not admit into its view any separation or opposition anywhere. For that reason a supramental creation would be a multifold harmony and not a separative process fragmenting or analysing the One into parts and setting these parts over against each other or else putting them contradictorily against each other and having afterwards to synthetise and piece them together in order to arrive at harmony or else to exclude some or all of the parts in order to realise the indivisible One.

You speak of the Vaishnava school emphasising the personal felicities, as in the classification of the *bhāvas*, and you say that these are short and quick feelings and lack in vastness or amplitude. No doubt, when they are first felt and as they are felt by the limited consciousness in its ordinary functioning and movement; but that is only because the emotional in man with this imperfect bodily instrument acts largely by spasms of intensity when it wants to sublimate and cannot maintain either the continuity or the extension or the sublimated paroxysm of these things. But as the individual becomes cosmic (the universalising of the individual without his losing his higher individuality as a divine centre is one of the processes which lead towards the supramental Truth), this disability begins to disappear. The truth behind the *dāsya* or *madhura* or any other *bhāva* or fusion of *bhāvas* becomes a vast and ample continuous state, — if by chance they lose something of their briefer intensities by this extension of themselves, they recover them a thousandfold in the movement of the universalised individual towards the Transcendence. There is an ever enlarging experience which takes up the elements of spiritual realisation and in this uplifting and transforming process they become other and greater things than they were and more and more they take their place by sublimation, first in the spiritual-cosmic, then in the all-embracing transcendent whole.

The difference of view between Shankara and Ramanuja and on the other side Chaitanya about Krishna arises from the turn of their experience. Krishna was only an aspect of Vishnu to the others because that ecstatic form of love and bhakti which had become associated with Krishna was not for them the whole. The Gita, like Chaitanya, but from a different viewpoint, regarded Krishna as the Divine himself. To Chaitanya he was Love and Ananda, and Love and Ananda being for him the highest transcendental experience, so Krishna too must be the Supreme. For the writer of the Gita, Krishna was the source of Knowledge and Power as well as Love, the Destroyer, Preserver, Creator in one, so necessarily Vishnu was only an aspect of this universal Divine. In the Mahabharat indeed Krishna comes as an incarnation of Vishnu, but that can be turned by taking it that it was through the Vishnu aspect as his frontal appearance that he manifested, for that the greater Godhead can manifest later than others is logical if we consider the manifestation as progressive, — just as Vishnu is in the Veda a younger Indra, Upendra, but gains upon his elder and subsequently takes place above him in the Trimurti.

I cannot say much about the Vaishnava idea of the form of Krishna. Form is the basic means of manifestation and without it it may be said that the manifestation of anything is not complete. Even if the Formless logically precedes Form, yet it is not illogical to assume that in the Formless, Form is inherent and already existent in a mystic latency, otherwise how could it be manifested? For any other process would be the creation of the non-existent, not manifestation. If so, it would be equally logical to assume that there is an eternal form of Krishna, a spirit body. As for the highest Reality, it is no doubt absolute Existence, but is it only that? Absolute Existence as an abstraction may exclude everything else from itself and amount to a sort of very positive zero; but Absolute Existence as a reality — who shall define and say what is or is not in its inconceivable depths, its illimitable Mystery? Mind can ordinarily conceive of the Absolute Existence only as a negation of its own concepts spatial, temporal or other. But it cannot tell what is at the basis of manifestation or what manifestation is or why there is any manifestation at all out of its positive zero — and the Vaishnavas, we must remember, do not admit this conception as the absolute and original truth of the Divine. It is therefore not rigidly impossible that what we conceive and perceive as spatial form may correspond to some mysterious power of the spaceless Absolute. I do not say all that as a definite statement of Truth, I am only pointing out that the Vaishnava position on its own ground is far from being logically or metaphysically untenable.

Love and Bhakti for Krishna

As for Krishna, why not approach simply and straight? The simple approach means trust. If you pray, trust that he hears. If the reply takes long in coming, trust that he knows and loves and that he is wisest in the choice of the time. Meanwhile quietly clear the ground, so that he may not have to trip over stone and jungle when he comes. That is my suggestion and I know what I am saying — for whatever you may say, I know very well all human difficulties and struggles and I know of the cure. That is why I press always on the things that would minimise and shorten the struggles and difficulties, — the psychic turn, faith, perfect and simple confidence and reliance. These, let me remind you, are tenets of the Vaishnava Yoga. Of course, there is the other Vaishnava way which swings between yearning and despair — ardent seeking and the pangs of viraha. It is that you seem to be following and I do not deny that one can arrive by that as one can by almost any way, if followed sincerely. But then those who follow it find a rasa even in viraha, in the absence and the caprice of the Divine Lover. Some of them have sung that they have followed after him all their lives but always he has slipped away from their vision and even in that they find a rasa and never cease following. But you find no rasa in it. So you cannot expect me to approve of that for you. Follow after Krishna by all means, but follow with the determination to arrive: don't do it with the expectation of failure or admit any possibility of breaking off half-way.

*

As for the "hostile forces", it is quite true that to persuade the sadhak to cut off outer contact with us on the plea of solitude and intense sadhana, is a favourite device of theirs and has often led to disaster. It gives them a freer field to bring in their own influence and represent it as the divine influence or as our own influence, and it ends often by a revolt and finally the sadhak cuts off the inner relation also or even turns hostile. This has happened fairly often and that is one reason why I have usually discouraged that or any kind of complete solitude. Absence from darshan for a short time if there is good reason for it, but more than that is inadvisable.

The direct approach to Krishna is not safe or easy; it can sometimes be terribly risky, if there is anything in the sadhak that interferes with the clarity and singleness of his attitude. In that case any wrong desire, vanity, pride, sexual impurity, ambition, or any other pronounced weakness may open the way to serious distortion of the sadhana, turning into wrong ways, breakdown or collapse, even to spiritual perdition. Krishna's own influence cannot be a wrong influence, if it is really his, but it is easy to mistake and accept some other influence as his. Especially, he is the Lord of Love and Beauty and Delight, and nothing is easier for men who are always going in the wrong way in search of these things, to bring their wrong ways into their search for him also. That experience must be one of the reasons why the seers insist on the approach through the guru and say that Krishna cannot be attained otherwise. It is the reason why they insist on vairagya, detachment from the ordinary aims and ends of human nature as so necessary. That is also why Krishna does not like to show himself until the field is clear for him! The intervention of some power or influence that represents itself as he, even puts on an imitation of his form or voice would be fatal if accepted; but even his real manifestation might bring about an upset in someone not really ready for it. One must be on guard against these dangers and it is the guru who can interpose himself as a shield against them.

The identification of the guru with the Divine is a common rule, not peculiar to the Vaishnava bhakti. Ordinarily, so far as the outer mind is concerned, it is a firm belief; the outer mind can believe, can by its faith have some feeling of it, can with the help of the heart worship, adore, serve with humility and fidelity; ordinarily, this is enough and it prepares besides for something deeper. But to realise the identity is another matter, [*incomplete*]

*

I do not know that I can answer your question about what Krishnaprem means by Krishna's light. It is certainly not what people ordinarily mean by knowledge. He may mean the light of the Divine Consciousness, or if you like, the light that is the Divine Consciousness or the light that comes from it or he may mean the luminous being of Krishna in which all things are in their supreme truth, — the truth of Knowledge, the truth of Bhakti, the truth of ecstasy and Ananda, everything is there.

There is also a manifestation of Light — the Upanishads speak of *jyotir brahma*, the Light that is Brahman. Very often the sadhak feels a flow of Light upon him or around him or a flow of Light invading his centres or even his whole being and body, penetrating and illumining every cell and in that Light there grows the spiritual consciousness and one becomes open to all or many of its workings and realisations. Appositely I have a review of a book of Ramdas (of the *Vision*) before me in which is described such an experience got by the repetition of the Rama mantra, but, if I understand rightly, after a long and rigorous self-discipline. "The mantra having stopped automatically, he beheld a small circular light before his mental vision. This yielded him thrills of delight. This experience having continued for some days, he felt a dazzling light like lightning, flashing before his eyes, which ultimately permeated and absorbed him. Now an inexpressible transport of bliss filled every pore of his physical frame." It does not always come like that — very often it comes by stages or at long intervals, at first, working on the consciousness till it is ready.

We speak here also of Krishna's light — Krishna's light in the mind, Krishna's light in the vital; but it is a special light — in the mind it brings clarity, freedom from obscurity, mental error and perversion; in the vital it clears out all perilous stuff and where it is there is a pure and divine happiness and gladness.

There are some however who seem to regard this invasion of Light not merely as a thing without value but a thing of evil or, possibly, one that can be such and so to be distrusted: for I have before me a letter describing an experience very similar to Ramdas's, but it was condemned by the writer's Guru as an attempt at possession by a devil to be dispelled by uttering the name of Ramakrishna!

But why limit oneself, insist on one thing alone and shut out every other? Whether it be by Bhakti or by Light or by Ananda or by Peace or by any other means whatsoever that one gets the initial realisation of the Divine, to get it is the thing and all means are good that bring it.

If it is Bhakti that one insists on, it is by Bhakti that Bhakti comes and Bhakti in its fullness is nothing but an entire self-giving, as Krishnaprem very rightly indicates. Then all meditation, all tapasya, all means of prayer or mantra must have that as its end and it is when one has progressed sufficiently in that that the Divine Grace descends and the realisation comes and develops till it is complete. But the moment of its advent is chosen by the wisdom of the Divine alone and one must have the strength to go on till it arrives; for when all is truly ready it cannot fail to come.

*

As to the point that puzzles you, it only arises from a confusion between the feeling of the devotee and the observation of the observer. Of course the devotee loves Krishna because Krishna is lovable and not for any other reason — that is his feeling and his true feeling. He has no time to bother his head about what in himself made him able to love, the fact that he does love is sufficient for him and he does not need to analyse his emotions. The Grace of Krishna consists for him in Krishna's very lovableness, in his showing of himself to the devotee, in his call, the cry of his flute. That is enough for the heart or, if there is anything more, it is the yearning that others or all may hear the flute, see the face, feel all the beauty and rapture of this love.

It is not the heart of the devotee but the mind of the observer that questions how it is that the Gopis were called or responded at once and others — the Brahmin women, for instance — were not called or did not respond at once. Once the mind puts the question, there are two possible answers, the mere will of Krishna without any reason, what the mind would call his absolute divine choice or his arbitrary divine caprice or else the readiness of the heart that is called, and that amounts to *adhikāri-bheda*. A third reply would be — circumstances, as for instance, the parking off of the spiritual ground into closed preserves. But how can circumstances prevent the Grace from acting? In spite of the parking off, it works — Christians, Mahomedans do answer to the Grace of Krishna. Tigers, ghouls must love if they see him, hear his flute? Yes, but why do some hear it and see him, others not? We are thrown back on the two alternatives, Krishna's Grace calls whom it wills to call without any determining reason for the choice or rejection, his mercy or his withholding or at least delaying of his mercy, or else he calls the hearts that are ready to vibrate and leap up at his call — and even there he waits till the moment has come. To say that it does not depend on outward merit or appearance of fitness is no doubt true; the something that was ready to wake in spite, it may be, of many hard layers in which it was enclosed, may be something visible to Krishna and not to us. It was there perhaps long before the flute began to play, but he was busy melting the hard layers so that the heart in its leap might not be pressed back by them when the awakening notes came. The Gopis heard and rushed out into the forest — the others did not — or did they think it was only some rustic music or some rude cowherd lover fluting to his sweetheart, not a call that learned and cultured or virtuous ears could recognise as the call of the Divine? There is something to be said for the *adhikāri-bheda*. But of course it must be understood in a large sense, — some may have the *adhikāra* for recognising Krishna's flute, some for the call of Christ, some for the dance of Shiva — to each his own way and his nature's answer to the Divine Call. *Adhikāra* cannot be stated in rigid mental terms, it is something spiritual and subtle, something mystic and secret between the called and the Caller.

As for the swelled head, the theory of Grace may no doubt contribute to it, though I should imagine that the said head never felt the Grace but only the magnanimity of its own ego. The swelling may come equally in the way of personal effort as by the craving for Grace. It is fundamentally not due to either, but to a natural predisposition to this kind of oedema.

*

If Krishna was always and by nature cold and distant (Lord, what a discovery — Krishna of all people!), how could human devotion and aspiration come near him — he and it would soon be like the North and South Pole, growing icier and icier, always facing each other but never seeing because of the earth's bulge. Also, if Krishna did not want the human bhakta as well as the bhakta wanting him, who could get at him? — he would be always sitting on the snows of the Himalayas like Shiva. History describes him otherwise and he is usually charged with being too warm and sportive.

*

If one wants Krishna, one gets Krishna — but he is a sufficiently trying Deity and does not come at once, though he may come suddenly at any time. But usually one has to want him so badly and obstinately that one is prepared to pay any price. One has to know how to wait as well as to want — to go on insisting and insisting without taking heed of even the longest denial. The psychic can do that — but the mind and the vital have to learn how to do it also.

*

Certainly Krishna is credited with much caprice, difficult dealings and a playfulness (lila!) which the played-with do not always immediately appreciate. But there is a reasoning as well as a hidden method in his caprices, and when he does come out of it and takes a fancy to be nice to you, he has a supreme attractiveness, charm and allurement which compensates and more than compensates for all you have suffered.

*

Well, why should not Krishna ride a horse if he so wants?[1] His actions or habits cannot be fixed by the human mind or by an immutable tradition. Especially Krishna is a law to himself. Perhaps he was in a hurry to get to the place where he wanted to flute.

*

The Gopis are not ordinary people in the proper sense of the word — they are extraordinary by their extremeness of love, passionate devotion, unreserved self-giving. Whoever has that, however humble his position in other respects, learning, external sanctity etc. etc., can easily follow after Krishna and reach him; that seems to me the sense of the symbol of the Gopis. There are many other significances, of course — that is only one among the many.

*

---

[1] *The correspondent wrote about a disciple who had a vision of Krishna galloping on a horse. — Ed.*

Radha is the personification of the absolute love for the Divine, total and integral in all parts of the being from the highest spiritual to the physical, bringing the absolute self-giving and total consecration of all the being and calling down into the body and the most material Nature the supreme Ananda.

*

The coming of sex on seeing the image of Krishna and Radha is due to the past association of sex with the cult of Radha-Krishna. But in fact the image has nothing to do with sex. The true symbol for it would not be the human sex-attraction, but the soul, the psychic, hearing the call of the Divine and flowering into the complete love and surrender that brings the supreme Ananda. That is what Radha and Krishna by their divine union bring about in the human consciousness and it is so that you must regard it, throwing aside the old sex-associations.

Love of Krishna and This Yoga

What you were told of the incompatibility of love and adoration of Krishna with this Yoga, is not true. There is not and cannot be any such incompatibility. Otherwise we would not have encouraged you in your aspiration. You can seek for him quite as well here as in Brindaban.

*

As regards Krishna and devotion, I think I have already answered more than once. I have no objection at all to the worship of Krishna or the Vaishnava form of devotion, nor is there any incompatibility between Vaishnava bhakti and my supramental Yoga. There is in fact no special and exclusive form of supramental Yoga: all ways can lead to the Supermind, just as all ways can lead to the Divine.

Certainly, I will help you and am helping and will always help you; the idea that I can stop doing it or will send you away has no sense in it. If you persevere, you cannot fail to get the permanent bhakti you want and the realisation you want, but you should learn to put an entire reliance on Krishna to give it when he finds all ready and the time come. If he wants you to clear out imperfections and impurities first, that is after all understandable. I don't see why you should not succeed in doing it, now that your attention is being so constantly turned on it. To see them clearly and acknowledge them is the first step, to have the firm will to reject them is the next, to separate yourself from them entirely so that if they enter at all it will be as foreign elements, no longer parts of your normal nature but suggestions from outside, brings their last state; even, once seen and rejected, they may automatically fall away and disappear; but for most the process takes time. These things are not peculiar to you; they are parts of universal human nature; but they can, do and will disappear.

*

But I have already told you more than once that I have no objection to your seeking Krishna or to your asking for Ananda or milan or anything else. I have never pressed you or others either to seek after Supermind or to accept me as an Avatar. These things have risen as an answer to questions put by yourself or others and I have treated them as matters of knowledge. But each must go by his own way and his own nature to his own goal. Ahaituki bhakti according to the Vaishnava ideal is the highest way and also the quickest, but if one does not feel equal to it, sahaituki bhakti will do well enough. Or if one has no turn for bhakti at all, there are plenty of other ways. Or if one does not care to follow any way, there is, as I said, in answer to X's question, the pressure of something in the nature to find the Self, if that is what it is after, or God or Krishna or the Mother or whatever it may be.

If you know the urge in you, well, follow it straight — there is no need of questioning or going this side or that. Follow the heart's urge till it reaches what it is seeking.

Chapter Nine

The Teachings of Some Modern Indian Yogis

Ramana Maharshi

According to Brunton's description of the sadhana he (Brunton) practised under the Maharshi's instructions,[1] it is the Overself one has to seek within, but he describes the Overself in a way that is at once the Psychic Being, the Atman and the Ishwara. So it is a little difficult to know what is the exact reading.

*

The methods described in the account [*of Ramana Maharshi's technique of self-realisation*] are the well-established methods of Jnanayoga — (1) one-pointed concentration followed by thought-suspension, (2) the method of distinguishing or finding out the true self by separating it from mind, life, body (this I have seen described by him [*Brunton*] more at length in another book) and coming to the pure I behind; this also can disappear into the Impersonal Self. The usual result is a merging in the Atman or Brahman — which is what one would suppose is meant by the Overself, for it is that which is the real Overself. This Brahman or Atman is everywhere, all is in it, it is in all, but it is in all not as an individual being in each but is the same in all — as the Ether is in all. When the merging into the Overself is complete, there is no ego, no distinguishable I, or any formed separative person or personality. All is *ekākāra* — an indivisible and undistinguishable Oneness either free from all formations or carrying all formations in it without being affected — for one can realise it in either way. There is a realisation in which all

---

[1] *The correspondent sent to Sri Aurobindo two paragraphs from Paul Brunton's book* A Message from Arunachala *(London: Rider & Co., n.d. [1936], pp. 205–7). — Ed.*

beings are moving in the one Self and this Self is there stable in all beings; there is another more complete and thoroughgoing in which not only is it so but all are vividly realised as the Self, the Brahman, the Divine. In the former, it is possible to dismiss all beings as creations of Maya, leaving the one Self alone as true — in the other it is easier to regard them as real manifestations of the Self, not as illusions. But one can also regard all beings as souls, independent realities in an eternal Nature dependent upon the One Divine. These are the characteristic realisations of the Overself familiar to the Vedanta. But on the other hand you say that this Overself is realised by the Maharshi as lodged in the heart-centre, and it is described by Brunton as something concealed which when it manifests appears as the real Thinker, source of all action, but now guiding thought and action in the Truth. Now the first description applies to the Purusha in the heart, described by the Gita as the Ishwara situated in the heart and by the Upanishads as the Purusha Antaratma; the second could apply also to the mental Purusha, *manomayaḥ prāṇaśarīra netā* of the Upanishads, the mental Being or Purusha who leads the life and the body. So your question is one which on the data I cannot easily answer. His Overself may be a combination of all these experiences, without any distinction being made or thought necessary between the various aspects. There are a thousand ways of approaching and realising the Divine and each way has its own experiences which have their own truth and stand really on a basis, one in essence but complex in aspects, common to all, but not expressed in the same way by all. There is not much use in discussing these variations; the important thing is to follow one's own way well and thoroughly. In this Yoga, one can realise the psychic being as a portion of the Divine seated in the heart with the Divine supporting it there — this psychic being takes charge of the sadhana and turns the whole being to the Truth and the Divine, with results in the mind, the vital, the physical consciousness which I need not go into here, — that is a first transformation. We realise it next as the one Self, Brahman, Divine, first *above* the body, life, mind and not only within the heart supporting them — above and free and unattached as the static Self but also extended in wideness through the world as the silent Self in all and dynamic too as the active Divine Being and Power, Ishwara-Shakti, containing the world and pervading it as well as transcending it, manifesting all cosmic aspects. But, what is most important for us, is that it manifests as a transcending Light, Knowledge, Power, Purity, Peace, Ananda of which we become aware above and which descends into the being and progressively replaces the ordinary consciousness by its own movements — that is the second transformation. We realise also the consciousness itself as moving upward, ascending through many planes physical, vital, mental, overmental to the supramental and Ananda planes. This is nothing new; it is stated in the Taittiriya Upanishad that there are five Purushas, the physical, the vital, the mental, the Truth Purusha (supramental) and the Bliss Purusha; it says that one has to draw the physical self up into the vital, the vital into the mental, the mental into the Truth Self, the Truth Self into the Bliss Self and so attain perfection. But in this Yoga we become aware not only of this taking up but of a pouring down of the powers of the higher Self, so that there comes in the possibility of a descent of the Supramental Self and nature to dominate and change our present nature and turn it from nature of Ignorance into nature of Truth-Knowledge (and through the supramental into nature of Ananda) — this is the third or supramental transformation. It does not always go in this order, for with many the spiritual descent begins first in an imperfect way before the psychic is in front and in charge, but the psychic development has to be attained before a perfect and unhampered spiritual descent can take place, and the last or supramental change is impossible so long as the two first have not become full and complete. That's the whole matter, put as briefly as possible.

*

The Upanishads do not say that about the Atman[2] — what they

---

[2] *That is, the Upanishads do not say that the Atman is situated in the core of the heart.* — Ed.

say about the Atman is that it is in all and all is in it, it is everywhere and all this universe is the Atman. What they speak of as situated in the deeper inner heart is the Purusha in the heart or Antaratman.[3] This is in fact what we call the psychic being, *caitya puruṣa*.

The heart spoken of by the Upanishads corresponds with the physical cardiac centre; it is the *hṛtpadma* of the Tantriks. As a subtle centre, *cakra*, it is supposed to have its apex on the spine and to broaden out in front. Exactly where in this area one or another feels it does not matter much; to feel it there and be guided by it is the main thing. I cannot say what the Maharshi has realised — but what Brunton describes in his book as the Self is certainly this Purusha Antaratma but concerned more with *mukti* and a liberated action than with transformation of the nature. What the psychic realisation does bring is a psychic change of the nature purifying it and turning it altogether towards the Divine. After that or along with it comes the realisation of the cosmic Self. It is these two things that the old Yogas encompassed and through them they passed to Moksha, Nirvana or the departure into some kind of celestial transcendence. The Yoga practised here includes both liberation and transcendence, but it takes liberation or even a certain Nirvana, if that comes, as a first step and not as the last step of its siddhi. Whatever exit to or towards the Transcendent it achieves is an ascent accompanied by a descent of the power, light, consciousness that has been achieved and it is by such descents that is to be achieved the spiritual and supramental transformation here. This possibility does not seem to be admitted in the Maharshi's thought, — he considers the Descent as superfluous and logically impossible. "The Divine is here, from where will He descend?" is his argument. But the Divine is everywhere, he is above as well as within, he has many habitats, many strings to his bow of Power, there are many levels of his dynamic Consciousness and each has its own light and force. He is not confined to his position in the heart or to the single cord of the psycho-spiritual

---

[3] *aṅguṣṭhamātraḥ puruṣo antarātmā.*

realisation. He has also his supramental station above the heart-centre and mind-centres and can descend from there if He wants to do so.

Swami Ramatirtha

I think Ramatirtha's realisations were more mental than anything else. He had opening of the higher mind and a realisation there of the cosmic Self, but I find no evidence of a transformed mind and vital; that transformation is not a result or object of the Yoga of Knowledge. The realisation of the Yoga of Knowledge is when one feels that one lives in the wideness of something silent, featureless and universal (called the Self) and all else is seen as only forms and names; the Self is real, nothing else. The realisation of "*my* self in other forms" is a part of this or a step towards it, but in the full realisation the "my" should drop so that there is only *the* one Self or rather only the Brahman. For the Self is merely a subjective aspect of the Brahman, just as the Ishwara is its objective aspect. That is the Vedantic "Knowledge". Its result is peace, silence, liberation. As for the active Prakriti, (mind, vital, body), the Yoga of Knowledge does not make it its aim to transform them — that would be no use as the idea is that if the liberation has come, it will all drop off at death. The only change wanted is to get rid of the idea of ego and realise as true only the supreme Self, the Brahman.

Swami Ramdas

I have not read Ramdas's writings nor am I at all acquainted with his personality or what may be the level of his experience. The words you quote from him could be expressions either of a simple faith or of a pantheistic experience; evidently, if they are used or intended to establish the thesis that the Divine is everywhere and is all and therefore all is good, being Divine, they are very insufficient for that purpose. But as an experience, it is a very common thing to have this feeling or realisation in the Vedantic sadhana — in fact without it there would be no Vedantic sadhana. I have had it myself on various levels of consciousness and in numerous forms and I have met scores of people who have had it very genuinely — not as an intellectual theory or perception, but as a spiritual reality which was too concrete for them to deny whatever paradoxes it may entail for the ordinary intelligence.

Of course it does not mean that all here is good or that in the estimation of values a brothel is as good as an Asram, but it does mean that all are part of one manifestation and that in the inner heart of the harlot as in the inner heart of the sage or saint there is the Divine. Again his experience is that there is one Force working in the world both in its good and in its evil — one Cosmic Force; it works both in the success (or failure) of the Asram and in the success (or failure) of the brothel. Things are done in this world by the use of the force, although the use made is according to the nature of the user, one uses it for the works of light, another for the works of Darkness, yet another for a mixture. I don't think any Vedantin (except perhaps some modernised ones) would maintain that all is good here — the orthodox Vedantic idea is that all is here an inextricable mixture of good and evil, a play of the Ignorance and therefore a play of the dualities. The Christian missionaries, I suppose, hold that all that God does is morally good, so they are shocked by the Taoist priests aiding the work of the brothel by their rites. But do not the Christian priests invoke the aid of God for the destruction of men in battle and did not some of them sing Te Deums over a victory won by the massacre of men and the starvation of women and children? The Taoist who believes only in the Impersonal Tao is more consistent and the Vedantin who believes that the Supreme is beyond good and evil, but that the Cosmic Force the Supreme has put out here works through the dualities, therefore through both good and evil, joy and suffering, has a thesis which at least accounts for the double fact of the experience of the Supreme which is All Light, All Bliss and All Beauty and a world of mixed light and darkness, joy and suffering, what is fair and what is ugly. He says that the dualities come by a separative Ignorance and so long as you accept this separative Ignorance, you cannot get rid of that, but it is possible to draw back from it in experience and to have the realisation of the Divine in all and the Divine everywhere and then you begin to realise the Light, Bliss and Beauty behind all and this is the one thing to do. Also you begin to realise the one Force and you can use it or let it use you for the growth of the Light in you and others — no longer for the satisfaction of the ego and for the works of the ignorance and darkness.

As to the dilemma about the cruelty of things, I do not know what answer Ramdas would give. One answer might be that the Divine within is felt through the psychic being and the nature of the psychic being is that of the divine light, harmony, love, but it is covered by the mental and separative vital ego from which strife, hate, cruelty naturally come. It is therefore natural to feel in the kindness the touch of the Divine, while the cruelty is felt as a disguise or perversion in Nature, although that would not prevent the man who has the realisation from feeling and meeting the Divine behind the disguise. I have known even instances in which the perception of the Divine in all accompanied by an intense experience of universal love or a wide experience of an inner harmony had an extraordinary effect in making all around kind and helpful, even the most coarse and hard and cruel. Perhaps it is some such experience which is at the base of Ramdas's statement about the kindness. As for the Divine working, the experience of the Vedantic realisation is that behind the confused mixture of good and evil something is working that he realises as the Divine and in his own life he can look back and see what each step, happy or unhappy, meant for his progress and how it led towards the growth of his spirit. Naturally this comes fully as the realisation progresses; before that he had to walk by faith and may have often felt his faith fail and yielded to grief, doubt and despair for a time.

As for my writings, I don't know if there is any that would clear up the difficulty. You would find mostly the statement of the Vedantic experience, for it is that through which I passed and, though now I have passed to something beyond, it seems to me the most thorough-going and radical preparation for whatever is Beyond, though I do not say that it is indispensable to pass through it. But whatever the solution, it seems to me that the Vedantin is right in insisting that one must, to arrive at it, admit the two facts, the prevalence of evil and suffering here and the experience of that which is free from these things — and it is only by the progressive experience that one can get a solution — whether through reconciliation, a conquering descent or an escape. If we start from the basis taken as an axiom that the prevalence of suffering and evil in the present and in the hard, outward fact of things, disproves of itself all that has been experienced by sages and mystics of the other side, the realisable Divine, then no solution seems possible.

Chapter Ten
Christianity and Theosophy

Christianity

The gospel of suffering, the obsessing sense of sin and the dramatic vital turn which goes with these things are certainly the most prominent defects of the Christian attitude, and they keep the religion even in its esoteric movements too much tied to a half-spiritualised vital movement. Christianity seems to me to have never clarified its intelligence by the spiritual light in the higher reaches of the mind; it is lacking in a spiritual philosophy and never really went beyond theology — in spite of one or two large thinkers who were the exception rather than the rule. One has to pass beyond even the higher mind, but not to have developed the spiritual light in it leaves the instrument defective and, instead of going above the mind, one is then apt to be content to remain below receiving whatever flashes and upliftings one can from a high and far-off and very much veiled Divine. And in such a state it is easier to mistake partial deities or even, if one is not careful, undivine Powers for the Supreme.

*

There is no connection between the Christian conception (of the Kingdom of Heaven) and the idea of the supramental descent. The Christian conception supposes a state of things brought about by religious emotion and moral purification; but these things are no more capable of changing the world, whatever value they may have for the individual, than mental idealism or any other power yet called upon for the purpose. The Christian proposes to substitute the sattwic religious ego for the rajasic and tamasic ego, but although this can be done as an individual achievement, it has never succeeded and will never succeed in accomplishing itself in the mass. It has no higher spiritual or psychological knowledge behind it and ignores the foundations of human character and the source of the difficulty — the duality of mind, life and body. Unless there is a descent of a new Power of Consciousness, not subject to the dualities but still dynamic which will provide a new foundation and a lifting of the centre of consciousness above the mind, the Kingdom of God on earth can only be an ideal, not a fact realised in the general earth-consciousness or earth-life.

*

I feel it difficult to say anything about X's Christ and Krishna. The attraction which she says people feel for Christ has never touched me, partly because I got disgusted with the dryness and deadness of Christianity in England and partly because the Christ of the gospels (apart from a few pregnant episodes) is luminous no doubt, but somewhat shadowy and imperfectly constructed in his luminosity; there is more of the ethical put forward than of the spiritual or divine man. The Christ that has strongly lived in the Western saints and mystics is the Christ of St. Francis of Assisi, St. Teresa and others. But apart from that, is it a fact that Christ has been strongly or vividly loved by Christians? Only by a very few, it seems to me. As for Krishna, to judge him and his revealing tradition by the Christ figure and Christ tradition is not possible. The two stand in two different worlds. There is nothing in the latter of the great and boundless and sovereign spiritual knowledge and power of realisation we find in the Gita, nothing of the emotional force, passion, beauty of the Gopi symbol and all that lies behind it, nothing of the many-sided manifestation of the Krishna figure. The other has other qualities: there is no gain in putting them side by side and trying to weigh them against each other. That is the besetting sin of the Christian mind even in those who are most liberal like Dr. Stanley Jones; they cannot get altogether free from the sectarian narrowness and leave each manifestation to its own inner world for those to follow who have the inner drawing to the one or the other. I have always refrained from these comparisons in my published writings in order to avoid this error. What I feel personally is for myself — I can't ask others to conform to my measure.

*

I do not gather from these extracts[1] the true nature of the transformation spoken of here. It seems to be something mental and moral with the love of God and a certain kind of union in separateness brought about by this divine love as the spiritualising element.

Love of God and union in separateness through that love and a transformation of the nature by realising certain mental, ethical, emotional, perhaps even physical possibilities (for the Vaishnavas speak of a new *cinmaya* body) is the principle of Vaishnava Yoga. So there is nothing here that was not already present in that line of Asiatic mysticism which looks to a Personal Deity and insists on the eternal pre-existence and survival of the individual being. A spiritual raising of the nature to its highest possibilities is a part of the Tantric discipline — so that too is not absent from Indian Yoga. The writer seems like most European writers to know only Illusionism and Buddhism and to accept them as the whole wisdom of Asia (*sagesse asiatique*); but even there he misinterprets their idea and their experience. Adwaita even in its extreme form does not aim at the extinction of existence, the adoption of nothingness, the end of the being and destruction of the essence. Only a certain kind of Nihilistic Buddhism aims at that and even so that Nothingness, Sunya, is described on another side of it as the Permanent. What these disciplines aim at is a passing from Time to Eternity, a putting off of the finite and putting on of the Infinite, a casting off of the bonds of ego and its results, desire, suffering, a falsified existence, in order to live in the true Self. These descriptions of the Christian writer betray an entire ignorance of the realisation which he decries, its infinity, freedom, surpassing peace, the ecstasy of the Brahmananda. It is an extinction of the limited individual personality but a liberation into cosmic and then into

---

[1] *Brief extracts from a book by Henri Massis,* Défense de l'Occident *(Paris: Librairie Plon, 1927), pp. 214–24. — Ed.*

transcendental consciousness—an extinction of thought and life but a liberation into an unlimited consciousness and knowledge and being. The personality is extinguished but in something greater than itself, not in something less nor in mere "*Néant*". If it be said that that negates earthly life, so does the Christian ideal, for the Christian ideal aims at the attainment of a celestial existence beyond the earth existence (beyond this single earth life, for reincarnation is not admitted), which is only a vale of sorrows and a passing ordeal. It insists on the preservation of the spiritual personality, but so do Vaishnavism and Shaivism and other "Asiatic" ideals. The writer's ignorance of the many-sidedness of Asiatic wisdom deprives his depreciation of it of all value.

The phrases which struck you as resembling superficially at least our ideal of transformation are of a general character and could be adopted without hesitation by almost any spiritual discipline, even Illusionism would be willing to include it as a stage or experience on the way. All depends on the content you put into the words, what actual change in the consciousness and life they are intended to cover. If the transformation be "from sin to sainthood" by the union of the soul with God "in an intellectual light full of love" — which is the most definite description of it in these extracts, — then it is not at all identical, but rather very far from what I mean by transformation. For the transformation I aim at is not from sin to sainthood but from the lower nature of the Ignorance to the Divine Nature of Light, Peace, Truth, Divine Power and Bliss beyond the Ignorance. It journeys towards a supreme self-existent good and leaves behind it the limited struggling human conception of sin and virtue; it is not an intellectual light that is the sun of its aspiration but a spiritual supra-intellectual supramental light; it is not sainthood that is its culmination but divine consciousness — or if you like, soul-hood, spirit-hood, conscious self-hood, divine-hood. There is therefore between these two kinds or two degrees of transformation an immense difference.

I. "*It is a heroic surrender in which the soul reaches the summit of free activity, the being is transformed and its faculties are purified, deified by Grace, without its essence being destroyed."*[2]

What is meant by free activity? With us the freedom consists in freedom from the darkness, limitation, error, suffering, transience of the ignorant lower Nature, but also in a total surrender to the Divine. Free action is the action of the Divine in us and through us; no other action can be free. That seems to be accepted in II and III; but this perception, this conception is as old as spiritual knowledge itself — it is not peculiar to Catholicism. What again is meant by the purification and deification of the faculties by Grace? If it is an ethical purification, that goes a very small way and does not bring deification. Again, if the deification is limited by the intellectual light, it must be a rather petty affair at the best. There was a similar aim in ancient Indian spirituality, but it had a larger sweep and a higher height than that. No spiritual discipline aims at purification or deification by the destruction of the essence — there can be no such thing, the very phrase is meaningless and self-contradictory. The essence of the being is indestructible. Even the most rigid Adwaita discipline does not aim at any such destruction; its object is the purest purity of the essential self. Transformation aims at this essential purity of the pure Spirit, but it asks also for the purity and divinity of the supreme Nature; it is not the essence of being but the accidents of our undeveloped imperfect nature that are destroyed and replaced by the manifestation of the divine Nature. The monistic Adwaita aims at the disappearance of the ego, not of the essence of the person; it arrives at its disappearance by identity with the One, by dissolution of the Nature-constructed ego into the reality of the eternal Self, for that, it says, not ego, is the essence of the person — *so'ham, tat tvam asi*. In our idea of transformation also there is the destruction of the ego, its dissolution into the cosmic and the divine consciousness, but by that destruction we recover the true or spiritual person which is an eternal portion of the Divine.

II. *"The contemplation of the Christian ... is inseparable*

---

[2] *This extract and those that follow appear here in translation. The original French extracts are given in the Note on the Texts. — Ed.*

from the state of Grace[3] and the divine life. Even when he annuls himself, his personality still triumphs by allowing itself to be torn away from all that is not itself, by breaking all the bonds that tie it to the flesh so that the living God may seize him, possess him and dwell in him."

III. *"Freedom means first to subordinate what is inferior in one's nature to what is superior."*

These passages can be taken in the above sense and as approximating to our ideal; but the confusion here is in the use of the word "personality". Personality is a temporary formation and to eternise it would be to eternise ignorance and limitation. The true "I" is not the mental ego or the present personality which is only a mask, but the eternal I which assumes various personalities in various lives. The Christian and European conception of a single life on earth tends to bring about this error by making our present personality appear as if it were our whole self... Again, it is not merely the bodily individuality to which ignorance ties us, but the mental individuality and vital individuality also. All these ties have to be broken, the imperfect forms of mind and life transcended, mind transformed into something beyond mind, life into divine life, if the transformation is to be real and not merely a new shaping or heightening of the lights of the Ignorance.

IV. *"This solitude of the soul [of the Asiatic ascetic] is not the true spiritual leisure, the active solitude in which the transformation from sin to sainthood takes place through the soul's union with God in an intellectual light full of love."*

I have commented already on this description of the transformation to be effected and have to add only one more reserve. The solitude of the self in the Divine has no doubt to be active as well as static and passive; but none who has not arrived at the silence and motionless solitude of the eternal Self can have the free and integral activity of the higher divine Nature. For the

---

[3] Grace is not a conception peculiar to the Christian spiritual idea — it is there in Vaishnavism, Shaivism, the Shakta religion, — it is as old as the Upanishads.

action is based on the silence and by the silence it is free.

V. " . . . *the Christian life, a mystic, progressive life which is an enrichment, an infinite enlargement of the human being.*"

This is not our idea of transformation — for the human person is the mental being limited by life and body. An enrichment and enlargement of it cannot go beyond the extreme limit of that formula, it can only widen and adorn its present poverty and narrowness. It cannot ascend out of the mental ignorance into a greater Truth and Light or bring that down in any fullness into earthly nature, which is the aim of transformation as we conceive it.

VI. "*For the Asiatic, the personality is the fall of man; for the Christian it is the very plan of God, the principle of union, the summit of the natural creation, and it calls wholly to the Grace.*"

The personality of this single life in man is a formation in the Ignorance, therefore a fall; it cannot be the summit of the being. We do not admit that it is the summit of the natural creation either, but say there are higher summits to which we have to climb and reveal their powers in earthly nature. The natural creation is an evolution of the hidden Divine Consciousness in Nature which is limited and disguised at first by the Ignorance. It has still to climb out of the Ignorance — therefore to get beyond the human person into the divine person. It is in this spiritual evolution that the Plan Divine (*dessein de Dieu*) manifests its central and significant line and calls all creation to the crowning Grace.

You will see therefore that the resemblance of the transformation here to our ideal is only on the surface, in the words, but not in the content of the words which is much narrower and of another order. So far as there is agreement and coincidence, it is because there is contained in them what is common (a certain conversion of the consciousness) to all spiritual disciplines; for all, in East or in West, have a common core of experience — it is in their developments, range, turn to this or that aspect or else their will towards the totality of the Truth that they differ.

Theosophy

It [*Theosophy*] is a movement that has taken from each previous movement European or Asiatic some of its knowledge and mixed it with much error and imagination of a rather vital character. It is that mixture and the mental character of its knowledge that prevent it from being a sound thing. Many start with it, but have to leave it if they want to get to real spiritual life and knowledge.

Note on the Texts

Note on the Texts

LETTERS ON YOGA — II, the second of four volumes, contains letters in which Sri Aurobindo speaks about the practice of his system of Yoga. The letters have been arranged in three parts dealing with these broad subject areas:

1. The Path of the Integral Yoga
2. The Synthetic Method of the Integral Yoga
3. The Integral Yoga and Other Spiritual Paths

The letters in this volume have been selected from the extensive correspondence Sri Aurobindo carried on with his disciples and others between 1927 and 1950. Letters from this corpus appear in seven volumes of THE COMPLETE WORKS OF SRI AUROBINDO: *Letters on Poetry and Art* (Volume 27), *Letters on Yoga* (Volumes 28–31), *The Mother with Letters on the Mother* (Volume 32), and *Letters on Himself and the Ashram* (Volume 35). The titles of these works specify the nature of the letters included in the volumes, but there is some overlap. For example, a number of letters in the present volume are also published in *Letters on Himself and the Ashram*.

The Writing of the Letters

Between 1927 and 1950, Sri Aurobindo replied to hundreds of correspondents in tens of thousands of letters, some of them many pages in length, others only a few words long. Most of his replies, however, were sent to just a few dozen disciples, almost all of them resident members of his Ashram; of these disciples, about a dozen received more than half the replies. Sri Aurobindo wrote most of these letters between 1931 and 1937, the prime period of his correspondence. Letters before and after this period were written on a more restricted scale and confined to a few persons for special reasons.

Disciples in the Ashram wrote to Sri Aurobindo on loose sheets or sent him the notebooks in which they kept diaries as a record of their spiritual endeavour and a means of communicating with him. These notebooks and loose sheets reached Sri Aurobindo via an internal "post" once or twice a day. Letters from outside which his secretary thought he might like to see were sent at the same time. Correspondents wrote in English if they knew the language well enough, but a good number wrote in Bengali, Gujarati, Hindi or French, all of which Sri Aurobindo read fluently, or in other languages that were translated into English for him. The disciples usually addressed their letters to the Mother, since Sri Aurobindo had asked them to do so, but most assumed that he would answer them. He generally replied in the notebook or on the sheets sent by the correspondent, writing beneath the correspondent's remarks or in the margin or between the lines; sometimes, however, he wrote his reply on a separate sheet of paper. In some cases he had his secretary prepare a typed copy of his letter, which he revised before it was sent. For correspondents living outside the Ashram, Sri Aurobindo sometimes addressed his reply not to the correspondent but to his secretary, who quoted, paraphrased or translated the reply and signed the letter himself. In these indirect replies, Sri Aurobindo often referred to himself in the third person.

While going through Sri Aurobindo's letters, the reader should keep in mind that each letter was written to a specific person at a specific time, in specific circumstances and for a specific purpose. The subjects taken up arose in regard to the needs of the person. Sri Aurobindo varied the style and tone of his replies according to his relationship with the correspondent; to those with whom he was close, he sometimes employed humour, irony and even sarcasm.

Although written to specific recipients, these letters contain much of general interest, which justifies their inclusion in a volume destined for the general public. For the reasons mentioned above, however, the advice in them does not always apply equally to everyone. Aware of this, Sri Aurobindo himself made some cautionary remarks about the proper use of his letters:

> I should like to say, in passing, that it is not always safe to apply practically to oneself what has been written for another.

Each sadhak is a case by himself and one cannot always or often take a mental rule and apply it rigidly to all who are practising the Yoga.

The tendency to take what I lay down for one and apply it without discrimination to another is responsible for much misunderstanding. A general statement, too, true in itself, cannot be applied to everyone alike or applied now and immediately without consideration of condition or circumstance or person or time.

It is not a fact that all I write is meant equally for everybody. That assumes that everybody is alike and there is no difference between sadhak and sadhak. If it were so everybody would advance alike and have the same experiences and take the same time to progress by the same steps and stages. It is not so at all.[1]

The Typing and Revision of the Letters

Most of the shorter items in this volume, and many of the longer ones, were not typed or revised during Sri Aurobindo's lifetime and are reproduced here directly from his handwritten manuscripts. A good number of the letters, however, as mentioned above, were typed for Sri Aurobindo and revised by him before sending. Other letters were typed by the recipients for their own use or for circulation within the Ashram. At first, circulation of the letters was restricted to members of the Ashram and others whom Sri Aurobindo had accepted as disciples. When these letters were circulated, personal references were removed. Persons mentioned by Sri Aurobindo were indicated by their initials or by the letters X, Y, Z, etc. Copies of these typed letters were kept by Sri Aurobindo's secretary and sometimes presented to Sri Aurobindo for revision before publication. These typed copies sometimes contained errors, most of which were corrected by him while revising.

---

[1] First and third passages: *Letters on Himself and the Ashram*, volume 35 of THE COMPLETE WORKS OF SRI AUROBINDO, pp. 473 and 475. Second passage: *The Mother with Letters on the Mother*, volume 32, p. 349.

Sri Aurobindo's revision sometimes amounted merely to making minor changes here and there, sometimes to a complete rewriting of the letter. He generally removed personal references if this had not already been done by the typist. When necessary, he also rewrote the openings or other parts of the replies in order to free them from dependence on the correspondent's question. As a result, some of these letters have an impersonal tone and read more like brief essays than personal communications.

The Publication of the Letters

Around 1933, Sri Aurobindo's secretary Nolini Kanta Gupta began to compile selections from the growing body of letters in order to publish them. During Sri Aurobindo's lifetime, four small books of letters were published: *The Riddle of This World* (1933), *Lights on Yoga* (1935), *Bases of Yoga* (1936) and *More Lights on Yoga* (1948). Sri Aurobindo revised the typescripts of most of the letters in these books. During this revision, he continued the process of removing personal references. A letter he wrote in August 1937 alludes to his approach to the revision:

> I had no idea of the book being published as a collection of personal letters — if that were done, they would have to be published whole as such without a word of alteration. I understood the book was meant like the others [*i.e., like* Bases of Yoga, *etc.*] where only what was helpful for an understanding of things Yogic was kept with necessary alterations and modifications.... With that idea I have been not only omitting but recasting and adding freely. Otherwise as a book it would be too scrappy and random for public interest. In the other books things too personal were omitted — it seems to me the same rule must hold here — except very sparingly where unavoidable.

A number of letters not included in the four books mentioned above were published in the mid and late 1940s in several journals associated with the Ashram: *Sri Aurobindo Circle*, *Sri Aurobindo Mandir Annual*, *The Advent* and *Mother India*. Many letters in these journals were revised by Sri Aurobindo before publication.

By the mid-1940s a significant body of letters had been collected, typed and revised. In 1945 plans were made, with Sri Aurobindo's approval, to publish a collection of his letters. The work of compiling and editing these letters was done under his guidance. At that time, many typed or printed copies of letters, some revised, some not, were presented to Sri Aurobindo for approval or revision. The resulting material was arranged and published in a four-volume series entitled *Letters of Sri Aurobindo*. Series One appeared in 1947, Series Two and Three in 1949 and Series Four in 1951. The first, second and fourth series contained letters on Yoga, the third letters on poetry and literature. In 1958, most of these letters on Yoga, along with many additional ones, were published under the titles *On Yoga II: Tome One* and *On Yoga II: Tome Two*, as Volumes VI and VII of the Sri Aurobindo International University Centre collection. The first tome, with further additions, was reissued in 1969. In 1970 a new edition of the letters was published under the title *Letters on Yoga*; this edition contained many new letters not included in *On Yoga II*. The three volumes of the enlarged edition constituted volumes 22, 23 and 24 of the Sri Aurobindo Birth Centenary Library.

The present edition, also titled *Letters on Yoga*, incorporates the Centenary Library letters, but also contains a large number of letters that have come to light in the four decades between the two editions. One source of new letters is the correspondences of several disciples which were published in books after the Centenary Library edition had been issued. Govindbhai Patel's correspondence was published in 1974 in a book entitled *My Pilgrimage to the Spirit*; an enlarged edition appeared in 1977. Nagin Doshi's correspondence, *Guidance from Sri Aurobindo: Letters to a Young Disciple*, was brought out in three volumes in 1974, 1976 and 1987. *Nirodbaran's Correspondence with Sri Aurobindo* came out in two volumes in 1983 and 1984. Sahana Devi's correspondence came out in 1985 in a book entitled *At the Feet of Sri Aurobindo and the Mother*. Prithwi Singh's correspondence came out in 1988 as *Sri Aurobindo and the Mother to Prithwi Singh*. Dilip Kumar Roy's correspondence was issued in four volumes in 2003, 2005, 2007 and 2011 under the title *Sri Aurobindo to Dilip*. A second source of new material is individual letters and small collections of letters published in Ashram journals and elsewhere after the Centenary Library had been issued. A third source is letters transcribed from manuscripts or from early typed copies. Many unpublished letters were discovered while reviewing correspondences long held by the Ashram; some of these had never been assessed to find letters for publication; others had been assessed, but relatively few letters were selected at the time. Additional letters were received by the Ashram upon the passing away of disciples. From the three sources mentioned above, many letters have been found that are worthy of publication. The present edition contains about one-third more letters than appear in the Centenary Library.

The Selection, Arrangement and Editing of the Letters

In compiling the present edition, all known manuscripts, typed copies or photographic copies of manuscripts and printed texts of letters were checked. From these sources, letters that seemed to be of general interest were selected. Electronic texts of the letters were then made and carefully checked at least twice against the handwritten, typed, photocopied, and printed versions of the texts.

The selected letters have been arranged according to subject and placed in the four volumes of the present edition. Each volume is divided and subdivided into parts, sections, chapters and groups with descriptive headings; each group, the lowest unit of division, contains one or more letters devoted to the specific subject of the group.

The present volume consists of 1163 separate items, an "item" being defined as what is published between one heading or asterisk and another heading or asterisk. Many items correspond exactly to individual letters; a good number, however, contain only part of the individual letters; a small number consist of two or more letters (or parts of them) that were joined together by early typists or editors and then revised in that form by Sri Aurobindo.

Whenever possible, the letters are reproduced to their full extent. In some cases, however, portions of the letters have been omitted because they are not of general interest. A number of letters, for example, begin with personal remarks by Sri Aurobindo unrelated to the more substantial remarks which follow; these personal openings have often been removed. In some letters, Sri Aurobindo marked the transition from one part of a letter to another with a phrase such as "As to"; these transitional phrases have often been retained and stand at the beginning of abbreviated letters — that is, letters in which the first part of the letter has been omitted or placed elsewhere.

A number of letters, or portions of them, have been published in more than one volume of THE COMPLETE WORKS OF SRI AUROBINDO. Most of this doubling of letters occurs between *Letters on Yoga* and *Letters on Himself and the Ashram*. The form of these letters is not always the same in both places. In *Letters on Himself and the Ashram*, the manuscript version of a given letter has often been used because it contains Sri Aurobindo's remarks on himself or the Mother or members of the Ashram. These personal remarks, as noted above, were usually removed by Sri Aurobindo when he revised the letter for publication as a letter on Yoga. This revised form of the letter has generally been reproduced in *Letters on Yoga*. Thus, a number of letters are available both in their original form and their revised form.

As in previous collections of Sri Aurobindo's letters, the names of Ashram members and others have often been replaced by the letters X, Y, Z, etc. In any given letter, X stands for the first name replaced, Y for the second, Z for the third, A for the fourth, and so on. An X in a given letter has no necessary relation to an X in another letter. Names of Ashram members to whom Sri Aurobindo referred not as sadhaks but as holders of a certain position — notably Nolini Kanta Gupta in his position as Sri Aurobindo's secretary — are given in full. Sometimes the names of people who played a role in the history of the period are also given.

In his letters Sri Aurobindo sometimes wrote Sanskrit words in the devanagari script; these words have been transliterated into roman script in this edition. Words in Bengali script have likewise been transliterated. This policy is in accord with the practice followed in Sri Aurobindo's lifetime.

The reader may note that Sri Aurobindo almost always spelled the word "Asram" without an "h" in his manuscripts. Around 1945, due to failing eyesight, he began dictating most of his writings to his amanuensis Nirodbaran; Nirodbaran sometimes spelled the word without an "h", sometimes with one. In the present edition, the word is always spelled as it occurs in the manuscripts, both those of Sri Aurobindo and of Nirodbaran. In headings and other editorial matter, the spelling "Ashram" has been used, since this is now the official spelling of the Sri Aurobindo Ashram.

Original French Texts of Six Extracts
Cited in the Letter on Pages 506–10

I. "*C'est un abandon héroïque, où l'âme parvient au sommet de l'activité libre, où la personne se transforme, où ses facultés sont épurées, déifiées par la grâce, sans que son essence soit détruite.*"

II. "*La contemplation du chrétien . . . est inséparable de l'état de grâce et de vie divine. S'il doit s'anéantir, c'est encore sa personnalité qui triomphe en se laissant arracher à tout ce qui n'est pas elle, en brisant tous les liens qui l'unissent à son individu de chair, afin que le Dieu vivant puisse s'en saisir, l'assumer, l'habiter.*"

III. "*Liberté qui consiste d'abord à subordonner ce qui est inférieur dans sa nature à ce qui lui est supérieur.*"

IV. "*Cette solitude de l'âme [de l'ascète asiatique] . . . n'est pas le vrai loisir spirituel, la solitude active où s'opère la transformation du péché en sainteté par l'union de l'âme avec Dieu dans 'une lumière intellectuelle toute pleine d'amour'.*"

V. "*. . . la vie chrétienne. Mystique progressive qui est un enrichissement, un élargissement infini de la personne humaine.*"

VI. "*Pour l'Asiatique la personnalité est la chute de l'homme; pour le chrétien, c'est le dessein même de Dieu, le principe de l'union, le sommet naturel de la création qu'il appelle tout entière à la grâce.*"